THE ASTROLOGY OF SUSTAINABILITY

The Challenge of Pluto in Capricorn

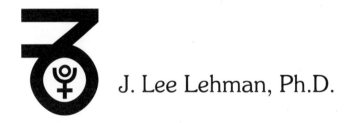

J. Lee Lehman, Ph.D.

Schiffer Publishing Ltd

4880 Lower Valley Road, Atglen, Pennsylvania 19310

Schiffer Books are available at special discounts for bulk purchases for sales promotions or premiums. Special editions, including personalized covers, corporate imprints, and excerpts can be created in large quantities for special needs. For more information contact the publisher:

Published by Schiffer Publishing Ltd.
4880 Lower Valley Road
Atglen, PA 19310
Phone: (610) 593-1777; Fax: (610) 593-2002
E-mail: Info@schifferbooks.com

For the largest selection of fine reference books on this and related subjects, please visit our website at

www.schifferbooks.com

We are always looking for people to write books on new and related subjects. If you have an idea for a book please contact us at the above address.

This book may be purchased from the publisher. Include $5.00 for shipping. Please try your bookstore first. You may write for a free catalog.

In Europe, Schiffer books are distributed by
Bushwood Books
6 Marksbury Ave.
Kew Gardens
Surrey TW9 4JF England
Phone: 44 (0) 20 8392 8585; Fax: 44 (0) 20 8392 9876
E-mail: info@bushwoodbooks.co.uk
Website: www.bushwoodbooks.co.uk

The Astrology of Sustainability:
The Challenge of Pluto in Capricorn

Outline

Table of Figures and Charts

Preface

ASTROLOGY TELLS THE STORY OF THE UNFOLDING OF THE UNIVERSE, WRIT ON THE CANVAS OF THE SKY. As a story, it is less about truth than about meaning. Because how can a story be true from all points of view? In Greek, Indian, or Celtic mythology, witness how many versions of the story of a hero or heroine, a goddess or god are contradictory – different family trees, different adventures. Each different interpretation gives us the chance to relate to the story in a personal way. Each version or retelling gives us a different perspective – a different meaning. One of the most difficult of perspectives is to walk through life with the sense that one's own existence has no meaning, value, or purpose. It is when we are imbued with a belief that "we" matter – whether the "we" is an individual, a tribe, or a nation – then the most amazing acts of courage, compassion and sacrifice are possible.

This book is about a major story of our time: the awareness that we must either reintegrate ourselves with the natural world and its rules, or perish as a species. I will not say this must be done by our generation: but it must be done soon. I will not say that famine and wars will result if we fail: but they could. I will also not say that there is no hope: because we simply don't know the detailed shape of the problems that we face.

In our present era, those people who use astrology at all, tend to use it as only a tool for self-understanding or spiritual development. Historically, astrology was so much larger. In the ancient days, the astrology of princes bridged the march across many lifetimes – because a prince was not successful unless his dynasty was. Astrology was not just a tool for a single life, but for generations – or even, if one dared to peek, the stretch back to the Creation itself. The ancient tools for this examination remain, and the skills for their use only need teaching, demonstrating, and honing.

If we are to understand the challenges of our day from an astrological perspective, we must first understand the tools that we can bring to examine our situation, not just in the *Now*, but within the patterns of unfolding that may exceed a single human lifespan. Much of this book is the process of explaining and demonstrating the tools, both within their historical development, and in application now.

This multidimensional work, blending history, ecology and astrology together, is designed to develop your level of proficiency in all three. In the end, I hope you will look at our times much differently than when you started. From that standpoint, this is a very radical book, because it challenges many assumptions.

As we develop sophistication in using the tools of mundane astrology, the ability to ask more difficult questions will also develop. The story will become more complex, more nuanced. As that happens, we can turn the perspective around from the collective and return to the question that is the most important for all of us individually: how do *we* fit into this story? Be prepared for a few surprises!

When I first conceptualized this book, I hadn't actually planned to go through the process of explicating Pluto through the elements. I was originally going to go from the earth signs directly to what is now Chapter 8. What had engaged me from the start was the crucial issue of the earth signs and political issues related to Planet Earth, which includes the question of sustainability. Then, I became intrigued by another question, which is the transition between signs. This issue of transition and sequencing is a topic that I believe has never been properly discussed in detail. Instead, it has been treated as the transitional sentences between *The Important Stuff*, namely, the signs themselves. But as I examined past transits of Pluto in Capricorn in my own quest for understanding, I found I could not place walls up between the signs and pretend that history started and stopped when it reached these barriers.

Watching the transition between Pluto in Sagittarius and Pluto in Capricorn reminded me of what Frank Herbert wrote in *Dune*, "A beginning is the time for taking the most delicate care that the balances are correct."[1] Astrologers have been refining themes for the Pluto sign periods almost from the point of its discovery. It is an interesting exercise to peruse some of the early writings on Pluto, which don't at all resemble our modern concepts. I am reminded of the performances that my old colleague in NCGR, Michael Lutin, presented as Pluto moved through each sign. Michael's characterizations – funny, tacky, haunting, disturbing – all pointed to how astrologers found it easy to characterize many of the likely qualities as the garbage disposal, Pluto, would progressively grind its way through a sign, "transforming" it. While many of the books on Pluto have emphasized its spiritual qualities, and the positive results, still, many astrology students are terrified of Pluto transits in a way fundamentally different from any other kind of transit.

Each transition has qualities of both signs – emphasized by the fact that a single-pass transition from sign to sign is next to impossible. This in turn brought up a question: when does Pluto in a new sign "start?" Does it start with the first entry, or the final entry after all the retrogrades? And what does one do with the retrogradation back into the "old" sign? Is there a language for these transitions?

The next question that bothered me was: when Pluto changes signs, does it just exchange its old marbles for new marbles, and go on its way? That is, after all, pretty much how we see it in natal consultation. The Sun moves into Aries, and at least once the Sun is past the first degree, that's it: bring on the Aries! The time in between is so ephemeral, so numinous, that we can't wait to skip over it to do new things. But perhaps the image is more like a paradigm shift, where a new idea or theory becomes dominant, but the old paradigm hangs out for a while, impeding the acceptance of the new idea, and slowing the transition.

Life flows; it is messy. Pluto went into Cancer, and bang! World War I started. Pluto went into Leo, and bang! World War II started. But there was no such major calamity when Pluto went to Virgo, although personally I would nominate Sputnik as the great harbinger of the change. And when Pluto went into Libra? What major world event then? Pluto had the audacity to go into Scorpio during Ronald Reagan's first term, thereby not marking the Reagan revolution. And when Pluto went into Sagittarius? Doesn't it seem a little trivial to attribute that to a Republican majority Congress going after Bill Clinton for adultery, not to mention the beginning of the criminal trial of O.J. Simpson? These were not culture-spanning, earth-shaking events!

As we witnessed the transition to Capricorn, the world economy tanked. But the visible symptoms of this occurred after Pluto touched Capricorn, and had retrograded back into Sagittarius, so how do we score this?

If we are to understand that one of the Pluto processes is to take a sign-complex to its extreme, then we can use this to develop a theory about transitions. For example, as Pluto passed into Sagittarius, one of the obvious readings for the period was religious extremism. The logic? Sagittarius is a Jupiter-ruled sign, and it has a long association with organized (hierarchical) religions. Given the up-tick in matters relating to fundamentalism of all sorts during the period of Pluto in Scorpio, it was an easy call to predict that matters would only become even more extreme. And there was evidence of this: not three weeks before the beginning of Pluto in Sagittarius in 1995, John Salvi opened fire at a Planned Parenthood Clinic and killed two people. Within a month after the Ingress, the Aum Shinrikyo religious cult in Japan staged a fatal nerve gas attack in the Tokyo subway.

As the Pluto in Scorpio period progressed and AIDS became a global epidemic, some astrologers predicted a cure for AIDS once Pluto went into Sagittarius, using the logic that AIDS, being sexually transmitted, was therefore to be classified as a blight of Pluto in Scorpio, and therefore curable when Pluto changed signs. It is true that drug cocktails to treat the symptoms did improve the subjective experience of AIDS sufferers enormously, although we are still left with the disease.

These observations lead me to propose the following ideas, which we shall elaborate and extend in the following chapters.

• Issues relating to the next sign of Pluto often begin to become obvious well before the sign change. This is really nothing different than the observation by many that the effects of the new solar return are often visible at least a month before the solar return actually occurs.

• There is a classical definition of the beginning of a cycle which addresses the issue of when to start counting, and we shall address that theory in Chapter 1, and then continue to test it through Chapters 4-8.

• There is a substantial amount of "clean-up" of the "messes" of the old sign that happens in the new sign – far more than most astrologers have factored.

The more you think about this idea of transition, the more it makes sense. If the function of Pluto in a sign is to push the limits of what that sign could be, how could reining in the extremes also be a part of the same function? If the function of Saturn in a sign is to bring about restructuring of the affairs of a sign, how could we expect that the breakdown, the restrictions, and the restructuring could be complete in less than three years? Suppose, for example, that Saturn is squaring my natal Sun position, and an eye problem manifests. And suppose, given the square aspect, that the operation is not entirely successful. If that's the case, I could well still be coping with that eye problem when Saturn goes in to the next sign. In that case, the next sign is acting to clean up the problem generated by the prior sign. If, as we saw with Pluto in Sagittarius, it takes years to set up the conditions that created the financial collapse from derivatives, how could we expect the effects to suddenly be over with the moment when Pluto entered Capricorn? In fact, a major portion of Pluto in Capricorn's agenda is cleaning up after Pluto in Sagittarius, just as a major portion of Pluto in Aquarius's job will be cleaning up after Pluto in Capricorn.

It was easy to see that a crash was coming when Pluto went into Capricorn. Back sometime in 1981-1982, I was teaching a class on astrology in which I predicted that the Social Security System would fail in 2008. Why did I make that prediction? Superficially, the answer is easy: I looked in an ephemeris and saw that Pluto was entering Capricorn that year. But why did I predict what I did? That's more complicated. My background as an ecologist/botanist had me interested in matters of overpopulation, and I was reading about the demographic impact of the Pluto in Leo generation (i.e., Baby Boomers) beginning to retire around this time – so the astrology fit the demographics.

But my prediction wasn't quite right – even if it was tantalizing. What I lacked then was sufficient knowledge of economic cycles – and experience with them – to even envision a crash of that magnitude. Because, more than anything else, astrologers can only predict what they can imagine as being possible. In Chapter 1, we shall see how astrologers missed the beginning of World War II, not because the traditional techniques failed, but largely because astrologers, as typical citizens of their own countries, shared the same reluctance to see the possibility of war as their non-astrological peers.

But more than economics or Social Security, the main signification that I could not get out of my mind is that Capricorn is *Earth* – and that means the world, materialism, and ecology. Humans have often made a career out of believing themselves different from and superior to the natural world. And yet, this has hardly been the dominant viewpoint throughout history.

Most traditional cultures see themselves as embedded within their environment, not superior beings with the god-given right to *subdue* their environment. Among astrologers, this issue has most passionately been addressed by Richard Tarnas[2], as well as Patrick Curry.[3] Using Greek terminology, Tarnas has contrasted the Apollonian and the Dionysian viewpoints, where the Apollonian perspective matches well with the rationalistic outer world, "arrow of time" perspective of the Enlightenment, while the Dionysian perspective is the cyclic, chaotic, inner-driven principle of many traditional societies. The same line was drawn dramatically in the television sci-fi series *Babylon 5* as the conflict between the Apollonian Vorlons and the Dionysian Shadows. This clash of positions has the advantage of being much less value-laden than good vs. evil dichotomies – even if a number of the religiously-based versions of the conflict have labeled the Dionysian position as evil.

And by the way, if you are a bit disturbed by the equation of cyclic and chaotic, consider the source. Both of these concepts, at first so superficially opposed, actually emerge from the realm of the nonhuman. The Apollonian perspective arises from the rational mind imposing rules on its playground – most prominently, the rule of cause and effect.

By contrast, the Dionysian world is seething with pulses of life. But it has an underlying rhythm in cyclic time. The drumbeat provides a structure, but the dance allows for improvisation. Again, to use my *Babylon 5* example, the Shadows periodically come out and knock over all the anthills, so to speak – but they do it *periodically*. There is still a rhythm under the chaos. In the universe of the Lord of the Rings, Sauron was merely the *last* of the great Dark Lords – periodically a new one would appear and the dark side would wax strong again. In the Star

Wars universe, there were two Sith (dark) lords – a master and an apprentice. Periodically, the apprentice would kill the master or the master would die by another means. A new age begins, but it maintains the form, because a new apprentice must be found. It is fascinating how frequently the Dionysian path is branded *evil* by the Apollonian. This form is really a flavor of dualism, because it is never clear that one path is truly stronger than the other. In *The Ultimate Asteroid Book*, I discussed the Mesoamerican dualistic mythology of Quezalcoatl and Tezcatlipoca;[4] Babylonian mythology was similarly dualistic with its paired antagonistic gods of Ahura Mazda and Angra Mainyu. Egyptian mythology has Seth and Osiris.

Walk with Pluto, and you will discover that you are walking on the dark side. Not necessarily evil – that is the branding of the Apollonian mind. But Pluto is literally so far out in the solar system, that the Apollonian light of the Sun truly is a distant star. Pluto, and the other Plutinos (the bodies in the same band as Pluto, outside the orbit of Neptune) rule matters complex, deep, old, and impersonal. These are matters too large for the human mind to comprehend rationally. These issues can be dangerous for people to encounter, especially unprepared. In this book, we shall take up some of the dynamics of this process in Chapter 3.

The theme of *Earth* will not be denied while Pluto is in Capricorn, even as there will also be cleaning up of the *excesses* of Pluto in Sagittarius. Simultaneously reading the data emerging from the studies of ecologists and the environmental movement, then seeing the concern of astrologers for the events of the 2010s and beyond, I could not help but see a convergence.

As these issues about this convergence developed, I realized that my dual background put me in a perfect position to bring these ideas to the astrological community. My science training is an asset, because it allowed me to conceive of a book which could address the ecological issues ahead using language from both disciplines. And the final part of this mix was my background in classical astrology, which allowed me to reformulate the question of astrological prediction in the mundane sphere – and therefore show how ancient ideas could apply to modern problems.

The structure of this book addresses several different techniques and applications:

Chapter 1 presents the history of mundane prediction techniques, with an emphasis on the use of the Aries Ingress, both individually and as a system for predictions for the effects of the longer Jupiter-Saturn and Mars-Saturn cycles.

Chapter 2 presents a primer on ecological and environmental concepts, so that the reader will have the language necessary to consider ecological matters in greater detail through the subsequent chapters.

Chapter 3 presents the dance of Neptune and Pluto. What many astrologers have missed about these two bodies is that their orbits make them a pair – and Uranus isn't far away in this slow cosmic dance.

Chapters 4-7 present Pluto through the elements. Much of the content of these chapters relates to environmental issues as they developed through the last pass of Pluto through each of these elements, emphasizing the point that each element contributes to the fate of Spaceship Earth.

Chapter 8 features the last two passes of Pluto through Sagittarius, Capricorn, Aquarius and Pisces, to examine more closely this issue of sign transition. We also get a chance to focus more clearly on the immediate patterns, and how previous passes through the same sign can provide ideas for what we can expect this time.

Chapter 9 wraps up what we can learn from these methods.

When my partner and stalwart editor, Maggie Meister, first began to read these chapters, she said: your voice has changed. She's right. It's been nine years since I wrote the *Martial Art of Horary Astrology*. That nine years has been mostly taken up with my duties at Kepler College. The challenge of applying myself to the development of curriculum in areas that have not been my own personal expertise has been both daunting and exhilarating. It has forced me to re-examine my own path.

But also, this last nine years has seen the time when our society has pushed itself in Sagittarian ways that my Virgo placements have found profoundly disturbing. While personally more comfortable in an Earth sign, I still have to acknowledge that society is often closer to precipices of its own making than all of us like to acknowledge. It is a personal blessing to live in times when food is plenty, and wars few, when the air is clean and the water fresh. The clash of outer planets over the next few years does not make the peace process easier, any more than global competition for resources makes for simple solutions. The status of countries rises and falls over time. And the only "corporations" that measure their longevity in millennia are churches, not businesses. Structures will change.

But it is my profound hope that, as astrologers and citizens, we can, through our understanding, change the center of gravity of our path, and ease our trajectory, if only a little.

A Word to the Modern Astrologer: Welcome!

I HAVE BEEN WORKING IN THE REALM OF CLASSICAL ASTROLOGY FOR LONG ENOUGH THAT I DON'T THINK MUCH ABOUT IT ANYMORE. However, the issues that I hope to present in this work are much broader than one's astrological preferences. The techniques involving the Aries Ingress are part of *your* inheritance as much as they are part of my world. I do not want to exclude you!

So I must apologize in advance for those times where I may forget you. This might be a difficult stretch if you've never had any exposure to classical astrology before. Appendix A is a glossary of both astrological and environmental terms, which will hopefully answer some of your questions as they arise. Appendix B is a table of essential dignities.

In attempting to characterize the difference between how classical astrologers and modern astrologers think, I would mention several key points

- Classical astrology has elaborate systems for measuring the strength of planets quite apart from the planets' aspects. Examples include: essential dignities, diurnal and nocturnal considerations, the Lots (or Arabic parts), conjunctions to fixed stars, angularity, and house rulership. While individual modern astrologers may use some or all of these, their use is much more variable in modern astrology.

- Malefic really does mean hard, and benefic really does mean easy. It's not a value judgment; it's a statement of fact. Malefics are harder to control, and we generally don't like what they bring.

- In many cases, approaching and separating aspects are distinguished.

- Classical astrology does not have psychology built in, apart from what we might derive from the historical temperament types. As such, classical astrology is less a tool for "Know Thyself" than for "Know what you're up against."

- Modern astrologers have sometimes characterized classical astrologers as too rigid and too fatalistic, denying free will. Classical astrologers would reply that theirs is the art of the possible, that by understanding a person's or entity's weaknesses and strengths, you can arrive at a course of action that is realistic.

I believe it is possible for one astrologer to be artful at both classical and modern astrology – but not without switching hats. I have taught classical methods to primarily psychological astrologers, and enjoyed the interaction – and I hope they have felt the same. I do not see that any one flavor of astrology is so overarching that it could (let alone should) dominate the rest.

Thus, I welcome you to this work, but I acknowledge that the language may at first be a bit of a stretch for you. My earlier book *Classical Astrology for Modern Living* is perhaps an easier place to start. But start anyway. There's much in this work which isn't exactly classical either!

And one specific tip. At Kepler College, we have taught the students several different styles of astrology – but always as discrete units. While it may be possible to create your own brand of modern astrology by mixing and matching techniques, it doesn't seem to work well to uncritically mix and match, like attempting to use the Vedic aphorisms in a tropical chart. When you are attempting to learn a technique, it's vital to first learn it within its original context. Only after you have understood its original meaning can you consider whether that technique can be artfully applied elsewhere, or whether the parameters of the technique clash too strongly with the rest of your method.

Techniques generally don't migrate well across zodiacs. But several of the Kepler professors who are modern astrologers have shifted to using the traditional rulerships – not through any pressure, but because they were challenged to think about the questions I raised about a planet in dignity: what does it do? How does it act differently? Does Pluto being in Scorpio supposedly dignified give you any unique insight into how Pluto works?

A number of modern astrologers have similarly found my section on planets at the Bendings (the points square the Nodes) in *Classical Astrology for Modern Living* to be sufficiently interesting to adopt. But neither of these particular techniques does any damage to an overall modern approach.

In the work I present here, you may find the old system of determining how much of the year the Aries Ingress actually rules to be a consideration you may want to adopt in your work. But first, before grabbing it, try to understand it within its original system. You should get more insights that way.

Endnotes: Preface

1. Herbert, Frank. *Dune*. New York: Ace Books, 2005, page 1.
2. Tarnas, Richard. *Cosmos and Psyche : Intimations of a New World View*. New York, N.Y.: Viking, 2006.
3. Most recently in Willis, Roy G., and Patrick Curry. *Astrology, Science, and Culture : Pulling Down the Moon*. 1st ed. Oxford, UK ; New York: Berg, 2004.
4. Lehman, J. Lee. *The Ultimate Asteroid Book*. Atglen, PA: Schiffer Press, 1988, Chapter 8.

Acknowledgments

SOME OF THIS WORK HAS ROOTS GOING BACK TO THE LATE 1960s – SO I FEEL AS IF PERHAPS I SHOULD ACKNOWLEDGE MANY OF THE PROFESSORS I HAD IN COLLEGE!

The first person I have to acknowledge is my father, Alan Lehman, who died in December 2005. Born into a family of Jews who had learned how to "pass," Dad's father Henry was born in Russia, and his mother Ida was born in the U.S.A. of Silesian parents. His father got a Bachelors from the City College of New York at a time when there were quotas on Jews, and then got a job as an engineer working on the New York City aqueduct construction in the Hudson Valley. They believed fervently in the American dream, and Henry insisted that both his sons get degrees in engineering. My Uncle Fred complied, but my father rebelled and got a degree in mathematics instead. The early death of their mother sent both boys into spiritual crises that made them attractive to the Christian Science proselytizers of the day: both converted, although Uncle Fred subsequently moved on to Lutheranism.

Both boys learned the family lesson of "passing" to such an extent that they took many of their memories of their early years to the grave, never sharing with their children – and allowing us to grow up believing that we were of German descent. My brother and I only discovered any of this family history the day after our mother died in 1998. Dad always believed in doing the right thing from a society standpoint: he volunteered for the Army in World War II, faking his eye exam to get in. He dressed way more conservatively than most of his professorial colleagues as the 1960s and 1970s unfolded. But in his mind, he was free. Dad embedded the liberal arts in my heart – the arts of free persons. His love of learning and inquiry taught us that no topic was sacrosanct. This work is, in many respects, one culmination of what I learned from Dad, combined with my own life experiences. I truly miss talking to him about it.

If Dad taught me inquiry, Mom taught me teaching. Kathryn's salt-of-the-earth (Moon in Taurus) Scottish background allowed her to connect with and inspire her students – and her children. Teaching is a calling every bit as much as astrology – and Mom exercised her calling well.

We do not walk this path alone, even when significant companions fall away. Once again, my partner, Maggie Meister, has worked to save you, the reader, from my more egregious lapses into personal soliloquies. Her continued dedication and assistance is invaluable. My friends Nicholas Campion and Karen Hamaker-Zondag have read portions of this manuscript, and I thank Karen especially for some excellent structural suggestions.

I would like to also thank David and Fei Cochrane of Cosmic Patterns Software. David has been extremely generous in working with me on the formats that appear in this book. David programmed the diagrams shown in Chapter 3, Figure 1 as a special request, and I thank him both for the time he spent doing it, and for his enthusiasm about the project. All charts shown here were generated by their program Sirius, either 1.0 or 1.2.

I have also presented data generated from Solar Fire Gold, by Esoteric Technologies Pty, Ltd. I would like to thank Stephanie Johnson, Neville Lang, and Graham Dawson for useful conversations over the years about the programming of mundane data.

One final note about computer programs. You would conclude correctly from the above that I use both Sirius and Solar Fire Gold regularly. Each could work as a comprehensive program, but I am spoiled enough to use both, utilizing the strengths of each.

One of the difficulties that astrologers face in the computer age is that, in purchasing a piece of software, one rapidly discovers that the program really knows a lot that you don't! But what this really means is that the software companies have consulted many experts in the field, and through this process, incorporated much more possible information into their programs than any one individual could utilize. However, in practice, no program can do what it has not been programmed to do. It is the responsibility of the individual astrologer to be aware of the default settings of the programs, and when those may not be the best for the situation at hand.

For example, my use of essential dignities in this volume is not the default settings in either of these excellent programs. I had the honor to consult with both companies on their implementation of these modules, but appropriately, mine was not the only voice, and in any case, as a historian of these methods, there are many historical variations with valid claims to being coded. So you will find that you need to adjust the settings in either program to match what you are seeing here in this volume. For Solar Fire users, I have created some formats that you can request from me at lee@leelehman.com. For Sirius, the settings I am using are the Dorothean Triplicities, with the essential dignities box in Page Designer adjusted to not allow Detriments and Falls to remove the Peregrine status. Even with these adjustments, I still don't always agree entirely with the calculations – and these are points where we humans do have the right to assert our opinions over our software.

For example, in Chart 68. Sun enters Aries 2010, Washington, D.C., which appears on page 265 in Chapter 8, I do not necessarily agree with the point assessment of Mars as +0 P. In Sirius, when a peregrine planet is in mutual reception by sign, the mutual reception takes away the -5 pointing for being peregrine. I would question whether this is an across-the-board rule, or one that only applies when the other planet has dignity. This may seem like a rather trivial quibble – and on a cosmic scale, it is. I do think it's important, though, to always remember that astrology did not develop in an environment of constant precision and mindless replicability. One of the most common admonitions of William Lilly was to "judge accordingly."

Finally, with regard to positions, please note that I am using Regiomontanus houses, and the Mean Node positions.

1

An Introduction to Classical and Not-so-Classical Mundane

ONE COULD MAKE A PRETTY GOOD CASE THAT MUNDANE MATTERS HAVE BEEN THE DRIVING FORCE BEHIND THE DEVELOPMENT OF COMPLEX ASTROLOGICAL SYSTEMS IN MANY CULTURES. Because traditional cultures since the beginning of history (not archeology) have been primarily agrarian in their economies, those mundane systems that predict the year and its surpluses or shortages became the most prized.

Weather Prediction

From this need and desire for information about the year, **astrometeorology** developed. Thus, as Bos and Burnett point out, the history of weather can be understood as astrometeorology.[5] Weather forecasting was a huge component of the early **parapegmata**, the compendia of events associated with different phases of the moon or the solar months. Weather predictions often included signs of rain, or wind – where the word "signs" is reminiscent of both biblical usage and also of astrology itself. If you care to consult Pliny's *Natural History* on-line (primarily Books 17-18), you will find a compendium of these types of signs, or predictions.

Whether by days, months, or the 28 stars used by the Arabs, weather patterns were observed and typical expectations developed. Thus, one can see weather prediction as establishing a base of seasonal patterns overlaid by deviations from the norm. Astrology, **scapulimancy**, or other divinatory signs were means to add communication with the gods into the equation.

That there was an involvement of the celestial bodies was clear, even if one simply meant the Sun's path through the zodiac. As one of the forms of natural astrology, astrometeorology was unaffected by the later religious condemnations of **judicial astrology**. The Sun's path marked the seasons, and the seasons in turn had typical weather.

It's worth stopping to consider just how logical it was to assume that the planets had such a contribution to make to the weather. As al-Kindi (c. 801-866) said:

"But if only the Sun effected this in this arrangement without the other planets, we would not see the nature of the seasons change, for thus the effects of the seasons would be equal: moisture and cold for the air in winter, coldness and dryness of the air in autumn, moisture alone in spring, and dryness of the air in summer, perpetually. And if we said that this was effected by the Sun and Moon but not the other planets, any day you like in one year would be similar in temperament and nature to any day you like in a second year, but this is something we do not see at all."[6]

This very ancient idea of an annual progression with seasonal variation is still embedded in any contemporary weather site you choose to visit on-line, which will show you the daily and monthly averages for high and low temperatures, and rainfall.

As critical to planning as weather prediction was, and as much as the monarch had more than a passing interest in the success of his farmers, the other great kingly activity was war. And just so, astrological systems were developed to enable the king or emperor to determine danger from his peers, or the best time to invade neighboring lands.[7]

The Babylonian Period

The earliest methods of the Babylonians, like the rest of their astrological systems, were primarily omen-based. But what is a mundane omen? This was also an issue for the Chinese. One answer to the question is that a mundane omen is a divinatory technique performed at an astronomically appropriate time, such as a lunation or ingress, or when an unscheduled celestial event occurred, such as a comet or **eclipse**. At these times in Shang China, the Emperor presided over one or more tortoise shell divinations that related to what sacrifices the Emperor needed to make to produce a good harvest or other positive result.[8] The wording of the question often appeared not unlike a horary question, by proposing a particular sacrifice, and asking if that would be appropriate.

In Mesopotamian cosmology, the gods and goddesses collectively decide upon future events, and then communicate these plans through the stars. The stars are read by diviners, who then communicate what they read to the king, who acts upon these messages.[9] As Campion points out, this process was participatory, in the sense that the king *acted* upon the omen, just as the Chinese Emperor acted upon the sacrifice of however many of his subjects or prisoners approved by the gods.[10] This issue of participation points out that the message was not merely from the deities to humans. Human action could change the future, just as surely as human inaction guaranteed that it would unfold as planned. As Campion says:

"Yet, we can see the entire astrological process as consisting of three phases, of which the first is the measurement or observation of celestial phenomena, and the second their interpretation or diagnosis. The third is the consequent action, the prescription, for there is no point in predicting the future unless it can be changed."[11]

One of the biggest challenges in mundane work, as evidenced as far back as the Babylonians, is *where* an effect will take place. The earliest answer to this question was to develop a quadrant system, then a zone system, and then a horoscopic system. Astrologers were painfully aware that, should an event call for the death of a king, not all kings of the world died. It was of critical importance to identify which king.

Hellenistic Mundane

The protocols of mundane astrology that we observe in Ptolemy's *Tetrabiblos* demonstrated methods using primarily lunations and eclipses. From these charts, certain predictions could be made, such as pinpointing the areas of life (houses) where the effect would be most marked. The second book of the *Tetrabiblos* remains one of the most important works historically for the study of mundane astrology. Even when the Arabs later developed the system of **major conjunctions,** the use of eclipses continued. Their interpretation was integrated into other systems as well, such as their use within the system of **revolutions**, which included the Aries and other ingresses of the Sun into the cardinal signs.

The problem raised by this horoscopic approach is that it is not entirely clear how ancient authors dealt with the fact that charts of the same eclipse could be drawn up for multiple countries – and how this fact should be interpreted. For example, charts of adjacent kingdoms might not have significantly different **angles**. If the interpretation was that a King of the West would die, and two kingdoms both had charts showing this, the question is: West of which? Does only the king of the furthest West kingdom die? Eclipses did have the further refinement of possibly only being effective if the eclipse could be seen – but authors are not unanimous on this point.

The Theory of the Great Conjunctions

The theory of **great conjunctions** added another nuance to mundane interpretation – one which will especially occupy us in this book. Great conjunctions are any series of conjunctions between **superior planets** only. This is the system in Western astrology that moved the study of mundane past the yearly agricultural cycles into the longer cycles necessary to understand culture as an historical process, not merely a seasonal one.

The idea of longer periods was not new: the Babylonians had divided the world into three time periods as early as 1000 B.C.E.[12] But it wasn't until a couple of centuries later that the Babylonians achieved the ability to predict the future planetary positions: an impressive technological advance, but one that drew away the power of the gods and goddesses to write new messages in the sky.[13]

What differed with the Arabic material was greater precision in the ability to calculate forward and backward, and its relation to only one astrological phenomenon: the successive conjunctions of Jupiter and Saturn. The full Jupiter-Saturn cycle was declared to be 960 years, which, at 20 years per conjunction is a total of 48 total conjunctions, averaging 240 years per element. Quickly doing the math, 12 conjunctions per element should mean four conjunctions in each sign per pass – but this doesn't work out so neatly in practice. For example, in the just completed Earth **Triplicity** mutation, there were actually nine conjunctions in Earth – three to each sign. According to Masha'allah (fl 762- ca. 815) in *On Conjunctions, Religions and Peoples*, each change of element was associated with changes in government.[14] These ideas were further elaborated to include both political and religious changes.[15] Not only was the Triplicity considered, but also the Quadruplicity:

"If their [Jupiter-Saturn] conjunction is in <one of> the tropical signs, it indicates universal changes. If it is in <one of> the fixed <signs>, it indicates the firmness of their condition, and the changes will be toward prosperity. If it is in <one of> the <bi> corporeal <signs>, the matter in this case is middling,

and this indicates that at the time of their conjunction most of the prosperity is in the countries of Jupiter, and the corruption in the countries of Saturn."[16]

It is almost impossible to overemphasize how important the triplicity of the conjunctions was in interpretation. Abu Ma'shar (c. 787-886) discussed this in detail in his work, *On the Great Conjunctions.*[17] He specifies that the sign in each triplicity that is furthest from Aries is strongest: thus, Sagittarius is the strongest fire sign, and the same for Pisces, Aquarius, and Capricorn. This idea of the relative strength of the three signs within an element is also applied in medical astrology.

Abu Ma'shar was clear in stating that the understanding of the Jupiter-Saturn cycle concerned *beginnings*, because this combination brings order. Mars added to the series shows destruction, which produces the end of things.[18]

How accurate is this description of the cycle using our modern astronomical equations? The results are shown in Table 1-1.

Year	Position	Years elapsed
25 B.C.E.	3 Leo	—
769 C.E.	0 Leo	794
1603	8 Sagittarius	809
2338	2 Sagittarius	735

Table 1-1. Iteration of the "960 year" Jupiter-Saturn cycle in practice. This shows the first conjunction within the fiery Triplicity in each era.

The first problem we encounter is the presumption that the first instance of the Fire signs, considered the starting point of this cycle, would always fall not only in Aries, but in the first **Face** (i.e., 10 degrees) of Aries, or at least *some* fire sign, it doesn't. For the cycle beginning 1603, *none* of the conjunctions occurred in the first ten degrees of Aries. So, does that mean that this mutation in fire doesn't count? We're in it still!

If we restrict the positions to the first Face of Aries, and not the first conjunction in the Fire signs, then we get the following results:

Year	Position	Years elapsed
114 C.E.	6 Aries	—
908	4 Aries	794
1702	6 Aries	794
2497	4 Aries	795

Table 1-1a. Iteration of the "960 year" Jupiter-Saturn cycle in practice, allowing only Aries as the starting Fire sign.

Here we see that the presumed length of the cycle of 960 years leaves a little bit to be desired when it comes to accuracy. In practice, this doesn't really change very much, except that the transition between elements can sometimes be a bit messy, with a couple of back and forths – and this challenges the definition of the cycles, especially since Aries is not necessarily the first Fire sign in these sequences. It also challenges history, because, as we shall see shortly, contemporary astrological writings confirm that 1603 was treated as the beginning of the new cycle.

Besides the 20 year elemental mutations, **great mutation** cycles, and all the seasonal ones, there were also Mars-Jupiter and Mars-Saturn cycles. The latter, which occur every couple of years, were used for shorter range forecasting. The Mars-Saturn especially was useful for determining which of the two **malefics** held greater sway over the next few years. This interpretation was best described by the later Medieval system of varying the interpretation of an aspect based on which of the two aspecting planets has the greater **essential dignity**.[19] According to al-Qabisi, the Mars-Saturn cycle was drawn out to a thirty year cycle by using the Mars-Saturn conjunction in Cancer as the starting point: this would be analogous to the 960 year cycle of Jupiter-Saturn. It is interesting that this cycle of malefics would be *started* in Cancer, where both are debilitated.[20]

Because the Jupiter-Saturn, Mars-Saturn and Mars-Jupiter cycles were all used, if Mars happens to conjoin Jupiter and Saturn during the period that Jupiter and Saturn themselves conjoin, that particular Jupiter-Saturn conjunction is called a major conjunction, and it was considered to be that much more significant in scope. As an example, the 2000 Jupiter-Saturn conjunction was of this type, but the 2021 is not.

The Jupiter-Saturn conjunctions since the earth sign element mutation are shown in Table 1-2.

If we follow the logic of these ancient astrologers, then we are in the midst of a transition which began in 1980 and will be completed in 2020. How do we tell the effects of this change? At the time of that series of conjunctions in 2000, the most obvious thing going on was the collapse of the tech stocks. But of course, 2000 was the election year in the U.S.A. that needed the Electoral College and the Supreme Court to decide it, and one could say that this Republican sweep set up a pattern which will continue to be felt, through action or reaction, until the next conjunction in 2020.

Year(s)	Position	Major Conjunction?
1802	2 Virgo	
1821	24 Aries	X
1842	8 Capricorn	
1861	18 Virgo	
1881	1 Taurus	
1901	14 Capricorn	X
1921	26 Virgo	
1940-1941	14, 12, 9 Taurus	
1961	25 Capricorn	
1980-1981	9, 8, 4 Libra	
2000	22 Taurus	X
2020	0 Aquarius	
2040	17 Libra	X
2060	0 Gemini	

Table 1-2. Jupiter-Saturn conjunctions since 1802. Data from Michelsen.[21]

On the other hand, it is very tempting to begin with 1980, because that was the year that President Reagan was elected and there is no question that the Reagan Presidency changed the paradigm for presidential power.[22] Within the model of Stephen Skowronek, the Reagan Presidency was a paradigm-setting presidency: one that set the tone through George W. Bush's Presidency – and possibly even beyond. Even more interestingly, Bush II was elected in the next transitional Jupiter-Saturn conjunctional year. Many of Abu Ma'shar's rules apply to examining the longevity of a dynasty of kings. It is not always easy to map these ideas to a democracy, where election cycles run in much shorter time periods than would be typical of monarchies. There are few democracies where a particular leader or even political party could have an absolute lock on power for the length of time that many royal dynasties did in the past. How we may adapt these ideas to the present will require more work, but utilizing a model something like Skowronek may be valuable – or other methods for looking for a preponderance of influence of one political party over time.

Using Abu Ma'shar's ideas about the Quadruplicity of the change-over, the Earth Triplicity began in the mutable sign Virgo in 1802, so that should have been middling in **quality**. And here, one idea might be that the advantages conveyed by this earth Triplicity were very favorable to some countries – but not to others. One possible interpretation of mutable is variable. The transition to the current Air sign period occurred with the conjunction in Libra in 1980, indicating a universal effect. In the modern age, we could expect nothing less, with the global economic linkages that were so strongly forged in the period of the previous Earth Triplicity.

Enter the Aries Ingress

However, we soon run into a methodological problem. Even as early as Masha'Allah, it was customary to draw up a chart to represent the conjunction and interpret it.[23] However, the chart that was used was the **Aries Ingress** for the year of the conjunction. Why? The answer is, it is hideously difficult to compute a conjunction chart for slowly moving bodies accurately – and that's assuming the level of astronomical accuracy that we now enjoy thanks to the equations derived from the Jet Propulsion Laboratory (JPL).[24] These equations include

estimates of gravitation effects of the other solar system bodies. The *Zij* calculations, which the Arabs had access to, recognized no gravitation effect, and were dependent upon assumptions of circular geocentric orbits with epicycles – an approximation, yes – but certainly not accurate enough to predict the precise time of the conjunction, and especially not going back to the alleged year of the Deluge (*i.e.*, Noah's flood) and to the alleged date of the birth of Jesus, as Masha'Allah did in his examples.

In Abu Ma'shar's system, the Mars-Saturn conjunction was also studied with respect to the Aries Ingress of the year: in fact, he gives extensive information for how to predict the result of the reign of a king based on the conditions of Mars, Jupiter, and Saturn for the Aries Ingress of the year of ascension.[25]

To help in studying the effect of the Mars-Saturn cycles as well as the Jupiter-Saturn ones, a compilation of the conjunctions of these two bodies is given in Table 1-3.

Date	Mars position	Saturn position
Dec 14 1901	15° Cp 42' D	15° Cp 42' D
Dec 20 1903	06° Aq 51' D	06° Aq 51' D
Dec 25 1905	28° Aq 43' D	28° Aq 43' D
Dec 30 1907	21° Pi 46' D	21° Pi 46' D
Dec 29 1909	16° Ar 27' D	16° Ar 27' D
Aug 16 1911	19° Ta 58' D	19° Ta 58' D
Aug 24 1913	16° Ge 55' D	16° Ge 55' D
Sep 10 1915	14° Cn 24' D	14° Cn 24' D
Oct 1 1917	11° Le 51' D	11° Le 51' D

Oct 24 1919	08° Vi 36' D	08° Vi 36' D		Feb 14 1964	25° Aq 30' D	25° Aq 30' D
Nov 13 1921	04° Li 07' D	04° Li 07' D		Feb 21 1966	17° Pi 47' D	17° Pi 47' D
Dec 1 1923	28° Li 14' D	28° Li 14' D		Mar 2 1968	11° Ar 18' D	11° Ar 18' D
Dec 14 1925	21° Sc 04' D	21° Sc 04' D		Mar 15 1970	06° Ta 17' D	06° Ta 17' D
Dec 26 1927	12° Sg 53' D	12° Sg 53' D		Mar 31 1972	02° Ge 42' D	02° Ge 42' D
Jan 3 1930	04° Cp 02' D	04° Cp 02' D		Apr 20 1974	00° Cn 08' D	00° Cn 08' D
Jan 11 1932	25° Cp 00' D	25° Cp 00' D		May 12 1976	27° Cn 51' D	27° Cn 51' D
Jan 17 1934	16° Aq 15' D	16° Aq 15' D		Jun 4 1978	25° Le 03' D	25° Le 03' D
Jan 24 1936	08° Pi 17' D	08° Pi 17' D		Jun 23 1980	21° Vi 05' D	21° Vi 05' D
Feb 1 1938	01° Ar 32' D	01° Ar 32' D		Jul 7 1982	15° Li 47' D	15° Li 47' D
Feb 11 1940	26° Ar 15' D	26° Ar 15' D		Feb 14 1984	16° Sc 18' D	16° Sc 18' D
Feb 22 1942	22° Ta 28' D	22° Ta 28' D		Feb 17 1986	08° Sg 57' D	08° Sg 57' D
Mar 6 1944	19° Ge 54' D	19° Ge 54' D		Feb 23 1988	00° Cp 45' D	00° Cp 45' D
Oct 26 1945	24° Cn 47' D	24° Cn 47' D		Feb 28 1990	22° Cp 06' D	22° Cp 06' D
Jan 20 1946	20° Cn 45' R	20° Cn 45' R		Mar 6 1992	13° Aq 29' D	13° Aq 29' D
Mar 20 1946	17° Cn 56' D	17° Cn 56' D		Mar 14 1994	05° Pi 18' D	05° Pi 18' D
Nov 12 1947	22° Le 13' D	22° Le 13' D		Mar 21 1996	28° Pi 00' D	28° Pi 00' D
Nov 30 1949	18° Vi 40' D	18° Vi 40' D		Apr 2 1998	21° Ar 56' D	21° Ar 56' D
Dec 18 1951	13° Li 47' D	13° Li 47' D		Apr 15 2000	17° Ta 16' D	17° Ta 16' D
Jan 1 1954	07° Sc 33' D	07° Sc 33' D		May 4 2002	13° Ge 53' D	13° Ge 53' D
Jan 14 1956	00° Sg 08' D	00° Sg 08' D		May 25 2004	11° Cn 18' D	11° Cn 18' D
Jan 23 1958	21° Sg 49' D	21° Sg 49' D		Jun 18 2006	08° Le 45' D	08° Le 45' D
Jan 31 1960	12° Cp 59' D	12° Cp 59' D		Jul 10 2008	05° Vi 26' D	05° Vi 26' D
Feb 6 1962	04° Aq 03' D	04° Aq 03' D		Jul 31 2010	00° Li 49' D	00° Li 49' D

Aug 15 2012	24° Li 49' D	24° Li 49' D
Aug 25 2014	17° Sc 40' D	17° Sc 40' D
Aug 24 2016	09° Sg 52' D	09° Sg 52' D
Apr 2 2018	08° Cp 57' D	08° Cp 57' D
Mar 31 2020	00° Aq 39' D	00° Aq 39' D
Apr 4 2022	22° Aq 24' D	22° Aq 24' D
Apr 10 2024	14° Pi 40' D	14° Pi 40' D
Apr 19 2026	07° Ar 51' D	07° Ar 51' D
Apr 30 2028	02° Ta 15' D	02° Ta 15' D
May 16 2030	27° Ta 59' D	27° Ta 59' D
Jun 3 2032	24° Ge 51' D	24° Ge 51' D
Jun 26 2034	22° Cn 17' D	22° Cn 17' D
Jul 19 2036	19° Le 29' D	19° Le 29' D
Aug 11 2038	15° Vi 44' D	15° Vi 44' D
Aug 30 2040	10° Li 36' D	10° Li 36' D
Sep 15 2042	04° Sc 04' D	04° Sc 04' D
Sep 26 2044	26° Sc 27' D	26° Sc 27' D
Oct 3 2046	18° Sg 09' D	18° Sg 09' D
Oct 2 2048	09° Cp 42' D	09° Cp 42' D

Table 1-3. Mars-Saturn conjunctions since 1900. Data generated from Solar Fire. EST +5:00

In considering the Mars-Saturn cycle from the standpoint of the U.S.A., it is interesting that, since the cycle length is a little more than two years, there will always be a different Mars-Saturn for each presidential term. However, this short length raises the question: what is it good for? It is too long for an agricultural cycle, and too short for many other things. The two year length might well be perfect for a political election cycle where the term in office is two years or more.

Abu Ma'shar delineated the Mars-Saturn conjunction by sign, specifying riots and war in the countries designated as being ruled by that sign.[26] He began with the conjunction in Cancer, noting that in this sign, both planets are debilitated. The Triplicity of the conjunction was also interpreted, giving something of the location of the major effects, as well as weather patterns associated with it.[27] He also interpreted the conjunction by house – but we need to remember that this is the house of the Aries Ingress for the year in which the conjunction occurs.[28]

Guido Bonatti

We can examine the transmission of Arabic ideas into the Latin West by examining Guido Bonatti (1207?-1296?). Bonatti's work follows the method of Abu Ma'shar fairly closely, although his emphasis has changed. The emphasis in the mundane section is completely on the Aries Ingress. This follows a definition which encompasses both the personal solar return and the Aries Ingress, defining them both as two categories of **revolutions.**[29]

This would seem to be a departure from the earlier Arabic material – but it isn't really. Consider: in all of the discussion about the great conjunctions, and even the longer cycles of them, the mode of interpretation was always to examine the Aries Ingress for the year of the conjunction. So a practical work on mundane astrology would necessitate a thorough understanding of the modes of delineating the Aries Ingress, which would then be coupled with a discussion of exactly what additional information one would glean from the Jupiter-Saturn cycles and Mars-Saturn cycles, both as delineated through the Aries Ingress. That is precisely what Bonatti produced.

Bonatti cites Abu Ma'shar repeatedly and positively in this section. He elaborates somewhat, as Bonatti is prone to highly detailed lists of considerations. In this case, he gives fifty-four considerations for finding the **Lord of the Year.** Abu Ma'shar's list was not so imposing, nor as systematically organized.[30] Bonatti proceeds to analyze the revolution using additional concepts of Abu Ma'shar, such as the Significator of the King, and when the Lord of the Year is made the **Significator of the King.** Throughout this discussion, Abu Ma'shar is cited repeatedly.[31] Bonatti continues the use of Ptolemy's system of *climata* for finding the location of the effects of the revolution that was used throughout the Arabic period.

Mostly, Bonatti follows Abu Ma'shar's work *On the Great Conjunctions.* But two places where he elaborates are, first, in giving the rules for electing to go to war,[32] and secondly, in systematically presenting the interpretation of the Arabic parts (or Lots) in revolution charts – although clearly, the latter wasn't meant to apply only to revolutions.[33]

William Ramesey

The 1653 work, *Astrologia Restaurata*, by William Ramesey (1627-1675/6) is the first comprehensive work on mundane astrology published in English.[34] It follows the structure of Bonatti quite strongly, even preceding the section on mundane with a section on electional, just as Bonatti had done with Treatises 7 and 8. One component of the earlier systems that had become vestigial by Ramesey's day is the location system of *climata*. Perhaps the discovery of the New World as well as Asian and Pacific exploration made the old system seem naively stunted as it defined a center of civilization that simply no longer applied. This would only be replaced wholesale in the modern period by new systems of pinpointing locations. But even by Ramesey's time, the *climata* were not strictly necessary, since Aries Ingress charts could be run for multiple locations. In any case, they had developed lists of countries and cities that were ruled by particular signs, and these listings had replaced the *climata*, although it remains to be determined how much of the lists had in fact been derived from them.

Where Ramesey and his other contemporaries differed was in beginning to lay greater emphasis on using the aspects besides the conjunctions of the superior planets. Thus, we see the following:

> *Wherefore then know, that years of War, Dissention, Quarrels and Bloodshed, are to be judged from the Conjunction of Saturn and Jupiter, as also from their Square and Opposition, also from the Ascendant and Angles of the Revolution of the year; for if these Superior Planets be either in Conjunction, Square or Opposition of each other, or applying to each other by any of these Configurations, wars are to be feared, and that they shall then begin when they are in Partil Conjunction or Aspect, if they are in Angles, or else they shall begin when Jupiter enters his exaltation or one of his houses [i.e., Pisces or Sagittarius], or any of the Angles of the Figure at the time of the Revolution; and judge that party to have Victory that is signified by the Planet most elevated in his excentrik; for if Jupiter be most elevated, and be exalted above Saturn, they shall overcome who make insurrection or begin the strike.*

Also if Mars be in any of the Angles at the time of the Revolution, whichsoever it be, he excites and stirs up wars according to his strength and power; for if he be strong and well dignified, it will be the more certain, also the strife and war will be the more invective and grievous; in like matter if he be in a Square of Saturn or Jupiter, because these are the Superior Planets; for take this as an approved Aphorism, that when any of the Superiors, viz. Saturn, Jupiter or Mars (who are thus termed because they are above the Sun) are in Conjunction, or any Malevolent Configuration one of another, there happens great and manifest Alterations in this Elementary world, according to their strength and natural and accidental Significations.[35]

Let's tease out the ideas here that were already present in the Arabic material.

- This quotation began by referencing the Jupiter-Saturn cycle as the source of wars and other contentions, which is exactly like the material we have already been examining from the Arabs. But immediately, Ramesey adds the other hard aspects to the conjunction as being significant. Now, instead of a twenty year cycle for Jupiter-Saturn, we are talking intervals of, on average, five years, depending upon the retrograde cycles. Also note that, since he references all the superior configurations, there is a guarantee of an approaching aspect of Mars-Saturn to consider in *every* Aries Ingress, unless Mars is retrograde, because now the 2+ year cycle of Mars and Saturn can be divided by four to give well less than a year. We should note that the Arabs recognized the hard aspects as being significant: Abu Ma'shar discussed them in *The Book of Flowers*.[36] One does detect a somewhat subtle shift, from the minor to the normal.

- An additional activation factor needed to make the promise of the hard aspect or conjunction come true is the presence of the superiors in angles; Abu Ma'shar discussed that in Part Seven of his work, *On the Great Conjunctions*. They still have signification over mischief by house placement regardless; it's just that the angles are more significant for actual war.

- The other additional factor, which comes right out of the Arabic material as well, is that Jupiter in his Exaltation can push things over the edge. Abu Ma'shar discussed the exaltations of the planets at length, giving the impression that the exaltations were at least as significant from the standpoint of strength as sign rulership. To our modern ears, we might not think of the exalted Jupiter as so warlike, but perhaps this is a function of overconfidence and self-righteousness on the part of the ruler. As a cultural artifact, it seems that moderns view war as an aberration of peace, whereas the ancient view was that war was the business of princes.

- The relative **elevation** of the superiors is also an Arabic concept: the planet most elevated is stronger. The Arabic material had gone so far as to specify combinations, according to which of the three was most elevated. Elevation is a measure in this case of proximity to the MC. Later, we shall see how bodies at the IC can be extremely unpleasant – just the flip side of the elevation idea.

Lest it be thought that Ramesey was putting too much emphasis on the Aries Ingress at the expense of the major conjunctions, his Chapter XI and the succeeding ones address these conjunctions directly. First, he lists the seven sorts of major conjunctions one needs to consider:

> *The first and greatest of all the rest, is the Conjunction of the two superiour Planets Saturn and Jupiter in the first term or degree of Aries, which happens but once in nine hundred and threescore years.*
>
> *The second is the Conjunction of Saturn and Jupiter in the first term or degree of every triplicity, and this is accomplished once in two hundred and forty years, yet once in twenty years, they come into Conjunction in one part or other of the Zodiack.*
>
> *The third is the Conjunction of Saturn and Mars in the first term or degree of Cancer, and this is once in thirty years.*
>
> *The fourth is the Conjunction of the three superiours, Saturn, Jupiter and Mars in one term or face of any sign.*
>
> *The fifth is the Conjunction of Jupiter and Mars, which is a mean and the least Conjunction of the superiours, and therefore is not the fore-runner of such great mischiefs as the other;...*
>
> *The sixth is the Conjunction of the Sun with any of the rest of the Planets at the time of his entrance into the first point of Aries.*
>
> *The seventh and last is the Conjunction of the Sun and Moon, which happens once every month."*[37]

Notice that points 1-3 follow exactly from Abu Ma'shar, with the addition in the enumeration of the specific definition of the first degree or Term of the sign in question.[38] The thirty year cycle of Mars-Saturn is mentioned twice in Abu Ma'shar.[39]

This material does raise a point that, in my opinion, was never addressed adequately in the classical literature. That question concerns malefics in dignity and debility. I refer specifically to the 44th Aphorism of Guido Bonatti:

> *The 44th is, to consider if the Significators, Fortune or* **Infortune***, be in his own House, Exaltation, Triplicity, Terms or Face (but the latter being not of that virtue with the rest, 'tis necessary it should be assisted with another Dignity, which is* **Hayz** *or Light); for in such case the Infortune loses his sting; and being rein'd in like a wild horse from doing mischief, his malice is converted into good, and though this seems strange, yet the ancients affirm and I myself have often found it true by experience.*[40]

The idea here is that malefics dignified behave rather well. This is an aphorism that I have used for years, because in horary, either Mars or Saturn dignified hardly need be counted as a malefic at all. When it reverts to a sign of no dignity, the change can virtually be described as catastrophic.

So the question that I am raising is this: from the standpoint of predicting calamities, what should one make of the dignities of the malefics? When Bernadette Brady and I did empirical studies on Mars and Saturn in predicting the outcome of sporting events, this aphorism loomed large. It was the malefics in debility that were especially strong as combatants.[41] Mars and Saturn dignified were more likely to produce losses than wins.

Our data definitely supported the idea of Aphorism 44. The problem is that, historically, while this idea percolated through iterations of method, it never seemed to be fully worked out in terms of its consequences. There is an analogous problem in medical astrology, which, I am told, also permeates *Jyotish*.[42] And that is: when a planet is said to rule an herb or a stone, how do you actually use that herb or stone in practice? For example, if my natal Mars is problematic, do I want to fortify that Mars by wearing an amulet or a bloodstone (ruled by Mars), or do I want to use something antagonistic, like a stone ruled by Venus? This concept of excess and deficiency, while present in the texts, is not consistently worked out in practice.

There is one hint of this recognition in the use of a Mars-Saturn cycle that begins with the conjunction in Cancer. As Abu Ma'shar had indicated that the purpose of studying these cycles at all was to observe beginnings and endings, perhaps having the malefics the most badly behaved represents some logic that things can't get any worse, so there is an upswing – a beginning of a sort.

Sir Christopher Heydon and Richard Edlyn

Before we leave the classical period, I want to cite two more authors. Richard Edlyn (1631-1677). Edlyn (sometimes spelled Edlin, and related to the later spelling Edelen) published two books on the major conjunctions, one on the Mars-Saturn and the other on the Jupiter-Saturn. In his earlier Mars-Saturn work, he nonetheless refers to the Jupiter-Saturn conjunction of 1603, and the two following. Why 1603? Because the 1603 conjunction, as we saw in Table 1-1, was the first conjunction in the fire signs, and hence, it was a mutation. The 1623 conjunction occurred in 6 Leo, and the 1643 conjunction occurred in 25 Pisces, while the 1663 one occurred at 12 Sagittarius. As we have already seen, the Jupiter-Saturn cycle isn't quite as regular as the Arabic descriptions imply, and here we have a case where there were two sequential

conjunctions in fire before there was one "retrogressive" conjunction in water, the element that preceded fire in the sequence. The 1603 conjunction was observed by the astrologer, Sir Christopher Heydon (d. 1623), and his correspondence concerning this was still considered relevant enough to reprint in 1650 and 1690.[43] Heydon refers to his observations being confirmed by Kepler.[44] Because he actually observed the conjunction, and because he confirmed his observation through Kepler, Heydon presented a chart for the actual moment of the conjunction, reproduced here as Figure 1.

This is the earliest discussion of an actual Jupiter-Saturn chart that I have found – but it may not in fact be the earliest such case. Heydon was cautious about describing the circumstances of his observations, suggesting that he felt the need to reference or justify this chart, not from ephemeris calculations, but from direct observation. This implies that he was aware that it was not possible to create a chart for the exact moment of the conjunction based on the existing calculational resources – a statement that is certainly true.

Heydon's initial discussion pertains to Kepler's New Star, the supernova he had described in Ophiuchus. While he did describe the position of *De Stella Nova* in this chart in more verbiage than his delineation of the chart itself, nonetheless, he did interpret it. He inserted the position of the eclipse from 1605 (you may see this in the 9th house), and he remarked on the conjunction being in the 12th house in London.

So we can conclude that, by the opening of the 17th century, astrologers were aware that they *could* interpret a chart for a major conjunction *if* they were reasonably sure of the accuracy of the data, which meant that it *must* be produced by direct sky observation. It's also worth mentioning that Heydon lived during

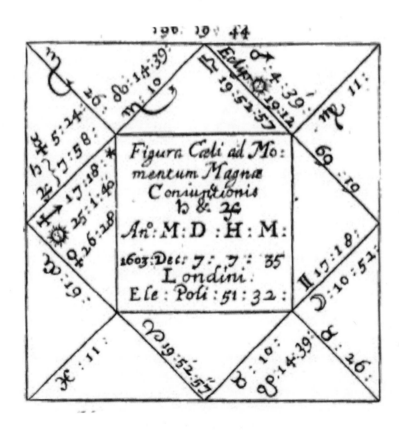

Figure 1. Heydon's chart of the
Jupiter-Saturn conjunction of 1603.[45]

the time when astronomical observational instruments were being massively improved by such as Tycho Brahe (1546-1601) and Gemma Frisius (1508-1555).[46]

Lest there be any doubt about this conclusion, Edlyn quoted Vincent Wing specifically on this point in his Mars-Saturn work. Wing (1619-1668), a student of William Lilly, was the foremost British mathematical astrologer of his day. His computations, which were based upon Kepler's heliocentric elliptical orbits, were much more accurate than similar ephemerides of even a century earlier. Edlyn said:

> How improbable it is to have the time of their Conjunctions, which is or ought to be understood, when they are in degree, minute and second at least; And thus likewise doth the intricacy of finding the said time by instrument appear, by which, though as large as ever any was, no man can observe to half a minute, if to a minute, and to this purpose Mr. Vincent Wing after the Calculation of the conjunction of Saturn and Jupiter: 1663, hath most judiciously expres'd himself by way of caution, whose words may take the better impression in the minds of all judicious Astrologians. I think it necessary here to repeat them.
>
> To erect a figure (saith he) for the time of this Conjunction is too great a curiosity for any to attempt, for if we could but judiciously consider the great difficulty in observing the true places of the stars and planets with instruments, we shall wave [sic.] such niceties, for I am confident the most curious Observator on Earth, though his instrument be never so large and exquisitely divided, may yet fail 2 or 3 minutes at some time in taking the place of any star, as Tycho himself hath sundry times experimented, who with his Coadjutors and Assistants did usually

> make several observations at once, in different places about taking the longitude and latitude of one and the same star, so that hence the (best) Tables built upon observation, must of necessity fail somewhat of truth, though not much, being directed by an able Artist, as in this Conjunction should we fail but one minute in the place of each planet, we should miss no less than 8 hours of the time of the conjunction, which with the best instrument that can be used is scarce discernable; the further proof whereof I leave to the consideration of the judicious, but not to the fancy of every practitioner.[47]

Edlyn's remarks reinforce the point that using an actual chart for the time of a Jupiter-Saturn conjunction was considered far too risky from the standpoint of accuracy. One can also note that the *idea* of using this chart would follow directly from interpreting New Moon charts, what we might call the minor conjunctions, to contrast them with the major conjunctions.

Edlyn went on to accept Heydon's observations, but then he noted that the calculation of the conjunction using Kepler's Rudolphine tables differed by 24 hours.[48] Wing's conclusion is that attempts to produce a correct chart have too many intrinsic difficulties, and he suggests using the preceding or subsequent lunation as the guide to the meaning of the conjunction.[49]

One of the techniques that is very clear in Edlyn's interpretation of the 1661 Mars-Saturn conjunction was that he still considered the degree of the 1603 Jupiter-Saturn conjunction to be significant, again, highlighting the importance of the mutation of element, and also the interconnectedness of the Mars-Saturn cycle interpretation with the more ponderous Jupiter-Saturn one.[50]

As for the interpretation of the Mars-Saturn, I will reproduce part of his text. The chart he is referring to is given in Figure 2.

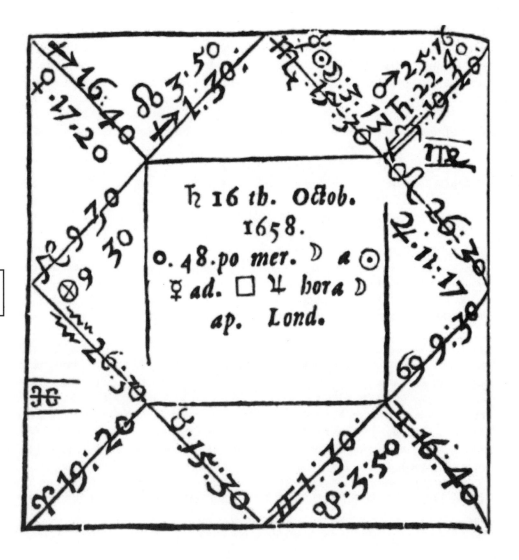

Figure 2. New Moon following Mars-Saturn conjunction in Edlyn (1659), p 46.

Please first observe that Edlyn has followed his own advice: he has not attempted to do a chart for the actual conjunction, but for the following New Moon. Edlyn spends a great deal of time attempting to decide whether Mars or Saturn has dominion over the conjunction.

We have seen that classical astrology allowed for a different interpretation of an aspect based on which planet had more essential dignity in that degree. But Edlyn brings in a whole series of arguments relating to dominion, and it's worth examining them here, in order to see the kinds of factors that were considered.

But for the more particular distinction of the Effects, we are advised (and with good reason) to consider that Planet who hath most dominion, whether it be a greater or lesser Conjunction, Eclipse, annual Revolution, &c.... Messah de Mag.... know saith he, that planet that is strongest shall be chief significator, who if he be of evil nature shall signify much tribulation and detriment, if he be a fortune, he signifies good, &c. he goeth further...., (i.e.) if these Planets be in their Exaltations, it signifieth good, the fitness of time, yet there will be much war and Commotion, and the shewing of wonders..., but also if they be in their depressions or falls, they signifie great detriment, corruption, drought, famine, or great scarcity, unless they be otherwise fortunate.

It seems to me somewhat dubious which of these Planets shall have most dominion in this Conjunction, for if we observe them barely at the Conjunction, viz. In the place where they are conjoyned, we shall find Saturn in his Exaltation, and Mars in his fall, so that as Saturn is essentially dignifyed, and Mars depressed, we might from thence judge Saturn to have the most dominion, and the rather for that in the conjunction of the Sun and Mars, and of the Sun with himself, he hath the like dominion, and

in respect of his more Northern latitude is said to be elevated above them both; ... Haly pars 8 Cap 23. (i.e.) when Saturn is elevated above Mars he hath the better signification, but Ioh. Escuidus from Albumazar hath it more fully and significantly; fol 30.... Saturn elevated above Mars in Libra, signifieth enmity and hatred among Kings &c. the ayre will be temperate & there will be a remission of cold,... when he is elevated above the Sun, he signifieth much drought, famine or scarcity in many Countries; there will be abundance of Rain in its Season, the death of Children, these are the judgements of the ancients when Saturn is elevated only over those Planets.

But whether Saturn or Mars shall have chief and sole dominion is the question, for the Resolving of which I say, that notwithstanding Saturn his essentiall dignity, his elevation, &c. whereby a moderate artist would judge that much of his evil is prohibited; yet I observe that Saturn is wholly passive in both the conjunction of Sol and with Mars, as being applied to and wholly afflicted by both; and that in an extraordinary manner, and that at the subsequent lunation he hath such principal dominion in the Angles of the figure, and the lunation it self as sole Ruler thereof, as also of the subsequent tropical ingress, viz. In December following.[51]

Edlyn's discussion has several departures from earlier material – and yet it is extremely valuable in demonstrating in some detail how he worked things out. I would like to mention specifically several points:

- Like his predecessors, he continued to be interested in determining whether Mars or Saturn was the principal ruler of the conjunction. Where he departs is in trying to integrate some of the ancient concepts in a complex system involving dignity, elevation, and **application**. There are a couple of problems with this. First, I'm not sure this list of factors is complete: these were merely the ones applying to this particular conjunction. Without knowing the entire list, one also doesn't know how the factors are weighted. In this case, Saturn is clearly the winner by essential dignity and elevation. However, if, as I pointed out earlier, Mars and Saturn can effectively be considered weak malefics when dignified, and real bad guys when debilitated, perhaps the argument here (since Edlyn clearly has decided that Mars is the winner) that a malefic in debility acts more strongly than a malefic in dignity. Second, and most importantly, I am troubled by his argument concerning the application of both the Sun and Mars to Saturn. His argument is that Saturn is passive (and thus weak) because it is the other planet that applies to Saturn. By this logic, a superior planet is almost always weaker than an inferior one, and a slower planet is weaker than a faster one. This conclusion does not fall out from traditional practice: in fact, the reverse is generally held to be true.

• Edlyn seems to have dispensed with the calculation of the Ruler of the Chart. Granted, Bonatti may have gone a shade overboard with his 53 considerations, but the point is well taken. The various classical methods of combining different factors to determine which planet was the ruler of a particular subject within a chart was well intentioned – and logically useful. The point of going through the trouble of calculating the Ruler of the Revolution, lunation, Eclipse, or Nativity, was to then allow a skillful elaboration of the situation based on that single planet – which avoids a lot of conflicting indications.

This is no different than my insistence in horary on having one Significator for each party, not several.[52] The issue, as I explain in *Martial Art of Horary Astrology*, is that one must have a methodology for sorting out conflicting arguments on the way to selecting that sole ruler. Bonatti did have such a procedure. I'm not sure Edlyn did.

• Edlyn preferred to use the lunations surrounding the Mars-Saturn conjunction: but he gave no consistent model for which of the four to pick: the New Moon before or after, or the Full Moon before or after. Without a consistent decision tree, there is the possibility for conflicting results. Furthermore, he gives no rationale for abandoning the traditional method of using the Aries Ingress prior to the event.

Edlyn's second book was on the Jupiter-Saturn conjunctions.[53] In this work, he gave the correct period for the great cycle of Jupiter and Saturn, namely 794+ years.[54] This was presumably because Edlyn had access to the more accurate Rudolphine Tables. He does not mention anything about a discrepancy with the Arabic authors, so this fact was presumably well known in his time – and not considered any kind of argument against Arabic method. Edlyn was also aware of the discrepancy between defining the great mutation as occurring in the beginning of Aries, and the fact that the beginning of the conjunctions within the Fire Triplicity did not necessarily occur in Aries. He incorrectly stated that it always begins in Sagittarius – which was true in his time, and will be true the next time, although the beginning before that in 764 was in Leo, which he missed, using instead the conjunction following it in 809 in Sagittarius.[55] I think the problem was that he had adopted the idea of a 199-year period within each element, but this does not account for retrograde cycles which can affect the transition between the Triplicities.

His chart for the 1663 eclipse is actually for the next lunation after the Jupiter-Saturn conjunction, as shown in Figure 3. Like the example that we showed in Figure 2, this is for the New Moon following the event. These two examples give us the impression that Edlyn preferred the New Moon after – but if this were the case, then why did he state the option of four possible lunations?

One point that this example does answer definitively: he refers to the 1663 Jupiter-Saturn conjunction as the third since the entry of the conjunctions into the Fire signs in 1603.[56] Since we know that the 1643 conjunction occurred in Pisces, then this nails the question of whether a run through an element starts the first time there is a conjunction in that element (as with the 1980 conjunction in Libra inaugurating the Air Triplicity period), or after the last "retrograde" back into the previous Triplicity (as would be the case if the Air Triplicity didn't begin until 2020). Within U.S. politics, we have two good pieces of evidence for the appropriateness of the 1980 Jupiter-Saturn as the true start of a new element:

I. The near universal agreement that Reagan's presidency represented a paradigm-shifting case.

II. The breakdown of Tecumseh's Curse, the observation of the death of Presidents elected in zero years, which had extended back to the beginning of the Jupiter-Saturn conjunctions in the Earth Triplicity, and which ended with President Kennedy following the 1960 election.

Edlyn mentions a comment by Lilly in his discussion for the 1603 conjunction concerning the Sabbatai Zevi, who was born about 20 years after this conjunction.[57] The changeover in element is often accompanied by a new religion according to Arabic theory. The Sabbatai had been hailed in his time by many Jews as the expected Messiah – the known mutation of the Triplicities undoubtedly played a role in the extremely high expectation for a Messiah at that time. This was just playing out in Lilly's day. As it turned out, the Sabbatai ended up converting to Islam and living out his days quietly – not as the One.

The Retrogression of the Conjunction

The **retrogression of the conjunction** into the water signs in 1643 was of profound interest to English and French astrologers, because that was during the English Civil War (1642-1649) – as well as the beginning of the reign of Louis XIV (the *Sun* King, fire imagery if there ever was!) in France. Edlyn says this about the 1663 conjunction:

> I cannot call this Conjunction Great, although it be as it were a restitution of the Fiery Trigon, considering that irregular one of the year 1643.[58]

Edlyn treats the 1643 conjunction in Pisces, and states boldly that it "should" have been in Aries, and, not having been so, was of a contrary nature:

> ...the kinds of men are made worse by the transmutations of those Conjunctions, when those that succeed are inimically configurated to those that are past. So I say did this preposterous

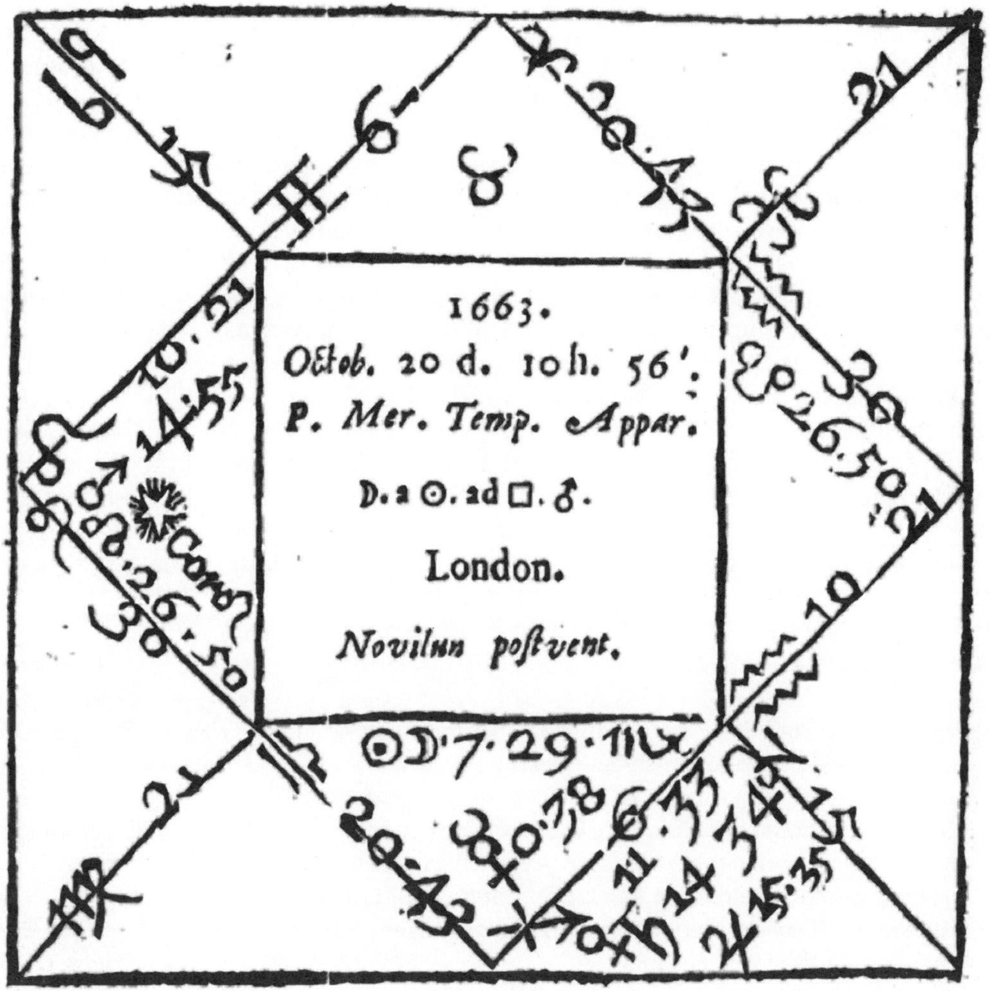

Figure 3. New Moon following Jupiter-Saturn conjunction in Edlyn (1664), p 21.

Effects, viz. The suppressing and abrogating of former Laws, Religion, Customs, Privileges, Governments, &c. which now from the effects of this Restitution, or returning again of the Superiours into the Fiery, First and Regal Triplicity, must all those exorbitant abuses both in Church and State be abolished, and all or most of those former Rights and Privileges, Laws and Customs, be restored and established upon their former principles and foundations.[59]

Don't hold back, Dick! What Edlyn was referring to in this rather strong diatribe was the restoration of Charles II to the throne in 1660 at the end of the Protectorate. In Edlyn's interpretation, the Jupiter-Saturn retrogression into the water signs provided an interlude when the portents of the Fiery Trigon were temporarily doused by a counterpoint. But it also points out the *easy* interpretation by astrologers that the ascension of Charles II to the throne *restored* the monarchy to its rightful place, as the Jupiter-Saturn conjunction in fire *restored* the pattern to its rightful type as fire.

We may observe that this same configuration of retrogression occurred in 2000. The disputed U.S. election in 2000, which went to the Supreme Court, could be taken as another example of this phenomenon.

So what we can see by the end of the Classical period is that a system of using major conjunctions developed which had a lot in common with the delineation of the minor conjunctions, *i.e.*, of the Sun and Moon. While there was variation from author to author, there was also significant continuity. At the end of the 17th century, there is a break in transmission in England for about fifty years – although it is not clear how complete this break actually was.

Ebinezer Sibly and the U.S. War of Independence

Years ago, I published a horary article based on the massive work of Ebinezer Sibly, *A New and Complete Illustration of the Celestial Science of Astrology*, in which I referred to Sibly's work as Rococo.[60] When I began, in the 1980s, to designate the astrology practiced before 1700 as classical, my actual rationale was as a musical reference, not a literary one. When we talk about classical music, it is still possible to compose in the classical style, but "classical" as a designation covers quite a few separate historical periods. But my designation of Rococo for Sibly was meant to convey something quite specific. Sibly is a pivotal figure in the history of astrology. He lived during the time when Uranus was discovered, and so he was among the first generation of astrologers to have to come to grips with this shocking change. And yet, he practiced primarily using classical methods. But Sibly learned his astrology from books, not from a living lineage, so while his work is definitely classical, there's a bit of a twist to some of it.

Sibly takes up the great conjunctions in his Third Part, which he styles "The Meteorological Part of Astrology." This section takes up all of mundane as well as the weather. There is some shift in emphasis, as seen in this statement:

After the impressive influx of the planetary configurations, the universal and particular effects of comets, eclipses, and great conjunctions, are next to be considered in this speculation.[61]

This is actually an excellent example of the problem of learning from books. Are we to infer that comets are the most important mundane consideration? We don't know whether this list is ordered by importance, or not. Actually, this seems to be one of the key issues when a lineage breaks: the following generations, should they want to regenerate the tradition, are often most stumped by the problem of multiple factors and their relative importance. To this point, Sibly has discussed eclipses and comets in great detail: not so the great conjunctions.

And yet – this is the section in which Sibly derives his chart for the 4th of July 1776, based on directing the Mars-Saturn conjunction earlier in the year. We see here his figures for the Aries and Cancer Ingresses of 1776 in Figure 4.

Sibly began with the Aries Ingress – which is precisely what Masha' Allah, Abu Ma'shar, Bonatti, or Ramesey would have done. Note that he presents the Cancer Ingress as well. As the Ascendant for the Aries Ingress in London is Sagittarius, which is a mutable or common sign, then the old rules state that only two ingresses per year are necessary, not four.[63] So the presentation here of the Cancer Ingress is extraneous, as the next chart to be used would have been Libra – which was too late for the events in question.

I have reproduced Sibly's own Aries Ingress chart in Figure 5. What is striking about this chart, having examined the development of these ideas, is how there has been some drift by the time it is in Sibly's hand. Let us examine his delineation on pp. 1052-1053 so that we can understand his method. While the quotation is broken up into parts, the entire quotation is given sequentially.

One of the things that's very hard to do when confronted by an example is to remember to view it critically, which means asking whether the statements within the text make sense, or whether they do or don't follow tradition. It's also important in examining mundane charts to assess them relatively. How notable is any one

Aries Ingress? So for that reason, I have included the 1775 and 1777 Aries Ingresses as well.

In the vernal equinox, we find Jupiter is lord of the Ascendant, and in his Detriment.

Since this chart is being done for London, this should make England the 1st House; and King George III the 10th house. Jupiter is indeed weak in Gemini, and in the house of open enemies, Jupiter/England is not initiating the action; the enemies are. But Sibly doesn't treat Jupiter as representing England at all! What is especially strange about this is that America was assigned to Gemini well before the U.S. war of independence, so a chart with Gemini on the 7th house in a period where trouble with America was brewing should have seemed extremely apt.

Mars we find in Aries, which is the ascendant of England, strong and powerful in his own house, but under the Earth.

Here, because England is an Aries country, Sibly automatically assigns Mars as England's ruler. But does this make sense? Considering the historical frequency of English wars with France, and France is traditionally ruled by Aries as well, what would we make of this? It appears that Sibly was determined to see the two combatants through the Mars-Saturn opposition, but his method of getting there was unique!

The Moon, who represents the common people, we find under affliction, being combust of the Sun; and Mars, being combust also, foreshows that England, though her internal strength is great and permanent, yet she will this year be

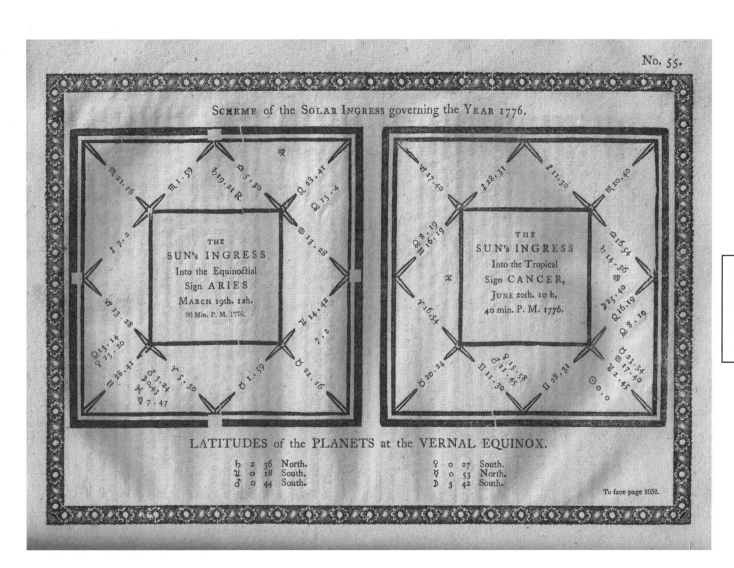

No. 55.

SCHEME of the SOLAR INGRESS governing the YEAR 1776.

THE
SUN's INGRESS
Into the Equinoctial
Sign ARIES
MARCH 19th. 12h.
20 Min. P. M. 1776.

THE
SUN's INGRESS
Into the Tropical
Sign CANCER,
JUNE 20th. 10 h.
40 min. P. M. 1776.

LATITUDES of the PLANETS at the VERNAL EQUINOX.

♄	2	36	North.	♀	0	27	South.
♃	0	18	South.	☿	0	53	North.
♂	0	44	South.	☽	3	42	South.

To face page 1052.

Figure 4.
Sibly's rendition of the Aries and Cancer Ingresses, 1776.[62]

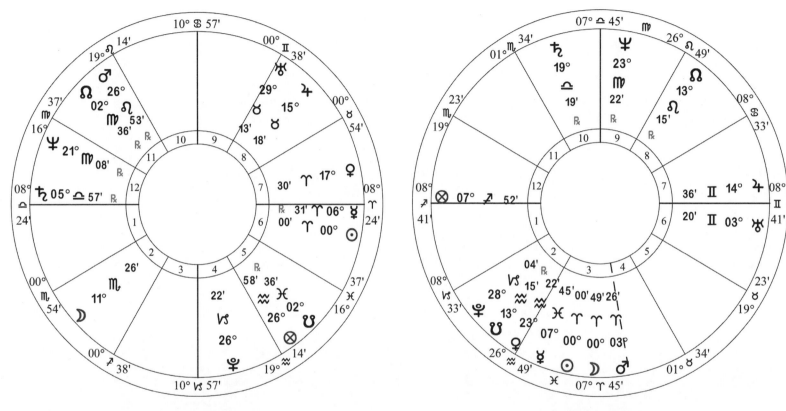

Sun enters Ari 3-20-1775
March 20, 1775
6:55:13 PM
London, England
51 N 30 0 W 10
Local Mean Time
Time Zone: 0 hours West
Tropical Regiomontanus
NATAL CHART

Figure 5. Aries Ingress for London, 1775-1777. Modern calculations.

Sun enters Ari 3-20-1776
March 20, 1776
12:36:02 AM
London, England
51 N 30 0 W 10
Local Mean Time
Time Zone: 0 hours West
Tropical Regiomontanus
NATAL CHART

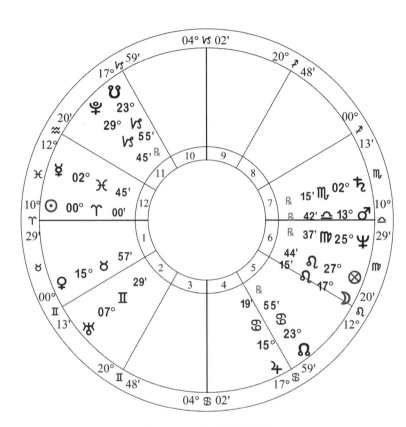

Sun enters Ari 3-20-1777
March 20, 1777
6:25:10 AM
London, England
51 N 30 0 W 10
Local Mean Time
Time Zone: 0 hours West
Tropical Regiomontanus
NATAL CHART

accidentally afflicted and depressed; more especially as we find Mars going to an opposition of Saturn, and Saturn uncommonly strong in the Midheaven, in his exaltation, and beheld by the two fortunes Jupiter and Venus; and consequently superior to Mars in power and dignity, who is under the Earth, and combust of the Sun, though located in his own house; which in this case serves however to show the permanency and stability of Great Britain during the whole of this trying conflict.

Sibly is correct in pointing out Moon and Mars are combust. He perhaps might have discussed the question of whether an ingress so close to a New Moon wasn't highly symbolic for the beginning of something. But the rest of this? Saturn is located in the 10th, exalted and elevated, albeit retrograde, so undoubtedly the best significator for the King. But the part I find hardest to swallow is that a cadent combust Mars (Sibly shows no evidence of using the **five degree rule** which would put a planet within 5° of the cadent side of an angle as still being angular) would show the "permanency and stability of Great Britain during the whole of this trying conflict." How can one single Aries Ingress argue the permanency of anything? And also, this is cardinal, not fixed – fixed would at least argue in the direction of permanency.

In this figure the planet Saturn is the significator of America, and Mars represents the people of Great Britain; as may very easily be seen by taking down the dignities of Saturn and Mars.... That Saturn hath the superiority of power, and that Mars and Saturn are inimical in their nature to each other, are facts too evident to be denied; and, as the aspect which is about to be formed between them is a malevolent one, namely, *a **partile** opposition, it declares the event shall be such as to cause a total and eternal separation of the two countries from each other.*

Again, why is America Saturn? Because Britain has dibs on Mars? One could argue the point that it was the colonists who were being belligerent at the time, and thus better described by Mars, with Saturn being "the old country." So in any Mars-Saturn opposition, house placement doesn't matter? Or alternately, countries or colonies cannot go to war when there's no Mars-Saturn opposition? How do we view the Aries Ingress from 1775, when there was tension between Mother England and her colonies, or 1777, when the two sides were at war? Was ever a Mars-Saturn aspect considered such a major combination as to produce "a total and eternal separation of the two countries from each other?"

*...and that the congress, which is represented by Saturn, will establish an independent and complete revolution, which shall be built upon a firm and durable foundation; and the increasing strength and durability of the new state is represented by Saturn in his exaltation, supported by the **benefic** rays of the two fortunes. And since there is a remarkable **reception** between the two planets Saturn and Venus, i.e., Venus in the house of Saturn, and Saturn in the house of Venus, supported by a propitious trine of Venus and Jupiter, while Jupiter and Saturn, and Saturn and Venus, with the three preceding planets, occupy and possess the whole expanse of the heavens; it is hence declared, that whatever is effected under this revolution of the Sun's ingress into Aries by the Americans, shall not only be permanent and durable, but shall be supported by those*

three grand pillars of state, wisdom, strength and unanimity; which are pointed out by those three planets, agreeable to their tendency and nature...

Again, isn't this a little grandiose for a single ingress? And really, if the Americans were so strong, why did the War last until 1783? If this interpretation was to be believed, the Yanks should have prevailed in a few months or less!

In my opinion, Sibly's delineation looks more like hindsight than foresight. Nonetheless, we see certain continuities of method that are worth mentioning as well as the breaks in transmission noted above.

Sibly interprets the superior planet configuration using an Aries Ingress. However, he seems to conflate the Mars-Saturn opposition into having the staying power of at least a turn of the elements within the Jupiter-Saturn cycle. As I mentioned earlier, the inability to prioritize may be symptomatic of the break in transmission of the method.

While I have not covered it here, he then uses primary directions to direct this Mars-Saturn opposition in order to find out when it will reach exactitude – and it comes to July 4, 1776. While there is no evidence that this method was ever used this way classically, nonetheless it is actually a beautiful example of the use of primary directions that has seldom been demonstrated in this level of detail.[64]

Sibly has inched away from using standard house rulers to using **natural rulers**, in rejecting the Ascendant for ruling England, and selecting instead the Mars of the approaching opposition.

Sibly discusses elevation and exaltation, both ideas going back to Arabic interpretation.

Luke Broughton

We next consider Dr. Luke Broughton (1828-1899), an Englishman who emigrated to the United States, and most importantly for our purposes, published the *Monthly Planetary Reader* from 1860-1869, neatly covering the U.S. Civil War. These periodicals give us a chance to examine his methodology over some period of time. His book, *Elements of Astrology*[65] shows a definite self-professed Ptolemaic influence that actually looks more like 17th century astrology than true Hellenistic.

His first issue was published in April 1860 – an election year. He wrongly predicted that Douglas would win over Lincoln. On page 7, he began his column "Predictions on the Fate of the Nation" which ran throughout the magazine's existence. He began by delineating the Aries Ingress, giving the angles, and declaring Jupiter to be Lord of the Year. In months without a cardinal ingress, he interpreted the New Moon; in the cardinal months, he also interpreted the ingress for the quarter in question. The fact that he knew to call Jupiter Lord of the Year shows that he was aware of the primacy of the Aries Ingress; the fact that he didn't follow the rule for determining how many ingresses per year to use may mean that he was unaware of the rule; or it may have been more convenient for journalistic purposes to always delineate all four quarters.

Examining his columns through the time of the magazine, the following pieces of methodology can be gleaned:

He used Uranus in his discussions, which obviously was not done in earlier works. But he does not use Neptune, despite its discovery in 1848.

He interpreted eclipses as well as ingresses and lunations. He held to the theory that eclipses not visible in a particular place result in little effect.

He worked with specific city and state rulerships: for example, Saturn in Leo being bad for Philadelphia, and Saturn in Virgo afflicting Boston and New England.

In examining important aspects for a time period, he would predict effects based on the nativity for the monarch of a particular country.

In February 1861, Broughton interpreted the square between Saturn and Uranus: *"These are significations of an evil nature. We do not look for any settlement of the present difficulties between the slave-holding and free states, but rather the square aspect of Saturn and Herschel [Uranus] will cause the breach to grow wider, and we are afraid that some fatal blow will be struck by the seceding states..."*[66]

Broughton consistently referred to the United States Uranus in Gemini as being an important factor in the Civil War, as it had returned to its natal sign. Here, we have the description of a mundane Uranus return, which is a definite shift in emphasis in mundane interpretation! Here is a good example: *"The Union has just lasted One Revolution of the Planet Herschel [Uranus] Round the heavens, and until Herschel gets out of Gemini, which will not be before July 1865, I do not look for any PEACE for this Country."*[67] It was implicit in classical delineation that the Aries Ingress was a return of the Sun to that placement – and accordingly, a return of any other body to a placement was not a huge stretch – it just wasn't a methodology commonly employed. But we already saw the use of the Jupiter-Saturn degree of 1603 by Lilly or Edlyn being treated as what would now be called a **sensitive point**. Rafael (Robert Cross Smith, 1795-1832) presaged the use of the Saturn return natally in his prognostications for 1824.[68] Thus, when Broughton talked about the return of Uranus to Gemini, it was not so much in the modern sense of attempting to construct a Uranus return, as the general influence of a recapitulation of an earlier time. Further, note that his prediction was for when Uranus *left* Gemini – not when Uranus *returned to its exact degree*. Broughton's prediction based on the ingress of Uranus into Cancer wasn't too bad. The Civil War ended in April 1865, with Uranus at 26 Gemini. The whole War took place with Uranus in Gemini.

• In the August 1861 issue, Broughton uses a **stellium** of planets in the 7th to denote that "*the Southern Rebels are determined to maintain their ground.*"[69] He does not use the word stellium, but neither does he spell out the exact relationships of the specific planets.

• He interprets a comet that was visible as the War Comet. In one of his columns on it, he messed up the chronology of the English Civil War, placing it twenty five years too late, thereby proving once again the utility of Wikipedia.

• He covered the Jupiter-Saturn conjunction at 18 Virgo that occurred in October 1861 in the November 1861 issue. He did not mention it in his discussion of either the Aries Ingress or the Cancer Ingress for that year.[70] He talked about the nature of buildings built under the conjunction, depending upon the quadruplicity of the conjunction itself.[71]

• He mentions unaspected planets.[72] While this was observed in the classical period, it was not a usual item of delineation, apart from the specifics of the **Void of Course Moon**.

• He predicted Lincoln's assassination, slightly cryptically, by saying the following: "*Some noted general or person in high office dies or is removed about the 17th or 18th day.*"[73] The date suggests that Broughton may well have done this by reading all the quarter moons, not just the new and the full, as illustrated in Figure 6. The debilitated Moon ruling the 10th at the 4th, square Saturn and at the **Bendings** with Venus ruling the 1st in the 8th near Algol, and retrograde Saturn at the Ascendant is a baleful combination. Lincoln actually died on April 15, 1865. The Quarter Moon itself showed a tight opposition of Mars and Jupiter, with the Ruler of the President (the 10th house, *i.e.*, Venus) in the turned 8th – although this is not the worst lunation for the war.

Broughton also never addressed the problem that I mentioned as existing even in the Babylonian era – that of interpreting mundane events when two countries are close together. Richmond, Virginia, the capital of the Confederate States, was just over 100 miles South from Washington, D.C. Thus, all mundane charts for these two capitals would have been almost the same. How, then to decide which one is valid?

How did Broughton do overall? Reading his predictions with the book in one hand, and a chronology of the Civil War in the other is revealing. While he had some excellent hits, I cannot say that most of what he said was consistently accurate. So is this a problem in the method – or the man? It's not entirely clear, but I believe that the structure of his predictions, derived from the necessity of publishing the Civil War equivalent of sound bites in a monthly, or later, quarterly

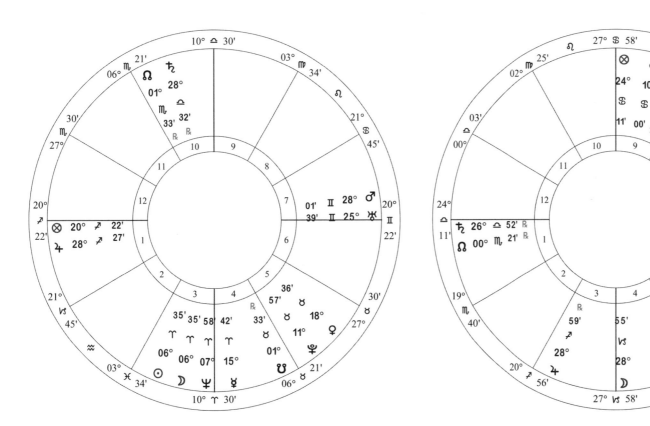

New Moon 03-27-1865
March 27, 1865
12:19:57 AM
Washington, D.C.
38N53'42" 77W02'12"
Local Mean Time
Time Zone: 0 hours West
Tropical Regiomontanus
New Moon (astrological)

Figure 6. New Moon and Third-Quarter Moon for the period of Lincoln's assassination.

3rd Q Moon Apr 18 1865
April 18, 1865
6:11:56 PM
Washington, D.C.
38N53'42" 77W02'12"
Local Mean Time
Time Zone: 0 hours West
Tropical Regiomontanus
NATAL CHART

format, produced some anomalies. His monthly synopses are generally far too terse to use as the basis of any judgment. Generally, his ingress discussions are longer and more accurate. It may be that lunations simply aren't the best technique for judging how many battles there will be – or how bloody. The season that included Antietam, the single bloodiest day in U.S. military history, was described in part this way: *"The war-like planet Mars so much afflicted in the sixth house (the house of sickness,) and being lord of the eighth, (the house of death,) will show that sickness and death caused by the war, will be very prevalent among the soldiers, in both the Northern and Southern armies, and that widows and orphans will be uncommon plentiful."* [74] This is a true enough statement, with 27,000 casualties occurring on the one day of Antietam. His prediction from the lunation that applied was simply, *"The aspects are uncommon evil for the Northern states."* [75]

To summarize Broughton's methods, he published mainly lunations and ingresses, with a smattering of comets and eclipses. He did not publish on all the eclipses that occurred during the Civil War. He primarily listed the positions of the planets and the houses they ruled, worked most extensively with the aspects of the planets in the figure, and occasionally referred to dignity or retrogradation. While he published an article on the Jupiter-Saturn conjunction, it did not appear to be a focus of his work. The Mars-Saturn conjunctions 1861, 1863, and 1865 were given no more prominence in the delineation than any other aspect. In fact, with the exception of the one token article on the Jupiter-Saturn, and the fact that a New Moon is by definition a conjunction of the Lights, there is no sense in Broughton's method that conjunctions were treated any differently than the aspects proper.

Sepharial and His Enduring Influence

As Broughton's method diverged from classical, we can see an even further divergence by the time of Sepharial (1864-1929). In his magazine *Coming Events*, we observe his column for November 1897. There are three subheadings: "Transits," "The Weather," and "The Lunation." Under transits, we read:

Jupiter and Venus are now passing through Libra, giving peace and strength to the armies of Austria, China, Japan, and India. But in this latter country other disturbing elements will arise. The transit of Saturn and Mars through the early degrees of Sagittarius will bring trouble to America, Spain, Arabia, and Hungary. The fortunes of Spain are in danger of complete wreck, but the country will not be without its supporters among the nations. Cuba, as we predicted in July last, will change its government. It is likely to pass into the hands of America, but only after much bloodshed and devastation of property. [76]

Under his lunation section, he says:

The lunation for November takes place at 11:28 p.m. on the 25th of October, when 28 Aries is on the midheaven, and the 16th degree of Leo rising. There are no less than five of the celestial bodies, Sun, Moon, Mars, Uranus, and Saturn, in the 4th house. Consequently, we may expect to see or hear of alarming colliery disasters, landslips, earthquakes, and wide destruction of property.... [77]

We can extract some important ideas of his methodology as follows:

- The sign placements of the planets have replaced any celestial conjunction as the top headline. When he mentions Jupiter and Venus in Libra, they aren't even conjunct. As of November 1st, Venus was 13 degrees ahead of Jupiter, so not even close! This is a transit left over from October. But Sepharial leaves it in anyway, because it allows him to focus on the affairs of countries ruled by Libra.

- The *"transit of Saturn and Mars through the early degrees of Sagittarius"* was actually the Mars-Saturn conjunction, which occurred 26 November 1897 at 3 Sagittarius. What is missing from this statement is any sense that a Mars-Saturn conjunction is an event worth analyzing in its own right. His delineation did bring up the U.S. and Spain – and this was a few months before the outbreak of the Spanish-American War, which was already festering at this time.

- His discussion of the lunation actually is touching upon a stellium in Scorpio – but instead of referring to it as such, he talks about the planetary conjunctions which will occur – but these conjunctions are largely inferior conjunctions to superior planet configurations already in play. The most significant of the superior configurations was Saturn separating from Uranus, and then Mars catching up to conjoin both of them in turn. That certainly was a volatile combination. That began January 6, 1897 at 27 Scorpio, and then repeated on Jun 1, 1897 at 26 Scorpio; completing on September 9th at 25 Scorpio. One could probably make a good case for that major conjunction being involved with the set-up

of the subsequent war – it's just that November 1897 did not represent any critical point in the process.

- Gone is any sense that superior conjunctions are in any way special – except possibly by activating particular countries ruled by the sign in question.

Sepharial wrote specifically on the interpretation of the Jupiter-Saturn Conjunction in *Transits and Planetary Periods*. In fact, this work should be seen as the genesis of the methods of working with the Jupiter-Saturn conjunction still being used in the 1920s and 1930s. In this work, he repeated the 960 year cycle figure that we have already dismissed as inaccurate, and developed a system for working with the **conjunctional chart**, and then following it through time with secondary progressions or directions.[78]

Is there any justification for this wholesale change in method since the classical period? In fact, there may be. The discovery of the New World, and European involvement in Asia profoundly changed the nature of what mundane astrologers were called upon to do. Suddenly, prognostications were needed for the entire globe, not a series of countries in Europe that had been facing off with each other for over a millennium. Sepharial's predictions for the December 1897 lunation included specifics for London (of course), but also East Africa, Asia Minor, Southern Russia, Arabia, Spain, Sydney, New York, and India.[79] Abu Ma'shar was never called upon to do this! The whole system of analyzing *where* the effects of a planetary configuration would occur most strongly broke down entirely, ultimately resulting in the development of astrocartography. While these techniques were invented during Sepharial's lifetime, their systematic utilization had to wait for the development of computers and their greater mathematical horsepower.

Having said this, I am not at all sure that the majority of the changes we see by Sepharial's time were conscious decisions taken to produce a more accurate or comprehensive result. And I am especially suspicious of those changes which were the result of the expediency of writing for a monthly magazine. It seems to me that matters of politics do not necessarily fall neatly into one month intervals. Any major piece of legislation takes months to enact; any war needs months to mobilize. Monthly predictions may be producing too much chatter, obscuring the major themes. We have already seen with Broughton that the monthly forecasting techniques may actually have decreased his accuracy.

The other obvious change that *had* to be addressed in the modern period was the discovery of yet more superior planets. Broughton was quite right to attempt to use the Mars-Uranus conjunction, just as Sepharial was right to use the Saturn-Uranus. The problem with more superior planets is that now there is much more going on in the way of transits – which really makes one reflect on just how much one can get from the aspects apart from the conjunctions in this new alphabet soup.

And I have to look at the shift in Sepharial's interpretations to the use of signs as being part of an attempt to re-envision how to get the "where" right. As I said, this seems transitional to astrocartography, but unfortunately, the emphasis on sign seems to have stuck as much for its convenience in generating copy for monthly deadlines as for producing real predictive power.

The methods that Sepharial was beginning to experiment with for approaching mundane as a truly global art only needed reinforcing as time went on. World War I (the Great War, as it was styled before World War II imposed a numbering system) was fought globally. The emergence of new world powers continued to challenge capabilities of astrology to keep up with globalization.

Between the wars, we can use the *Astrological Quarterly* to understand these developments. I examined the various mundane articles in Volume 1. The Editor, Charles Carter, continued to write extensively on mundane, but this will serve as a guide to the development of the ideas that were circulating in astrology generally at that time.

The first piece to examine was by L. Protheroe Smith, entitled "The Year 1927," which featured the Jupiter-Saturn conjunction of 1921.[80] He begins his article by saying:

> I make no apology for once more drawing your attention to the forgoing figure, for the conjunction of Jupiter and Saturn in the year 1921. I have discussed it here before, and I shall do so again whenever I am asked to speak on National Astrology during the period over which it rules. Because, although perhaps less is known concerning this branch of our work than almost any other, yet there is reason to believe that national destiny runs in cycles; and we get, I think, a glimpse of this cyclical process in the Jupiter-Saturn conjunctions which recur at intervals of approximately 20 years. (page 4)

So far, this could have been written by Masha' Allah – except for the phrase "national destiny." We have moved into the period of democracies and other governmental forms, where the Head of State may differ from the Head of Government, and where the Head of Government may only last in that role for a few years – rarely for life.

However, a close examination of the article reveals major differences. First of all, his year is a calendar year: not a year as defined by the Aries Ingress. In fact, there are no cardinal ingresses to be seen at all. What is present is a chart purporting to be for the exact moment of the conjunction – something we have already seen has some serious astronomical challenges associated with it. His chart, shown recomputed by a modern program as Figure 7, comes out to approximately twelve hours off of exactitude, as computed by Solar Fire. But the chart has the deceptive *appearance* of correctness, because both Jupiter and Saturn are in the same minute of arc. Jupiter was moving by 13' per day, and Saturn by 7' – this is a good illustration of the degree of uncertainty of these conjunction charts – and exactly why Vincent Wing warned about this problem over two centuries earlier. Uncertainty by twelve hours wrecks havoc with the houses! So we must begin by being suspicious of anything he says about the Jupiter-Saturn that is house-based.

Since he is not using ingresses, eclipses, or lunations, what is he doing to predict 1927? Why, he's progressing this already suspect Jupiter-Saturn conjunctional chart, using the method pioneered by Sepharial!

Secondary progressions did not exist until the 17th century when Placidus invented them in an attempt to reproduce Ptolemy's method of directing. I don't object to their use here because they are new. The genesis of the idea for doing something like this exists in the classical material, which mentions directing revolutionary charts – although this would have been by primary direction. But if the method is going to shift, it's important to test it out. How can one test it out on a chart which is already suspicious?

Protheroe Smith used the progression to focus on the progressed Moon, by sign and house placement. He also does transits from the year to the progressed placements, and aspects of the progressed Moon to the dubious conjunctional chart.

I should mention that Protheroe Smith's articles continued to grace the *Quarterly* for some years to come. And both he and his editor clearly believed that he was getting good results from such a tenuous method. How can this be? This methodological problem does not negate transits by themselves, nor does it negate the importance of the planetary placements at the time of the Jupiter-Saturn conjunction itself – a conjunction Protheroe Smith clearly had come to know intimately. He talked about labor problems in 1926 that he attributed to the 1926 progressed Ascendant opposite Uranus – but 1926 had a Mars-Uranus conjunction which would have been an equal argument. The difficulty of assuming that there is only one possible explanation for an event is truly a huge problem in attempting to sort out mundane method.

Just following Protheroe Smith's article, an anonymous "American Student" published the "Aries Ingress for the United States," which showed knowledge of the adage about a mutable rising chart not being adequate for predicting the entire year. The student makes reference to the Gemini Ascendant in recapitulating the Gemini rulership of the U.S. The student determined that Mercury retrograde (we would add, in Detriment in Pisces) in the 10th, and ruling the 1st, would result in endless meaningless talk within Congress, with no action. The student used the conjunction of the Sun to Uranus in the chart to indicate that change was wanted – and so then-President Coolidge would not be re-elected: this turned out to be entirely correct, as Coolidge himself chose not to run.[81] We conclude from this that the traditional means of interpreting ingresses was still extant, although clearly other techniques were being tried.

The next mundane example was "Uranus in Aries: Notes and Predictions," by YKRAAMIS.[82] She/he takes the new Moon in Sagittarius, when Uranus has just crossed into Aries, and creates a "world chart" by creating an equal house chart for the moment for the New Moon, with the Ascendant equal to the New Moon. Since this is not for a particular location, it becomes a metaphor for the meaning of Uranus in Aries. This is an overtly spiritual rendition,

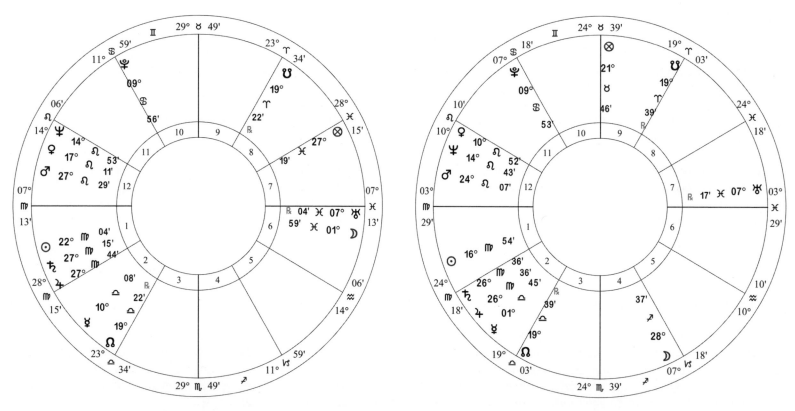

Jupiter-Saturn conj
Calc: September 15, 1921
11:39:11 AM GMT
London, England
51 N 30 0 W 10
Greenwich Mean Time
Time Zone: 0 hours West
Tropical Regiomontanus
Secondary Progression for January 1, 1927 at 12:00 AM GMT

Figure 7. Most likely incorrect chart for Jupiter-Saturn conjunction, reproducing Protheroe Smith's time.

Jupiter-Saturn conj
September 10, 1921
5:15:12 AM
London, England
51 N 30 0 W 10
Daylight Saving Time
Time Zone: 0 hours West
Tropical Regiomontanus
NATAL CHART

without predictions in the outer world. There is an aspectarian for principal events, culminating in Uranus transiting into Taurus in 1934. The author expected the New Order to manifest itself. Unfortunately, Nazism manifested instead.

In the same issue, "Taurus" reported on the total eclipse, visible in London on 29 June 1927.[83] After a review of the astronomy, the eclipse was interpreted astrologically, using aspect patterns. Planets are used exclusively through their house positions: no house rulerships are noted at all.

As you can see, this foray into 1927 demonstrates a lot of experimentation going on, with that experimentation in many respects paralleling the development of modern natal astrology, with its simplification of the ancient systems, along with a much heightened dependence upon the aspect patterns as the primary method of delineation.

From here, we can pick up the history as it is presented in Baigent, Campion, and Harvey. As Nicholas Campion pointed out in his chapter, "The National Horoscope: Mundane Astrology and Political Theory," the current modern reliance on the national horoscope is quite new. It was impossible in Europe until only a few centuries ago, with the development of the modern state.[84] He also discusses the relationship of the state to the national leader, *"the birth chart of the leader becomes a working horoscope for the collective"* (page 109). As Campion has pointed out elsewhere, the development of the national horoscope as a preferred method for the analysis of mundane effects came in the wake of the failure of British astrologers to predict World War II. We can see it in use in the lead-up as well, witness C.E.O. Carter's references to a chart for the Fascist Regime and to the French Republic in the March-April-May 1939 issue of the *Quarterly*.[85] The theory has been presented that incorrect predictions by R.H. Naylor and others concerning

the war led to a wholesale re-evaluation of mundane methods, leading to two primary developments:

- Greater utilization of national charts to pinpoint hot spots

- Work by Barbault and Gouchon initially, then buttressed by Baigent, Campion, and Harvey to elaborate the meanings of the new superior planet cycles involving Uranus, Neptune, and Pluto.

While this is undoubtedly true, I suggest also examining a chart for the Aries Ingress 1939, shown in Figure 8.

Either way you cut it, an Aries Ingress with Mars exalted in a partile square to the Sun looks like a war. And yet, in an article in the *Quarterly* by Estelle Gardner entitled "National Astrology," she reviews that chart – and does not so much as mention the word "war." Doing the chart for London, she merely remarks that the Pluto Rising may denote the association of Pluto with National Socialism and Fascism![86] How did she miss this? It's worth remembering that England at this time was strongly neutral and anti-war. There was also a significant political faction favoring the Nazis. One sure-fire way to mess up your predictions is to hold too dearly to your own pet theory of How Things Are. If you cannot imagine war, then you cannot predict it either.

Charles Carter himself joined in the prediction of "no-war-in-1939!" in the June-July-August 1939 issue of the *Quarterly*, using as his evidence the Jupiter-Saturn conjunction for 1901 – a chart which is as flawed in its calculation as the 1921 chart that I discussed in relation to Protheroe Smith's article. Then, adhering to the same method, Carter used secondaries to progress the chart to 1939, divining easy aspects for the immediate future.[87] And yet, in his following Editorial that he wrote on August 1st, he said:

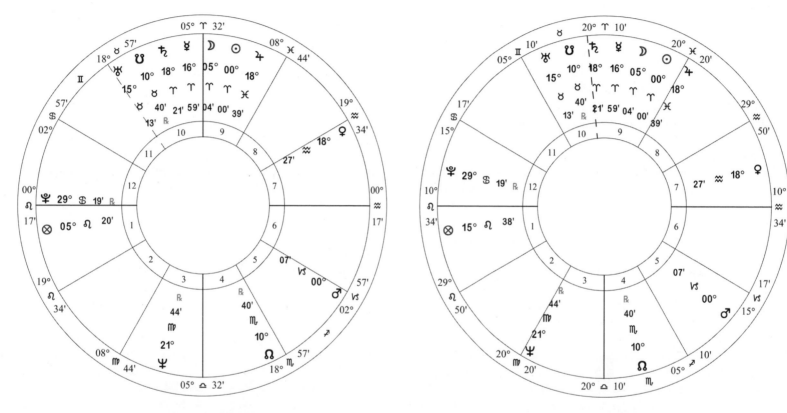

Sun enters Ari 3-21-1939
March 21, 1939
12:28:30 PM
London, England
51 N 30 0 W 10
Standard Time
Time Zone: 0 hours West
Tropical Regiomontanus
NATAL CHART

Figure 8. Aries Ingress 1939, calculated for Berlin and London.

Sun enters Ari 3-21-1939
March 21, 1939
1:28:30 PM
Berlin, Germany
52 N 30 13 E 22
Standard Time
Time Zone: 1 hours East
Tropical Regiomontanus
NATAL CHART

I am writing this on the first day of August, with the atmosphere around me somewhat milder (under the influence of Jupiter stationary) than it was a few weeks ago (under Mars stationary). Nevertheless there is a widespread belief that things will move rapidly and dangerously at least or about the end of the month. And the August lunation is a strange one; Sun and Moon rise at Berlin, square Uranus in M.C.[88]

It would seem that the sudden beginning of the invasion of Poland looked exactly like that lunation. It was only strange if you couldn't envision war as the meaning. What failed the British astrologers was not the ancient techniques, but Sepharial's modification of them, combined with unwillingness to interpret what they were seeing, but couldn't believe.

Fast forward one more time. By 1960, Brigadier Firebrace was experimenting with maps that he published in *Spica* – maps that were the immediate predecessors of Jim Lewis's Astro*Carto*Graphy® – maps that Lewis began publishing systematically in the late 1970s.[89] By the late 1980s, Nicholas Campion had published his *Book of World Horoscopes*,[90] which became the master reference for horoscopes of countries. By the 1990s, any astrologer who wanted to work in this field had access to computer software that did not only maps, but ingresses, lunations, and eclipses as far back or as far forward as you wanted. The tools were now in place.

The advent of these tools allowed astrologers to research the mundane techniques that we so sorely need if we are going to continue to make progress in finding answers to the two great mundane questions: *where* and *when*. Hopefully, you will find this work to be one more step in that progress.

Endnotes: Chapter 1

5. Kindi, Gerrit Bos, and Charles Burnett. *Scientific Weather Forecasting in the Middle Ages : The Writings of Al-Kindi: Studies, Editions, and Translations*. Sir Henry Wellcome Asian Series. London; New York; New York: Kegan Paul International; ; Distributed by Wiley, 2000, p 2.

6. Bos & Burnett, p 166.

7. A good example of how this was developed in Ancient China is given in: Pankenier, David W. "Applied Field-Allocation Astrology in Zhou China: Duke Wen of Jin and the Battle of Chengpu (632 B. C.)." *Journal of the American Oriental Society* 119.2 (1999): 261-79.

8. Allan, Sarah. *The Shape of the Turtle : Myth, Art, and Cosmos in Early China*. Suny Series in Chinese Philosophy and Culture. Albany, NY: State University of New York Press, 1991, pp 117-123.

9. Campion, Nicholas. *The Great Year: Astrology, Millenarianism, and History in the Western Tradition*. London, England ; New York, N.Y., U.S.A.: Arkana, 1994, page 45.

10. Campion, Nicholas. *The Dawn of Astrology : A Cultural History of Western Astrology. Vol. 1, the Ancient and Classical Worlds*. London; New York: Continuum, 2008, p 57.

11. Campion, 2008, p 62.

12. "B.C.E." stands for "Before Common Era" and is the currently preferred term for what used to be called "BC." The date source is: Campion, 1994, pp 86-87.

13. Campion, 2008, p 75.

14. Kennedy, E. S., et al. *The Astrological History of Masha' Allah*. Harvard Monographs in the History of Science. Cambridge, Mass.,: Harvard University Press, 1971.

15. Burnett, Charles, Keiji Yamamoto and Michio Yano. *Al-Qabisi (Alcabitious): The Introduction to Astrology*. London: Warburg Institute, 2004.

16. Abu, Ma'shar, Keiji Yamamoto, and Charles Burnett. *On Historical Astrology: The Book of Religions and Dynasties (on the Great Conjunctions)*. Islamic

Philosophy, Theology, and Science,. 2 vols. Leiden ; Boston: Brill, 2000, p 55.

17. Abu, Ma'shar, Keiji Yamamoto, and Charles Burnett, 2000, beginning p 31.

18. Abu, Ma'shar, Keiji Yamamoto, and Charles Burnett, 2000, p 7.

19. You can see an example of these ideas worked out here: Salmon, William. *Horæ Mathematicæ, Seu, Urania the Soul of Astrology, Containing That Art in All Its Parts ... : The Whole Work a New Thing, the Like Never yet Extant*. London: Printed by, 1679, pp 65-83. On the mundane side, one work devoted entirely to the interpretation of the Mars-Saturn is: Edlyn, Richard. *Observationes Astrologicae, or, an Astrological Discourse of the Effects of a Notable Conjunction of Saturn and Mars by Richard Edlyn...* London: Printed by J.W. For B. Billingsley, and O. Blagrave... 1668. The earlier mundane reference is: Abu; Ma'shar, Keiji Yamamoto, and Charles Burnett, 2000.

20. Burnett, Charles, Keiji Yamamoto and Michio Yano, p 109.

21. Michelsen, p 91.

22. For a very insightful view of how a political scientist can study paradigms for presidential power, see Skowronek, Stephen. *The Politics Presidents Make: Leadership from John Adams to Bill Clinton*. Cambridge, Mass.: The Belknap Press of Harvard University Press, 1997.

23. Kennedy and Pingree give sixteen charts that Masha'Allah included in his text, the majority of which were charts for the Aries Ingresses of the years of Jupiter-Saturn conjunctions.

24. Mark Pottenger has estimated that it takes a minimum of 8-11 decimal places to compute the accuracy of a planetary position to within one second of accuracy – again assuming that the equations used are that accurate in the first place. We should note that, at the time that Pottenger wrote this article, the 8-11 decimal places was greater than single precision numbers as defined by computer programs of the time. At that time, in order to achieve double precision numbers with reasonable time responses, an additional math chip was needed. The greater horsepower of our present computers easily handles the greater precision – but

then, the planetary calculation algorithms used must reflect this. Pottenger, Mark, Editor. *Astrological Research Methods Volume I: An ISAR Anthology (Vol. I)*. Los Angeles: International Society for Astrological Research, 1995, his article is entitled "Accuracy," pp 159-176; the specific citation is p 160.

25. Abu, Ma'shar, Keiji Yamamoto, and Charles Burnett, Vol 1, pp 82-157.

26. Abu, Ma'shar, Keiji Yamamoto, and Charles Burnett, Vol 1, pp 131-135.

27. Abu, Ma'shar, Keiji Yamamoto, and Charles Burnett, Vol 1, pp 137-147.

28. Abu, Ma'shar, Keiji Yamamoto, and Charles Burnett, Vol 1, p 147.

29. Bonatti, Guido. *The Book of Astronomy by Guido Bonatti*. Trans. Benjamin N. Dykes. Golden Valley, MN: Cazimi Press, 2007, p 816.

30. Bonatti, pp 826-829. For Abu Ma'shar's method, see Holden, pp 13-14.

31. Bonatti, pp 830-838.

32. Bonatti, pp 899-902.

33. Bonatti, pp 1040-1105.

34. Ramesey, William. *Astrologia Restaurata*. London,: Printed for R. White, 1653.

35. Ramesey, pp 280-281.

36. Holden, James Herschel. *Five Medieval Astrologers*. Scottsdale, AZ: American Federation of Astrologers, 2008.

37. Ramesey, p. 327.

38. Abu, Ma'shar, Keiji Yamamoto, and Charles Burnett, 2000, p 11.

39. Abu, Ma'shar, Keiji Yamamoto, and Charles Burnett, 2000, p 11 and 149. The authors have a rather curious footnote on the later page questioning what was going on with the thirty year cycle and weakness: I would read it as simply referring to the weakness of both planets in the sign Cancer.

40. Lilly, William, Guido Bonatti, and Girolamo Cardano. *Anima Astrologiae: Or, a Guide for Astrologers. Being the Considerations of the Famous Guido Bonatus, Faithfully Rendred into English. As Also the Choicest Aphorisms of Cardans Seaven Segments, Translated and Methodically Digested under Their Proper Heads. With a New Table of the Fixed Stars, Rectified for Several Years to Come, and Divers Other Necessary Illustrations*. microform.

Printed for B. Harris at the Stationers Arms in Sweethings Rents near the Royal Exchange, London,, 1676, pp 22-23.

41. Brady, Bernadette and J. Lee Lehman. Twelfth century castle besiegement in sport. The Astrological Journal 39(3): 27-44, 1998.

42. Jack Hauck, personal communication.

43. Heydon, Christopher, and Nicholas Fiske. *An Astrological Discourse with Mathematical Demonstrations, Proving the Powerful and Harmonical Influence of the Planets and Fixed Stars Upon Elementary Bodies, in Justification of the Validity of Astrology. Together with an Astrological Judgment Upon the Great Conjunction of Saturn & Jupiter 1603. Written by That Worthy Learned Gentleman Sir Christopher Heydon, Knight, and Now Published by Nicholas Fiske, Jatromathematicus.* London,: Printed by J. Macock for N. Brooks, 1650.

44. Heydon, p. 101.

45. Heydon, p 103.

46. For further information about the development of astronomical instrumentation during this period, consult: Broecke, Steven Vanden. *The Limits of Influence : Pico, Louvain, and the Crisis of Renaissance Astrology.* Medieval and Early Modern Science. Leiden; Boston: Brill, 2003.

47. Edlyn (1659), pp 40-41.

48. Edlyn (1659), p 43.

49. Edlyn (1659), p 45.

50. Edlyn (1659), p 52.

51. Edlyn (1658), pp 73-76.

52. Lehman, J. Lee. *Martial Art of Horary Astrology.* Atglen, PA: Schiffer Press., 2002 p 94.

53. Edlyn, Richard. *Prae-Nuncius Sydereus an Astrological Treatise of the Effects of the Great Conjunction of the Two Superiour Planets, Saturn & Jupiter, October the Xth, 1663, and Other Configurations Concomitant : Wherein the Fate of Europe for These Next Twenty Years Is (from the Most Rational Grounds of Art) More Than Probably Conjectured, and the Success of the Present Design of the Turk against Christendome Occasionally Hinted At.* London: Printed by, 1664.

54. Edlyn (1664), p 8.

55. Edlyn (1664), pp 10-12.

56. Edlyn (1664), p 21.

57. Edlyn (1664), p 20.

58. Edlyn (1664), p 25.

59. Edlyn (1664), pp 43.44.

60. Lehman, J. Lee. A Rococo Horary with a Critique using Classical Methods. Aspects 14(3): 9-13 (1989).

61. Sibly, E. *A New and Complete Illustration of the Celestial Science of Astrology: Or, the Art of Foretelling Future Events and Contingencies, by the Aspects, Positions, and Influences of the Heavenly Bodies. In Four Parts.* 11th, or posthumous ed. London: Hamblin and Seyfang, 1813, p 1044. The first edition came out in 1784; I have examined several editions and found the text to be identical in the portions I have examined.

62. Sibly, p 1052, facing. I have developed a Learning with Lee instruction CD going through the detail of how he derived his Sagittarius rising chart of the U.S.A. here: *www.leelehman.com.*

63. There are multiple citations we could use for this, but here are three: Abu, Ma'shar, Keiji Yamamoto, and Charles Burnett., Vol 1, p 489; Holden (2008), p 34; Bonatti (2007), Vol 2, pp 880-882. We have already seen that this rule transmitted consistently through the classical period.

64. I have covered this detail elsewhere, in my Learning with Lee cd series, as cd#20, "Mundane Directions. Sibly Chart."

65. Broughton, Luke Dennis. *The Elements of Astrology.* New York,: The author, 1898.

66. Broughton's *Monthly Planetary Reader,* Vol 2. No. 2, p 6.

67. Broughton's *Monthly Planetary Reader,* Vol 2. No. 7, p 21.

68. *The Astrologer of the Nineteenth Century.* 6th ed. London,: W. C. Wright, 1825, p 142.

69. Broughton's *Monthly Planetary Reader*, Vol 2. No. 8, p 25.

70. Broughton's *Monthly Planetary Reader*, Vol 2. No. 11, pp 35-36.

71. Broughton's *Monthly Planetary Reader*, Vol 2. No. 12, pp 40-41.

72. For example, Broughton's *Monthly Planetary Reader*, Vol 2. No. 11, p 36.

73. Broughton's *Monthly Planetary Reader*, Vol 6. No. 2, p 15.

74. Broughton's *Monthly Planetary Reader*, Vol 3. No. 5, p 19.

75. Broughton's *Monthly Planetary Reader*, Vol 3. No. 5, p 21.

76. *Coming Events: The Astrological Monthly*, November 1897, p 45.

77. *Coming Events: The Astrological Monthly*, November 1897, pp 45-46.

78. Sepharial. *Transits and Planetary Periods; a Book of Practical Hints to Students of Astrology*. New York,: S. Weiser, 1970, pp 70-81.

79. *Coming Events: The Astrological Monthly*, December 1897, pp 100-102.

80. Astrological Quarterly, Vol. 1, No. 2, pp 4-11.

81. *Astrological Quarterly*, Vol. 1, No. 2., pp 11-14.

82. *Astrological Quarterly*, Vol. 1, No. 3., pp 23-26.

83. *Astrological Quarterly*, Vol. 1, No. 3., pp 29-33.

84. Baigent, Michael, Nicholas Campion, and Charles Harvey. *Mundane Astrology. An Aquarian Astrology Handbook.* Wellingborough, Northamptonshire: Aquarian Press, 1984. The chapter referred to is pp 95-111.

85. P 1.

86. Gardner, Estelle. National Astrology. *Astrological Quarterly*, Vol 13, No 1, 1939, pp 3-8.

87. Carter, C.E.O. Editorial. *Astrological Quarterly*, Vol 13, No 2, pp 45-47.

88. Carter, C.E.O. Editorial. *Astrological Quarterly*, Vol 13, No 3, p 89.

89. This work culminated in the book: Lewis, Jim, and Gail Guttman. *The Astro-Carto-Graphy Book of Maps : The Astrology of Relocation : How 136 Famous People Found Their Places*. The Llewellyn Modern Astrology Library. 1st ed. St. Paul, Minn., U.S.A.: Llewellyn Publications, 1989.

90. Campion, Nicholas. *The Book of World Horoscopes*. Aquarian Astrology Handbook. Wellingborough, Northamptonshire, England; New York, N.Y.: Aquarian Press ; Distributed by Sterling Pub. Co., 1988.

2

A Primer of Environmental Science and Concepts

You probably have opinions about everything. So do most people. Does that mean that all opinions are equal? No. Some opinions are based on facts. These carry more weight than do those based only on what someone feels. You need information to form a reasonable opinion.... It is perfectly all right to not have an opinion about something, but it is important to know when you need to gather more information before you form an opinion or make a decision.[91]

—Sharon La Bonde Hanks

AT FIRST, IT MAY SEEM RATHER STRANGE THAT I AM INTERRUPTING AN ASTROLOGY BOOK TO TALK ABOUT SCIENCE. However, I view these first two chapters as vital to having the basic tools and concepts to understand the rest of the book.

Science has been used as a metaphor almost since science broke away from natural philosophy in the 18th century. Helena Blavatsky forever changed the understanding of metaphysicians by incorporating the term "**evolution**" into the spiritual process. There is no evidence that the term was ever used spiritually before

Darwin and Wallace published the scientific theory. And yet, it immediately struck a very deep chord among spiritual practitioners, because it so precisely explained the process of the spiritual quest, and its various stages. But the concept of evolution, coming from the Enlightenment, implies a directionality – that things move *up* or *out*. Blavatsky almost immediately needed the concept of *devolution* to express the idea of moving back. But these words diverge from the original cyclic perspective of any **cosmos** based on astrological principles.

I do believe that depth ecology, as it is sometimes called, will provide the vital metaphor for the time of Pluto in Capricorn. And since I believe in approaching the subject of this book systematically, it is vital that you and I, Reader and Author, make sure that we are in the place of understanding about what is meant when vocabulary from environmental science is used.

This chapter also touches on a bit of personal history – history I only began to understand when I was preparing this book. I would argue that my academic training in ecology pre-wired me for my later interest in astrology – and that the reverse may also be true.

Astrology and ecology share the use of holistic thinking, a systems approach (although astrology has not defined it rigorously nor mathematically, the systems approach in astrology is to state that isolated chart components do not mean much in isolation, as saying that the Sun sign is only part of the psychological make-up), and the constant reminder of the power of the **Law of Unintended Consequences.** Stated somewhat loosely, that law means that, without complete knowledge of an **ecosystem** or other unit of life, doing something which on the surface seems right, moral, or just a good idea, often produces effects that are the reverse, because of the interdependence of elements of the system that don't act in anticipated ways.

So we will share a journey that is part history, and part science. The quote at the beginning of the chapter comes from a college text entitled *Ecology and the Biosphere : Principles and Problems.* This text was designed for non-science majors, in order to explain the science behind ecology to those who often don't study it. I would recommend this text for learning more about this subject, and I shall refer to concepts within it in this chapter.

Definitions of Science

Oftentimes, scientists begin their books with a definition of science that is operational: it defines science by how it is *done* rather than what it *is*. By such definitions, science branched off from natural philosophy when its practitioners adopted the **scientific method** – twin systems of inquiry into the natural world that were proposed by Frances Bacon and René Descartes. What these two methods share is the choice to only study subjects and ideas that can be studied empirically. It was this choice that has made it so very difficult to integrate astrology into science as most scientists

would understand it: because the "good stuff" in astrology is mostly non-quantitative in the way usually understood by scientists.

I do not want to quibble with the definition of science here, in great part because I think the practitioners of a field do have the default right to define what it is that they are doing. We astrologers would resent scientists telling us what we can and cannot study and how – so why should we impose our ideas on them?

Early Ideas on the Natural World

As far back as Aristotle, long before science was science, individual natural philosophers were interested in the natural world, and how different species managed to live together. Because Aristotle presented a world that was permanent – it had not been created and it was not going to be destroyed – a lot of what followed was a description of what is. His world was more static than dynamic. However, Aristotle certainly never postulated that change was impossible, and his great work, *On Coming to Be and Passing Away* directly addresses change and how it occurs.

This view of the world clashed dramatically with the Jewish, and then Christian Cosmos, in which God created the world — and in the Christian vision of Revelation, God would destroy it too. This Christian vision had significant consequences that continue to reverberate in environmental matters because of one particular passage in Genesis:

And God blessed them, and God said to them, "Be fruitful and multiply, and fill the earth and subdue it; and have dominion over the fish of the sea and over the birds of the air and over every living thing that moves upon the earth." (Gen 1:28, Revised Standard Version)

Aristotle's Cosmos does not presume an elevated place for humans as overseers of the world. Once Christianity won out as the dominant religion of Western Europe, at least until about the 15th century, anytime that Faith clashed with Reason, Faith won. So Genesis trumped Aristotle.

Historical Environmental Problems

Even so, people gradually increased their knowledge of the Earth, its creatures, and natural processes. Animal and plant breeding is an old idea in most human cultures, and both bring with them the understanding that offspring resemble their parents – to a degree. People also got to observe what we would call environmental devastation. There are many historical examples. Rivers drying up can be devastating, as likely happened to the Indus Valley Civilization. **Overgrazing** can create desert. The bible refers to the cedars of Lebanon – the modern visitor would be hard-pressed to imagine this.

Environmental catastrophes, whether from flooding after **clear-cutting**, the collapse of a mine, or the destruction of grasslands by over-grazing, were considered isolated events. And most importantly, the Christian viewpoint that God had given Man a unique Soul meant that, while his body might have properties in common with animals, his soul changed the equation so drastically that rules for animals did not necessarily apply.

Besides, human beings through the Middle Ages were generally only capable of causing serious environmental damage on a limited scale. Population densities were orders of magnitude lower than today. For millennia, a high civilization such as Ancient Egypt or Mesopotamia could construct terracing, or create irrigation canals on only a limited geographical scale. Throughout the Middle Ages,

water- and windmill construction technologies improved, but not so much that land use shifted. The Chinese, who were far ahead of Europe technologically, developed steel manufacturing as well as other fairly advanced technologies, but not so systematically as to destroy river valleys.

Industrialization and Its Consequences

But by the Early Modern Period (15th century), the equation changed entirely, as Europe already used coal, and began to develop the inventions that would usher in the industrial revolution. In 1765, Frederick the Great commissioned a land reclamation project for draining the Prussian fens along the Rhine River. Few people today realize that the original land around the Rhine was mainly marsh. For centuries, small scale marsh reclamation schemes were tried, but Frederick's engineers attacked the fen on a massive scale, eventually resculpting that entire region of Germany.[92] The development of civil engineering in the Enlightenment completely changed the attitude of humans toward the environment. Before, "land improvement" was difficult: expensive undertakings that could only be done sporadically. The success of civil engineering allowed deliberate planning to "tame" Mother Nature – and, as Carolyn Merchant has pointed out, the juxtaposition of feminine names for nature and the image of rape is completely interconnected.[93]

Unfortunately, changes this massive produce many unintended effects. In Germany, the destruction of marshlands changed the animal species entirely. But civil engineering took the position that they were improving the land for human use, primarily through land reclamation, flood control, and similar benefits. And because the measure was *human* benefit, these improvements could be completely catastrophic for *every other species* impacted, but they would nonetheless be rated successful because humans benefited.

The efforts of 18th and 19th century civil engineers increased agricultural and pastoral productivity. Fens and marshes are remarkably productive ecosystems, but not for humans. This change to field and pasture increased the wealth of Prussia, allowed for a greater population, whose productivity also increased the country's wealth. So the economists and aristocracy were happy. But these extra people only lived hard lives at a subsistence level, not enjoying the wealth that flowed to the top. And with the reclamation of the lands, these same lands became more accessible and useful for industry, leading to rampant pollution from the increased pasture land, which spawned Samuel Taylor Coleridge's famous poem about the Rhine entitled "Cologne:"

> *The river Rhine, it is well known,*
> *Doth wash your city of Cologne;*
> *But tell me, nymphs! what power divine*
> *Shall henceforth wash the river Rhine?*[94]

But beyond the memorable lines of the Romantic poets, there were rumblings of other viewpoints besides engineering progress. In 1798 Thomas Malthus's *An Essay on the Principle of Population* was published, the first philosophical work to address the issue of overpopulation.

In the past, human activity which degraded an ecosystem too catastrophically resulted in human migration away from the scene of the crime. Eventually, the land would recover – or not. While humans may not have entirely created the Sahara Desert, human activity massively expanded it. In the 16th and 18th centuries, when deforestation destroyed the fertility of a river valley or weather produced a potato famine, the people affected could move on to the New World.

The Study of Organisms as Groups

Biology is an odd science, when you get down to it. It's messy. There's no neat set of categories to study. Do you study the organisms in isolation? Are you trying to classify them? Understand how they function? Understand how they function with others? Once upon a time, all organisms slotted into either botany or zoology – plants or animals. But microscopic work broke down these neat barriers. Genetics cut across species and even animals and plants. So did cell biology. So does ecology. Ecology works with organisms as a whole, not pieces of them – and even organisms in groups: yet knowledge of physiology, genetics, and taxonomy can be vital. But working with individual organisms as units that fit into a landscape or habitat can be vital to understand how these unintended effects come about.

Ecologists of the early 20th century were not primarily environmental activists of the flavor of the 1970s. Their goals often related to specific human problems as well, such as what are the adaptations of plants native to desert regions that could aid the farming of those regions. At that time, one of the great ecological problems in the U.S. was how to adapt agriculture to the arid West. Water utilization and reclamation were huge topics in ecology as well as engineering.

In the 20th century, the U.S. Army Corps of Engineers went from being heroes to being reviled by environmentalists. What happened? First, a lot of the things that civil engineers did, like straightening rivers, came under question, both for environmental reasons, and for economic ones when it was discovered that meandering rivers were *less* susceptible to flooding than straight ones. In other words, the engineering was making the problem worse, not better.

Ecosystems

During this period, people began to realize that these large problems could only be understood by treating a large number of pieces as a whole. **Systems theory** became a major new area of study in the second half of the 20th century, when computer programs were developed to do the number crunching that such studies often entailed. But earlier in the century, less rigorous quantitative methods began to be developed that applied to one form of system: the **ecosystem**. The concept of ecosystems is this: if we are to understand what happened when they drained the German fens, we have to not just look at a bird species here, a marsh grass there, but at all the plants, animals, and substrate that comprise the environment of a given place. This is an ecosystem. There are marsh ecosystems, and aquatic ecosystems, and grassland ecosystems, and many more. While the terrain, climate and species differ, the concept is the same. If foxes feed on field mice, then anything that affects the mice will also affect the foxes. The theory of evolution applies to species: an ecosystem contains many species. So if the mice produce more offspring than can survive (according to one of the tenets of evolution), then on the level of the ecosystem, too many mice for the environment produce stress on the grass that they eat, resulting in less food for all the mice. The foxes have a field day, eating all the mice. But then the foxes produce too many offspring

too, and these excess foxes keep eating the mice until the mouse population crashes. Now the foxes don't have enough to eat, and they starve. The mouse population is low, the fox population is low, and the grasses recover. They then recover so much that now there's lots of mouse food, and so the mice get fat, happy, and reproduce – and the cycle continues.

A **self-sustaining community or ecosystem** is one in which the building blocks that the aggregate of organisms need is either generated internally, or where what comes in and goes out is roughly the same. These building blocks are carbon, nitrogen, oxygen, and some minerals. Our grass-mouse-fox community above is a simplified case, but add some other species like bacteria and fungi to break down dead matter, and you approach this idea. But notice: the absolute and relative population of all the species is not the same all the time. This ecosystem could be at the stage where grass is especially abundant – or foxes are. The question is: could these processes go on indefinitely?

There are larger units or systems than ecosystems. The largest unit is the **biosphere**, which is the region of the Earth where life is possible. This runs from pole to pole, as high as the atmosphere where spores can exist, to the deepest ocean trenches where specialized bacteria can convert inorganic chemicals into energy. Notice that this zone contains much nonliving material as well: but the atmosphere, and the **hydrosphere** (the water more or less at the surface of the earth) and the **lithosphere** (the soil and surface rocks) provide the substrate for life, and many chemicals necessary for life to exist.

It is at the level of the biosphere that the **Gaia Hypothesis** rests. This theory of James Lovelock's says that, since the biosphere is **bioregenerative** (*i.e.*, self-sustaining, in that the biological and non-biological components of the biosphere recycle into each other), that the living components regulate the nonliving substrate, thereby changing it. It is *as if* the entire biosphere were one large organism. This metaphor of the entire earth as alive is not unlike the metaphor of the zodiac as a series of "living" animals.

Ecology is the study of the biosphere, from the Greek words for "home" (*oikos*) and study of (*logos*). That's not how the term was originally defined, but it works pretty well now. Ecologists may study at the biosphere level, the ecosystem level, or the population level, but they only study individual organisms as they relate to these higher units.

Dropping down from the level of the biosphere, major climatic regions are classified as **biomes**: these are zones such as grasslands, tropical rainforests, desert, and tundra, that share similar temperature and rainfall, and have similar species worldwide. This is why the Western Coast of California looks similar to the Eastern Coast of Australia.

Each biome has multiple ecosystems within it. The ecosystem is the major unit studied by ecologists. Each ecosystem has organisms classified as producers (also called **autotrophs**) and consumers (also called **heterotrophs**): producers are the plants and certain bacteria that "fix" carbon and store energy from radiant or chemical processes. The vast majority of production is from **photosynthesis**, the series of chemical reactions carried on within a plant which capture energy from light into organic compounds and stored energy. **Consumers** eat other organisms or dead organisms in order to gather their carbon and energy.

A somewhat more detailed analysis classifies the consumer organisms of an ecosystem into four functions:

- **Herbivores** eat the producers directly

- **Carnivores** eat other animals, whether herbivore or carnivore

- **Omnivores** sometimes eat plants, and sometimes eat animals

- **Saprovores** consume dead organisms, or non-living organic matter

A particular ecosystem could lack herbivores, carnivores or omnivores (the consumers), but a self-sustaining ecosystem would have to have producers as well as saprovores.

Population Dynamics

Ecology studies how all these parts work together to produce a stable result. What has been verified in all the ecosystems studied is that population dynamics are the key to stability. In our example above, the conclusion is that a particular ecosystem cannot support an infinite number of foxes. However, in a particular ecosystem, and for a particular organism, population growth may be unlimited – for a time. For example, when that first hypothetical fox couple migrated to a new grassland full of field mice, the foxes might not be limited at all – for some generations. Lots of food, no predators – the foxes had it easy. Foxes would still die of injury or disease. But eventually, as more foxes were born, the population density reached a point where the fox population could not grow any more without causing a crash in the mouse population, which then caused a crash in the fox population. This population level where stability results is called the **carrying capacity** of a particular species – and this varies from ecosystem to ecosystem, and over time.

The Effect of Humans on Ecosystems

This is how it works when you leave humans out of the picture. What has happened with most ecosystems where humans live is precisely what happened when Frederick drained the marshes: the total measure is human benefit. This tends to produce unstable ecosystems because we don't require an ecosystem to be self-sustaining. Instead, we can come in and cut down the trees in the Amazon and farm the land, and then, after a few years, when the land no longer produces crops, we just move on, and leave the abandoned land to its own devices. Or, when the soil in a farming area becomes depleted, we add artificial fertilizers. In other words, we may be able to compensate for some of the instability of an area by importing energy or substances such as fertilizers. But we are only compensating to aid the species we are fostering – crops or farm animals. The other species are either deliberately destroyed through pesticides, herbicides or fungicides, or left to fend for themselves amidst the changed conditions. These lands now stay productive, as long as we keep artificially adding to them. If we stop, the land ceases to produce anything of human value, and once again, the land is abandoned. Perhaps this wasn't that much of a problem when there were still continents that were seriously underpopulated by humans. But no more. Because now, what happens in South America can affect what is going on in Europe. And what is also not superficially apparent is that adding substances like fertilizers translates into energy expenditures of fossil fuels. It takes energy to mine the rock, pulverize it, convert it to the specific chemicals used in fertilizers, transport it, and apply it.

The Clash of Ecology with Traditional Religion

It is at this point that the findings of ecology become controversial, because ecology assumes that human beings are also animals. Talking about the carrying capacity of foxes is one thing, but humans? This is where science and some religions clash. Within the monotheistic definition, if we are special because God made us so, why should or would these rules apply to us? The answers to these questions at this point vary from denomination to denomination. Many of the mainstream Protestant denominations have accepted the scientific arguments. The Catholic Church and a number of evangelical and fundamentalist groups have not.

But even examining the position of the groups that prefer a biblical to a scientific approach, a simple point is clear. If you accept the biblical account, then *God created a finite Earth*. There is only so much land, no more. There is only so much space, fuel, and food. So the only difference between the scientific and the biblical points of view is how *extreme* the numbers would have to be for the finiteness of the Earth to limit the human population.

The question, as we will see over the later part of this book, is not *whether* there are limits, but *where* and *when* those limits will kick in. In Chapter 5, we will examine the process by which systems theorists attempted to characterize these limitations.

Global Warming

But before we resume the astrological subject of this book, I want to take up the question of global warming, which has been the other controversial environmental idea in the news.

The theory of global warming is simple: the question is how important it is. Here's the background.

One of the astronomical puzzles of our solar system is why our climate is so different from that of Venus, a similar-sized planet that presumably started with more or less the same composition as the Earth. Yes, Venus is closer to the Sun, but does that account for the massively hotter climate on Venus? Venus has an extremely thick atmosphere, and the theory developed that its atmosphere is actually keeping heat *in*, thereby running up the surface temperature. Gases which would have that property are called **greenhouse gases**, and the conditions on Venus have been designated a **runaway greenhouse effect**. One known greenhouse gas is carbon dioxide, which is also present in trace levels in Earth's atmosphere: almost all living beings produce carbon dioxide in respiration.

This would be an interesting but irrelevant fact, except for one thing. I mentioned the civil engineering works begun under Frederick the Great earlier, but I didn't mention how that was possible in the 18th century, when it hadn't been possible in, say, the 5th century. Until the last few centuries, humans derived all their power from physical human labor, combined with a certain amount of animal work. As I mentioned, watermills and windmills supplemented this, but still, human labor can produce an impressive monument like the Greek Parthenon, the Roman Coliseum, or the Gothic cathedrals, but it's not enough to massively change the contours of the land over areas of hundreds of square miles. Greater power was necessary for this – as for the industrial revolution in general. That power came from coal. Coal had been mined and used in Roman times in Britain in iron-making.[95] Its use dropped out in the early Middle Ages, and then began to make a comeback when fuel wood prices began to rise, about the 13th

century. Its use began to shoot up even more in the 18th century when cast iron, wrought iron, and steel-making in the industrial revolution took off, because coal was necessary to produce the higher temperatures for smelting.

Iron and steel were necessary to build engines, bridges, mills, rails, ships, and so much more. This massive increase in iron working could not happen without power – and power meant burning fuel, which produces carbon dioxide. So it was the industrial revolution which began the process by which human activities really impacted the globe. First, deforestation had driven up the cost of wood and charcoal. Then coal burning accelerated the production of carbon dioxide and other waste gases. Deforestation destroyed ecosystems, while mining was often devastating for the land as well.

Our modern age is characterized by greater power usage than that of all humanity before us. But, to use the terminology of ecology, we need to remember that we are energy *consumers*, not energy *producers*. Our society talks about oil "production," but what we call "production" is actually mining. Botanical plants produce – we consume. Coal and petroleum are deposits. They are no longer being produced. Whatever the arguments about how much is left, once we use up the deposits, they are gone, and there is no more.

Because petroleum and coal originally came from animals and plants that used to live on the Earth, they are carbon-based. And being carbon-based, burning them for energy produces carbon dioxide. And there is no question that human activity is increasing the amount of carbon dioxide in the atmosphere.

Controversy happens when we consider the next question: how much carbon dioxide can we humans add to the atmosphere without poisoning ourselves? I am not using the word "poison" incorrectly here, because carbon dioxide *does* become poisonous for animals beyond a certain trace level. If you saw the movie *Apollo 13*, you might recall the scene where the astronauts had to improvise a carbon dioxide filter or die.

But there are two possible "poisons." Carbon dioxide itself is poisonous to animals, just like carbon monoxide is, although carbon monoxide is much more poisonous at lower levels. But if there is enough carbon dioxide to trigger climatic changes (because it is a greenhouse gas), then, the theory goes, we could inadvertently change the climate of the entire Earth, which could change agricultural production, change hurricane and other weather patterns, and possibly, send the Earth into a runaway greenhouse effect, like that which may have made Venus such a noxious place.

Because the effect of greenhouse gases is to increase the average temperature (*i.e.*, produce **global warming**), environmentalists and climatologists have been looking for evidence that global temperatures are rising. This has been observed. One piece of evidence is that there is melting of the arctic ice caps.[96]

But, the argument goes, Earth historically has experienced ups and downs in its average temperature. Even if human activity is releasing greenhouse gases, it doesn't mean that this activity is driving the temperatures higher than they have ever been in the history of the Earth.

Since the 1960s, there has been a steady increase in the development of computer software to model climate. What many of these models predict is a tipping point – that up to a certain point, the changes produced are minor or incremental, but that when the **tipping point** is reached, catastrophic effects result that are virtually irreversible. Because these conclusions are based on modeling about what hasn't happened yet, there is going to be controversy, especially since changing our behavior on a global scale can only happen with major economic disruptions. And beyond the question of just how much the climate shifts is another simple fact, also documented in Brown: the higher the temperature, the less the agricultural productivity.[97] So even if humans were to actually enjoy the higher temperatures, less agricultural capacity means less food.

What do you think is the risk of a catastrophic climate event, versus the risk of being killed in a terrorist attack, versus being killed in a car crash? How you answer this question determines your political priorities.

Overpopulation

There is one other factor which goes right along with the climate change question. If we can agree that human activities affect the Earth, even if we don't collectively agree on how much, then the more people, the greater the environmental impact of the human race. I mentioned earlier that Thomas Malthus's 1798 publication made the argument that human reproduction can easily outstrip food supply. Let me re-work his argument as it has been refined through ecological studies.

Malthus was part of the inspiration for Darwin's statement: more offspring are born into an environment than can survive. We see this over and over in nature: fish that produce thousands of eggs for every one organism that survives to adulthood. Any time you plant seeds in the garden, you discover that you had better plant a lot more carrot seeds than the number of carrot plants you want!

This was true for humans as well, up through the 19th century, and in many places today in the developing world.

Go into your genealogical records, and you will discover that a family with a dozen children might result in only two or three adults. But now, in industrialized countries, we consider any infant mortality at all to be tragic, and we expect it to be uncommon. What happened?

The first half of the 20th century had two major advances that drastically reduced infant and childhood mortality. The first was the improvement of sanitation as a result of separating sewage from drinking water. Clean water massively reduces mortality. The second was the advent of antibiotics, which reduced many childhood diseases that used to be killers to the level of petty annoyance. Measles, mumps, scarlet fever, whooping cough, pneumonia – all these were routine killers less than a century ago. My mother lost a brother and a sister to these diseases when she was growing up – and she almost died of scarlet fever as a child. Check your own family tree, and stories like this are probably closer than you might think.

Lesser infant mortality without a similarly drastic reduction in number of children born per couple will result in rapid population growth. And this is what has happened all over the world: reduction in childhood mortality resulted in major population growth. But many countries reduced their population growth, even to negative levels, because people chose to have fewer children. This is something that we can *choose* to control. But many more have not. The medical miracles we exported to the developing countries in the form of vaccines and antibiotics were applied without any heed to how the larger families which would then ensue could impede and guarantee the maintenance of poverty and misery for far more people. Unchecked human population growth has doomed billions to lives of poverty, hunger, disease, rape, violence, and ignorance.

How Did All This Happen Right in Front of Us?

This was not supposed to be what happened. Flash back to the late 1940s and 1950s. America and the Western democracies had just emerged victorious from what was perceived of as a just war. Antibiotics had changed the face of medicine, seemingly forever. Other medical discoveries gave hope that many of mankind's most dreaded diseases would be eliminated. The development of new farming methods based on the use of chemical fertilizers and pesticides was just taking off, promising huge increases in crop yields, promising to feed the millions, and then billions, ending forever the cycle of poverty worldwide. Nuclear energy was about to bring in an era of energy so cheap that it could be delivered without even having to meter it.

Science and reason were going to fix everything. They didn't. What happened? Here, we return to the Law of Unintended Consequences that I referred to toward the beginning of this chapter. Call this a measure of the fact that humans cannot claim to omniscience.

- The burgeoning of antibiotics occurred before any biologists had considered the possibility that bacteria would develop immunity to the antibiotics, thereby producing strains that were much more dangerous and damaging.

- The technology to produce a vaccine for one disease didn't always cross over to other diseases. Additionally, diseases like heart disease, diabetes, and cancer proved much more difficult to eradicate than was originally projected. That cure for cancer that was only twenty years away in the 1960s? We're still waiting for it, right along with flying cars. There was also little to no understanding at the time how many of these diseases had environmental or lifestyle components to them. The increased use of sugars in food has driven the rates of diabetes up, not down, despite all the medical research on it. The relationship between smoking and lung cancer had not even been imagined.

• There really was a massive increase in agricultural productivity. However, increases in productivity mostly ended about half a Saturn cycle ago. Since then, the growth of cities, overgrazing and over-intensive farming has reduced arable land per capita, water tables are dropping worldwide and now, competition with the use of foodstuffs to produce biofuel has produced a permanent increase in the cost of food. Up until 1997, these agricultural wonders were reducing hunger worldwide, but, since then, hunger is growing again.[98] The current agricultural darling, genetic modification, has yet to be demonstrated as resulting in any significant increase in agricultural productivity. Genetically modified crops are technically defined as fungicides, not plants, and their principal benefit is that they guarantee a continuous market for their manufacturers, because they are also genetically designed *not* to be able to reproduce, thus guaranteeing a continuous market for their seed.

• Nuclear energy did not turn into the panacea that was hyped in large part because the industry consistently downplayed the poisonous qualities of radioactive substances, while never developing any truly permanent storage facilities for the toxic waste that inevitably accumulated. The tragic accidents in Chernobyl and Three Mile Island were in the future. The simple fact that radioactivity is a potent carcinogen has been a consistent blind spot of both the scientists and the industry as it developed, with a number of the early pioneers experiencing earlier death due to their toxic side effects. When nuclear power faltered, fusion became the next great solution, but one that has never come to market. Cheap "inexhaustible" energy remains elusive, as every day we reduce the quantity of remaining fossil fuel, while suffering from its by-products.

While one might question the motives of some of the scientists and captains of industry in not revealing or publicizing detrimental health effects resulting from their industries, I think we cannot question their original motives and enthusiasm. What they all failed to grasp was perhaps one of the most basic rules that falls out of both ecology and the 2nd Law of Thermodynamics: there is no such thing as a free lunch. Put bluntly, energy cannot be free, because there is always waste energy in the form of heat: and it has to go somewhere. On the level of matter, the creation of phosphorus or nitrogen fertilizer which makes those substances no longer the limiting element, simply means that the next most scarce substance becomes the limiting factor.

Human ingenuity has a curious blindness. You see a problem: you come up with a way to solve the problem. You don't think in terms of the ways that your solution creates still more problems.

These well-intentioned plans simply were not formulated with the other major consequence they were creating: population growth. Food or disease had not been the only check on population. Wars and economic downturns impact population as well, whether there is modern contraception or not. People who really do not want to have children will find a way, whether through abstention, abortion, infanticide, or late marriage.

The equation is simple and uncontroversial: the more people, the more consumption, the more energy use, the more pollution. The problem is that, in the U.S. and many other countries, it has become so ingrained that children are good and population growth is good, that we are incapable as a society in seeing that there can be a downside to growth.

There is no example of indefinite population growth in nature or otherwise. And in nature, there is no example where indefinite population growth doesn't ultimately result in a population crash when the carrying capacity of the environment is exceeded. We can delay it, through our increased power usage, but all that may do is make the crash bigger when it happens. And in the meantime, every problem relating to resources – air pollution, water pollution, soil erosion – becomes worse, the more people contribute to it.

The facts are so simple, but so hard to apply. We are finite. Our world is finite. Each resource that we use is finite. At some point, something will run out. Then, we may be able to come up with a substitute, but that will only delay the problem until something else runs out. That is the lesson of ecology.

Endnotes: Chapter 2

91. Hanks, Sharon La Bonde. *Ecology and the Biosphere: Principles and Problems*. Boca Raton, Fla: St. Lucie Press, 1996., p xix.

92. Henderson, W.O. *Studies in the Economic Policy of Frederick the Great*. Oxford: Taylor & Francis, 2006, p 82.

93. Merchant, Carolyn. *The Death of Nature : Women, Ecology, and the Scientific Revolution*. New York: Harper & Row, 1989.

94. http://www.online-literature.com/quotes/quotation_search.php?author=Samuel Taylor Coleridge

95. Hatcher, John, Michael. W. Flinn, David Stoker, Roy Church, Alan Hall, John Kanefsky, Barry Supple, William Ashworth, and Mark Pegg. *The History of the British Coal Industry*. Oxford: Clarendon Press, 1984, Volume 2, p 17.

96. While there has been quite a bit of controversy about the actual specific temperature figures associated with global warming, the melting of the icecaps is not controversial: it is demonstrable. For a synopsis of the observations, see Brown, Lester Russell, and Lester Russell Brown. *Plan B 4.0: Mobilizing to Save Civilization*. New York: W. W. Norton, 2009, pp 61-66.

97. Brown, 2009, pp 56-61.

98. Brown, Lester, 2009, Chapter 1.

3

The Dance of Neptune and Pluto

In the Preface, I mentioned the Plutinos, and I specifically defined them as the bodies outside Neptune's orbit. A couple of years ago, the International Astronomical Union reclassified Pluto as a dwarf planet, not a "true" planet – and a lot of astrologers were rather miffed. So you might well be wondering: first, I'm a classical astrologer, so why am I talking about Pluto anyway? And then I mention Plutinos, and you have to wonder if I'm not somehow downgrading Pluto doubly. Believe me, I'm not.

From my viewpoint, the traditional planets have their meanings, functions and their roles. We know that comets were interpreted, so there is a precedent for additional bodies. I would simply say, all these extra bodies can be interpreted, but don't rule signs of their own.

About the Plutinos. Historically, Pluto was the first one: it was a Plutino before there were Plutinos, because the very name implies plurality. Beyond the historical pride of place as the First One, Pluto has another quality that sets it apart: its orbital relationship to Neptune. For this, I thank both Robert Hand and David Cochrane for influencing my thinking. The ratio in the orbits of Neptune to Pluto is an almost perfect 3:2 ratio. What do I mean by this? The Jet Propulsion Laboratory gives the orbital period of Neptune as 164.79132 years. They give the orbital period of Pluto as 247.92065 years.[99] So: multiply the Neptune period by 3, and you get 494.37396 years. Multiply the Pluto period by 2 and you get 495.8413 years. Almost identical. Given the uncertainty in the orbital elements of Pluto, the actual may be even closer. From our human perspective of a life span on the lower side of a century, this is close enough to a perfect 3:2 relation. So what, you say? In music, there is a name for that ratio, it's a **sesquialter**, which musicians know better as a fifth – a very harmonic ratio. (By the way: if you're wondering whether this term somehow relates to **sesquiquadrate**, the 135° aspect, it does. The prefix "sesqui" refers to "and a half." A sesquiquadrate is "a square [quadrate] and a half:" 90 + 45 = 135. You may have seen the expression sesquicentennial for a celebration of an entity as being 150 years old.)

From this, we see that Neptune and Pluto are not separate concepts, but a fugue, a chord, a relationship. It is a theme with variation, because Pluto's orbit is much more eccentric and inclined than Neptune's, which means there is a much greater disparity in the time that Pluto spends in each of the signs. Each other Plutino will have a different harmonic relationship to Neptune, although few will have the simplicity of the pairing of Neptune and Pluto. Whether planet, dwarf planet, Plutino, or some other Apollonian classification, Pluto will have its say.

In Figure 1, you can see the graphical representation of the transit of Pluto through Sagittarius, Capricorn, Aquarius, and Pisces for the last three historical periods, including our own. Observe how the map of the 1st and 3rd passes have almost identical positions of Neptune for a given Pluto position. The orbital length of Uranus's cycle is just more than half that of Neptune's – 50.1%, to be exact. So observe how each successive Pluto cycle, Uranus has crept a little bit to the right – it is advancing slightly quicker than the Neptune-Pluto pairing.

In the Pluto in Sagittarius period beginning in 1502 and 1995, Neptune spent most of its time in Aquarius. The time in between, beginning in 1748, Neptune was mainly in Leo. The signs aren't always precisely opposite, because Pluto's eccentric orbit means that it spends much more time in Taurus than in Scorpio. These ratios between the planetary orbits, while not exact, mean that every other pass of Pluto in a sign will bear a strong resemblance to each other in terms of outer planet effect.

The fugue manifests in many ways, and we shall see this underlying theme throughout this book as we examine charts from different historical periods. It is exceptionally rare to consider the long-term cycles of Neptune and Pluto, because we mostly pay attention to the here and now. Then, whenever we experience a sign change of these bodies, we go into our computer programs or the ephemeris, and dig out the last few passes of that planet in the upcoming sign. Because we do it in a haphazard way, we tend to miss the long-term cycles as well as the harmonic relationship we have discussed just now. And in this particular case, if we are that haphazard, we will also tend to be wrong. If we go back only one Neptune-Pluto pass, we will miss the symmetry that becomes obvious by going back two passes, and then confirming that every other pass really does have the same sign pairs.

The relationship between Neptune and Pluto has been treated as one type of outer planet synodic cycle. Thus, Charles Harvey said:

"We would suggest that in some sense [Neptune and Pluto] relate to the higher ideas and ideals of the time, and to the larger spiritual, cosmic and human purposes which are coming into manifestation. As noted, this cycle sets the tone of the underlying and compelling aspirations of the time."[100]

Neptune-Pluto hard aspects are rare: they occur on average once a century – and sometimes less. Because of Pluto's unusual orbit, the intervals are not regular. Because of the close ratio between the orbits of Neptune and Pluto, between 1 – 2500 c.e., they have always occurred in the mutable signs: with only two exceptions. These periods are shown in Table 3-1 on page 73.

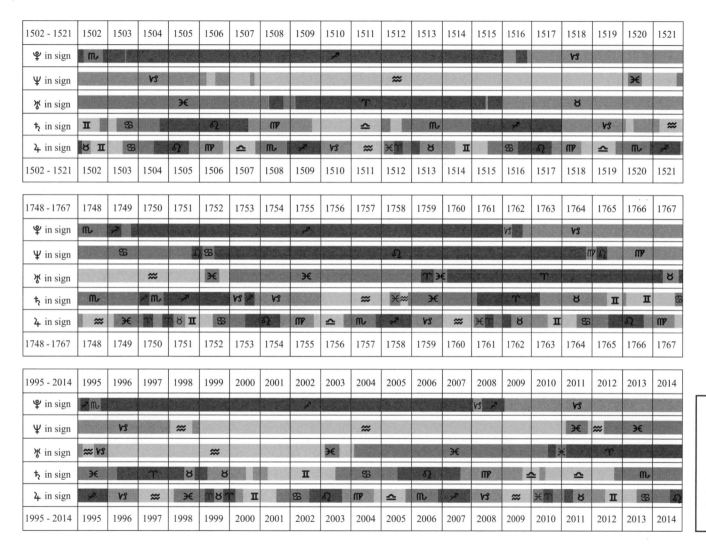

Figure 1. The last three passes of Pluto through Sagittarius, Capricorn, Aquarius, and Pisces. Data derived from Sirius, Version 1.2.

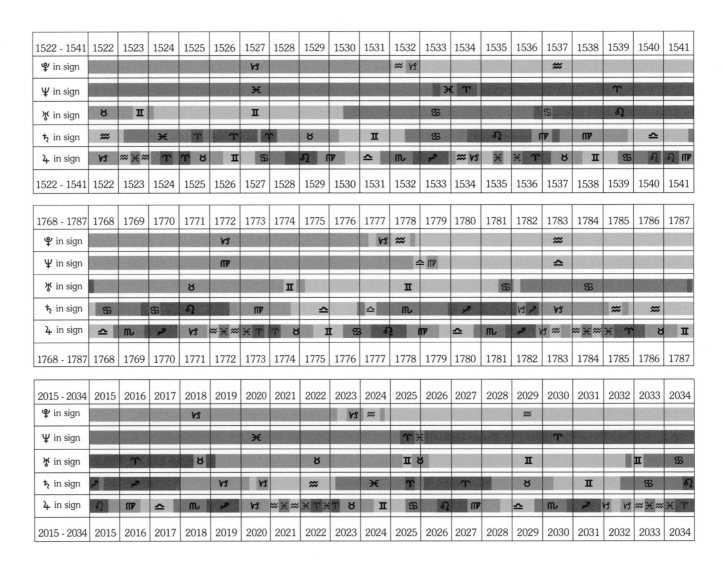

1542 - 1561	1542	1543	1544	1545	1546	1547	1548	1549	1550	1551	1552	1553	1554	1555	1556	1557	1558	1559	1560	1561
♇ in sign					♒						♓ ♒	♓				♓				
♆ in sign			♈			♉							♉						♊	♉ ♊
♅ in sign	♌	♌			♍				♎		♎				♎			♏		
♄ in sign	♏		♏	♐		♑	♑		♒		♓	♓			♈		♉		♊	♋
♃ in sign	♍	♎	♏	♐	♑	♓	♈	♉	♊	♋	♌ ♍	♍	♍ ♎	♎ ♏	♐ ♏ ♐	♑ ♐ ♑	♒	♓	♈	♉
1542 - 1561	1542	1543	1544	1545	1546	1547	1548	1549	1550	1551	1552	1553	1554	1555	1556	1557	1558	1559	1560	1561

1788 -1807	1788	1789	1790	1791	1792	1793	1794	1795	1796	1797	1798	1799	1800	1801	1802	1803	1804	1805	1806	1807
♇ in sign						♒				♓ ♒	♓			♓						
♆ in sign				♎		♏		♏											♏	♐
♅ in sign	♋			♌			♍	♌		♍				♍		♎				♎
♄ in sign	♒	♓	♈	♈	♈		♉		♊		♋		♌		♍		♎	♎		♏
♃ in sign	♊ ♋		♌ ♍	♍ ♎	♎ ♏	♏ ♐	♐ ♑	♒ ♑	♒ ♓	♈	♉	♊	♊ ♋	♋ ♌ ♍	♌ ♍	♎ ♎	♎ ♏	♐ ♏ ♐	♑ ♑	♒
1788 -1807	1788	1789	1790	1791	1792	1793	1794	1795	1796	1797	1798	1799	1800	1801	1802	1803	1804	1805	1806	1807

2035 - 2054	2035	2036	2037	2038	2039	2040	2041	2042	2043	2044	2045	2046	2047	2048	2049	2050	2051	2052	2053	2054
♇ in sign					♒				♓ ♒						♓					
♆ in sign		♈		♉ ♈					♉									♉	♊	
♅ in sign			♋		♌				♌		♍	♌			♍			♍	♎	
♄ in sign	♌		♌	♍		♎			♏	♏	♐		♑	♑			♒	♓	♓	
♃ in sign	♉	♊	♋	♌	♌ ♍	♍ ♎	♎ ♏	♏ ♐	♑ ♐	♑ ♒	♓	♈	♉		♊	♋ ♌	♍ ♎	♎	♏	♐ ♏ ♐
2035 - 2054	2035	2036	2037	2038	2039	2040	2041	2042	2043	2044	2045	2046	2047	2048	2049	2050	2051	2052	2053	2054

Legend:

- Fire
- Earth
- Air
- Water

Legend:

Fire

Earth

Air

Water

1562 - 1581	1562	1563	1564	1565	1566	1567	1568	1569	1570	1571	1572	1573	1574	1575	1576	1577	1578	1579	1580	1581
♇ in sign								♓								♈ ♓	♈		♈	
♆ in sign						♊							♊ ♋				♋			
♅ in sign	♏	♐ ♏				♐			♑	♑						♒	♒			
♄ in sign	♋		♋ ♌		♌	♍		♎		♏	♏			♐	♐	♑		♒ ♑	♒	
♃ in sign	♉ ♊ ♋	♋ ♌	♌	♍ ♍ ♎	♎	♏ ♏	♐	♑	♒	♓	♈	♈ ♉	♋		♌	♍	♎	♏	♐	♑
1562 - 1581	1562	1563	1564	1565	1566	1567	1568	1569	1570	1571	1572	1573	1574	1575	1576	1577	1578	1579	1580	1581

1808 - 1827	1808	1809	1810	1811	1812	1813	1814	1815	1816	1817	1818	1819	1820	1821	1822	1823	1824	1825	1826	1827
♇ in sign							♓								♈	♈		♈		
♆ in sign						♐							♑				♑			
♅ in sign			♏				♐ ♏	♐						♑			♑			
♄ in sign	♏	♐ ♏	♐		♑		♑	♒		♓ ♒	♓	♓	♈			♉		♊	♋	♋
♃ in sign	♒ ♓	♈	♉	♊ ♋	♋ ♌		♍	♎	♏	♐	♑	♒	♓	♈ ♈	♉ ♊	♊	♋	♌	♍	♎
1808 - 1827	1808	1809	1810	1811	1812	1813	1814	1815	1816	1817	1818	1819	1820	1821	1822	1823	1824	1825	1826	1827

2055 - 2074	2055	2056	2057	2058	2059	2060	2061	2062	2063	2064	2065	2066	2067	2068	2069	2070	2071	2072	2073	2074
♇ in sign						♓						♓	♈	♓			♈			
♆ in sign					♊						♋	♊			♋					
♅ in sign		♎			♏		♏				♐ ♏		♐					♑ ♐	♑	
♄ in sign		♈	♉	♉	♊	♊		♊	♋		♌		♍		♎		♎	♏		♐
♃ in sign	♑ ♑	♒	♓	♈	♉ ♉	♊ ♋	♋ ♌	♌	♍	♎	♏	♐	♑	♒	♓	♈	♉ ♊	♊ ♋		♌ ♍
2055 - 2074	2055	2056	2057	2058	2059	2060	2061	2062	2063	2064	2065	2066	2067	2068	2069	2070	2071	2072	2073	2074

Years	Aspect	Ne Sign	Pl Sign	# Exact hits
88 – 92	Square	Gemini	Pisces	9
163 – 167	Opposite	Scorpio	Taurus	11
336 – 340	Square	Sagittarius	Pisces	9
411 – 412	Conjunct	Taurus	Taurus	3
582 – 586	Square	Gemini	Pisces	9
657 – 660	Opposite	Scorpio	Taurus	11
830 – 833	Square	Sagittarius	Pisces	7
905	Conjunct	Gemini	Gemini	1
1075 – 1079	Square	Gemini	Pisces	9
1150 – 1154	Opposite	Scorpio	Taurus	
		Sagittarius	Gemini	9
1323 – 1327	Square	Sagittarius	Pisces	9
1398 – 1399	Conjunct	Gemini	Gemini	3
1568 – 1572	Square	Gemini	Pisces	9
1644 – 1648	Opposite	Sagittarius	Gemini	11
1816 – 1820	Square	Sagittarius	Pisces	9
1891 – 1892	Conjunct	Gemini	Gemini	3
2061 – 2065	Square	Gemini	Pisces	9
2137 – 2141	Opposite	Sagittarius	Gemini	11
2309 – 2312	Square	Sagittarius	Pisces	
		Capricorn	Aries	9
2385	Conjunct	Gemini	Gemini	1

Table 3-1. Hard aspects of Neptune and Pluto, 1 – 2500 C.E.

What we can see from this table, which includes five complete synodic cycles of Neptune and Pluto, is that when Pluto goes into Pisces, there will be a Neptune square Pluto. When Pluto goes into Gemini, there will be either a Neptune conjunction, or a Neptune opposition – with one exception. This is yet one more indication that you cannot simply look at the last ingress of Pluto into a sign to predict its significance in the coming pass: you have to look at previous transits through that sign to get the picture. Was Harvey's description of this cycle relating to "ideas and ideals" in part a function of the conjunction between them occurring in Gemini, an air sign relating very much to ideas?

In this book, we will discuss the historical periods of the 1568-1572, 1816-1820, and 1891-1892 hard aspects. We will also anticipate some of what might occur with the next one in 2061-2065.

Beyond just the symmetry we have shown above, we can also examine this relationship between Neptune and Pluto in terms of the repetition of sign patterns. Again, this is a road not generally taken, but easily available, should you choose to run long-term sign ingresses on your computer. In Table 3-2, to extract the essence of this Neptunian/Plutonian dance, I have listed all the sign positions of Pluto where Neptune spent at least eight years of its transit through its corresponding sign: the dominant Pluto sign for a particular sign of Neptune. For example, Neptune spent ten years in Aquarius while Pluto was in Sagittarius, from 1998-2008. Then again, Neptune will be in Pisces from its ingress in 2011, until Pluto leaves Capricorn in 2023.

From Table 3-2, we can see that the sign combinations are drifting slowly over time, but each sign pair repeats several times and in a pattern. Every other time Pluto is in a particular sign, Neptune will be in the same sign, or the adjacent one. So Pluto alternates between Neptune signs on each successive pass. Thus, if we want to predict what Pluto will do in Aquarius after 2023, we should go back not to the last time that Pluto was in Aquarius, 1777-1797, but to the previous time, 1532-1552.

Neptune Sign	Pluto Sign	Years
Aries	Aquarius	61-73, 551-564, 1042-1056, 2026-2038
Aries	Leo	224-235, 715-727, 1206-1218, 1697-1710, 2188-2202
Aries	Taurus	389-401, 878-892, 1370-1383, 1861-1874, 2353-2365
Taurus	Aquarius	73-84, 564-573, 1533-1547
Taurus	Pisces	1552-1560, 2043-2051
Taurus	Virgo	237-247, 728-739, 1219-1232, 1710-1724, 2202-2215
Taurus	Taurus	401-412, 893-905, 1383-1394, 1874-1882
Taurus	Gemini	2371-2379
Gemini	Pisces	87-100, 578-591, 1069-1082, 1560-1573, 2051-2065
Gemini	Libra	250-259, 741-751, 1233-1243, 1724-1736, 2217-2228
Gemini	Gemini	418-427, 906-919, 1396-1410, 1887-1901, 2379-2392
Cancer	Pisces	100-112, 591-600
Cancer	Aries	1088-1096, 1577-1587, 2066-2078
Cancer	Scorpio	264-272, 755-763, 1246-1255, 1737-1748, 2229-2241
Cancer	Gemini	427-441, 919-932, 1410-1423, 1901-1912, 2392-2402
Leo	Aries	114-127, 605-618, 1096-1109, 1587-1600, 2078-2092
Leo	Sagittarius	277-287, 768-778, 1259-1269, 1751-1762, 2242-2254
Leo	Cancer	446-455, 934-946, 1423-1437, 1914-1928, 2406-2419
Virgo	Aries	127-141, 618-630, 1109-1118
Virgo	Taurus	1606-1614, 2095-2105
Virgo	Capricorn	291-305, 782-795, 1273-1286, 1764-1777, 2255-2269
Virgo	Cancer	455-465, 946-956, 1437-1447, 1928-1937, 2419-2428
Libra	Taurus	143-155, 632-646, 1123-1137, 1614-1628, 2105-2119

Libra	Aquarius	306-319, 796-810, 1287-1301, 1778-1792, 2270-2283
Libra	Leo	468-481, 959-972, 1450-1464, 1942-1955, 2433-2447
Scorpio	Taurus	155-169, 646-660, 1137-1150, 1628-1638, 2119-2127
Scorpio	Aquarius	319-328, 810-817, 1307-1315
Scorpio	Pisces	1797-1806, 2288-2297
Scorpio	Virgo	482-493, 973-985, 1464-1478, 1956-1970, 2448-2461
Sagittarius	Gemini	174-183, 662-674, 1151-1165, 1642-1656, 2133-2148
Sagittarius	Pisces	333-347, 824-838, 1315-1329, 1806-1820, 2297-2311
Sagittarius	Libra	496-505, 987-997, 1478-1490, 1971-1983, 2464-2475
Capricorn	Gemini	183-197, 674-688, 1165-1178, 1656-1668, 2148-2157
Capricorn	Pisces	347-356, 838-844
Capricorn	Aries	844-852, 1332-1343, 1822-1834, 2312-2325
Capricorn	Sagittarius	517-524
Capricorn	Scorpio	1001-1009, 1493-1502, 1984-1995, 2476-2488
Aquarius	Sagittarius	33-42, 524-532, 1015-1024, 1506-1515, 1998-2008
Aquarius	Cancer	200-210, 689-701, 1180-1192, 1670-1684, 2161-2175
Aquarius	Aries	361-374, 852-865, 1343-1356, 1834-1847, 2325-2339
Pisces	Capricorn	47-60, 538-550, 1029-1041, 1520-1532, 2011-2023
Pisces	Cancer	210-220, 701-711, 1192-1201, 1684-1692, 2175-2183
Pisces	Aries	374-387, 865-874
Pisces	Taurus	1362-1370, 1851-1861, 2340-2352

Table 3-2. Neptune and Pluto combinations, where both planets are in the same sign pairing for at least eight years, 1 – 2489 c.e. Rows with red text show where there has been a gradual change in the sign pair.

When we compare the structure of Tables 3-2 and 3-3 — Table 3-2 sorted by Neptune sign, and Table 3-3 sorted by Pluto sign — we arrive at another view of the harmonic cycle between these two bodies. Typically, there are three different Pluto signs for each sign of Neptune, with the signs slowly drifting over time. Therefore, in the roughly twenty-five hundred years represented by this table, there are seven of the 36 combinations that have changed. (There are thirty-six combinations when you multiply three per sign.)

Neptune Sign	Pluto Sign	Years
Cancer	Aries	1088-1096, 1577-1587, 2066-2078
Leo	Aries	114-127, 605-618, 1096-1109, 1587-1600, 2078-2092
Virgo	Aries	127-141, 618-630, 1109-1118
Capricorn	Aries	844-852, 1332-1343, 1822-1834, 2312-2325
Aquarius	Aries	361-374, 852-865, 1343-1356, 1834-1847, 2325-2339
Pisces	Aries	374-387, 865-874
Aries	Taurus	389-401, 878-892, 1370-1383, 1861-1874, 2353-2365
Taurus	Taurus	401-412, 893-905, 1383-1394, 1874-1882
Virgo	Taurus	1606-1614, 2095-2105
Libra	Taurus	143-155, 632-646, 1123-1137, 1614-1628, 2105-2119
Scorpio	Taurus	155-169, 646-660, 1137-1150, 1628-1638, 2119-2127
Pisces	Taurus	1362-1370, 1851-1861, 2340-2352
Taurus	Gemini	2371-2379
Gemini	Gemini	418-427, 906-919, 1396-1410, 1887-1901, 2379-2392
Cancer	Gemini	427-441, 919-932, 1410-1423. 1901-1912, 2392-2402
Sagittarius	Gemini	174-183, 662-674, 1151-1165, 1642-1656, 2133-2148
Capricorn	Gemini	183-197, 674-688, 1165-1178, 1656-1668, 2148-2157
Leo	Cancer	446-455, 934-946, 1423-1437, 1914-1928, 2406-2419
Virgo	Cancer	455-465, 946-956, 1437-1447, 1928-1937, 2419-2428
Aquarius	Cancer	200-210, 689-701, 1180-1192, 1670-1684, 2161-2175
Pisces	Cancer	210-220, 701-711, 1192-1201, 1684-1692, 2175-2183
Aries	Leo	224-235, 715-727, 1206-1218, 1697-1710, 2188-2202
Libra	Leo	468-481, 959-972, 1450-1464, 1942-1955, 2433-2447

Taurus	Virgo	237-247, 728-739, 1219-1232, 1710-1724, 2202-2215
Scorpio	Virgo	482-493, 973-985, 1464-1478, 1956-1970, 2448-2461
Gemini	Libra	250-259, 741-751, 1233-1243, 1724-1736, 2217-2228
Sagittarius	Libra	496-505, 987-997, 1478-1490, 1971-1983, 2464-2475
Cancer	Scorpio	264-272, 755-763, 1246-1255, 1737-1748, 2229-2241
Capricorn	Scorpio	1001-1009, 1493-1502, 1984-1995, 2476-2488
Leo	Sagittarius	277-287, 768-778, 1259-1269, 1751-1762, 2242-2254
Capricorn	Sagittarius	517-524
Aquarius	Sagittarius	33-42, 524-532, 1015-1024, 1506-1515, 1998-2008
Virgo	Capricorn	291-305, 782-795, 1273-1286, 1764-1777, 2255-2269
Pisces	Capricorn	47-60, 538-550, 1029-1041, 1520-1532, 2011-2023
Aries	Aquarius	61-73, 551-564, 1042-1056, 2026-2038
Taurus	Aquarius	73-84, 564-573, 1533-1547
Libra	Aquarius	306-319, 796-810, 1287-1301, 1778-1792, 2270-2283
Scorpio	Aquarius	319-328, 810-817, 1307-1315
Taurus	Pisces	1552-1560, 2043-2051
Gemini	Pisces	87-100, 578-591, 1069-1082, 1560-1573. 2051-2065
Cancer	Pisces	100-112, 591-600
Scorpio	Pisces	1797-1806, 2288-2297
Sagittarius	Pisces	333-347, 824-838, 1315-1329, 1806-1820, 2297-2311
Capricorn	Pisces	347-356, 838-844

Table 3-3. Neptune and Pluto combinations, where both planets are in the same sign pairing for at least eight years, 1 – 2489 C.E., sorted by Pluto sign.

Earlier, I mentioned that Uranus has an orbital period roughly half that of Neptune. In practice, what this works out to is a slippage of roughly 15-23 degrees each Neptune cycle, as shown in Table 3-4.

Date of Neptune in Aries	Uranus Position
3 May 60	23 Sagittarius
12 Apr. 224	8 Sagittarius
8 Jun. 387	15 Scorpio
6 May 551	0 Scorpio
13 Apr. 715	14 Libra
19 Jun. 878	21 Virgo
6 May 1042	4 Virgo
13 Apr. 1206	17 Leo
26 Mar. 1370	0 Leo
14 May 1533	11 Cancer
30 Apr. 1697	24 Gemini
13 Apr. 1861	9 Gemini
30 Mar. 2025	24 Taurus
23 May 2188	10 Taurus
6 May 2352	26 Aries

Table 3-4. Degree position of Uranus at the first entrance of Neptune into Aries in each cycle, 1 – 2400 c.e.

The numbers are not identical from cycle to cycle because of the retrograde patterns, as well as the fact that the orbits of the planets are not circular, but elliptical.

Expressed in terms of Pluto cycles, the results are shown in Table 3-5.

Date of Pluto in Capricorn	Uranus Position
5 Jan. 42	4 Libra
21 Jan. 287	3 Virgo
23 Feb. 532	0 Leo
21 Jan. 778	5 Cancer
4 Jan. 1024	11 Gemini
25 Dec. 1269	18 Taurus
24 Dec. 1515	26 Aries
7 Jan. 1762	5 Aries
25 Jan. 2008	16 Pisces
27 Feb. 2254	28 Aquarius

Table 3-5. Degree position of Uranus at the first entrance of Pluto into Capricorn in each cycle, 1 – 2400 c.e.

Going back to Figure 1, Table 3-5 tells us that for *every* pass of Pluto, Uranus "slips" about a sign. In the 1515 pass of Pluto in Capricorn, Uranus occupied Aries, Taurus, Gemini, and Cancer. In the 1762 pass, Uranus was in Aries, Taurus, and Gemini. In the current pass, Uranus occupies Pisces, Aries, and Taurus. Depending on which sign of Pluto (remember the eccentric orbit) and depending on the retrograde cycles, Uranus occupies 3-4 signs per Pluto sign. We can see from these tables that this provides some significant overlaps in Uranus signs between successive Pluto occupations of the same sign.

I know it's very easy to go bleary-eyed on all the numbers I have presented in these tables, so let me also discuss their significance.

Perhaps the biggest idea is that *all three outer bodies presented here have certain constraints in their orbital patterns that astrologers seldom consider*. For example, if my Pluto is in Virgo, I don't tend to think about the fact that my Neptune *could only be* in Scorpio or Taurus during a long slice of historical time. We are used to thinking that any of the planets (except Mercury and Venus) can be anywhere in the chart – that each planet's position is actually independent of the position of all the others. *What these tables demonstrate is that this assumption isn't correct.*

While there may not be independence, there are symmetrical patterns. An 18th century version was **Bode's Law** (or Titius-Bode's Law), which expressed the mean distances of the planets from the Sun as a ratio. The Law was formulated before the discovery of Uranus, and the location of Uranus corresponded to the next position predicted. The absence of a body between Mars and Jupiter corresponding to the "right" point was a justification for the search which resulted in the discovery of the asteroids.[101] Neptune's position does not correspond to this law, and so, from a scientific standpoint, the law is disproved. Curiously, Pluto does fit the pattern. From a scientific perspective, the single exception negates the rule. From an astrological standpoint, we may choose to interpret this ratio as one component of the harmony of the spheres – and Neptune's "deviation" may tell us a great deal. And perhaps Pluto's adherence to the pattern tells us something again

about Neptune and Pluto – with Pluto being necessary to restore the balance, so to speak. This is speculation – but we may yet find ways to understand this matter more clearly.

What are we to make of this slowly shifting pattern of outer planet constraints that we have observed? As a teacher, I am reminded that few people are capable of learning a complex pattern based on a single repetition. When I was studying Tai Kwon Do, I ran across the hypothesis that one had to repeat a bodily motion something like 5,000 times in order to be able to make its use instinctual. And when I took that rule of thumb and applied it to the various moves and estimated which moves one could be said to have mastered by the time the average person receives a black belt, it was an interesting insight. If we apply it to astrological education, again we see the need for multiple examples to really understand a point.

But as a human species? Does everyone alive at a particular time constitute a repetition of a planetary configuration? How many times do humans have to experience a pattern for us to "learn" it? In Chapter 8, we will examine the last two passes of Pluto in Sagittarius through Pisces, while also discussing the current pass. By necessity, that means we will also examine Neptune in Capricorn through Gemini, and in Cancer through Scorpio. Throughout this book, we will examine the "lessons" of Pluto through the signs by element, emphasizing how these lessons apply specifically to our interface with our home planet Earth.

Our attitudes and beliefs bring us back to Neptune. When does the positive side of a sign come out, and when the negative? This is always a difficult question. Once the pattern is established one way, it takes more than inertia to change it. The ingress of Neptune or Pluto into a new sign gives the opportunity to reset the clock, so to speak. Unfortunately, these transitions are often marked by stress, and stress doesn't always bring out the best in people.

In Jared Diamond's book *Collapse: How Societies Choose to Fail or Succeed*, he discusses at length a number of societies that experienced environmental devastation, and lost.[102] The fact that we are here having this bookish conversation means that, at least to date, not all societies have failed. Different societies in different locations and times have been more or less aware that it is *we* who must adapt – not the Earth. Some of the societies that he discussed only lasted in a particular environment for a couple of hundred years. But consider that this time period is the length of the existence of the United States: which is also roughly the length of a Pluto cycle.

A successful society must be able to learn the lessons of all twelve Pluto signs – and then be able to do it again with the second set of Neptune signs. Neither the U.S.A. nor our current global society dependent upon fossil fuels has done this. As astrologers, we can only point out the patterns – we cannot solve the problems by ourselves. Hopefully, the rest of this book will provide the ammunition.

Endnotes: Chapter 3

99. *http//www.ssd.jpl.nasa.gov/?planet_phys_par*

100. Baigent, Michael, Nicholas Campion, and Charles Harvey. 1984, p 178.

101. The fact that Jupiter's gravitational pull was too great to allow a stable planet to exist at this distance from Jupiter was unknown at the time.

102. Diamond, Jared M. *Collapse: How Societies Choose to Fail or Succeed.* New York: Viking, 2005

4

Incarnation in Matter: Pluto in the Earth Signs

SUSTAINABILITY IS AN EARTH ELEMENT CONCEPT. It would be easy to simply do a fairly detailed analysis of Pluto in Virgo, when Earth Day started, and then extrapolate to Pluto in Capricorn. But major themes are seldom that simple, and there are many good reasons to back things up. There is a concept in classical medical astrology whereby the extremity of a condition by element is measured as follows: the first sign of that element, beginning with Aries, is the least extreme; and, within any one sign, the early degrees of any sign are less extreme than the later ones. Using this same type of analysis, it makes sense to begin our survey with the last time that Pluto was in Taurus, the first of the earth signs by this system of reckoning.

Before proceeding to the most recent trilogy, let us first observe the difference in time that Pluto spends in each of the three signs. Because of its eccentric orbit, Pluto is in Taurus longer than in either of the other two signs. In fact, Pluto is in Taurus a bit longer than in the other two signs combined. Pluto is in Virgo for less time than in Capricorn.

What does this mean? Lilly does not list Taurus as a fertile sign, but based on horaries I have done related to pregnancy, I do. And at least in the Northern Hemisphere, it makes sense. As a sign of Spring, the seasonal influence is Hot and Wet, which, from an Aristotelian perspective, combines the male principle of heat with the female principle of wetness. On the other hand, Virgo is a barren sign. While Capricorn is not classified as either fertile or barren, one has to assume that its rulership by Saturn limits its fecundity, and the fact that it's a sign of winter doesn't help either. So if we consider Capricorn to be trending toward barren, at least in the Northern Hemisphere, there is about an equal distribution of time by the planet Pluto within the earth signs of fecundity (Taurus) and sterility (Virgo and Capricorn).

While there is a Judeo-Christian admonition to be fruitful and multiply, if one accepts cyclic analysis as a higher calling, then one simply sees these two sides of the coin as the natural ebb and flow of life. From a more Ecclesiatical perspective, there is a time to sow and a time to reap.

What is interesting is that this ebb and flow has a triangular theme, not a binary one. The arc of fertility is a long note, while the arc of barrenness is two shorter notes. We could also envision

Taurus	Virgo	Capricorn
21 Jun – 11 Sep 1118	23 Oct 1218 – 12 Jan 1219	31 Dec 1269 – 18 Jul 1270
2 May – 6 Nov 1119	19 Aug 1219 – 15 Apr 1220	1 Nov 1270 – 5 Mar 1286
20 Mar 1120 – 25 Jun 1150	5 Jun 1220 – 3 Oct 1232	29 Jun 1286 – 10 Jan 1287
	23 Sep 1287 – 1 Nov 1287	
20 Jun 1362 – 9 Sep 1362	18 Oct 1464 – 17 Jan 1465	2 Jan 1516 – 18 Jul 1516
1 May 1363 – 5 Nov 1363	16 Aug 1465 – 21 Apr 1466	2 Nov 1516 – 12 Feb 1532
20 Mar – 29 Jun 1364	31 May 1466 – 21 Oct 1478	29 Jul 1532 – 21 Dec 1532
2 Nov 1394 – 16 May 1395	25 Mar 1479 – 19 Aug 1479	
27 Dec 1395 – 29 Mar 1396		
7 Jul 1606 -22 Aug 1606	17 Oct 1710 – 19 Jan 1711	7 Jan 1762 – 8 Jul 1762
10 May 1607 – 26 Oct 1607	17 Aug 1711 – 19 Apr 1712	9 Nov 1762 – 3 Apr 1777
28 Mar 1608 – 9 Jul 1638	1 Jun 1712 – 14 Nov 1724	28 May 1777 – 26 Jan 1778
22 Oct 1638 – 24 May 1639	22 Feb 1725 – 9 Sep 1725	21 Aug 1778 – 1 Dec 1778
15 Dec 1639 – 10 Apr 1640		
20 May 1851 – 14 Oct 1851	20 Oct 1956 – 15 Jan 1957	26 Jan 2008 – 14 Jun 2008
7 Apr 1852 – 12 Dec 1852	19 Aug 1957 – 11 Apr 1958	27 Nov 2008 – 23 Mar 2023
14 Feb 1853 – 21 Jul 1882	10 Jun 1958 – 5 Oct 1971*	11 Jun 2023 – 21 Jan 2024
9 Oct 1882 – 2 Jun 1883	17 Apr 1972 – 30 Jul 1972	1 Sep 2024 – 19 Nov 2024
4 Dec 1883 – 19 Apr 1884		

Table 4-1. Pluto Ingresses by Sign. Data from Michelsen, 1990, pp 63-64.

this musically as Point, Counter-point, Counter-point. We shall see how this rhythm works out in the current period.

However, in the study of any historical period, whether through Pluto or any other planet, it's always worth remembering that the people who populate that age generally do not share the planet in question by natal position. At the end of Pluto in Taurus, those people with Pluto in Taurus natally had reached at most their early thirties. They might be Congresspeople – but they weren't the Presidents of the Pluto in Taurus period. They were the Presidents of Pluto in Gemini and Pluto in Cancer. There is always a lag, where the people of earlier placements become the lens of the current placements, always attempting to understand and adapt to something that is personally foreign to a greater or lesser degree. Thus, it is the people of Pluto in Leo and Virgo who are the prime movers for Pluto in Capricorn. The Plutos in Cancer have almost all retired. With a different age distribution (as was typical historically, when the people in power were often in their teens and twenties), it would have been the Plutos in Sagittarius who would be trying to figure out Pluto in Capricorn.

Pluto in Taurus

The technological achievements of the 19th century were so vast that many people of the early 20th century believed that they were on the threshold of a new era. And well they should have! The Steam Age and the first major uptick in the utilization of fossil fuel sources meant that the 19th century looked unlike any century before it. Pluto in Taurus ran from 1851-1883, and encompassed major discoveries in science: the theory of evolution, the founding of genetics, the development of the atomic table, the discovery of the linkage between electricity and magnetism; not to mention such practical achievements as the light bulb, the phonograph, the chemistry to fractionate and utilize petroleum, the Transcontinental Railroad in the U.S.A. and the Suez Canal. The transportation boom, which began with the steam engine, accelerated even further when Pluto went into Gemini, and the automobile and the airplane were developed.

The entire 19th century represented a time of rapid population increase in the U.S., with a large contribution of immigration, as the vast land area of the continent was exploited. The U.S. experience may have had correlates with other parts of the Americas, but the issues presented to other regions and countries were different. One common factor for all the regions that had participated in the Industrial Revolution of the centuries before was that these policies had resulted in greater urbanization, although rural populations were still the majority. More efficient exploitation of the land resulted in higher populations, which then put still more pressure on the land.

Heretofore, increases in agricultural production occurred mainly through increased land in cultivation, and periodically through the invention of a new type of plow. But in the 1850s, the steam plow, and then steam tractor were developed – radically changing agricultural productivity. At first, this increased productivity was literally from horsepower, as heavier equipment that was too large for humans to handle unaided was harnessed. Later, those horses became mechanized. From this point on, worldwide increases in agricultural production were accomplished through the use of increased energy. Even the increase in artificial fertilizers like nitrate and phosphate is actually possible because of fossil fuel energy to first manufacture the fertilizer, and then to transport it.

Oil Exploitation in Europe

With the exploitation of petroleum in the 1850s, a new resource was developed that would push the human envelope where it had never gone before. Kerosene had been produced by the alchemist al-Razi in the 9th century, but for much of the 19th century, whale oil exceeded petroleum for energy exploitation. Coal was already fueling the industrial revolution. Still, none of this had really changed agricultural methods. 1878 saw the development of the first oil tanker to transport Russian oil, which at that time was at least half the world's production. At first, the refined oil was used to produce machine oils, lubricants, asphalts, and kerosene – in other words, not as a major energy source, but for useful derivatives. Plastics were also invented around this time.

While the idea of petroleum as an energy source may be relatively new, it was a known substance in the ancient world. Known under several names, the most common one was naphtha, for which it has in fact been assigned the rulership Mars, presumably either from its odor or its flammability. Naphtha was mined in Russia by the Arabs as early as 1003.[103] It was early recognized as both a fuel and a medicine. Toward the end of the 18th century, mining activity in Russia had increased. The Russian source at Baku had been taken over from the local khan in 1820. This was the background to the planned refinery in Galicia, a territory in modern Poland. The revenue from this mining doubled after 1850.[104] So we see that the successful exploitation of petroleum really did accelerate with Pluto in Taurus.

Chart 1 is the chart for the Aries Ingress in the period where the oil refinery in Jaslo, Galicia, now in Poland, was being built. This was a very early refinery, before demand had shifted from other heating fuels to petroleum, and long before petroleum had been discovered to be not only a fuel, but the basis for such a large chemical industry.

The first question that this chart raises is: what rules petroleum? Diana Stone says Neptune and Pluto.[105] I can see a dual logic for this selection: petroleum is a liquid (granted, a very viscous one) and hence Neptune; it comes from the ground, the world of Hades, and therefore Pluto. Diana, like me, is a horary astrologer, although our methodologies differ. A horary astrologer will generally tell you that she would rather see the item show up in some horary charts to feel confident of the attribution. And in over two decades of horary work, I cannot say that I've ever had a chart that pivoted on the question of the rulership of petroleum. It's not a common horary concern! So, the next possible choice for finding or verifying the rulership is mundane charts.

We also have the mundane problem that picking a time for the "birth" of the petroleum refineries in Galicia is problematic at best. The oil in Galicia had been known for centuries; it had been applied medically for the treatment of rheumatism under the name mountain balsam.[106] In 1848, a sample was sent out for analysis, but the chart here for 1854 represents the beginning of construction for the refineries, which were finally brought into full production in 1858 – a chart we shall examine shortly.

The 1854 chart has certain intriguing features about it. First of all, the Mars-Pluto trine for that ingress brings to my mind the demand to list Mars as at least a co-ruler of petroleum. My reasons? First of all, I don't automatically assume that items discovered or exploited after the Outer Planets were discovered are necessarily ruled by Outer Planets. But more importantly, the principal application of petroleum has been as an energy source – and I cannot think of a better signature for that than Mars. Stone's logic in *The Rulership*

NATAL CHART
Sun enters Ari 3-20-1854
March 20, 1854
11:45:44 PM
Jaslo, Poland
49 N 45 21 E 29
Local Mean Time
Time Zone: 0 hours West
Tropical Regiomontanus

Chart 1. Sun enters Aries 1854, Jaslo, Poland.

Day of ☽	Hour of ♂
Last Hr ♃	- 39 mins
Next Hr ☉	+21 mins

FIXED STARS	
♆☌ Achernar	0°47's
♆☌ Ankaa	0°35's
♀☌ Fomalhaut	0°07's
♀☌ Sadalmelik	0°22'a
♄☌ Alcyone	0°31'a

Hs	Alm. (Dor)
1	♃
2	♃
3	☿
4	♂
5	♂
6	☽
7	☿
8	☿
9	☉
10	☿
11	☿♀
12	♂

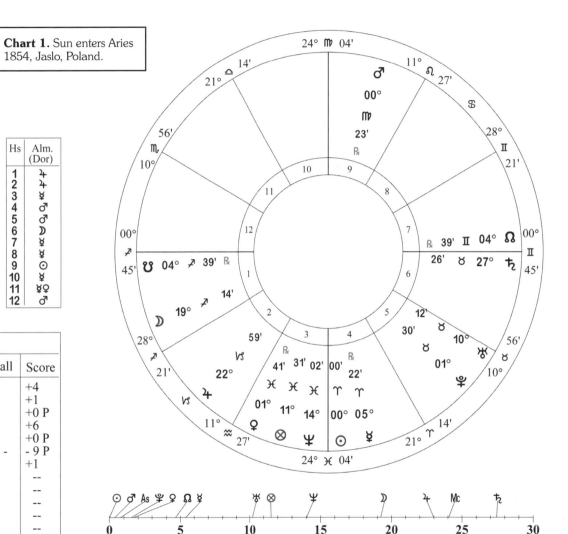

ESSENTIAL DIGNITIES (Dorothean)

Pl	Ruler	Exalt	Tripl	Term	Face	Detri	Fall	Score
☉	♂	☉ +	♃	♃	♂ m	♀	♄	+4
☽	♃	☋	♃ m	♄	☽ +	☿	--	+1
☿	♂ m	☉	♃	♃	♂	♀	♄	+0 P
♀	♃	♀ +	♂	♀ +	♄	☿	☿	+6
♂	☿ m	☿	☽	☿	☉ m	♃	♀	+0 P
♃	♄	♂	☽ m	♂	☉	☽	♃ -	- 9 P
♄	♀	☽	☽	♂	♄ +	♂	--	+1
☊	☿	☊ +	☿	☿	♃	♃	--	--
⊗	♃	♀	♂	♃	♃	☿	☿	--
As	♃	☋	♃	♃	☿	☿	--	--
Mc	☿	☿	☽	♂	☿	♃	♀	--
☋	♃	☋	♃	♃	☿	☿	--	--

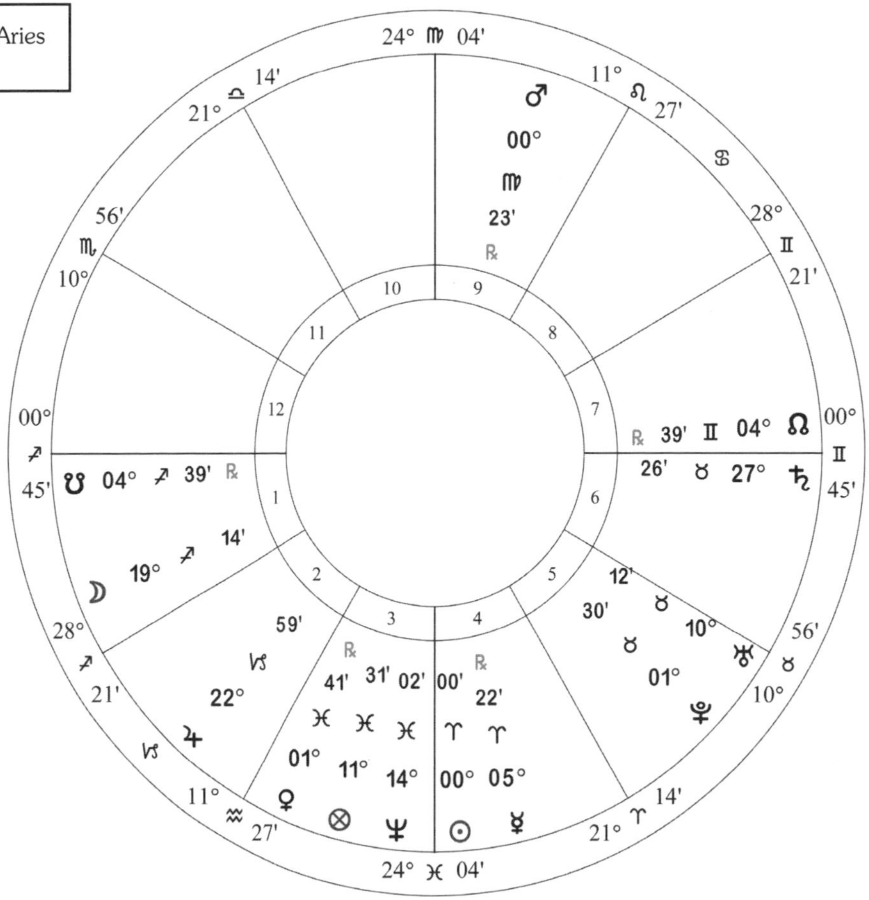

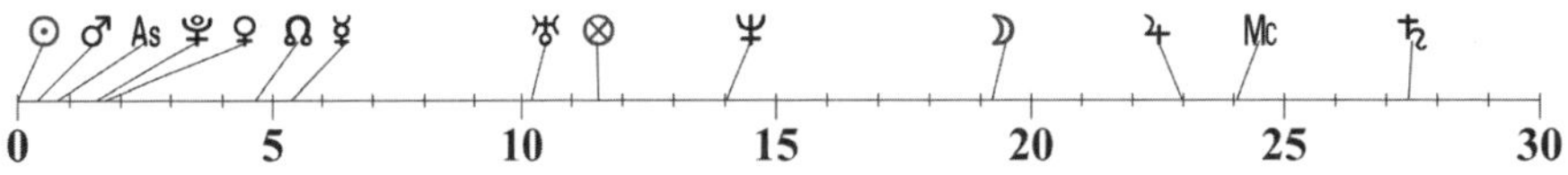

Book was what we would call the Doctrine of Signatures. This is a completely historical system of assigning rulership. It asks, what does something look like? It was especially common with plants. But as I detailed in *Essential Dignities*, while the Doctrine of Signatures gets the most lip service among astrologers for justifying rulership choices, when you actually study the assignments, you discover that functionality is a more common explanation.[107] Mars makes sense from a functionality point of view. In Chapter 8, we shall see the reasoning that supported the logic of functionality: it derived from the belief that God had created the entire world for our benefit.

So if we accept Mars as a co-ruler of petroleum, then what does this chart tell us? We see the Nodes very close to the Ascendant-Descendant axis. Venus and Mars are in a pretty tight opposition with each other, and both are dignified by Triplicity, with Venus also dignified by Exaltation, although retrograde. Mars would be considered debilitated because of the retrograde – in fact, the technical term is **imbecilic**. However, Mars is elevated and would be **rendered** by Venus, except that Venus herself is retrograde. **Rendering** occurs when an imbecilic planet (one which is either **Combust** or retrograde) is aspected by another planet which (1) disposes the imbecilic planet, and (2) is itself dignified. What a rendering accomplishes is that the rendering planet stabilizes Mars, so that Mars can function more normally.

So we have an enterprise being built that could well be characterized by that Mars-Pluto trine, with a nodal-Ascendant combination, and the doubly imbecilic Mars-Venus opposition at the Bendings (the points square the Nodes). How do we put this all together?

One approach is to examine the question: would projects initiated in this time and place be successful? The presence of the South Node near the Ascendant makes the long-term success questionable, although the Nodes don't precisely land on the angles. However, the Nodes have a compulsion about them – this is going to be a very appealing thing to do.

The Mars-Venus opposition, however, is partile square the Ascendant-Descendant axis, making this a very direct hit in this location. Something important is going on here: but the imbecilic quality again argues for problems. Mars rules the 12th and 5th; Venus rules the 11th and 6th. The 5th house includes speculation, as in stock for investing; and the 2nd house is ruled by Jupiter in Fall in the 2nd house. This venture will have costs which are inflated (Jupiter in the 2nd house) compared to their profit (Jupiter is in Fall as well). Pluto is in the 5th of speculation and gambling. I would agree with many modern interpretations that Pluto in general does relate to large profit, but it's large profit with a risk. And further, there's the question of whether the large profit is the meaning, or Pluto as a ruler of oil is the meaning. Because the alternate reading for this combination would be: there will be investment in matters relating to affairs ruled by this Pluto, which would include petroleum. Saturn near the 7th house cusp and dignified only by Face makes it unlikely that the partners will fully profit from this venture – or at least, that Saturn will slow the project down.

The 5th house is ruled by Mars here – the Mars that we are already connecting to petroleum itself. A chance (gambling) could pay off largely (Pluto), especially in an industry like petroleum (Mars-Pluto), but stupid mistakes (imbecility) could negate the possibility.

The Sun is angular, making this a more significant chart. Being in the house of buried treasure is completely apt for this scenario – but might not be ideal for some other business activity proposed at this time.

We next consider Chart 2, the Aries Ingress for 1858, the year the Galaician facilities were completed.

NATAL CHART
Sun enters Ari 3-20-1858
March 20, 1858
10:57:41 PM
Jaslo, Poland
49 N 45 21 E 29
Local Mean Time
Time Zone: 0 hours West
Tropical Regiomontanus

Chart 2. Sun enters Aries 1858, Jaslo, Poland.

Day of ♄ Hour of ♂
Last Hr ♃ - 51 mins
Next Hr ☉ + 9 mins

FIXED STARS	
As♂ Agena	0°10's
♄♂ Pollux	0°09'a
♅♂ Hamal	0°24'a
♇♂ Schedar	0°32'a

Hs	Alm. (Dor)
1	♂♃
2	♃
3	♄
4	♃
5	☉♂
6	☽♀
7	☽
8	☿
9	☿☽
10	☿
11	♀
12	♂

ESSENTIAL DIGNITIES (Dorothean)

Pl	Ruler	Exalt	Tripl	Term	Face	Detri	Fall	Score
☉	♂	☉ +	♃	♃	♂	♀	♄	+4
☽	☿	☊	☿	♃	♂	♃	--	- 5 P
☿	♃	♀	♂	♂	♂	☿ -	☿ -	- 14 P
♀	♂	☉	♃	♃	♂ m	♀ -	♄	- 10 P
♂	♂ +	--	♂ +	♄	♀ m	♀	☽	+8
♃	♄	☽	♄	♃ +	☽	☿	--	+2
♄	♃	♃	♀	♀	☽	♄ -	♂	- 10 P
☊	♃	♀	♂	☿	♀	☿	♀	--
⊗	☿	☿	☽	♀	♀	♃	♀	--
As	♂	--	♂	♀	♀	♀	☽	--
Mc	☿	☿	☽	♀	♀	♃	♀	--
☋	♃	♃	☽	♃	♀	♃	♀	--

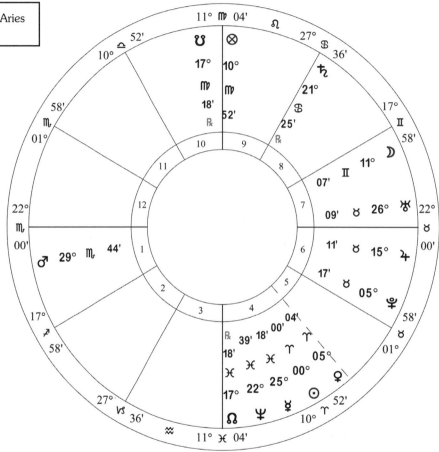

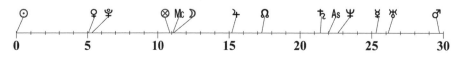

A brief reminder of the geopolitical circumstances: petroleum use was increasing, and in 1858, Russia remained the world's largest miner of petroleum. The opening of the Galician refinery, combined with the local supplies of oil, meant that Europe now had a closer source geographically, although the availability of tankers on the Black Sea from Russia did have a certain appeal. Also, Galicia was part of the Austro-Hungarian Empire, a major geo-political force within Europe at this time.

What is striking about this chart for 1858 is Mars sitting right there in the 1st house in its own sign of Scorpio – how perfect for these facilities now coming fully on-line! This time, the Nodes line up fairly closely along the MC/IC axis, with the North Node in the 4th house of buried treasure. However, this chart also shows that there are some problems with the future associated with this project. The Mars is strong: but it's at 29 degrees. In 1859, Pennsylvania became a player in petroleum reserves: and the United States shortly shot up to become the biggest supplier of petroleum in the world.

Oil Exploitation in the U.S.A.

In the United States, the first map which showed oil in Pennsylvania was produced in 1755.[108] There is some evidence to suggest that Native Americans were aware of petroleum, as they used it in religious ceremonies and for medicinal purposes.[109] While its flammability was known, the utilization of oil for lamps or heating wasn't feasible until after fractionation was developed, because the odor of the oil burning was simply intolerable. In the United States, fractionation experiments to produce a viable lamp oil began only in 1857 – again, after Pluto had gone into Taurus.

In Pennsylvania, the first oil lease occurred on July 4, 1853.[110] This is shown in Chart 3 as a noon chart.

At the time of this lease, the commercial applications were still pretty sketchy. Oil was still thought of primarily for its medical uses and drilling was still so inefficient that half of the output of oil went back into powering its own extraction. (This issue of how much oil has to go into powering its own extraction is now becoming an issue again with the exploitation of Canadian oil shale and other sources of petroleum that are more geologically challenging than the oil fields of an earlier time, which were relatively easy to exploit.) This chart doesn't scream success! Venus, Ruler of the noon Ascendant does have Triplicity, and Jupiter is dignified if retrograde. The Moon is Void of Course, and in a barren sign of no dignity. If this were the only company to have invested in oil, the industry would have died right there.

However, there are a couple of notable fixed stars: Mars conjunct the royal star Aldebaran, and Saturn, Ruler of the 4th, conjunct Alycone. What happened was that samples of the oil got shown around, and after several more rounds of talking up the possibilities of an oil industry, the Pennsylvania Rock Oil Company of New York was incorporated on December 30, 1854.[111] This company then bought the tract where the lease had occurred. Its chart is shown as Chart 4.

NATAL CHART
First Oil Lease - noon
July 4, 1853
12:00 PM
Titusville, Pennsylvania
41N37'37" 79W40'26"
Local Mean Time
Time Zone: 0 hours West
Tropical Regiomontanus

Chart 3. First Oil Lease – noon

Day of ☽   Hour of ♀

Last Hr ☉ - 71 mins
Next Hr ☿ + 4 mins

FIXED STARS	
☊♂Bellatrix	0°31's
☉♂Sirius	0°29's
♂♂Aldebaran	0°02's
♆♂Ankaa	0°12'a
♄♂Alcyone	0°14'a
☉♂Canopus	0°23'a
♆♂Achernar	0°24'a
Mc♂Sirius	0°27'a
♅♂Menkar	0°31'a
⊗♂Alkes	0°58'a

Hs	Alm. (Dor)
1	♀♄
2	♂
3	♂
4	♂♄
5	♄
6	♀
7	☉
8	♀
9	☿
10	♃
11	☉
12	☿

ESSENTIAL DIGNITIES (Dorothean)							
Pl	Ruler	Exalt	Tripl	Term	Face	Detri	Fall	Score
☉	☽	♃	♀	♃	☿	♄	♂	- 5 P
☽	☿	☊	♄	♄	☉	♃	--	- 5 P
☿	☉	--	☉	♄	♄	♄	--	- 5 P
♀	☽	♃	♀ +	♀ +	☽	♄	♂	+5
♂	☿	☊	♄	♃	♃	♃	--	- 5 P
♃	♃ +	☊	☉	☿	☽	☿	--	+5
♄	♀	☽	♄	♂	♄ +	♂	--	+1
☊	☿	☊ +	♀	♀	☿	♃	--	--
⊗	☿	☿	♀	♄	☿	♃	♀	--
As	♀	♄	♄	♀	☽	♂	☉	--
Mc	☽	♃	♀	♃	☿	♄	♂	--
☋	♃	☊	☉	☿	☽	☿	--	--

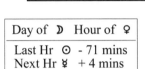

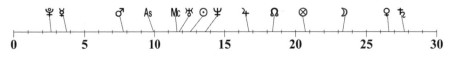

NATAL CHART
PA Rock Oil Company of NY
December 30, 1854
12:00 PM
Albany, NY
42N39'09" 73W45'24"
Local Mean Time
Time Zone: 0 hours West
Tropical Regiomontanus.

Chart 4. Pennsylvania Rock Oil Company of New York.

Day of ♄ Hour of ☿
Last Hr ♀ - 42 mins
Next Hr ☽ + 3 mins

	FIXED STARS	
☽ ♂ Alcyone	0°21's	
♆ ♂ Achernar	0°17's	
♆ ♂ Ankaa	0°05's	
♅ ♂ Acumens	0°11'a	
♀ ♂ Vega	0°25'a	
♅ ♂ Menkar	0°36'a	

Hs	Alm. (Dor)
1	☉
2	♀
3	☿ ♃
4	♃
5	☽
6	☉
7	♄
8	♂
9	♃
10	♄
11	♄
12	♄

	ESSENTIAL DIGNITIES (Dorothean)							
Pl	Ruler	Exalt	Tripl	Term	Face	Detri	Fall	Score
☉	♄	♂	♀	☿	♃	☽	♃	- 5 P
☽	♀	☽ +	♀	♂	♄	♂	--	+4
☿	♃	☊	☉	♂	♄	☿ -	--	- 10 P
♀	♄	♂	♀ +	♃	♂ m	☽	♃	+3
♂	♄	--	♄	♄	♀ m	☉	--	- 5 P
♃	♄	--	♄	♄ m	♀	☉	--	- 5 P
♄	♃	☊	♄ +	♃ m	♀	♃	--	+3
☊	♀	☽	♀	♀	☽	♂	--	--
⊗	☿	☿	♀	☿	☉	♃	♀	--
As	♂	☉	☉	☿	☉	♀	♄	--
Mc	♄	♂	♀	☿	♃	☽	♃	--
☋	♂	--	♀	♀	☉	♀	☽	--

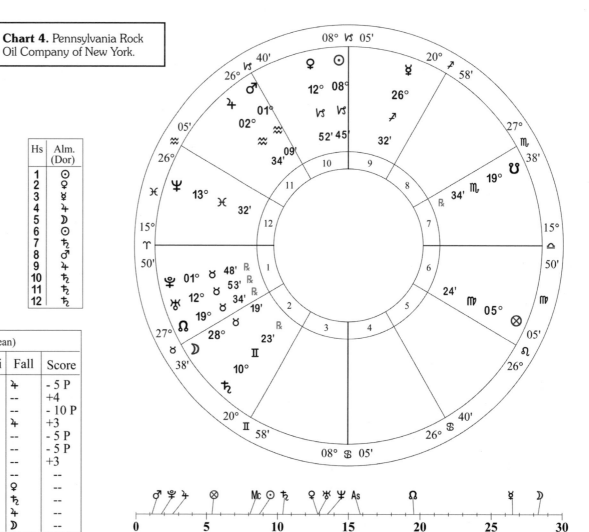

This chart looks much better than the oil lease chart – but maybe not so ideal for the subject of the incorporation. Here, we have Pluto in the 1st house: front and center. Unfortunately, it's in a square to Mars. There's a lot of fixity in this chart, and that is actually what manifested. The main accomplishment of this corporation was to commission a report on the future of petroleum as a commodity. They produced a brilliant report, but investors grew nervous about certain features of New York corporate law and demanded that the company be reincorporated in Connecticut, which had laws more favorable to investors at that time. Perhaps that is the meaning of the second Void of Course Moon. This corporation established the promise of petroleum, not its exploitation. And the production of the report took a lot longer than most people expected at the time.[112]

As a result of investor demand, the next corporation was the Pennsylvania Rock Oil Company of Connecticut, incorporated 18 September 1855.[113] This is shown as Chart 5.

Finally, a chart without a Void of Course Moon! However, this is still not an ideal chart. Having a dignified Ruler of the Ascendant, which also rules the 4th house, is very good, but Jupiter has dignity by participating Triplicity, and it is retrograde: and so dispositors could render the imbecility. But none do. Saturn might have been able to, except that Jupiter and Saturn are doubly separating because of the retrograde. So quite literally, Jupiter acts stupidly – imbecilic, in other words. Also note that Jupiter is in the 3rd – which at first may seem a little odd.

Consider the circumstances. Connecticut is a neighboring state to New York, but technically further from the trenching in Pennsylvania, which was how they did oil wells in those days. The whole point of moving the company to Connecticut was a legal ploy. It had nothing to do with the operation of the well. Saturn ruling the 2nd and in the 7th, was the money of the corporation: the initial sale of stock had been decent – but Saturn is almost ready to leave Gemini, where it has Triplicity, and proceed into Cancer, where it is in Detriment. Furthermore, the Moon is coming to the opposition of that Saturn!

What happened was that the Board of Directors dragged its feet on making capital improvements to increase the productivity of the stake. Here, the Board of Directors is shown by the 11th house: ruled by a dignified, but retrograde Venus! Imbecilic again! Mercury, which also shares the Air Triplicity and is conjunct Venus, is in a position to render her. But who is Mercury? Mercury rules the 10th house, and this conjunction is taking place in the 10th house. The people who had put together this whole deal were being out-maneuvered when the corporation moved to Connecticut, because, while they remained majority stock-holders, the corporate law required the Board to be dominated by Connecticut residents. So, these 10th house guys hit upon the idea of re-leasing the land, and picking up a payout for themselves in the process! Which is a good way of reminding us astrologically: when somebody needs to come in and rescue you, don't assume the rescuer has altruistic motives!

But render Venus, Mercury did – and these charts can work in mysterious ways. The economy of the 19th century was not noted for its stability, and during the Panic of 1857, the group that was going to lease the property bailed out, and then it was discovered that the original sale of the land had title irregularities. Remember that Jupiter retrograde in the 3rd house, ruling the 4th? Jupiter, unlike Venus, was not rendered. In stages, the new Board Chair decided two things: first, they had to properly clear the title, and secondly, they should drill for oil.[114]

NATAL CHART
PA Rock Oil Company of CT
September 18, 1855
12:00 PM
Hartford, Connecticut
41N45'49" 72W41'08"
Local Mean Time
Time Zone: 0 hours West
Tropical Regiomontanus

Chart 5. Pennsylvania Rock Oil Company of Connecticut.

Day of ♂	Hour of ♃
Last Hr ♄	- 6 mins
Next Hr ♂	+55 mins

FIXED STARS	
As☌Antares	0°17's
☊☌Schedar	0°05's
☊☌Hamal	0°03'a
♂☌Acubens	0°35'a
⊗☌Sadalmelik	0°39'a

Hs	Alm. (Dor)
1	♃
2	♄
3	♄
4	♀
5	☉♂
6	♀
7	☿
8	♃
9	☉
10	☿
11	♄
12	♂

ESSENTIAL DIGNITIES (Dorothean)

Pl	Ruler	Exalt	Tripl	Term	Face	Detri	Fall	Score
☉	☿	☿	♀	♂	☿	♃	♀	- 5 P
☽	♃	☋	☉	☿	☽ +	☿	--	+1
☿	♀	♄	♄	♃	♄	♂	☉	- 5 P
♀	♀ +	♄	♄	♃	♄	♂	☉	+5
♂	☉	--	☉	☿	♃	♄	--	- 5 P
♃	♄	--	♄	♃ +	☽	☉	--	+2
♄	☿	☊	♄ +	♂	☉	♃	--	+3
☊	♀	☽	♀	♀	☿	♂	--	--
⊗	♃	♀	♀	♀	♄	☿	☿	--
As	♃	☋	☉	♀	☿	☿	--	--
Mc	☿	☿	♀	♂	☿	♃	♀	--
☋	♂	--	♀	♂	♂	♀	☽	--

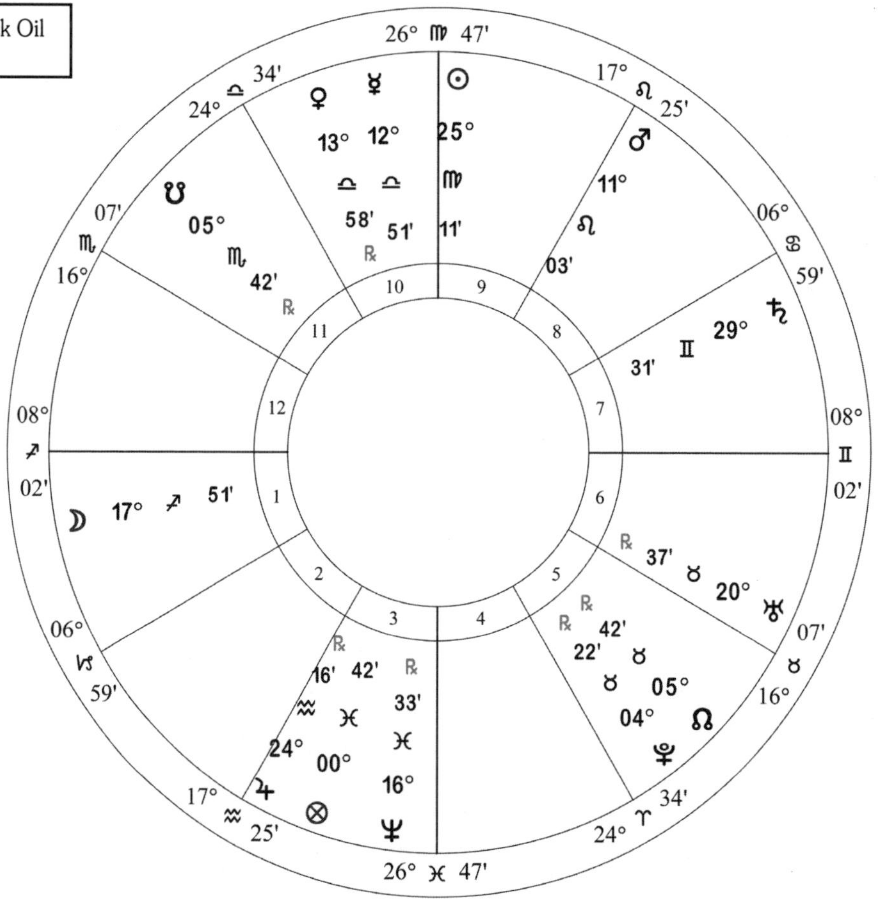

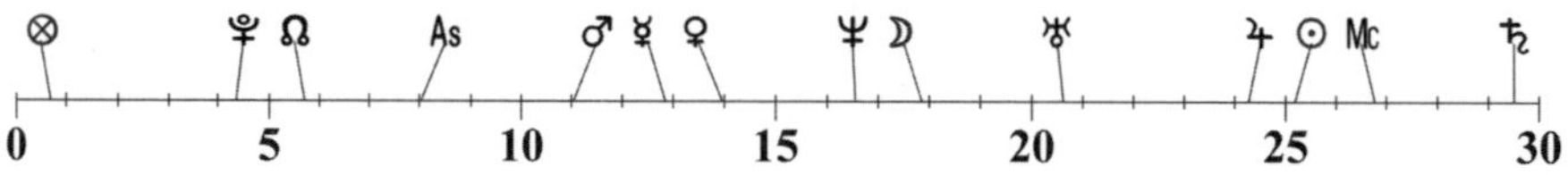

Drill for oil? *Nobody* drilled for oil in those days – only water. James Townsend was declared crazy by many for even proposing it. They leased the newly cleared property in 1858, and formed the Seneca Oil Company of Connecticut on March 23, 1858, shown as Chart 6.[115]

In this chart, one immediately is struck by the Moon-Saturn conjunction at the Ascendant. At first, this played out in a very literal way. The weather that Spring was extremely wet, and it didn't dry out until Summer! But we can see that this sequence of charts is gradually moving toward better ones. Here, the Ascendant is ruled by a highly dignified Moon – but unfortunately, it is also immediately applying to a bodily conjunction with Saturn. The Sun rules, and is **Almuten** of the 2nd and 10th – in the sign of its exaltation, Aries. The Sun is not afflicted by malefics. One should pause and note that if we are using Mars as at least the co-ruler of oil, it's doubtful it is operating here as a malefic, but the Sun is separating from the trine to Mars anyway. Venus is combust, and thus imbecilic: and Venus rules the property. However, the Sun, source of the imbecility, also renders Venus at the same time.

Eventually, after reaching the end of his support, the driller struck oil – or to be exact, discovered oil from the previous day's work late in the afternoon on Sunday, August 28, 1859, shown as Chart 7.[116]

Because of the vagueness of the time, we can't entirely trust the house cusps or Part of Fortune, but at least the planets' positions should be approximately correct. It looks like the actual strike occurred very close to a New Moon eclipse. This means that, in terms of predictive charts, we can examine both the Aries Ingress for the year, as well as the eclipse.

I would also point out the Mercury retrograde. Often, modern astrologers seem to get very nervous around Mercury retrograde, virtually implying that nothing of substance can be accomplished until after the next Mercury station! In the histories of the oil industry, this 1859 date is taken as the birth of American oil production.

Jupiter probably is the 2nd house ruler – and Jupiter is technically the second-most dignified planet, but Mercury's imbecility probably makes Jupiter the most functional planet. A dignified 2nd house ruler makes a lot of sense for this chart.

So let us examine the Aries Ingress for 1859, drawn for Titusville, Pennsylvania, Chart 8. First, we note the fixed Ascendant, telling us that this is the only chart we need to produce for the year 1859 in this location. This chart shows a Mars-Pluto conjunction in the 6th and the North Node at the IC. Remarkable! Getting this oil well drilled at all was hard, tedious work – and it was only successful because the man hired as the driller kept at it, even as the funding was drying up. Another less stubborn man would already have packed his tents, so to speak. Jupiter in Gemini rules both 2nd and 5th – the immediate profit and the investment.

The eclipse, Chart 9, is very revealing. It occurred very close to midnight local time, as evidenced by the Sun-Moon so close to the IC. Mercury, strongly dignified but retrograde, rules both IC and Ascendant, the two active angles in this particular story. One of the meanings of a planet retrograde according to William Lilly is a sudden denouement.[117] In this particular case, the discovery couldn't be more sudden – it was discovered after the crucial digging had already occurred.

From the time of the Aries Ingress to the time of the eclipse, Jupiter had moved from its Detriment in Gemini to its Exaltation in Cancer. Jupiter, ruler of the 2nd, is located near the 2nd house cusp. The result of this discovery was the immediate implementation of the same technologies in drilling yet more wells: this activity

NATAL CHART
Seneca Oil Co. of CT
March 23, 1858
12:00 PM
Hartford, Connecticut
41N45'49" 72W41'08"
Local Mean Time
Time Zone: 0 hours West
Tropical Regiomontanus

Chart 6. Seneca Oil Company of Connecticut

Day of ♂	Hour of ♄
Last Hr ☽	- 54 mins
Next Hr ♃	+ 7 mins

FIXED STARS	
♄☌Pollux	0°09's
♇☌Hamal	0°20'a
☽☌ Pollux	0°26'a
♇☌Schedar	0°29'a
As☌Pollux	0°58'a

Hs	Alm. (Dor)
1	☽
2	☉
3	☿
4	♄
5	♂
6	♃
7	♂
8	♄
9	♀
10	☉
11	♀
12	☿♄

ESSENTIAL DIGNITIES (Dorothean)

Pl	Ruler	Exalt	Tripl	Term	Face	Detri	Fall	Score
☉	♂	☉ +	☉ +	♃	♂	♀	♄	+7
☽	☽ +	♃ m	♀	♀	☽ +	♄	♂	+10
☿	♂	☉	☉	♃	♂ m	♀	♄	- 5 P
♀	♂	☉	☉	♀ +	♂	♀ -	♄	- 3
♂	♃	☋	☉	♃	☿ m	☿	--	- 5 P
♃	♀	☽ m	♀	♃ +	☽	♂	--	+6
♄	☽	♃	♀	♀	☽	♄ -	♂	- 10 P
☊	♃	♀	♀	☿	♃	☿	☿	--
⊗	♂	--	♀	♃	♂	♀	☽	--
As	☽	♃	♀	♀	☽	♄	♂	--
Mc	♂	☉	☉	♃	♂	♀	♄	--
☋	☿	☿	♀	♃	♀	♃	♀	--

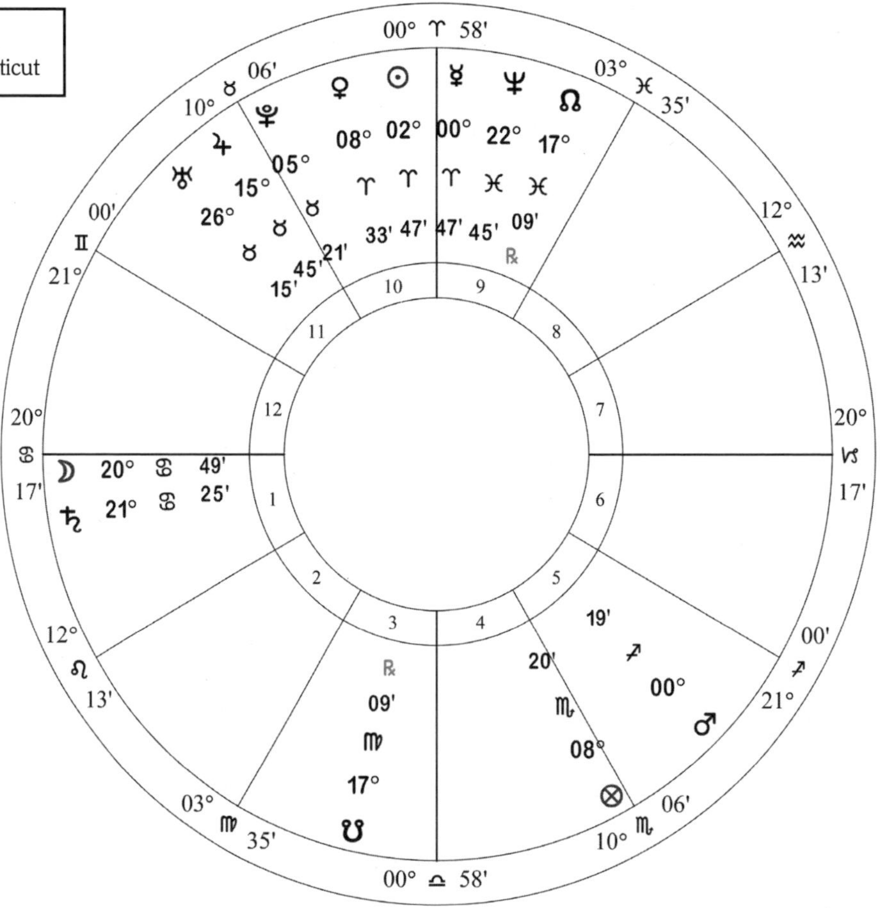

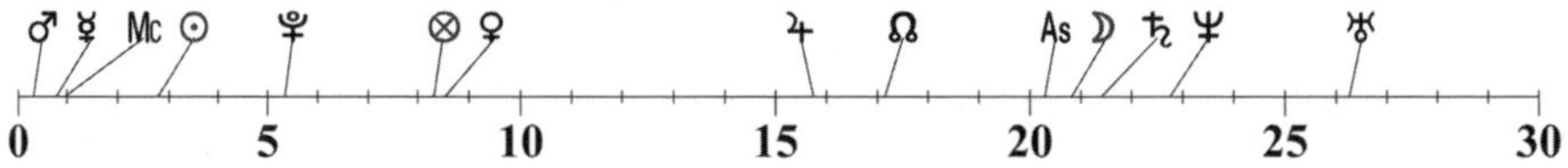

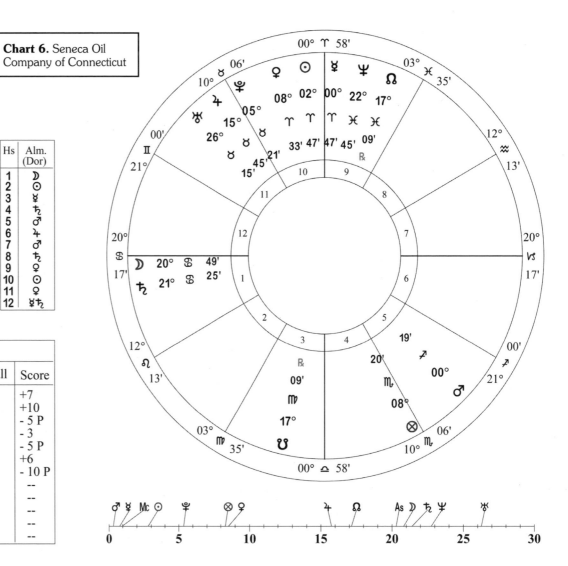

NATAL CHART
Discovery of Oil
August 28, 1859
5:00 PM
Titusville, Pennsylvania
41N37'37" 79W40'26"
Local Mean Time
Time Zone: 0 hours West
Tropical Regiomontanus

Chart 7. Discovery of Oil, Titusville, PA. Time approximate.

Day of ☉	Hour of ☽
Last Hr ☿	- 36 mins
Next Hr ♄	+30 mins

FIXED STARS	
As☌ Altair	0°39's
♅☌ Aldebaran	0°12'a
♀☌ Regulus	0°57'a

Hs	Alm. (Dor)
1	♄
2	♀
3	☉
4	♀
5	☿
6	☽
7	☉
8	☿
9	♄
10	♂
11	♃
12	♀♄

ESSENTIAL DIGNITIES (Dorothean)

Pl	Ruler	Exalt	Tripl	Term	Face	Detri	Fall	Score
☉	☿	☿	♀ m	☿	☉ +	♃	♀	+1
☽	☿	☿	♀	♃	♀	♃	♀	- 5 P
☿	☿ +	☿ +	♀	☿ +	☉	♃	♀	+11
♀	☉	--	☉ m	♂	♂	♄	--	- 5 P
♂	☉	--	☉	♃	♂ +	♄	--	+1
♃	☽	♃ +	♀	☿	☿	♄	♂	+4
♄	☉	--	☉	♀	♃	♄ -	--	- 10 P
☊	♄	--	♄	♀	☿	☉	--	--
⊗	♄	--	♄	☿	☿	☉	--	--
As	♄	--	♄	♄	♀	☉	--	--
Mc	♂	--	♀	☿	♀	♀	☽	--
☋	☉	--	☉	♃	♃	♄	--	--

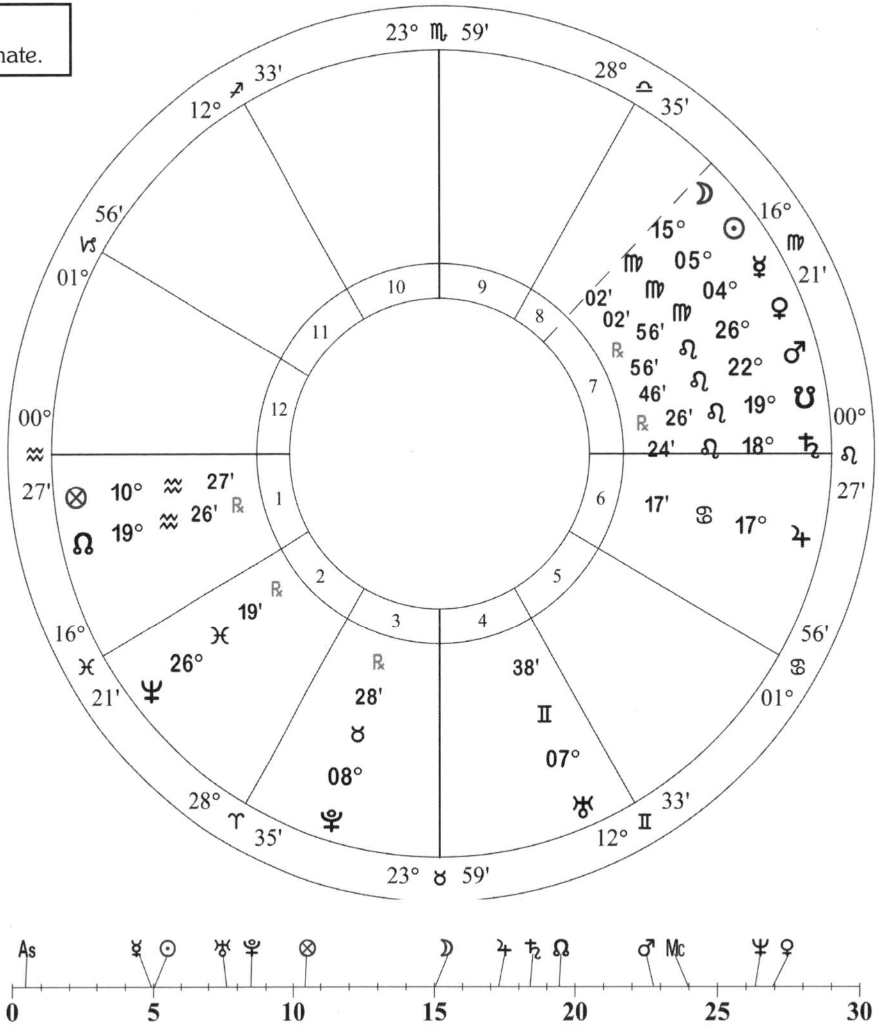

NATAL CHART
Sun enters Ari 3-21-1859
March 20, 1859
9:59:41 PM
Titusville, Pennsylvania
41N37'37" 79W40'26"
Local Mean Time
Time Zone: 0 hours West
Tropical Regiomontanus

Chart 8. Sun enters
Aries 1859, Titusville, PA

Day of ☉ Hour of ♀		
Last Hr ☉ - 52 mins		
Next Hr ☿ + 8 mins		

Hs	Alm. (Dor)
1	♂
2	♃
3	♂♄
4	♄
5	♄♃
6	♂
7	☽
8	☽
9	☽
10	☉
11	☿
12	☿

FIXED STARS		
♇♂Hamal	0°32's	
Mc♂Alphard	0°27's	
♇♂Schedar	0°24's	
♅♂Mirfak	0°06's	
♂♂Hamal	0°19'a	
♃♂Rigel	0°20'a	
♀♂Sualocin	0°24'a	
♂♂Schedar	0°27'a	
☿♂Alpheratz	0°31'a	

ESSENTIAL DIGNITIES (Dorothean)								
Pl	Ruler	Exalt	Tripl	Term	Face	Detri	Fall	Score
☉	♂	☉ +	♃	♃	♂	♀	♄	+4
☽	♀	♄	☿	♂	♃	♂	☉	- 5 P
☿	♂	☉	♃ m	♀	☉	♀	♄	- 5 P
♀	♄	--	☿	♀ +	☿	☉	--	+2
♂	♀	☽	☽	♀	☿	♂ -	--	- 10 P
♃	☿	☊	☿ m	♀	♂	♃ -	--	- 10 P
♄	☉	--	♃	♄ +	♄ +	♄ -	--	- 2
☊	♂	☉	♃	♂	☽	♀	♄	--
⊗	♂	☉	♃	♀	☉	♀	♄	--
As	♂	--	♂	♀	♀	♀	☽	--
Mc	☉	--	♃	♂	♂	♄	--	--
☋	☉	--	♃	♂	♂	♄	--	--

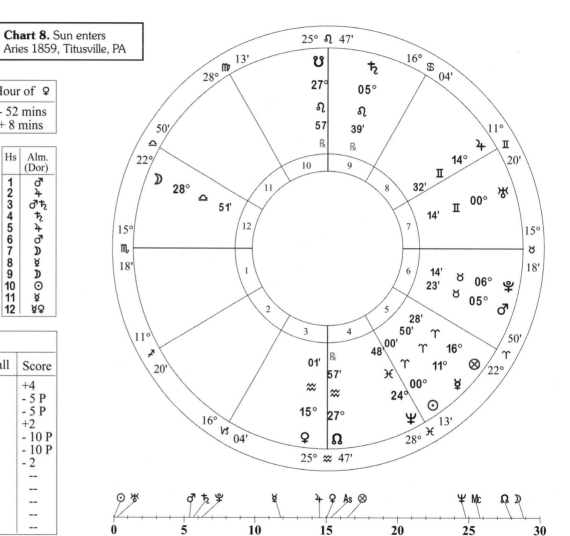

Solar Eclipse (astrological)
Solar Eclipse 08-28-1859
August 27, 1859
11:55:39 PM
Titusville, Pennsylvania
41N37'37" 79W40'26"
Local Mean Time
Time Zone: 0 hours West
Tropical Regiomontanus

Chart 9. Solar Eclipse 28 August 1859, Titusville, PA

Day of ♄	Hour of ☉
Last Hr ♂	- 48 mins
Next Hr ♀	+ 6 mins

Hs	Alm. (Dor)
1	☿
2	☽
3	☉
4	☿
5	♀
6	♂
7	♃
8	♂
9	☿
10	♀
11	♂
12	☽

FIXED STARS	
Mc☌Fomalhaut	0°58's
⊗☌Betelgeuse	0°53's
As☌Betelgeuse	0°53's
♀☌ Alphard	0°44's
♅☌ Aldebaran	0°13'a
Mc☌Deneb Adige	0°33'a

ESSENTIAL DIGNITIES (Dorothean)

Pl	Ruler	Exalt	Tripl	Term	Face	Detri	Fall	Score
☉	☿	☿	☽	☿	☉ +	♃	♀	+1
☽	☿	☿	☽ +	☿	☉	♃	♀	+3
☿	☿ +	☿ +	☽	☿ +	☉	♃	♀	+11
♀	☉	--	♃	♂	♂	♄	--	- 5 P
♂	☉	--	♃ m	♃	♂ +	♄	--	+1
♃	☽	♃ +	♂ m	☿	☿	♄	♂	+4
♄	☉	--	♃	♀	♃	♄ -	--	- 10 P
☊	♄	--	☿	♀	☿	☉	--	--
⊗	☿	☊	☿	♂	☉	♃	--	--
As	☿	☊	☿	♂	☉	♃	--	--
Mc	♃	♀	♂	♀	♄	☿	☿	--
☋	☉	--	♃	♃	♃	♄	--	--

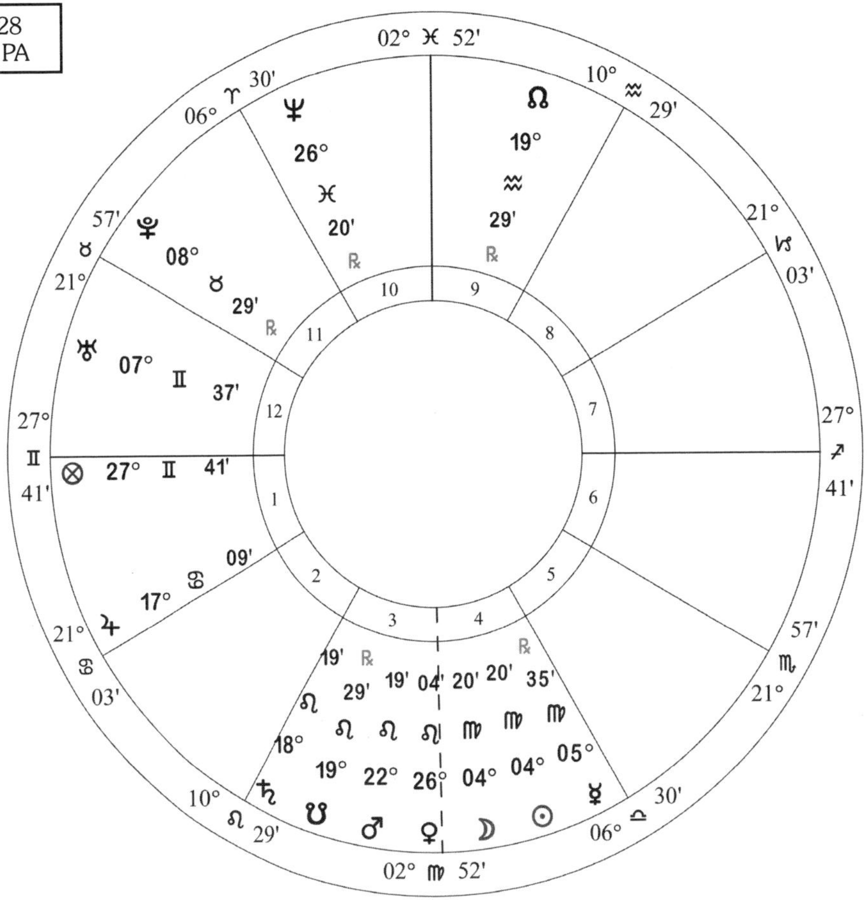

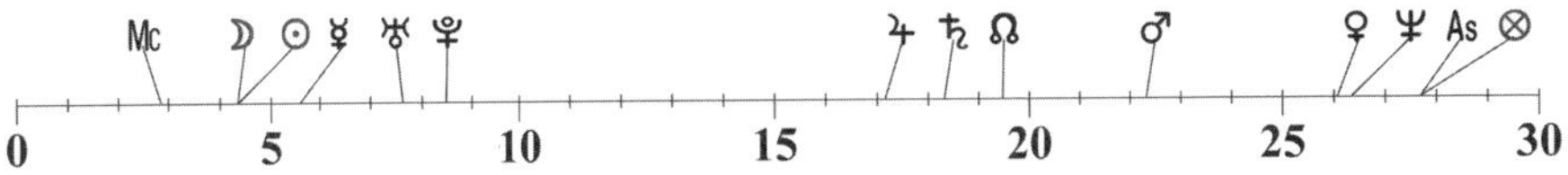

resulted in more production than demand, which in turn drove the price down.[118] What we might notice here is that Venus, ruler of the 5th house of speculation, is without dignity and **Under Beams** – the exuberance of Jupiter goes a bit too far. We see a fascinating reversal of this theme in the Aries Ingress, where the Jupiter in Gemini in the 8th house of debt is ruling the 2nd, which warns of cash flow problems at the least (and there were – until oil was discovered).

The period of Pluto in Taurus marked the early phase of petroleum exploitation in which the primary means of extraction changed to drilling, rather than surface collection. This resulted in a major increase in production, and a shift in where petroleum was being produced. The fractionation of oil resulted in more ways to use oil, but it was the production of motor-driven transportation in the Pluto in Gemini period that would cement the world's love affair with oil.

Evolution

Before we leave Pluto in Taurus, I want to take up one more theme: evolution. I don't mean to imply that the idea of evolution, as defined as one species giving rise to new ones, is uniquely a Pluto in Taurus phenomenon, or even uniquely earth. I think the connection is not so much the theory, as the pragmatism in its development and application. But I do want to touch upon the reactions to Darwin's and Wallace's theories, as much as the development of the theories themselves.

Most histories of biology will begin their discussion of evolution with the 18th century, when several factors converged:

- The system of biological classification that was promulgated in Linnaeus in order to add discoveries from the New World already emphasized relationships between different animals and plants. This made it very easy to envision that similar species from different parts of the world really could be related to each other, and thus, one could have led to the other.

- The Baconian and Cartesian systems which became the scientific method had had well over a century to allow scientists to think about problems of science in a completely secular way. Gone was the earlier tendency to see God as actively engaged in the minutiae of ordinary life.

- The concept of positivism as enunciated by Comptes assumed a form of linear progression, which could easily be seen as logical improvement over time. Along with this, there was a general breakdown of the traditional mode (which included astrology) of seeing time as cyclic, to one of seeing time's directional arrow.

- Biologists such as Erasmus Darwin (Charles' grandfather) and Lamarck were already commenting on the plasticity of species and how a few changes in traits could lead to a new species.

- Geologists were beginning to posit an Earth significantly older than the few thousand years that had been agreed to by Christian theologians.

One could argue the point that evolution as a scientific theory could have been enunciated pretty much any time after 1820 – the pieces were in place. But Charles Darwin and Alfred Russell Wallace didn't publish their theories until 1859. What happened? From 1820 on, many biologists already accepted in principle that species evolved from other species. What Darwin especially achieved was a painstakingly detailed iteration of the necessary components that explained how this process could be accomplished: that there is variability within a species; that more offspring are produced than can survive; that this leads to a struggle for existence in which those best adapted not only survive, but pass on their traits to the next generation.

The Aries Ingress for 1859, Chart 10, shows the circumstances surrounding the propagation of these ideas. What is evolution from an astrological perspective? It's got to be Venus-Mars: fecundity and the struggle for existence.

Here we see a chart that looks a lot like the petroleum charts we have just been examining – and of course, it's the same historical period. But now, Mars means something else entirely! I am struck by the Mars-Pluto conjunction here because of how many modern astrologers have targeted Pluto in terms of reproduction and regeneration. That symbology is present in this chart. What is also striking is that the Mars-Pluto conjunction occurs in the 3rd house. We have already observed that while both the 3rd and 9th houses were mentioned in the classical period as relating to religion, it was the 3rd house that could justifiably be nominated as the house of heresy.[119] Here is the Mars-Pluto conjunction in the 3rd house, partile square Saturn: the Establishment! The publication of this theory invoked a firestorm of protest from many in the Christian religious establishment.

It's interesting. For decades, as I mentioned, many, if not most biologists, had clearly anticipated something like the theory of evolution – if not its full contours. Geologists had routinely begun to speculate about what was called uniformitarianism (the Earth develops gradually) *vs.* catastrophism (Earth changes are sudden and dramatic). And all this speculation was more or less ignored by the religious establishment. Then, this moment arrives – and everything is thrown into chaos.

In trying to think deeply about the connection of this eruption as related to Pluto in Taurus, and specifically Mars-Pluto in Taurus square Saturn in Leo, one of the most fundamental tenets of the Christian churches that was challenged was the uniqueness and specialness of Man. Fire may bring us awareness of the Spirit of Man, but Earth evokes our basic materiality. Many religious people couldn't handle it. The effect of this theory hit so hard that we still see a substantial minority today that simply refuse to even consider the possibility that the theory *might* be correct.

So to summarize, what lessons for the now and coming era of Pluto in Capricorn can we glean from this earlier period of Pluto in Taurus, the "first" of the earth signs? Pluto in Taurus brought us exploitation of the Earth in ways that had never before been dreamed. Pluto in Taurus also brought a materialistic view of humanity that still reverberates today.

Pluto in Virgo

"Sustainability," with its older sister "green," are both ideas and concepts derived from an environmental movement which has now passed its first Saturn return. Born just a little after the Gay Rights Movement, both of these political movements appear to be bearing some significant fruit at more or less the same time.

How long does it take a political movement to become effective, especially one like the environmental movement, which

NATAL CHART
Sun enters Ari 3-21-1859
March 21, 1859
3:18:23 AM
London, England
51 N 30 0 W 10
Standard Time
Time Zone: 0 hours West
Tropical Regiomontanus

Chart 10. Sun enters Aries 1859 London

Day of ☉	Hour of ☉
Last Hr ♂	- 11 mins
Next Hr ♀	+49 mins

Hs	Alm. (Dor)
1	♂♄
2	♀
3	♂
4	☽
5	☿
6	☿
7	☽
8	☿
9	♀
10	♂
11	♃
12	♃

FIXED STARS	
⊗☌Rigel	0°56's
♇☌Hamal	0°32's
♇☌Schedar	0°24's
♅☌Mirfak	0°06's
As☌Rukbat	0°02'a
♂☌Hamal	0°19'a
♃☌Rigel	0°20'a
♀☌Sualocin	0°24'a
♂☌Schedar	0°27'a
☿☌Alpheratz	0°31'a

ESSENTIAL DIGNITIES (Dorothean)

Pl	Ruler	Exalt	Tripl	Term	Face	Detri	Fall	Score
☉	♂	☉ +	♃	♃	♂	♀	♄	+4
☽	♀	♄	☿	♂	♃	♂	☉	- 5 P
☿	♂	☉	♃ m	♀	☉	♀	♄	- 5 P
♀	♄	--	☿	♀ +	☿	☉	--	+2
♂	♀	☽	☽	♀	☿	♂ -	--	- 10 P
♃	☿	☊	☿ m	♀	♂	♃ -	--	- 10 P
♄	☉	--	♃	♄ +	♄ +	♄ -	--	- 2
☊	♄	--	☿	♂	☽	☉	--	--
⊗	☿	☊	☿	♀	♂	♃	--	--
As	♄	♂	☽	♃	♂	☽	♃	--
Mc	♂	--	♂	♀	♀	♀	☽	--
☋	☉	--	♃	♂	♂	♄	--	--

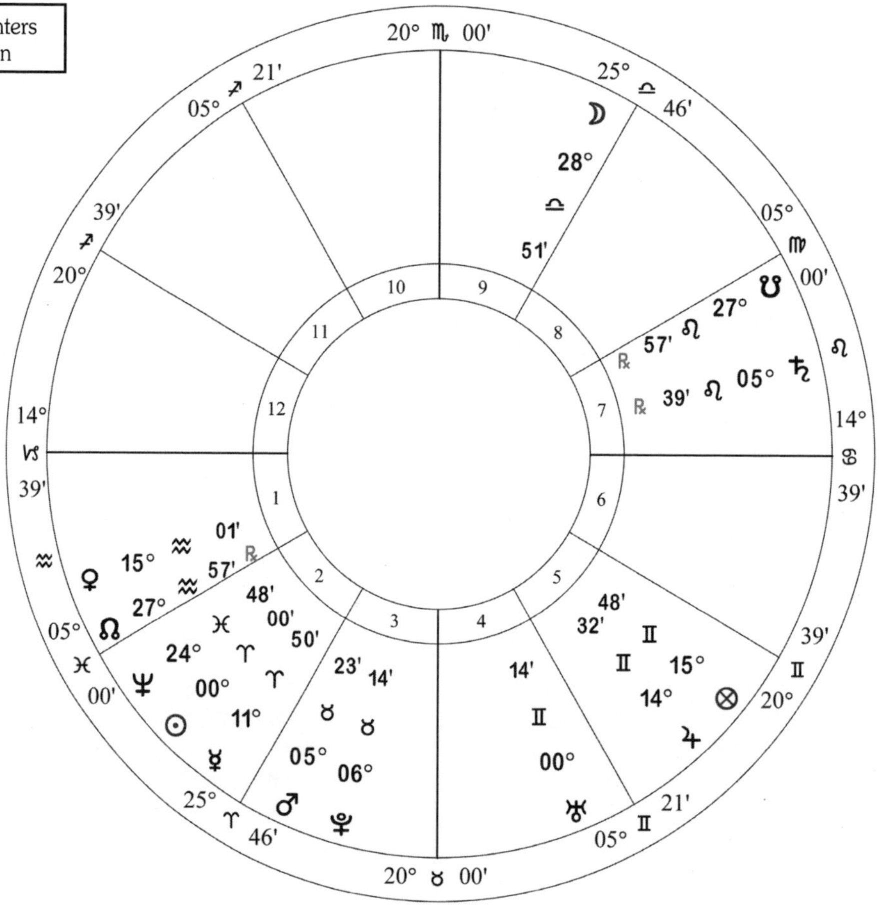

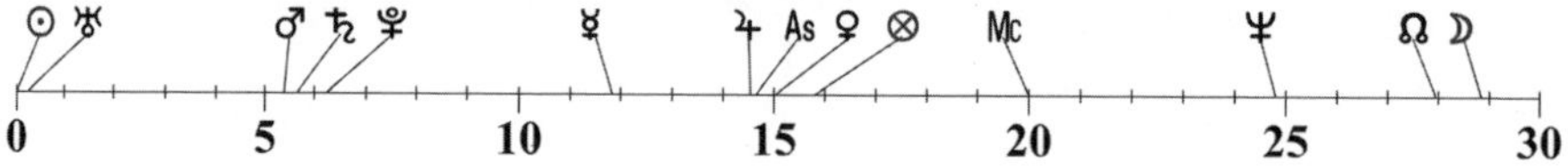

did have early accomplishments, but just never seemed to become entirely mainstream until recently? This section is the story of that movement – but it also addresses a larger question: how does it work astrologically when an idea is "before its time?"

The effects of a political movement will rarely be apparent when the movement is formed – and it may be decades before it is clear whether the movement has succeeded – or not. And as astrologers, we would hypothesize that a successful political movement must be able to continue to operate with the outer planet configurations present at the time the movement started. This may be more crucial than one would think at first. The reason is that finding one single "starting time" may be very difficult, especially if the idea for the movement is very diffuse. Without an agreed-upon "birth," there is no single chart for the movement, although valid charts of organizations within the movement may act as proxies.

Nick Campion would aver that countries often have multiple significant moments – thus, potentially, several alternate charts. For the United Kingdom, is the Norman Invasion the "moment" of the country? Or the unification with Scotland? Or with Scotland, Northern Ireland, and Wales? Or the monarch of the moment?

However, countries are much different than movements. Movements are based primarily around an idea – whether the need to live sustainably, or the desire for civil rights. They cannot give citizenship – but organizations may have members. They don't levy taxes, but organizations may charge dues. Thus, we see that there may be an analogy between organizations and countries – but a movement? That depends on whether a movement appears to come out of an organization, or becomes an organization, or is more grassroots in nature.

The date that everyone has come to celebrate for the beginning of the environmental movement is Earth Day – 22 April 1970. We will examine that chart – but one thing is obvious. Earth Day was an event, but not the birth of a movement. The movement had to already have been there to plan the event. But finding the *first* official organization of the *first* group to *think about* presenting Earth Day – that may be impossible to procure.

I was already active in the environmental movement in 1969 – and I remember that the two most influential forerunners of Earth Day both published highly significant works in 1968: Paul Ehrlich's *Population Bomb*, and Garrett Hardin's "The Tragedy of the Commons."[120] These works, in turn, didn't come out of a vacuum either. Hardin had been addressing overpopulation as early as 1959.

Why 1959? This actually gives us a hint, because 1957 marked the end of the transition of Pluto from Leo to Virgo that began the previous year. Elsewhere, I have traced the development of the space program and the Moon race, which are particular icons of Pluto in Virgo.[121] But Pluto in a sign has more than one effect. Most astrologers were far more prepared for the issue of religious fundamentalism as a major theme of Pluto in Sagittarius, than the additional theme of economic extremism, and ultimately, economic meltdown.

The Modern Environmental Movement

I would propose that the formation of the modern environmental movement was a child of Pluto in Virgo, and that with Pluto's ingress into Capricorn, the strongest of the earth signs, the issues enunciated then will become even more important. But first, let's consider how the environmental movement fits under the rubric of Virgo. Then we can proceed to see how that Virgoan mandate will be modified by the sign of Capricorn.

The relationships between *Earth* Day and the *Earth* sign Virgo seem clear enough. But it gets better. An even better specific in this case is that Virgo is a barren sign. This fact is extremely important, because, unlike all previous back-to-nature movements, the environmental movement from the beginning had overpopulation as one of its core issues, even if that wasn't always the side put forward to the public. As noted above, Garrett Hardin, enshrined through his article on the tragedy of the commons, was speaking out first about overpopulation, and overpopulation is a major theme of that most famous article – although that fact has been forgotten by many.

The interpretation of Pluto in any one sign is modified or reinforced by outer planet hard aspects. The aspect may not be exact at the moment of the event, but these passages mark times when the energy of the outer planets can be released as a crisis point. From October 1965 to June 1966, Uranus and Pluto conjoined, once in 17 Virgo, and twice at 16 Virgo. This conjunction marked a crisis point for Pluto in Virgo – a crisis that was not fully appreciated for about two years. 1968, the year of student riots and revolutions, was one such marker. Within the space program, the marker was the Apollo 1 tragedy of 27 January 1967, where three astronauts were incinerated during a test at Cape Canaveral.

In 1967, Paul Ehrlich spoke to the Commonwealth Club on overpopulation, and this exposure resulted in his first popular article on the subject, published in *New Scientist* in December 1967. *The Population Bomb*, based on that lecture, came out the following year.

What these works addressed was that human impact on the environment was not only becoming worse, it was becoming *much* worse. The single greatest environmental work of Pluto in Virgo did not address population directly, but pesticides: it was Rachel Carson's classic *Silent Spring*.[122] Ehrlich himself lists Carson as one of his great heroines.[123] Biologists especially had the intuition that humanity was at a tipping point: that unthinking development and utilization of chemicals in agriculture was allowing the human population to rise too rapidly, while environmental devastation was likely to produce catastrophic results in the not-too-distant future.

If we want to examine the impact of the Uranus-Pluto period, what chart do we pick? This question falls under the conundrum we discussed in Chapter 1, relating to the difficulty of computing an accurate time for an outer planet conjunction. More recently, Mark Pottenger confirmed Vincent Wing's 17th century computations, and concluded mathematically that the slower the two bodies, the harder it is to come up with an exact time of the conjunction.[124] Pluto is even more complicated, as there are different equations for its orbital motion – so different programs will even differ on the exact time of its sign ingress, depending on which orbital equation the programmer chose to use. The problem is that your computer program may dutifully compute a time, whether that time is accurate or not. So to substitute for this, I have used the Aries Ingresses (Chart 11 & Chart 13) computed for Washington, D.C., for 1965 and 1966, to see the influences of this time period.

NATAL CHART
Sun enters Ari 3-20-1965
March 20, 1965
3:04:47 PM
Washington, D.C.
38N53'42" 77W02'12"
Standard Time
Time Zone: 5 hours West
Tropical Regiomontanus

Chart 11. Sun enters Aries 1965, Washington, D.C.

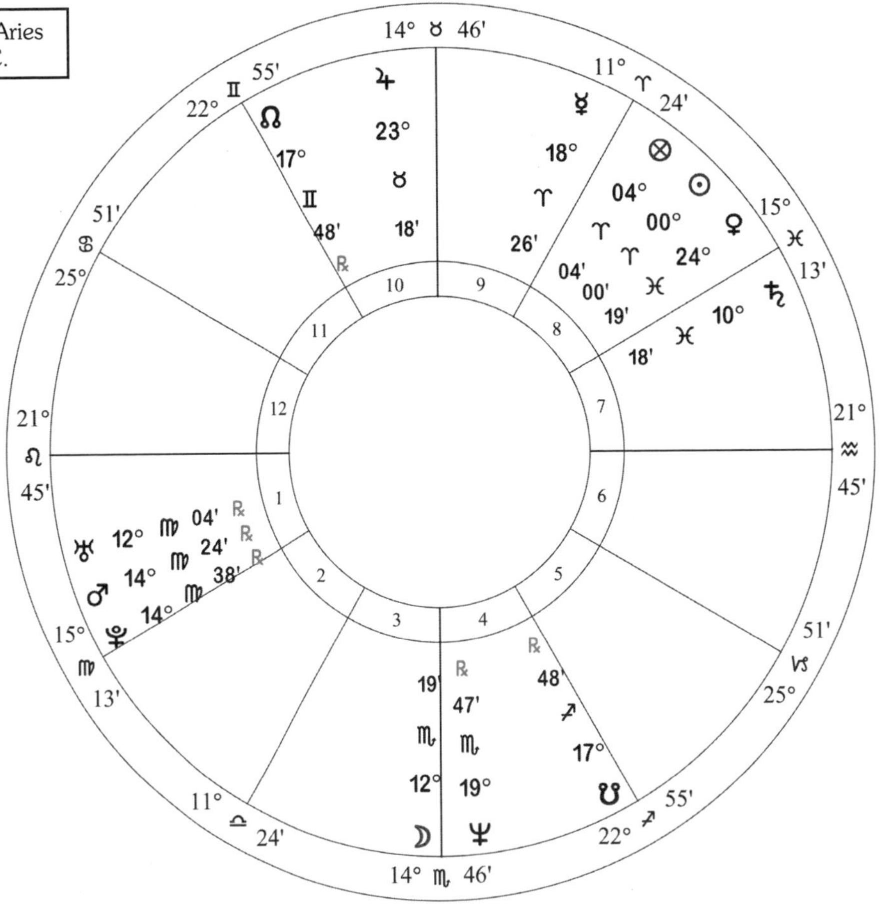

Day of ♄	Hour of ♃
Last Hr ♄	- 49 mins
Next Hr ♂	+11 mins

FIXED STARS	
Mc☌Menkar	0°56's
☽☌ Acrux	0°56's
☽☌ Alphecca	0°31's
♃☌Capulus	0°25'a
♆☌N Scale	0°54'a

Hs	Alm. (Dor)
1	☉
2	☿
3	♄
4	♂
5	♃
6	♄
7	♄
8	♀
9	☉
10	♀
11	☿♄
12	☽

ESSENTIAL DIGNITIES (Dorothean)

Pl	Ruler	Exalt	Tripl	Term	Face	Detri	Fall	Score
☉	♂	☉ +	☉ +	♃	♂	♀	♄	+7
☽	♂	--	♀	♃	☉	♀	☽ -	- 9 P
☿	♂ m	☉	☉	☿ +	☉	♀	♄	+7
♀	♃ m	♀ +	♀ +	♂	♂ m	☿	☿	+12
♂	☿ m	☿	♀	♃	♀ m	♃	♀	+0 P
♃	♀ m	☽	♀	♄ m	♄ m	♂	--	+0 P
♄	♃	♀	♀	♃ m	♃ m	☿	☿	- 5 P
☊	☿	☊ +	♄	♀	♂	♃	--	--
⊗	♂	☉	☉	♃	♂	♀	♄	--
As	☉	--	☉	♃	♂	♄	--	--
Mc	♀	☽	♀	☿	☽	♂	--	--
☋	♃	☋	☉	☿	☽	☿	--	--

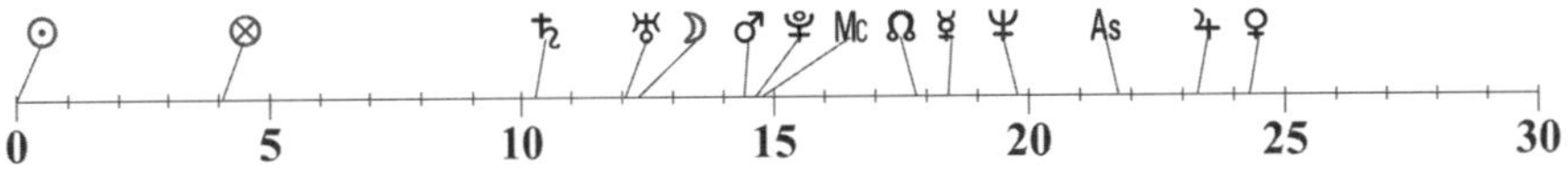

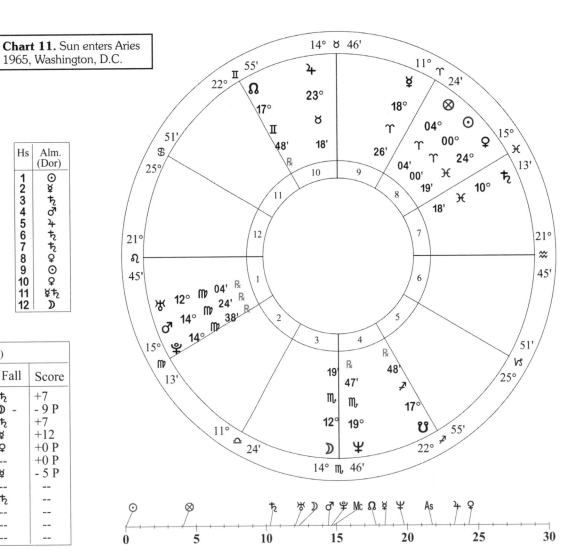

For the 1965 Aries Ingress, Chart 11, Mars was also conjunct Uranus-Pluto, making this a Great Conjunction in classical parlance. (The astrological eye also observes Saturn opposite that whole group, which needs to be considered in delineation, but is not part of the definition of Great Conjunction.) Which means, among other things, that the Uranus-Pluto cannot be interpreted in the absence of Mars. This chart is actually a very martian one, given that the Moon is also in Scorpio, applying to Neptune in Scorpio. This makes sense. Venus, ruler of the MC, was in Pisces, the sign of its exaltation. Metaphorically, the king was exalted. President Lyndon Johnson had just won a landslide victory over Barry Goldwater. Remember that exaltation as a dignity has the quality of having things done for it? The reason Johnson had won the landslide victory was because of the assassination of President Kennedy. Johnson had the election handed to him quite literally as a gift. But this exalted Venus was in the 8th house of Death – opposite by sign from the Uranus-Pluto. The President started out popular, but the conduct of the Vietnam War (how Mars can you get?) and the deaths of Americans there would come to undermine that popularity. At this point in time, however, Moon-Neptune had conjoined the IC – the problem was still mostly underground.

For our purposes in examining this in relation to the environment, the water signs are considered fruitful; while Virgo is barren. While the Moon is fruitful in Scorpio, it is also in Fall – but sextile the triple conjunction – and with Saturn, the planet of limitation, in a separating trine. Remember that the early issue driving the development of the environmental movement was overpopulation – and here, the contrast between the fertile and barren signs is fascinating. Specifically related to the U.S.A., you might notice that the 5th house cusp was Sagittarius – and Jupiter, its ruler, was in the fertile sign of Taurus. The U.S.A. was well above **replacement fertility** at that time: in other words, its population was still growing.

If the environment and population issues were generally below the radar for the vast majority of Americans, it was academic biologists who began to see the problem clearly. Notice that Mars ruled the 9th house, with Mercury there – in Mars's sign. Academics (Mars, or Mercury as natural ruler) became suddenly aware (Uranus) of the need for fertility (Moon–Saturn–Pluto) reduction (barren Virgo). But this was also the beginning of the teach-in movement against the Vietnam War – another 9th house effort. Academics became warriors, exactly matching that Mars.

But elsewhere, the effect of Pluto in barren Virgo was making itself felt – although this fact went almost unnoticed at the time. In Europe, at least four countries dropped below replacement fertility in the period of Pluto in Virgo: Bulgaria, Russia, Czechoslovakia, and Germany.[125] It would have been easy at the time for Western demographers to dismiss this trend as relating to Communism (the German data combines East and West Germany). However, the rest of Europe followed when Pluto was in Libra, with only Ireland holding out until Pluto was in Scorpio. This drop in fertility rate had not been seen since a brief period relating to World War II – but interestingly, the previous downward trend that was *not* related to a war was in the 1890s – the period of Pluto in Gemini, another barren sign. The difference is that the reduction in fertility at the turn of the 20th century did not hold, and population rates increased exponentially in the 20th century, except for temporary set-backs, and then, since the 1960s, in certain parts of the world.

As a check of this idea, we can examine Chart 12 for the Vernal Equinox for Sofia, Bulgaria in 1963, the year this country became the first in Europe to drop below replacement level fertility. In this chart, there's a partile Venus-Saturn conjunction (how perfect!) in

NATAL CHART
Sun enters Ari 3-21-1963
March 21, 1963
10:19:43 AM
Sofia, Bulgaria
42 N 41 23 E 19
Standard Time
Time Zone: 2 hours East
Tropical Regiomontanus

Chart 12. Sun enters Aries 1963, Sofia, Bulgaria

Day of ♃	Hour of ♀
Last Hr ☉	- 45 mins
Next Hr ☿	+15 mins

FIXED STARS	
♇☌ Zosma	0°25's
As☌ Bellatrix	0°03'a
♆☌ S Scale	0°48'a
As☌ Capella	0°58'a

Hs	Alm. (Dor)
1	☿
2	☽
3	☉
4	☉
5	♂
6	♂
7	♃
8	♂♄
9	♂♄
10	♄
11	♀
12	♀

	ESSENTIAL DIGNITIES (Dorothean)							
Pl	Ruler	Exalt	Tripl	Term	Face	Detri	Fall	Score
☉	♂ m	☉ +	☉ +	♃	♂	♀	♄	+12
☽	♄	--	♄	♄	♀	☉	--	- 5 P
☿	♃	♀	♀	☿ +	♂	☿ -	☿ -	- 7
♀	♄	--	♄	♀ +	☿	☉	--	+2
♂	☉ m	--	☉	♄	♄	♄	--	+0 P
♃	♃ +	♀	♀	♄	♂	☿	☿	+5
♄	♄ +	--	♀ +	♀	♀	☽	♂	+8
☊	☽	♃	♀	♀	♂	♄	--	--
⊗	♂	☉	♀	♂	♀	♀	♄	--
As	☿	☊	♄	♀	☉	♃	--	--
Mc	♄	--	♄	♃	☽	☉	--	--
☋	♄	♂	♀	♄	☉	☽	♃	--

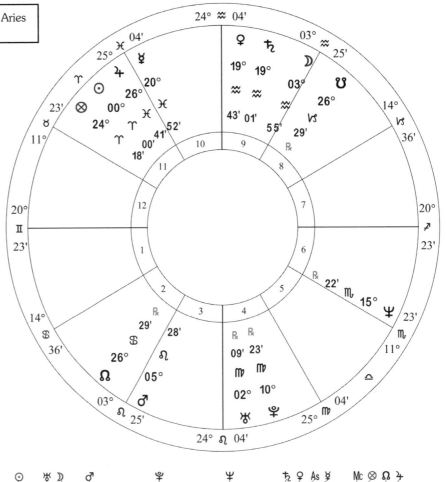

Saturn's sign of Aquarius, very close to the MC. The barren sign Virgo is on the 5th house cusp, while the barren sign Gemini is on the Ascendant. While Aquarius is not a barren sign, the planet Saturn is – so this chart is actually a *very* barren one.

As we continue to follow the path of the Uranus-Pluto, we arrive at the Aries Ingress for 1966, Chart 13. Of course, once again Uranus and Pluto are retrograde – as they must be, given that they are in a sign more or less opposite the Sun. But in 1966, Uranus was ahead of Pluto, on its way to stationing direct at 15 Virgo with Pluto in that same degree. For the Aries Ingress, the Moon-Saturn conjunction in the 5th house is in fertile Pisces – no awareness of population issues here! Except that the Moon is in a partile opposition to Uranus – things are going to change. And this is another Martian focus chart, with Scorpio rising and Mars so strong in Aries. The Vietnam War trumps much of the rest of the news. This was the year that Paul Ehrlich did a series of public lectures on the material that would become the *Population Bomb*. While Ehrlich's warning about overpopulation was not heeded at this time, note the ambiguity of the 5th house indicators. While today we talk about Pluto and fertility – and also regeneration – historically, Saturn would be seen as the planet of barrenness, or *infertility*. This was the time when the general American attitude about children was that couples should have as many as they wanted or could afford – but this was also around the time of the birth of the second wave of feminism – when child-bearing began to be seen as a feminist issue.

Through Rudhyar's and Ruperti's analyses of synodic cycles, we have come to understand that the opposition represents the time when problems, flaws, or difficulties begin to become apparent: the issues that will ultimately lead to the new cycle must be enunciated as the issues of the existing cycle are taken to their extreme. While 1965–1966 does mark the beginning of the Uranus-Pluto cycle, it also represents the culmination of the Saturn-Pluto cycle. There may be many meanings to the Saturn-Pluto cycle, but optimism isn't one of them. Saturn and Pluto are both terribly difficult and wrenching planets to experience on a personal level, let alone magnified through mass experience. Collectively, they bring out the worst of our fears and anxieties. This is, after all, the cycle that later manifested as 9-1-1.

Just as a new Uranus-Pluto cycle was starting at the conjunction, Saturn-Pluto culminated (the opposition). The opening square of that cycle? In 1956 at 29 Leo, just before the initial ingress of Pluto into Virgo. This Saturn-Pluto cycle began in Leo in 1947, representing the beginning of the Baby Boom, which demographically resulted from population pressures, both from the end of the Great Depression and the deferral of reproduction during World War II. And later it would be one of only two Baby Boom presidents who would preside over 9-1-1.

These two hard aspects in Pluto cycles coincided to produce the late 1960s: a time of political action around the world that shook the power base of Western society before mostly dissipating. What happened? The challenge to power doesn't necessarily topple it. An earlier example of the Uranus-Pluto conjunction occurred with the riots and political upheavals of 1848. Once again, students and others were on the move. Once again, governments were challenged, and a few toppled. But mostly, things returned to "normal" afterward. In fact, one can make a pretty good case that things got more conservative, because people got scared by the radical rhetoric of a time that they looked back upon as dangerous. In other words, the effect of the unrest of 1848 on the body politic was to send it in the opposite direction from what the radicals wanted.

NATAL CHART
Sun enters Ari 3-21-1966
March 20, 1966
8:52:56 PM
Washington, D.C.
38N53'42" 77W02'12"
Standard Time
Time Zone: 5 hours West
Tropical Regiomontanus

Chart 13. Sun enters Aries 1966, Washington, D.C.

Day of ☉	Hour of ☉
Last Hr ♂	- 38 mins
Next Hr ♀	+22 mins

FIXED STARS	
♃☌ El Nath	0°58's
♃☌ Alnilam	0°05's
⊗☌S Scale	0°40'a

Hs	Alm. (Dor)
1	♂
2	♂
3	♃
4	☿♄
5	♃
6	♂
7	☽♀
8	☽
9	☿
10	☉
11	☿
12	♀

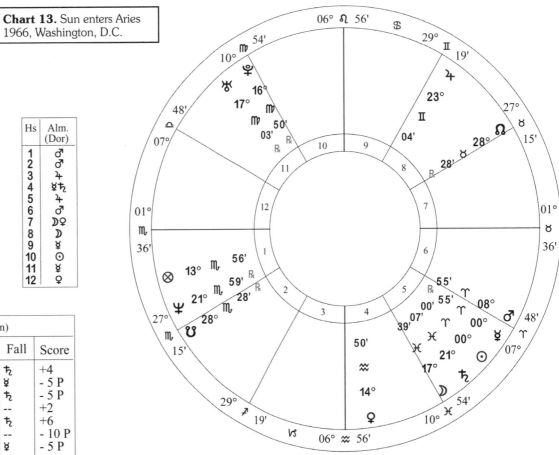

ESSENTIAL DIGNITIES (Dorothean)

Pl	Ruler	Exalt	Tripl	Term	Face	Detri	Fall	Score
☉	♂	☉ +	♃	♃	♂	♀	♄	+4
☽	♃	♀	♂	☿	♃	☿	☿	- 5 P
☿	♂	☉	♃ m	♃	♂	♀	♄	- 5 P
♀	♄	--	☿	♀ +	☿	☉	--	+2
♂	♂ +	☉	♃	♀	♂ +	♀	♄	+6
♃	☿	☊	☿ m	♄	☉	♃ -	--	- 10 P
♄	♃	♀	♂	☿	♂	☿	☿	- 5 P
☊	♀	☽	☽	♂	♄	♂	--	--
⊗	♂	--	♂	♃	☉	♀	☽	--
As	♂	--	♂	♂	♂	♀	☽	--
Mc	☉	--	♃	☿	♄	♄	--	--
☋	♂	--	♂	♄	♀	♀	☽	--

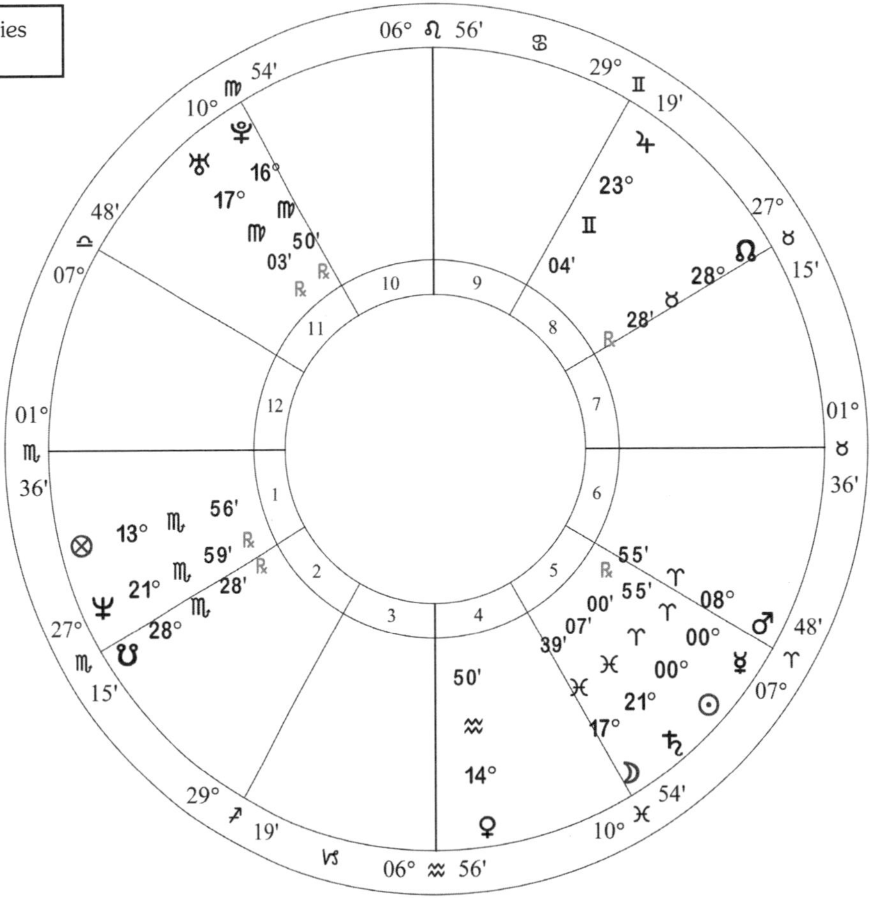

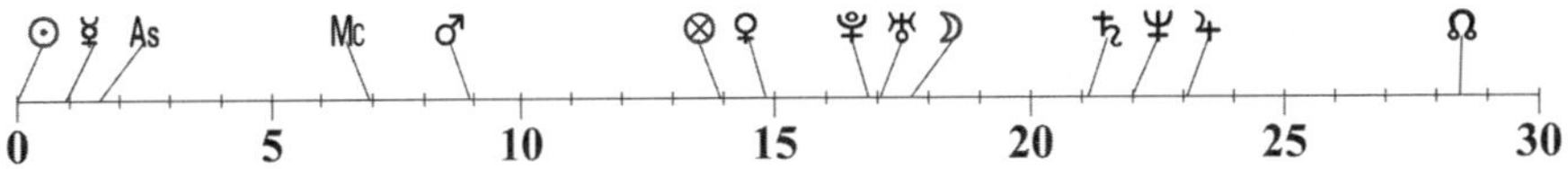

Consider the metaphor of an earthquake. The ground oscillates, buildings and roads may collapse, some people are killed, there is mass destruction of property if the quake is big enough. But then, what's the thing most survivors want to do? Rebuild and go on with their lives just as they were before. The same thing happens following a hurricane. Both earthquakes and hurricanes are primarily regional phenomena: one doesn't get hurricanes in Kansas and one doesn't get earthquakes in Wisconsin. Yet do we see a mass exodus to other places after a major disaster? Mostly, no. And yet – there are a few people who can take these times of trouble as revelation. It is possible to change.

People mostly react to disaster by attempting to cope, and then attempting to forget. There's scant evidence to suggest that people react to it by changing their minds about the nature of reality. Changes come in small increments. It's the daily exposure of co-workers of multiple ethnicities to the reality that their differently colored peers are not really so different after all. It's that life goes on after the election of the first woman mayor or governor or senator. It's the discovery that your favorite Uncle Roger is really gay – and you still love him. The little pebbles of everyday experience are unrelenting. The massive boulders of disaster are easy to dismiss as one-time occurrences best forgotten.

Thus we see how the paradox of the major transits works: for those confronted with the energy "out of the blue," the planetary tension is seen as a disaster which must be buried as rapidly as possible. For those already along the pathway, the planetary tension is the opportunity to strike out in a different direction.

In the 1960s, the vast majority of people were not ready to strike out in a new direction. And yet, incremental change that broke down racial and gender barriers began to happen. But some people really did "turn on, tune in, and drop out." The stereotype of the aging hippie is real, even if the majority of the people who experienced the 1960s didn't adopt that lifestyle as permanent.

The crossfire of 1960s politics around the world was incredibly complex. There was an unpopular war, several civil rights movements, and the nascent beginnings of environmental awareness. Is it any surprise that this level of political involvement suffered from non-sustainability? By the end of the 1960s, most people wanted to move back to their lives and business as usual.

And while some people began to experience environmental awareness, given the truly subversive nature of its message, it's amazing how entrenched it did become. In many countries, environmental departments and bureaucracies were created. The concept of "environmental impact" never existed before the 1970s as a governmental concept. And as we have already observed, a lot of individual families, especially in Europe, quietly changed their personal reproductive patterns. But more about these ideas with Pluto in Capricorn in Chapter 8!

To understand what happened, we need to skip forward to the 1970s. Ehrlich and Harden's books and articles continued to ignite interest, mostly on college campuses. By 1970, there was sufficient grass-roots interest to spark Earth Day celebrations.

On 22 April 1970, the Sun was in Taurus, appropriate for our Earth theme. It was also approaching a Sun-Saturn conjunction there. In modern astrological usage, this chart shows a stellium in Taurus, appropriate to this theme. As an event, however, the Moon and Jupiter in Scorpio opposed that stellium.

Earth Day was the day after a Full Moon. It would be a mistake to see this as the beginning of the environmental movement: clearly, somebody (actually, a lot of somebodies) had to organize this in the first place! Speaking for myself, I had joined our new campus chapter of Zero Population Growth in September 1969, and it was our chapter that went to participate on Earth Day. However, it was Earth Day that brought awareness of the growing strength of the movement to the rest of the U.S. population. As such, the Full Moon symbolism seems completely apt, as we see in Chart 14.

By definition, the Full Moon in Taurus has the Moon in Scorpio. But this particular one was Moon conjunct Jupiter as well. The Sun rules the Ascendant, and was Almuten of the 10th – the planet with the most points of essential dignity there. The presence of Saturn in this configuration and in the 10th house was important. Put simply, the major purpose of the environmental movement is to point out that people need to *voluntarily cut back* – a Saturn idea, if ever there was. The Mercury-Venus conjunction surely was in part the burgeoning awareness that overpopulation represented the key to the whole problem.

But was this a successful event? Venus trine Pluto is the only dignified planet – but as a planet of reproduction, this is not a bad thing. I'm sure that a number of students through this teach-in (the major type of event of the original Earth Day) made decisions about future family size that stuck. There is a lot of fixed energy in this chart, which would tend to extend its "life expectancy" with or without dignity.

What did happen as a result of this outpouring was the establishment of governmental structures that at least had a titular responsibility in this area. This was the Nixon administration, and it was under that presidency that both the Environmental Protection Agency as a cabinet agency and the Council on Environmental Quality within the White House were established.

The Environmental Protection Agency was formed as part of Reorganization Plan Number 3, which was signed into law on 9 July 1970. The chart shown is for noon. This chart has a Moon-Pluto conjunction at 23-24 Virgo, with the Moon ruling the 10th. The first degree of Libra rising suggests a new beginning: but a very amorphous one with zero degrees. In fact, it's doubtful that anybody in Washington had any concept how this agency was going to work. Venus, ruling the Ascendant, was in Leo – a barren sign – and square Neptune.

The Moon does have nighttime Triplicity in the earth signs – so this is reasonably strong by essential dignity. It is also translating the light between Saturn and Pluto. Which brings us to the realization that the Saturn-Pluto opposition of the charts we were examining from the 1960s has moved on to the Saturn-Pluto closing trine. Same theme, different implementation. What was tough for people to even register in the 1960s is now beginning to achieve respectability.

But is it the resource aspect – or the overpopulation aspect? Within the environmental movement, groups like Zero Population Growth had become driving factors. But outside the movement itself? The emphasis shown here with the 10th house cusp being Cancer, a fertile sign, suggests that the overpopulation theme wasn't getting through to the government at all.

We can see even more clearly how the mandate has shifted from the priorities of the activists to the politicians when we examine the chart for the actual opening of the EPA, Chart 16.

Full Moon (astrological)
Full Moon 04-21-1970
April 21, 1970
11:21:18 AM
Washington, D.C.
38N53'42" 77W02'12"
Standard Time
Time Zone: 5 hours West
Tropical Regiomontanus

Chart 14. Full Moon 21 April 1970, Washington, D.C.

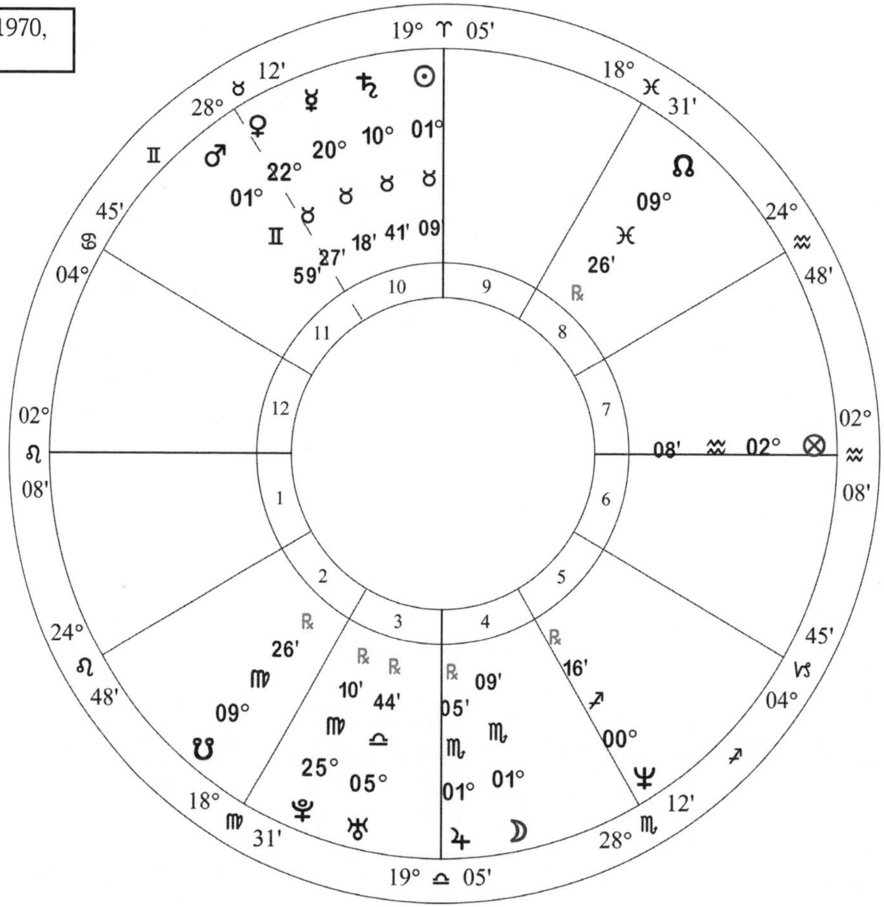

Day of ♂	Hour of ♄
Last Hr ☽	- 21 mins
Next Hr ♃	+46 mins

FIXED STARS	
⊗☌Altair	0°46's
♂☌Mirfak	0°19's

Hs	Alm. (Dor)
1	☉
2	☉
3	☿
4	♄
5	♂
6	♀♄
7	♄
8	♄
9	♀
10	☉
11	♀
12	☽

ESSENTIAL DIGNITIES (Dorothean)

Pl	Ruler	Exalt	Tripl	Term	Face	Detri	Fall	Score
☉	♀	☽	♀	♀	☿	♂	--	- 5 P
☽	♂	--	♀	♂	♂	♀	☽ -	- 9 P
☿	♀	☽	♀	♃	♄	♂	--	- 5 P
♀	♀ +	☽	♀ +	♄	♄	♂	--	+8
♂	☿	☊	♄	☿	♃ m	♃	--	- 5 P
♃	♂	--	♀	♂	♂ m	♀	☽	- 5 P
♄	♀	☽	♀	☿	☽	♂	--	- 5 P
☊	♃	♀	♀	♃	♄	☿	☿	--
⊗	♄	--	♄	♄	♀	☉	--	--
As	☉	--	☉	♄	♄	♄	--	--
Mc	♂	☉	☉	☿	☉	♀	♄	--
☋	☿	☿	♀	♀	☉	♃	♀	--

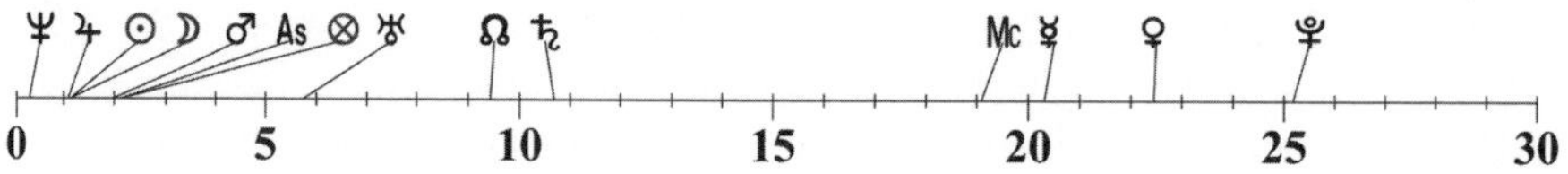

NATAL CHART
Reorganization Plan No. 3
July 9, 1970
12:00 PM
Washington, D.C.
38N53'42" 77W02'12"
Daylight Saving Time
Time Zone: 5 hours West
Tropical Regiomontanus

Day of ♃ Hour of ☿	
Last Hr ♀ - 73 mins	
Next Hr ☽ + 0 mins	

FIXED STARS		
♆♂Toliman	0°43's	
♅♂Castor	0°27's	
♀♂Alphard	0°08'a	
☽♂Alkes	0°16'a	
☊♂Deneb Adige	0°19'a	
♂♂Procyon	0°57'a	

Hs	Alm. (Dor)
1	♄
2	♄ ♃
3	♂ ♄
4	♀ ♄
5	♄ ♀
6	♄
7	☉
8	☉ ♂
9	♀
10	☽
11	☿
12	☿

ESSENTIAL DIGNITIES (Dorothean)

Pl	Ruler	Exalt	Tripl	Term	Face	Detri	Fall	Score
☉	☽	♃	♀ m	☿	☿	♄	♂	- 5 P
☽	☿ m	☿	♀	♄	☿ m	♃	♀	+0 P
☿	☽ m	♃	♀	♀	☽ m	♄	♂	+0 P
♀	☉	--	☉ m	♂ m	♂	♄	--	- 5 P
♂	☽	♃	♀	♄	☽ m	♃	☉	- 9 P
♃	♀	☽	♀	♂	♃ +	♂	☉	+1
♄	♀	☽	♀	♃	☽	♂	--	- 5 P
☊	♃	♀	♀	♀	♀	☿	☿	--
⊗	♃	☋ +	☉	♃	♀	☿	--	--
As	♀	♄	♄	♄	☽	♂	☉	--
Mc	☽	♃	♀	♂	♀	♄	♂	--
☋	☿	☿	♀	☿	☉	♃	♀	--

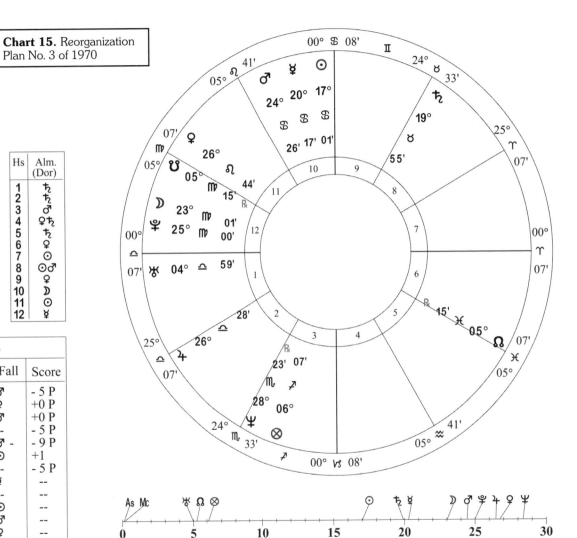

Chart 15. Reorganization Plan No. 3 of 1970

NATAL CHART
EPA Opens
December 2, 1970
9:00 AM
Washington, D.C.
38N53'42" 77W02'12"
Standard Time
Time Zone: 5 hours West
Tropical Regiomontanus

Chart 16. Environmental Protection Agency Opens

Day of ☿	Hour of ♄
Last Hr ☽	- 12 mins
Next Hr ♃	+35 mins

FIXED STARS	
☉☌ Antares	0°37's
☿☌ Acumens	0°30's

Hs	Alm. (Dor)
1	♀♄
2	♄
3	♀
4	☉♂
5	♀
6	☿
7	☽
8	☉
9	☿
10	♄
11	♂
12	♃

ESSENTIAL DIGNITIES (Dorothean)

Pl	Ruler	Exalt	Tripl	Term	Face	Detri	Fall	Score
☉	♃	☋	☉ +	♀	☿	☿	--	+3
☽	♄	♂	♀	♄	☉	☽ -	♃	- 10 P
☿	♃	☋	☉	♂	♄	☿ -	--	- 10 P
♀	♂ m	--	♀ +	♃	♂	♀ -	☽	+3
♂	♀ m	♄	♄	♂ +	♃	♂ -	☉	+2
♃	♂	--	♀	☿	♀	♀	☽	- 5 P
♄	♀	☽	♀	♃	☽	♂	--	- 5 P
☊	♄	--	♄	♂	☽	☉	--	--
⊗	♄	--	♄	♃	☽	☉	--	--
As	♄	♂	♀	♀	♃	☽	♃	--
Mc	♀	♄	♄	♂	♃	♂	☉	--
☋	☉	--	☉	♂	♂	♄	--	--

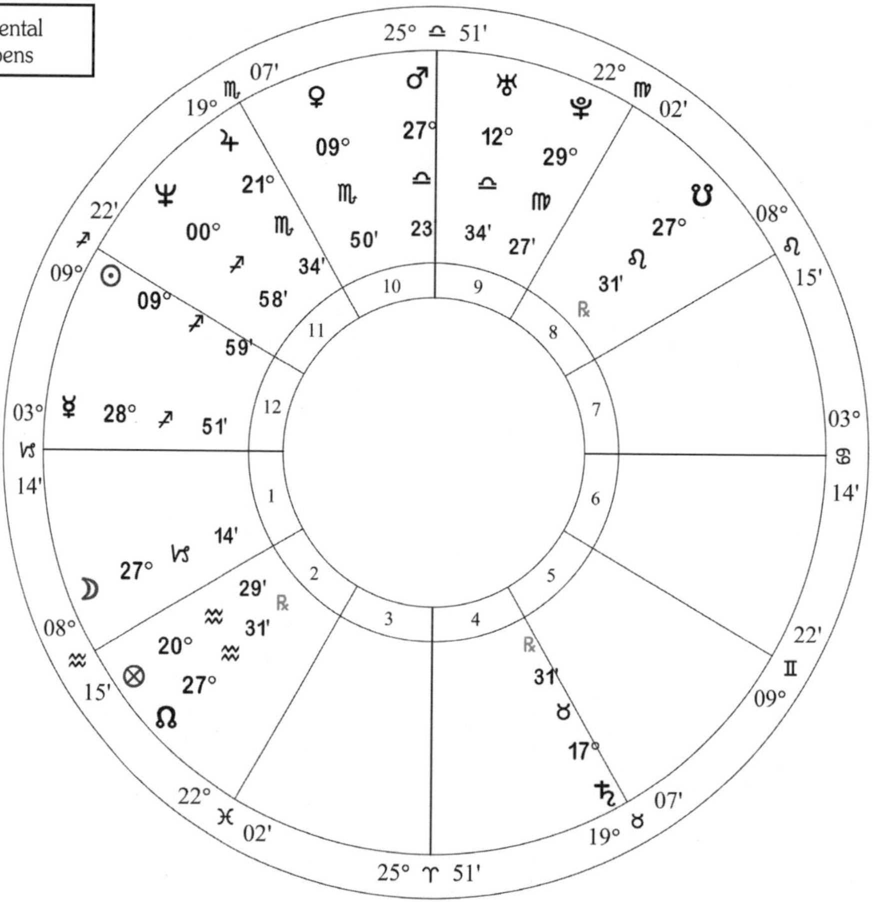

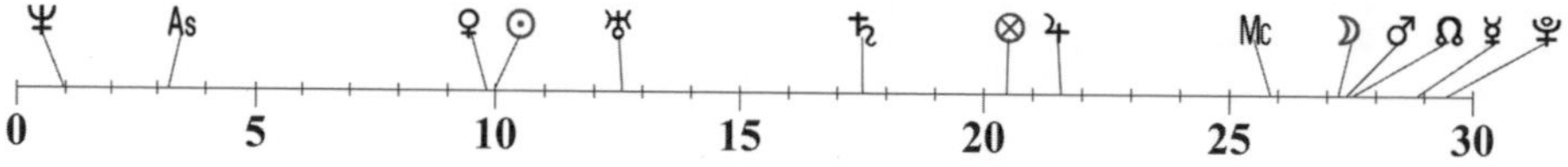

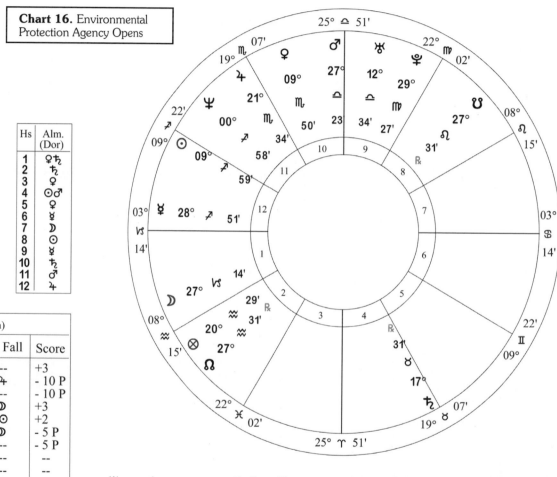

Here we see a time with Capricorn rising and the Moon in Capricorn. This seems appropriate enough. But what do we make of Libra on the MC? What the establishment of the EPA accomplished was the creation of a legal entity – a bureaucracy devoted to what is *legal* in environmental *law* and *regulation*. What brings a matter into public policy is the creation and administration of laws that relate to the area in question.

However, note the Pluto at 29 Virgo – it's just about done with its time in Virgo, but it adds a supporting argument to our statement above, being in the 9th house of this chart – legal affairs. Do we interpret the 29 Virgo as "too late," as we might in a horary? Not exactly. The idea, as mentioned earlier, borrowed from medical astrology, is that the characteristics of the sign become more extreme the further into the sign the planet is by degree. So by that interpretation, 29 Virgo is about as extremely Virgo as you can get.

Before we leave this chart, though, I want to ask the question again: does this say anything about overpopulation as an issue? For the formation of the EPA, there was a Jupiter-Saturn opposition. That about sums up the problem. Outside of environmental circles, there is a huge mythology that growth in population is an almost universal good.

We could follow the fact that, during this period of Pluto in Virgo, the pill became an increasingly popular and successful form of contraception. With the pill, family planning went from deciding how many children to have to a significant number of couples opting to have no children at all. The formation of the EPA with Saturn loosely conjunct the 5th house cusp *could* have indicated some push toward population issues – but it was a **peregrine** and thus weak Saturn – no essential dignity. Furthermore, Saturn was retrograde. These factors mitigate against the effectiveness of Saturn. And just so, overpopulation continued to take a back seat to environmental degradation as the topic for the EPA.

Aspect	Date	Pos1	Pos2
Sat – Sqr – Nep	Feb 18 1963	15° Aq 39' D	15° Sc 39' R
Sat – Opp – Ura	Apr 1 1965	11° Pi 37' D	11° Vi 37' R
Sat – Opp – Plu	Apr 23 1965	13° Pi 55' D	13° Vi 55' R
Sat – Opp – Plu	Aug 17 1965	15° Pi 18' R	15° Vi 18' D
Sat – Opp – Ura	Aug 27 1965	14° Pi 32' R	14° Vi 32' D
Ura – Cnj – Plu	Oct 9 1965	17° Vi 09' D	17° Vi 09' D
Sat – Opp – Plu	Feb 19 1966	17° Pi 34' D	17° Vi 34' R
Sat – Opp – Ura	Feb 24 1966	18° Pi 06' D	18° Vi 06' R
Ura – Cnj – Plu	Apr 4 1966	16° Vi 27' R	16° Vi 27' R
Ura – Cnj – Plu	Jun 30 1966	16° Vi 06' R	16° Vi 06' D
Sat – Opp – Ura	Nov 8 1966	23° Pi 12' R	23° Vi 12' D
Sat – Opp – Ura	Jan 6 1967	24° Pi 23' D	24° Vi 23' D
Sat – Opp – Nep	Jun 25 1971	00° Ge 51' D	00° Sg 51' R
Sat – Opp – Nep	Nov 27 1971	02° Ge 52' R	02° Sg 52' D

Summary for the period when Pluto was in Virgo:
    Saturn square Neptune (1 pass)
    Saturn opposite Uranus (5 passes)
    Saturn opposite Pluto (3 passes)
    Uranus conjunct Pluto (3 passes)
    Saturn opposite Neptune (2 passes)

Table 4-2. Sequence of Aspects, Saturn to Pluto, for the Period when Pluto was in Virgo, 1956 – 1972. Data calculated by Solar Fire Gold.

The formation of the government agencies marked the end of the period of Pluto in Virgo. Can we anticipate how this will impact the period we have just entered with Pluto in Capricorn? By

Aspect	Date	Pos1	Pos2
Sat – Opp – Ura	Feb 5 2009	20° Vi 39' R	20° Pi 39' D
Sat – Opp – Ura	Sep 15 2009	24° Vi 42' D	24° Pi 42' R
Sat – Sqr – Plu	Nov 15 2009	01° Li 42' D	01° Cp 42' D
Sat – Sqr – Plu	Jan 31 2010	04° Li 21' R	04° Cp 21' D
Sat – Opp – Ura	Apr 26 2010	28° Vi 46' R	28° Pi 46' D
Sat – Opp – Ura	Jul 26 2010	00° Li 25' D	00° Ar 25' R
Sat – Sqr – Plu	Aug 21 2010	02° Li 55' D	02° Cp 55' R
Ura – Sqr – Plu	Jun 24 2012	08° Ar 23' D	08° Cp 23' R
Ura – Sqr – Plu	Sep 19 2012	06° Ar 57' R	06° Cp 57' D
Ura – Sqr – Plu	May 20 2013	11° Ar 14' D	11° Cp 14' R
Ura – Sqr – Plu	Nov 1 2013	09° Ar 25' R	09° Cp 25' D
Ura – Sqr – Plu	Apr 21 2014	13° Ar 34' D	13° Cp 34' D
Ura – Sqr – Plu	Dec 15 2014	12° Ar 35' R	12° Cp 35' D
Ura – Sqr – Plu	Mar 16 2015	15° Ar 18' D	15° Cp 18' D
Sat – Sqr – Nep	Nov 26 2015	07° Sg 02' D	07° Pi 02' D
Sat – Sqr – Nep	Jun 17 2016	12° Sg 02' R	12° Pi 02' R
Sat – Sqr – Nep	Sep 10 2016	10° Sg 24' D	10° Pi 24' R
Sat – Cnj – Plu	Jan 12 2020	22° Cp 46' D	22° Cp 46' D
Sat – Sqr – Ura	Jun 14 2021	13° Aq 06' R	13° Ta 06' D
Sat – Sqr – Ura	Dec 24 2021	11° Aq 05' D	11° Ta 05' R

Table 4-3 *continued on the following column.*

Summary for the period when Pluto will be in Capricorn:
    Saturn opposite Uranus (4 passes)*
    Saturn square Pluto (3 passes)
    Uranus square Pluto (7 passes)
    Saturn square Neptune (3 passes)*
    Saturn conjunct Pluto (1 pass)+
    Saturn square Uranus (2 passes)

* Same aspect as with Pluto in Virgo

+ Aspect pair not present under Pluto in Virgo

Table 4-3. Sequence of Aspects, Saturn to Pluto, for the Period when Pluto will be in Capricorn, 2008 – 2024. Data calculated by Solar Fire Gold.

examining these charts for the 1960s, we can see what planetary combinations triggered, and which of these combinations are triggering again now that Pluto is in Capricorn. But unlike most of the commentary that has registered so far, I want to compare the aspects upcoming to those of the 1960s. Because, as we saw, that was a very intense time as well.

While the Pluto in Virgo period extended back to 1956, we can see that the focal point of these aspects was the period from 1965–1966.

Let's now compare this to the sequence of aspects ahead of us with Pluto in Capricorn. But before we do, let's also please note that Pluto spends a bit more time in Capricorn than it does in Virgo, due to the eccentricity of its orbit.

When we compare the two lists, the similarities are quite striking. These are the differences:

- In the Pluto in Virgo period, there was a concentration of aspects from 1965-1966, whereas in the Pluto in Capricorn period, the aspects are much more spread out through the entire period.

- The Uranus square Pluto for the Pluto in Capricorn period runs for almost 3 years, with seven passes – a bit extreme! However, by contrast, in the case of Neptune-Pluto, eleven passes have happened in historical time.

What do we make of this? I would assert that the similarity of aspect patterns suggests that many if not most of the issues that were thematic in the 1960s will return as themes in the Teens. These issues would include:

- Unpopular wars in intractable places (Vietnam? Afghanistan?)

- Civil rights

- Civil unrest

- Technological advances (remember the Space Race?)

- Environmental concerns

Astrologically, the big difference between Pluto in Virgo and Pluto in Capricorn is that Mercury rules Virgo, and Saturn rules Capricorn. The Space Race of the 1950-1960s had a real Mercury flavor to it, with all the engineering and technological whiz kids becoming heroes. The image of Saturn is far different: the Grim Reaper and the planet of scarcity. Saturn is a malefic; Mercury is not. How can we seriously expect that there won't be a down side to this transit?

Because the Mercury rulership so perfectly fit the race to the Moon, I think we can presume that technological innovations will not be the front burner issue this time. But everything else on the list is already poised to be significant.

Since we are considering environmental issues here, the obvious difference between 1965 and 2009 is that in 1965, the world population was 3.3 billion, and oil mining was still increasing. In 2009, the world population is about 6.7 billion, and oil mining plateaued some time ago. By the time that Pluto leaves Capricorn, the world population is estimated to be around 8 billion. Whatever else is going on, this continued population growth puts pressure on all development, infrastructure, and consumption. We will need to develop more conscious approaches to cope with and succeed amidst these circumstances.

We shall examine these questions more fully in Chapter 8, when we see the passage of Pluto through Sagittarius to Pisces.

Endnotes: Chapter 4

103. Brannt, William T., Hans Höfer, and Alexander Veith. *Petroleum; Its History, Origin, Occurrence, Production, Physical and Chemical Constitution, Technology, Examination and Uses; Together with the Occurrences and Uses of Natural Gas.* Philadelphia: H.C. Baird & co.; [etc., etc.], 1895, pp 20-23.

104. Brannt, William T., Hans Höfer, and Alexander Veith, p 23.

105. Bills, Rex E. *The Rulership Book; a Directory of Astrological Correspondences.* Richmond,: Macoy Pub. & Masonic Supply Co., 1971.

106. Brannt, William T., Hans Höfer, and Alexander Veith. The section on Galicia's early history of petroleum is found pp 30-32.

107. Lehman, J. Lee. *Essential Dignities*. Atglen, PA: Schiffer Press, 1989, pp 67-93.

108. Brannt, William T., Hans Höfer, and Alexander Veith, p 5.

109. Brannt, William T., Hans Höfer, and Alexander Veith, pp 5-7.

110. Williamson, Harold Francis, and Arnold Daum. *The American Petroleum Industry; The Age of Illumination, 1859-1899*. Evanston [Ill.]: Northwestern University Press, 1959, p 64.

111. Williamson & Daum , p 68.

112. Williamson and Daum, pp 70-72.

113. Williamson and Daum, p 72.

114. This whole complicated story is given in Chapter 4 of Williamson and Daum.

115. Williamson and Daum, p 77.

116. Williamson and Daum, p 79.

117. Lilly, William. *Christian Astrology Modestly Treated of in Three Books : The First Containing the Use of an Ephemeris, the Erecting of a Scheam of Heaven, Nature of the Twelve Signs of the Zodiack, of the Planets, with a Most Easie Introduction to the Whole Art of Astrology : The Second, by a Most Methodicall Way, Instructeth the Student How to Judge or Resolve All Manner of Questions Contingent Unto Man, Viz., of Health, Sicknesse, Riches, Marriage ... : The Third Containes an Exact Method Whereby to Judge Upon Nativities*. London: Printed by, 1647, p 211.

118. Williamson and Daum, pp 13-14.

119. Lehman, 2002, pp 35-36.

120. Ehrlich, Paul R. *The Population Bomb*. New York: Ballantine Books, 1968.
Hardin, Garrett. "The Tragedy of the Commons." *Science* 13 Dec 1968: 1242-48.

121. Lehman, J. Lee, "Hope in the Time of Pluto in Capricorn," *//leephd. blogspot.com/, 2009.*

122. Carson, Rachel, Lois Darling, and Louis Darling. *Silent Spring*. Boston; Cambridge, Mass.: Houghton Mifflin ; Riverside Press, 1962.

123. *http//www.grist.org/article/ehrlich/*

124. Pottenger, Mark, 1995, pp 159-176

125. Douglass, Carrie B. *Barren States : The Population "Implosion" In Europe*. Oxford; New York, N.Y.: Berg, 2005; page 13. This table lists the demographics for Norway, Germany, Czech Republic, Russia, Bulgaria, Greece, Italy, Spain, France and Ireland. I have not checked the demographics for other countries there, so I may be missing some examples.

5

The Limits to Growth: Pluto in the Air Signs

One of the penalties of an ecological education is that one lives alone in a world of wounds. Much of the damage inflicted on land is quite invisible to the layman. An ecologist must either harden his shell and make believe that the consequences of science are none of his business, or he must be the doctor who sees the marks of death in a community that believes itself well and does not want to be told otherwise.

—Aldo Leopold [126]

WHEN GOING BACK AND CONTEMPLATING THE SPACE RACE THAT OCCURRED WITH PLUTO IN VIRGO, AND HOW IT WAS SOLD TO THE AMERICAN PEOPLE, ONE OF THE BENEFITS AMERICANS WERE GIFTED WAS ALL OF THE INVENTIONS FOR THE TRIP TO THE MOON THAT WOULD HAVE APPLICATIONS IN CIVILIAN LIFE. In other words, space technology was seen to boost innovation, and innovation in turn had distinct values for society as a whole in the form of practical technology.

This argument is one that "pure" science has often made to justify its costs: that serendipitous applications fall out of it sufficiently frequently to justify the up-front expense. But the Moon landings should be understood primarily as an engineering feat, not pure science. While this distinction may at first seem subtle, what it actually speaks to is the fact that not all science as practiced is theoretical in nature: and most, in fact, is not.

When I referred to the landing as an engineering feat, what I meant was that, long before Pluto reached Virgo, the theoretical grounds for the Moon trip had already been established. For that matter, when Jules Verne wrote *From the Earth to the Moon* in 1865, when Pluto was in Taurus, most of the science necessary to go to the Moon had been envisioned. What was lacking were practical matters, such as a workable propulsion system, and means of working in the cold and vacuum of space. Apart from that, even Wikipedia gives an uncanny series of parallels between Verne's description of the journey and the actual Apollo program. [127]

Gemini	Libra	Aquarius
25 Jun – 8 Nov 1150	3 Oct 1232 – 19 Apr 1233	5 Mar – 29 Jun 1286
13 May 1151-3 Jan 1152	27 Jul 1233 – 24 Dec 1243	10 Jan – 23 1287
24 Mar 1152 – 9 Jul 1178	13 Mar – 13 Oct 1244	1 Nov 1287 – 27 Mar 1307
30 Dec 1179 – 23 May 1180		10 Aug 1307 – 7 Feb 1308
		23 Oct – 4 Dec 1308
29 Jun – 2 Nov 1394	21 Oct 1478 – 25 Mar 1479	12 Feb 1532 – 29 Jul 1532
16 May – 27 Dec 1395	19 Aug 1479 – 5 Nov 1490	21 Dec 1532 – 30 Mar 1552
29 Mar 1396 – 11 Aug 1423	19 May – 28 Aug 1491	15 Oct – 12 Dec 1553
22 Nov 1423 – 22 Jun 1424		
19 Jan – 5 May 1525		
9 Jul – 22 Oct 1638	14 Nov 1724 – 22 Feb 1725	3 Apr 1777 – 28 May 1777
24 May – 15 Dec 1639	9 Sep 1725 – 5 Dec 1736	26 Jan – 21 Aug 1778
10 Apr 1640 – 24 Jul 1668	4 Apr – 1 Oct 1737	1 Dec 1778 – 11 Apr 1797
8 Dec 1668 – 8 Jun 1669		21 Jul 1787 – 17 Feb 1798
10 Feb – Apr 13 1670		28 Sep – 26 Dec 1798
21 Jul 1882 – 9 Oct 1882	5 Oct 1971 – Apr 1972	23 Mar 2023 – 11 Jun 2023
2 Jun 1883 – 4 Dec 1883	30 Jul 1972 – 5 Nov 1983	21 Jan 2024 – 1 Sep 2024
19 Apr 1884 – 10 Sep 1912	18 May – 28 Aug 1984	19 Nov 2024 – 9 Mar 2043
20 Oct 1912 – 9 Jul 1913		
28 Dec 1913 – 26 May 1914		

Table 5-1. Pluto Ingresses by Sign. Data from Michelsen, 1990, pp 63-64.

Pluto in Gemini (1882-1914)

The period of the 1890s was a significant era in science – and this will give us the perfect lead-in to considering how the period of Libra actually advanced the cause of the environmental movement. The key to what at first may seem like an odd conclusion is actually quite simple. Theory and practice go together, the old "hand in glove" idea. What the astrology tells us is different from our stereotyped idea. Our stereotype of how science happens is that great scientists like Newton and Pasteur think great thoughts and propose theories – and then science advances through the next generation of maybe not so brilliant minds chasing down all the alleys opened by that single Great Mind.[128] What is more realistic can actually be seen from the life of Charles Darwin: that he spent decades observing nature, *then* he derived his theory of evolution from those observations. Observation, tinkering – engineering, if you will – precedes theorizing. And that's the sequence of Earth followed by Air. The theorizing can only happen when there is sufficient good information to theorize about.

In fact, the explosion of "pure science" in the 1890s was only possible because of the massive amount of more practical work of the Pluto in Taurus period – for example all those engineering applications leading to greater power, which in turn meant that more powerful and sophisticated scientific instruments could be built.

And what was this explosion? In 1885, Pasteur tested the first successful rabies vaccine – a huge advance in medicine. In 1887, the Michaelson-Morley experiment proved that the speed of light did not vary with motion. In 1895, Roentgen discovered what will later be named X-rays. In 1897, Thompson discovered the electron. In 1898, the Curies announced their discovery of radium. In 1899, Hoffman received a patent for aspirin. Hugo De Vries proposed the theory of genetic mutation in 1903. In 1905, Einstein proposed the special theory of relativity, with the famous expression $E=mc^2$. In 1913, Bohr proposed the quantum theory of the hydrogen atom. All of these discoveries appear in the brief history in beginning textbooks of these fields because they are considered to be so fundamental.

This period marks the invention of the automobile, zeppelin, airplane, cameras with roll film, radio, genetics, ecology, Bakelite plastic, the discovery of both the North and South Poles, and the nucleus of the atom.

In fact, the Jungian view of the Air element may be necessary to fully understand the intellectual processes, because the Air element is not just the sanguine party animal. Air plays with ideas, and can apply quite ruthless logic to them. The stereotype of the physicist at the blackboard writing endless equations is air incarnate. But as any mathematician will tell you, you have to start from somewhere. Earth provides the ground for Air's equations.

The world view that greeted Pluto in Gemini was Imperialism and, with it, the Victorian Age. European males expected to dominate the world as part of the natural order – and they believed that this was because of real superiority.[129] It was in the era dominated by these values that the United States began to emerge more forcefully onto the world stage. The timing of U.S. entry is pretty clear: it was the Spanish-American War. However, what chart to use for that war illustrates some of the difficulty that astrologers have had in putting together a coherent system of mundane astrology.

Here's the difficulty: astrologers are drawn to event charts like moths to flame. Event charts have been used for predictive purposes for at least two thousand years. But if I'm a political astrologer during a war, how do I interpret the patterns of the war? If I have to wait for a battle to occur, how useful is my prognostication? This goes back to the Babylonian question that Campion raised: what's the use of a celestial prediction if it isn't part of a conversation in which the events can be changed? An Aries Ingress, a lunation, an eclipse, a treaty or law with a "start date" in the future, or a sporting event actually meets the Babylonian standard: these are all charts that can be viewed, "divined," and then acted upon. A chart for an event that is unscheduled really is more like a horary than many people acknowledge, because the divination possible is only about the particular event *in the past*. In the words of Ambassador Kosh on Babylon 5: "The avalanche has already started, it's too late for the pebbles to vote."[130]

The Spanish-American War

Here, we will illustrate this point by considering the war in the Pluto in Gemini period that put the U.S. on the map, on its way to super-power status in the next century: the Spanish-American War. While American and other astrologers have disagreed vehemently on which U.S. chart to use, the earliest references to "America" in the astrological literature pre-date the U.S. War of Independence, and give Gemini as the ruler. In following Luke Broughton's logic from the Civil War, his use of the Gemini Rising chart for the U.S. was probably less because of any knowledge of an actual signing time for the Declaration of Independence, than a way to highlight the significance of Uranus in Gemini as a symbol for the U.S.: especially as the U.S. Civil War happened as Uranus was again transiting Gemini. If the transit of Uranus through Gemini was so significant, we would also expect that the transit of Pluto through Gemini would also be significant for the U.S. It was.

What caused the Spanish-American War? To a large extent, it depends upon your point of view. One prominent factor was the Monroe Doctrine, named after President James Monroe. The Doctrine states that the Americas (meaning the Western Hemisphere, both North and South) are for Americans – and that the United States will view any new meddling by other powers as a provocation against the U.S. itself. In 1898, the only significant European power in the Western Hemisphere was Spain. While the Doctrine had not called for Spain to renounce its existing colonies, the intent had been to prevent anybody else from taking advantage of independence movements in those colonies. In the 1890s, the issue that more specifically prompted the War was the struggle for independence in Cuba, and the well publicized atrocities committed by the Spanish Captain General (i.e., military governor) in an attempt to put down the rebellion. These atrocities began after the Captain General was appointed in 1896: so, theoretically, the War could have broken out any time after this. In 1896, American business and the political apparatus was not yet supportive of war as the solution to the problem. It took another two years to change this assessment.

In February of 1898, an explosion sank the USS Maine in Havana harbor. The time of the explosion is well documented, and shown in Chart 17.

The question I would ask is: what does this chart actually show? For interpretation, we can turn to William Lilly's section on ships at sea (see Appendix D), to see what the classical interpretation of this chart would be. In going through Lilly's rules, one of the issues of a shipwreck is the Ruler of the Ascendant in an ill configuration with the Lord of the 8th. Here, the Ruler of the 1st and the 8th are the same: leading to the perennial horary interpretation question: what if the rule calls for the Significators of two houses to be in aspect, but they are, in fact, the same planet? I have tended to interpret this as being of the nature of "yes," but I don't have good historical evidence to back up that presumption. Normally, one would be happy to see Venus, but this is a Venus in the heart of the Sun – or is it? According to Bonatti, Cazimi only occurs when the planet is conjunct the Sun in both longitude and latitude by less than 16'.[131] Without the conjunction in both coordinate systems, this proto-cazimi is judged combust, and thus debilitated – imbecilic, to be exact. And so, this is bad for the ship – which it was. The Moon under the Earth (i.e, in houses 1-6) is another argument that the ship is lost.[132]

We know the ship exploded, so where is that? Mars is always suspect. Here we have Mars in the 4th – and Lilly specifically mentioned malefics in angular houses as representing a danger to the ship.[133] Likewise, the ruler of the Ascendant combust is a specific danger. The Moon, which is also ruler of an angle, cadent, is also a danger. The South Node in Cancer in an angular house, in the sign that rules the bottom of the ship (i.e., Cancer), is an argument of a serious leak. Lilly says: "If the unfortunate Signes

Sinking of the Maine
February 15, 1898
9:40 PM
Havana, Cuba
23 N 08 82 W 22
Standard Time
Time Zone: 5 hr 30 min

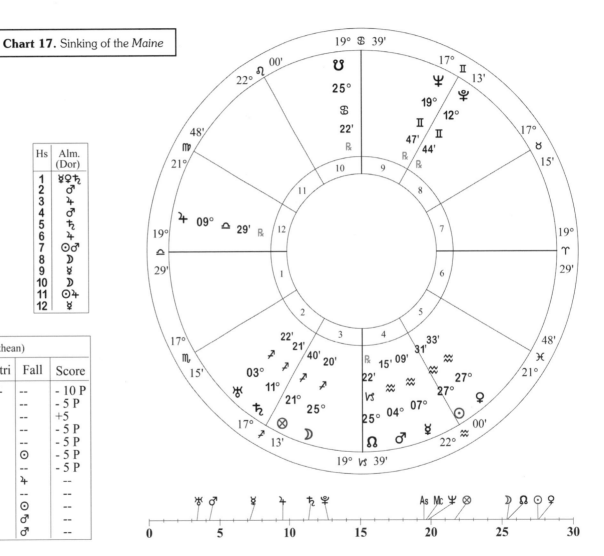

Chart 17. Sinking of the *Maine*

Day of ♂	Hour of ☉
Last Hr ♂	- 37 mins
Next Hr ♀	+26 mins

FIXED STARS	
♆☌Phact	0°58's
Mc☌Castor	0°49's
♆☌Capella	0°40's
⊗☌Rasalhague	0°38's
♆☌Bellatrix	0°15'a
♃☌Vindemiatrix	0°58'a

Hs	Alm. (Dor)
1	☿♀♄
2	♂
3	♃
4	♂
5	♄
6	♃
7	☉♂
8	☽
9	☿
10	☽
11	☉♃
12	☿

ESSENTIAL DIGNITIES (Dorothean)

Pl	Ruler	Exalt	Tripl	Term	Face	Detri	Fall	Score
☉	♄	--	☿	♂	☽	☉ -	--	- 10 P
☽	♃	☋	♃	♂	♄ m	☿	--	- 5 P
☿	♄	--	☿ +	☿ +	♀	☉	--	+5
♀	♄	--	☿	♂	☽	☉	--	- 5 P
♂	♄	--	☿	♄	♀	☉	--	- 5 P
♃	♀	♄	☿	♀	☽	♂	☉	- 5 P
♄	♃	☋	♃	♀	☽ m	☿	--	- 5 P
☊	♄	♂	☽	♄	☉	☽	♃	--
⊗	♃	☋ +	♃	♄	♄	☿	--	--
As	♀	♄	☿	☿	♄	♂	☉	--
Mc	☽	♃	♂	☿	☿	♄	♂	--
☋	☽	♃	♂	♀	☽	♄	♂	--

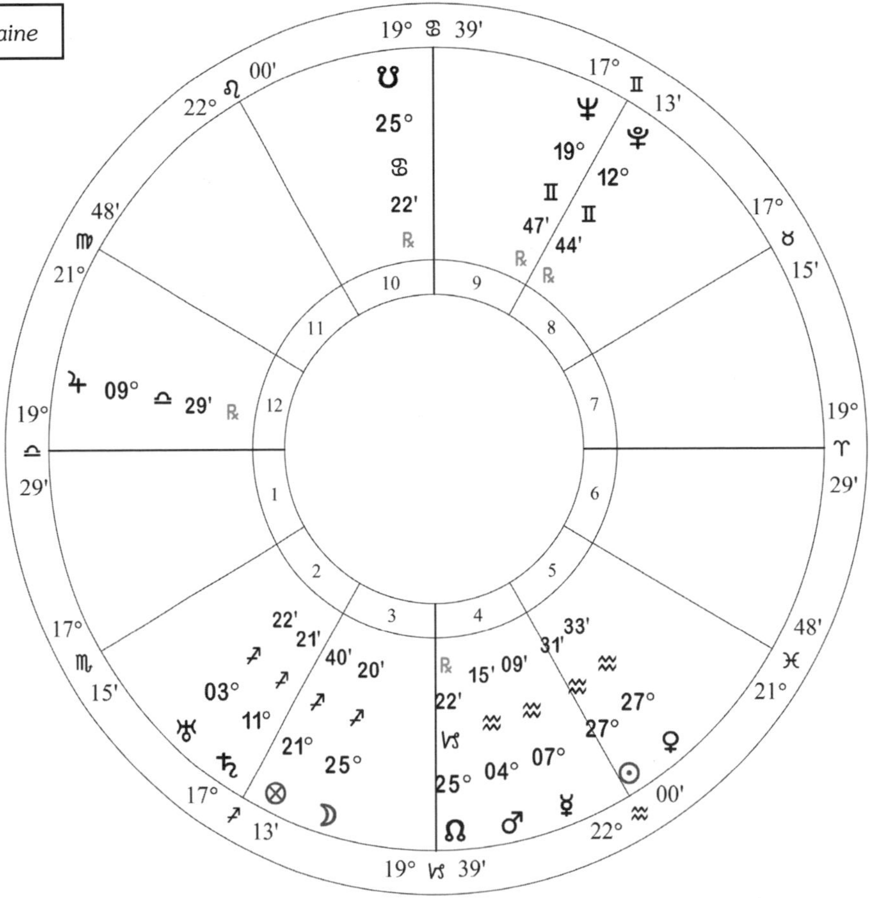

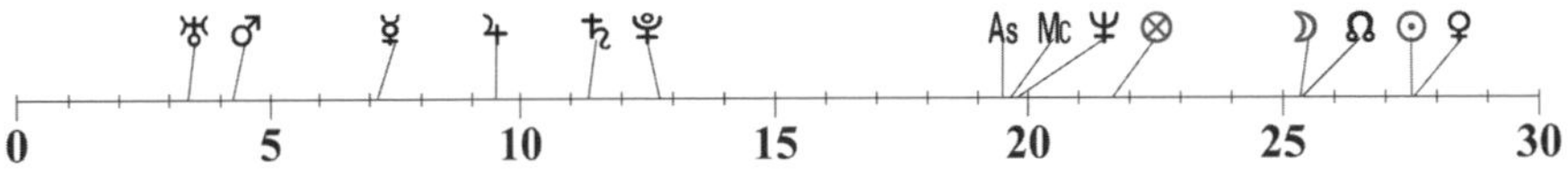

(viz., those which are afflicted by the presence of Saturn, Mars, or South Node) be those which signifie the bottom of that part of the Ship which is under Water, it's an argument of the breaking and drowning thereof, or receiving some dangerous Leak..."[134] Here, we have Mars unfortunating the bottom of the ship: the 4th house.[135]

Mars specifically is a problem – because we can get two different interpretations out of it. There were in fact two theories of what happened to the *Maine*. The first, favored by the U.S. at the time, was that the *Maine* had been mined and that a mine had exploded underneath. The Spanish conducted their own investigation, and they concluded that the evidence did not support this, and that most likely, the explosion was a coal fire internally. The latter would also implicate the lower section of the ship as the site of the explosion.

So if we take Mars as the general ruler of explosions, and Mars is in the 4th house in Aquarius, we have a dangerous peregrine Mars in the sign of the master or captain[136] – and being in Aquarius (the Water Bearer), it sounds like the boiler – and possibly some procedure ordered by the captain that inadvertently caused the explosion. But that is not the only interpretation, because Mars is the Ruler of the 7th. While the U.S. was not formally at war with Spain at this time, the *Maine* was moored in Havana as a show of force – a threat to Spain, in other words. So it is no stretch to see Spain as a good 7th house candidate. Since Mars does not afflict any of the angle rulers, there is not an argument of piracy – and I could see extending the rules for piracy to sabotage as well.[137] However, the rules also fit an attack. As Lilly says: *"If that Signe wherein Mars or the unfortunate Planet be the Signe of the fourth house, it notes firing of the Ship in the bottom of her; but if Mars be*

there, and the Signe humane, viz., either Gemini, Libra or Aquarius, that fire or burning of the Ship shall proceed from a fight with Enemies, or they shall cast fire into her..."[138] Human signs show human intervention: and a mistake by the crew is also possible. The Moon in Sagittarius highlights the crew (the sign Sagittarius[139]) – so again, we get a mixed read.

It's unfortunate that both scenarios proposed can be argued so well. I'd give the balance to the attack theory, but this is not entirely convincing either way.

Taking this chart one step further, does this event look like the beginning of a war? War is a 1st – 7th matter. Since this is an event chart, the 1st house rules the *Maine*, and by extension, the U.S. Venus and Mars are both in Aquarius, with Venus separating from Mars, already out of orb. This is the U.S. moving away from Spain. But the Moon *does* translate the light between them. However, it is not a dignified Moon, and there's not a whole lot of cross disposition either: the Moon is in Mars's **Term**, but that's pretty weak. This event alone could not have provoked the war, despite whatever claims of the so-called yellow journalists of the time, who were attempting to foment a war.

If we want to look at the reasons behind why the war started only in 1898, we shall have to look elsewhere. We can do that by examining a series of Aries Ingresses. Since the concentration camps created by the Spanish Captain General really do seem to be a factor in the U.S. fury over Spain's reaction to the rebels, we can start with 1896. If we do, we get the following series of Aries Ingress charts for Washington, D.C.

Table 5-2 shows the outer planet aspects for the period. We can immediately note that a full examination of the period would require only the Aries Ingress for 1896, all four ingresses for 1897, the Aries and Libra Ingresses for 1898, and only the Aries Ingress for 1899, based on the quadruplicity of the sign on the Ascendant. However, in the charts we are examining, the clearest indication of war is given by afflictions to the 1st and 7th – the country and its enemies. However, let's examine the Aries Ingresses for 1896-1899, in Chart 18.

In 1896, Saturn retrograde in the 1st house shows the U.S. focusing inward. The period of 1893-1894 had been a depression: the country had only recently gone into recovery. Here, that is shown by a very late Jupiter exalted in Cancer ruling the 2nd house: a good recovery, but probably spotty, given the retrograde. Retrogrades may not only deny, they may also upset the timing.

Pl 1	Aspect	Pl 2	Date	Pl 1 Position	Pl 2 Position
Jup	Sqr	Sat	Jul 7 1896	12° Le 28' D	12° Sc 28' R
Jup	Sqr	Ura	Aug 14 1896	20° Le 33' D	20° Sc 33' D
Sat	Cnj	Ura	Jan 6 1897	27° Sc3 9' D	27° Sc 39' D
Sat	Cnj	Ura	Jun 1 1897	26° Sc 5' R	26° Sc 25' R
Jup	Sqr	Plu	Aug 15 1897	14° Vi 34' D	14° Ge 34' D
Sat	Cnj	Ura	Sep 9 1897	25° Sc 34' D	25° Sc 34' D
Jup	Sqr	Nep	Sep 21 1897	22° Vi 33' D	22° Ge 33' D
Sat	Opp	Plu	Dec 6 1898	14° Sg 42' D	14° Ge 42' R
Sat	Opp	Nep	Feb 16 1899	22° Sg 02' D	22° Ge 02' R
Sat	Opp	Nep	May 2 1899	22° Sg 57' R	22° Ge 57' D
Sat	Opp	Nep	Dec 14 1899	25° Sg 41' D	25° Ge 41' R

Table 5-2. Outer planet aspects for the period 1896-1899.

The enemies of the U.S. are given by Venus exalted in Pisces, in the 4th. The Moon is in a partile square to Venus: Americans are becoming aware of the situation in Cuba and not liking it. Mars, the ruler of the Ascendant is conjunct the IC: the American focus is at home.

In 1897, Saturn again is associated with the 1st house, with Venus (Almuten of the 2nd) in Taurus. The recovery continues. The Sun in the 2nd shows where the attention is. The South Node in the 7th bodes badly for potential enemies. The Moon in Libra ruling those enemies in their 3rd house (the radix 9th) shows their attention is elsewhere besides the U.S.A. anyway.

In 1898, there is an abrupt shift. Now the 7th house is active: Saturn is there, in a partile opposition to Pluto in the 1st house. The Saturn-Pluto opposition then is the same aspect that was implicated in 2001 in the World Trade Center bombings – which also got us into war. The Uranus on the 7th house cusp also suggests volatility. I want to see the Neptune in the 1st as the journalistic deception of the period – but that may be hindsight. Also, Mars is angular, and just before entering one of the signs of its Triplicity: war is in the air, so to speak. It's interesting that the Sun is in the 11th house, because the Congress (i.e., legislature, 11th house) was quicker to get on the war bandwagon, that built after the explosion on the *Maine* and after business interests lined up for the war, than was the President. From this standpoint, it's also another argument of war with the rulers of the 1st and 7th in a doubly approaching opposition.

1899 again lacks the belligerency of the 1898 chart – and why not? The war was over by this time. Venus is now conjunct the 7th house cusp – a much more benign configuration.

I mentioned earlier that, in 1898, because the Ascendant was in a mutable sign, the Aries and Libra Ingresses would be

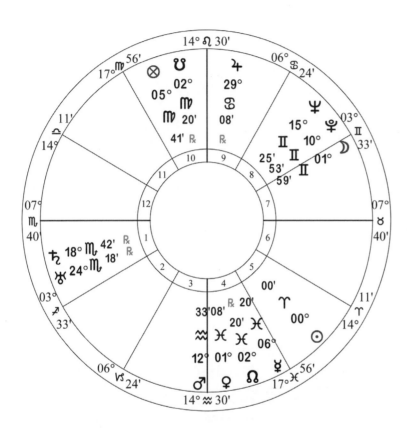

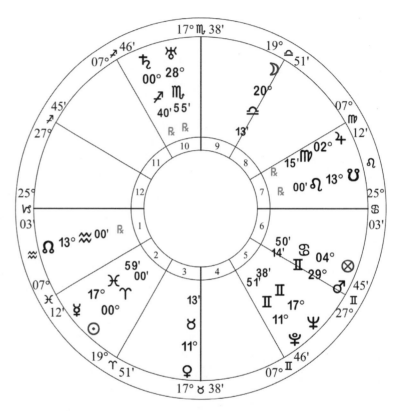

Sun enters Ari 3-20-1896
March 19, 1896 9:23:34 PM
Washington, D.C.
38N53'42" 77W02'12"
Standard Time
Time Zone: 5 hours West
Tropical Regiomontanus
NATAL CHART

Chart 18. Sun enters Aries
1896-1899, Washington, D.C.

Sun enters Ari 3-20-1897
March 20, 1897 3:16:21 AM
Washington, D.C.
38N53'42" 77W02'12"
Standard Time
Time Zone: 5 hours West
Tropical Regiomontanus
NATAL CHART

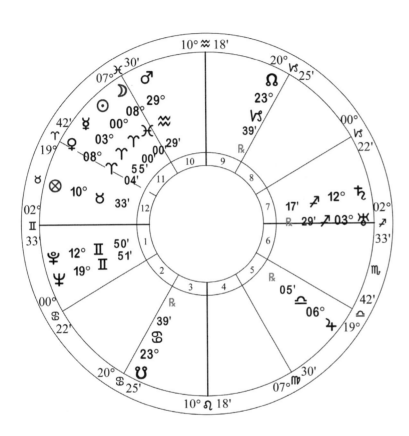

Sun enters Ari 3-20-1898
March 20, 1898 9:06:39 AM
Washington, D.C.
38N53'42" 77W02'12"
Standard Time
Time Zone: 5 hours West
Tropical Regiomontanus
NATAL CHART

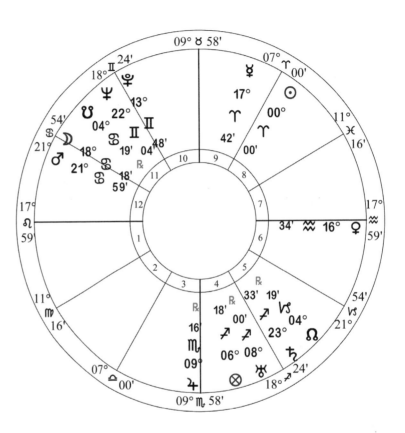

Sun enters Ari 3-20-1899
March 20, 1899 2:45:52 PM
Washington, D.C.
38N53'42" 77W02'12"
Standard Time
Time Zone: 5 hours West
Tropical Regiomontanus
NATAL CHART

necessary to interpret the entire year. Here I have presented them together: and the differences are quite clear. It's the Aries Ingress that shows the war. Now what is fascinating was that this was literally true, because it was an exceptionally short war, running from April to August. By the time the Libra Ingress had rolled around, hostilities had ceased, and peace negotiations were in progress, leading to a treaty under which the United States received Spain's overseas territories, putting the U.S.A. squarely into the Imperialist camp. This is shown in Chart 19.

Let's examine the Libra Ingress chart briefly. Venus in Scorpio, ruling the Ascendant, is in the 7th. As we have already seen, Mars and Venus in debility may actually be more powerful there when the issue at hand is conflict. This chart has both of them in Fall. Mercury in Virgo rules the 2nd – these developments are *very* good for business.

One thing the two charts have in common is the North Node in the 9th. While the war may not have started out that way, this certainly represents gain by foreign policy. And gain, the U.S. did, through the foreign territories. The Libra Ingress chart further has Mars, ruling the 7th, conjunct the South Node: loss for the U.S.'s open enemies.

If this interlude into the discussion of a war may seem a bit off-topic, consider what we have learned:

- The chart for a very famous event leading up to the war doesn't really show either the certainty of war, or its outcome. It actually doesn't even give a clear read on the event itself, because the astrology of the two suspected scenarios is so close in how they would be interpreted.

- It's more useful to examine the prospect for an event when viewing successive Aries Ingresses together than by focusing in on a single one.

These two conclusions are very important to astrological delineation. The first probably applies more to horary than to any other field, because a horary astrologer is oftentimes expected to be able to distinguish between multiple possibilities. If those possibilities are too similar, it is impossible to distinguish between them, unless some alternate means of delineation can be applied. For example, in Chapter 13 in *The Martial Art of Horary Astrology*, I give some of the rules if someone asks about several similar things together, like the question, "Should I take Job A or Job B?" Asked together, there are ways to distinguish the two jobs. However, if a Querent calls me at 1 pm Tuesday and asks about a job, and then calls me back at the same time on Wednesday, and the answer is no, and that Querent now asks about a different job – the chart is practically the same. If the Moon wasn't a significator, is the second question valid? This is like trying to figure out how to assign meaning to the Ascendant and Midheaven in sports events that always begin at the same time: it's not impossible, but one really does have to think about the logic of the situation.

The second point – the need to examine multiple Aries Ingresses (or years) together is a huge one. This is often neglected both in mundane astrology and in natal astrology. The problem is this. When astrologers are called upon for their yearly predictions, the tendency is to pull out the ephemeris for the year in question, maybe examine the eclipses and the ingresses, and then predict accordingly. I would then ask this

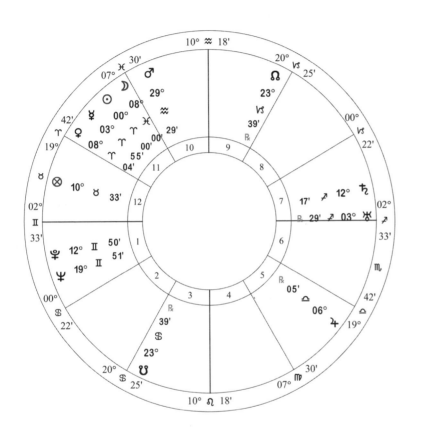

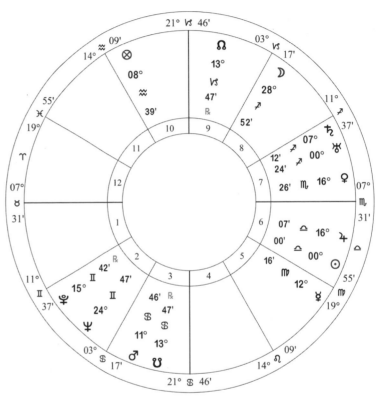

Sun enters Ari 3-20-1898
March 20, 1898
9:06:39 AM
Washington, D.C.
38N53'42" 77W02'12"
Standard Time
Time Zone: 5 hours West
Tropical Regiomontanus
NATAL CHART

Chart 19. Sun enters Aries and Libra 1898, Washington, D.C.

Sun enters Lib 9-23-1898
September 22, 1898
7:34:43 PM
Washington, D.C.
38N53'42" 77W02'12"
Standard Time
Time Zone: 5 hours West
Tropical Regiomontanus
NATAL CHART

question: how can the astrologer tell when a particular year is going to stand out? 1896, 1897, and 1899 were not as memorable years for the U.S.A. – and yet, things happened. And this is the problem: you or I could have taken the Aries Ingress chart for, say, 1897, and spent a good deal of time delineating every possible point. Astrologers can talk endlessly about any chart. And it's not that these discussions would necessarily have yielded garbage, either. Look at all those hard aspects of the outer planets I included in Table 5-1! The hypothetical astrological conference convener would have had to name the conference after the Saturn conjunct Uranus! But 1897 in retrospect was a set-up year for 1898. Quick! Name five important events from 1897! You cannot learn how to see the difference between the big years and the average years if you don't look at the charts comparatively.

The Development of the U.S. Conservation Movement

The period of Pluto in Gemini also had its own environmental theme. Because it is in this period that twin endeavors begin to bear fruit in the U.S.: the development of scientific field ecology, and the development of the conservation movement, culminating in Yellowstone National Park being established as the first national park in 1890. A huge influence on this emerging movement was the force and impact of the writings of John Muir (1838-1914), a great transitional figure between the Pluto in Taurus and Gemini periods. The conservation movement itself grew out of plans for water use and conservation in the West – ideas that embraced development, where to "conserve" was to use water wisely, as in to "store" flood water and to promote irrigation. These were ideas relating to land *use*, not necessarily land *preservation* in its natural state.[140] Because these policies allowed for multiple land uses (how Gemini!) one of those uses could be wilderness. Congressional support to survey water use in the West was first passed in 1888. Congress later set aside one million acres for each of the Western states to carry out irrigation projects.[141] These two ideas – wilderness and water preservation – were completely linked, because it was recognized that wilderness preserved water quality. President Theodore Roosevelt, a great believer in conservation, created the Reclamation Service within the Geological Survey, and it began its first four projects in 1903. While many in the environmental movement in the 1970s would look back on this period wistfully, it's important to observe two things. First, as Hays noted, this was primarily an issue of land development, which assumed continued growth. And secondly, a lot of what happened concretely was in the form of passage of laws, and development of administrative infrastructure. While legal structures may look a lot more like Libra than Gemini, I would argue that law is a natural outgrowth of Air, because laws are a human construct. Yet another factor was at work as well, because 1890 is considered by historians to be the approximate date for the closing of the American frontier: not that all the land was settled, but that there were no more huge gaps between settled areas.[142]

These dates are very interesting astrologically, because 1891-1892 marked the Neptune-Pluto conjunction in 7-8 Gemini: the placement that was early proposed as the Ascendant for the U.S., but which is certainly the Uranus of the U.S. for any of the July 4, 1776 charts.

It is also worth observing that it was directly out of the issue of water reclamation and conservation that we see the development of the mandate for the U.S. Army Corps of Engineers. This is a group that would factor greatly in the federal implementation of land and water use policy throughout the 20th century.

At the same time that the conservation movement reached as far as the White House, there were also changes in American biology. The professionalization of botany was accelerated in the 1890s, as botany acquired a research base, and largely moved out of being an avocation and into being a serious academic discipline. (It is perhaps worth noting that the disciplines of botany and zoology largely became backwaters in the 1980s and 1990s as cellular and molecular biology flourished.) This process gained momentum in the 1890s precisely because American science needed patronage in order to develop the professional infrastructure that had been largely lacking in American science until this time.[143] One of the immediate outgrowths of this philanthropy was the founding of the New York Botanical Garden in 1891. The founding of this institution, and other botanical gardens, allowed for the development of systematic study of plants within their evolutionary context, and not merely as species.

How would we see this development astrologically? That's a good question! The chart shown is the Aries Ingress for 1891, calculated for Albany, NY, as the founding of the garden resulted from a state statute, which allowed for the donation of the land. This is shown as Chart 20.

Science is not an endeavor that has a traditional rulership. The word "science" itself is a construct of the Enlightenment: before that, it was part of natural philosophy. When I saw this chart, I was immediately struck by the observation of the Gauquelins, who noted that the planet which showed a significant distribution among successful scientists was Saturn.[144] Here, in the Aries Ingress for the year of the founding of the Botanical Garden, what do we see but Saturn sitting right on the Ascendant, with Pluto on the MC.

So we could say from this that Saturn on the Ascendant would be emblematic for any scientific institution that the New York legislature would establish that year. But what about Pluto? Many of the keywords that have been proposed for Pluto don't seem to apply here, given what we know about the history of the Botanical Garden. Pluto has been seen for some time as a rather dangerous planet: either great wealth creation or destruction, for example. In this case, that's a possible theme, because the Garden was a result of a donation of significant "plutocratic" wealth.

As far as what the Garden itself represents, is it renewal or regeneration? Couldn't be, because it followed immediately on the heels of the Missouri Botanical Garden, founded in 1889. The plan for the New York Botanical Garden was loosely modeled on Kew Gardens in London. Was it evolutionary? Maybe – because one of the immediate outgrowths of the professionalization of botany which the Garden promoted was the integration of botany with evolutionary theory. And as for the destructive qualities sometimes attributed to Pluto – well, the Garden is still here.

I would like to suggest a different interpretation. As we have been examining the influence of Pluto in the various signs of the zodiac, perhaps having Pluto on an angle in a mundane chart is actually illustrating that the chart in question is a signature chart for the era. In other words, the angular Pluto here is

NATAL CHART
Sun enters Ari 3-20-1891
March 20, 1891
4:25:03 PM
Albany, New York
42N39'09" 73W45'24"
Standard Time
Time Zone: 5 hours West
Tropical Regiomontanus

Chart 20. Sun enters Aries 1891, Albany, NY

Day of ♀	Hour of ♄
Last Hr ☽	- 22 mins
Next Hr ♃	+38 mins

FIXED STARS	
♃☌ Fomalhaut	0°39's
♀☌ Sualocin	0°22's
☊☌ Aldebaran	0°46'a
Mc☌ Aldebaran	0°50'a
♃☌ Deneb Adige	0°51'a
☿☌ Scheat	0°58'a

Hs	Alm. (Dor)
1	☿
2	♄
3	♂
4	♃
5	♂♄
6	♄
7	♃
8	☉
9	♀
10	☿
11	☽
12	☉

ESSENTIAL DIGNITIES (Dorothean)

Pl	Ruler	Exalt	Tripl	Term	Face	Detri	Fall	Score
☉	♂	☉ +	☉ +	♃	♂	♀	♄	+7
☽	☉	--	☉	☿	♄	♄	--	- 5 P
☿	♃	♀	♀	♄	♂ m	☿ -	☿ -	- 14 P
♀	♄	--	♄ m	♀ +	☿	☉	--	+2
♂	♀	☽	♀	☿	☿ m	♂ -	--	- 10 P
♃	♃ +	♀	♀	♀	♄	☿	☿	+5
♄	☿	☿	♀ m	♀	♀	♃	♀	- 5 P
☊	☿	☊ +	♄	♃	♃	♃	--	--
⊗	♄	♂	♀	♂	☉	☽	♃	--
As	☿	☿	♀	♀	♀	♃	♀	--
Mc	☿	☊	♄	♃	♃	♃	--	--
☋	♃	☋	☉	♀	☿	☿	--	--

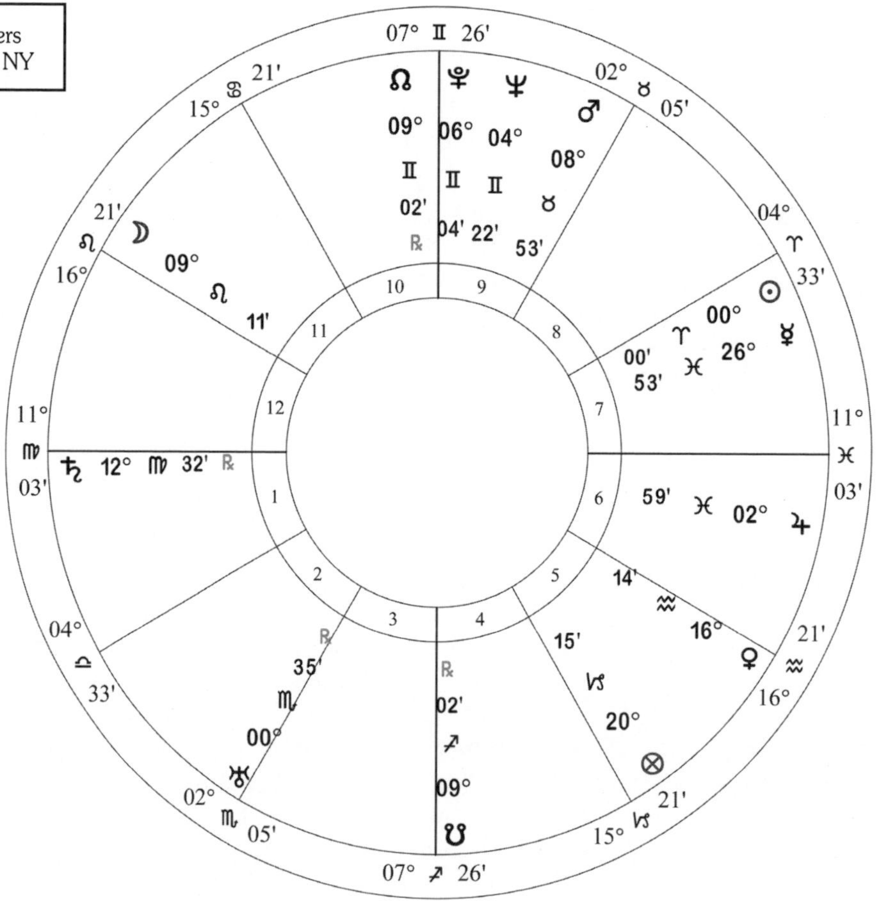

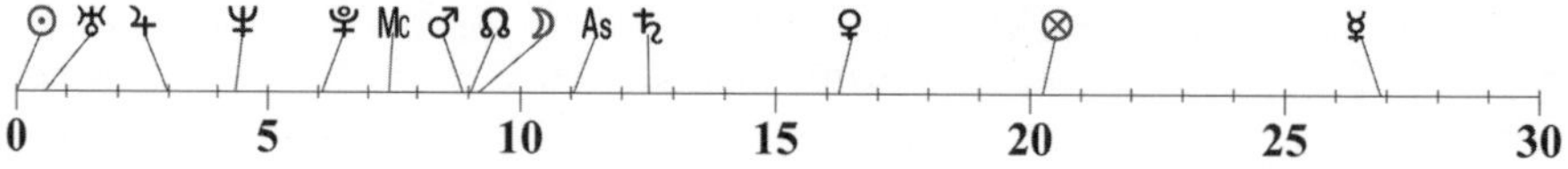

highlighting the significance of this time and place for the theme of professionalization which is unfolding. The formation of the Botanical Garden is therefore more important than what it might first seem to be. And along that theme, these may be the institutions or events that then create the change represented by that Pluto. Thus, one could argue that the New York Botanical Garden and its resources helped along the evolution (I can't resist it!) of naturalists into botanists – and from there, into ecologists. And there were other parallel institutions forming in this period, especially in agriculture. Agriculture too was moving out of random experiments performed by individual farmers and breeders into a systematic approach to agricultural education, experimentation, and research. And 1893 was the year that the Botanical Society of America was formed.

While the original research focus of the New York Botanical garden included experimental research and ecology, as well as taxonomy and field work, this mix did not last past the period of Pluto in Gemini.[145] By the end of Pluto in Gemini, the Garden had acquired a worldwide reputation.[146] The more traditional functions of taxonomy and field research completely predominated as Pluto went into Cancer. However, Kingsland contends that it was precisely this focus on ecology at the major gardens of the U.S. that guided the field of ecology into a discipline, rather than just a passing fad.[147] The name ecology had been coined by the great German morphologist, Ernst Haeckel (1834-1919), to denote the study of the mechanisms of Darwin's proposition that there is a struggle for existence. At first, the name did not catch on, although biologists began to work in this field. It was in the 1890s that the field began to achieve critical mass, suggesting to us that it is yet another function of the Neptune-Pluto conjunction.[148]

In the opening years of the 20th century, water problems in the West were a prime area for ecological research. In 1902, the Carnegie Institute was founded, and their botanical section proposed that very topic. Later in the same year, Congress passed the National Reclamation Act, which earmarked sales of federal land to be used to build irrigation and other water reclamation works.

In the Aries Ingress for 1902, Chart 21, we see that the most prominent feature is Saturn in Capricorn at the 10th house cusp. The President (i.e., the king) was Theodore Roosevelt, hero of the Spanish-American War, but also ardent conservationist. His federal appointments would drive this early wave. And as we have seen, this is the era when big businessmen were contributing to finance the science that was creating the field of ecology.

Saturn in Capricorn is a marvelous symbol for this early type of conservation. It has become commonplace to see big business in the sign Capricorn, and preserving vital resources (mostly water in this case) looks like a positive, hence dignified, use of Saturn.

Here Pluto sits on the 2nd house cusp. The science is about the money. Learning how the environment works so that man can get more of what he wants. What I found particularly interesting was the Moon in Leo. This configuration might seem strange at first – but consider. Leo is a barren sign – and it's hot and dry in nature. I have mentioned how frequently the placement of the Moon shows what people are really concerned about: drought!

As a result of the Carnegie study, the Desert Laboratory was opened in Tucson in 1903 in order to study these water adaptation applications rigorously. The Ecological Society of America was formed in 1915, just after Pluto went into Cancer.

NATAL CHART
Sun enters Ari 3-21-1902
March 21, 1902
8:16:41 AM
Washington, D.C.
38N53'42" 77W02'12"
Standard Time
Time Zone: 5 hours West
Tropical Regiomontanus

Chart 21. Sun enters Aries 1902, Washington, DC

Day of ♀	Hour of ☽
Last Hr ☿	- 1 mins
Next Hr ♄	+59 mins

FIXED STARS	
☿☌ Sadalmelik	0°42's
☽☌ Regulus	0°28's
☿☌ Fomalhaut	0°13's
♅☌ Rasalhague	0°11's
♀☌ Sadalsuud	0°59'a

Hs	Alm. (Dor)
1	♀
2	☿
3	♃
4	☽
5	☉
6	♄
7	♂
8	♃
9	♄
10	♄
11	♄
12	☉

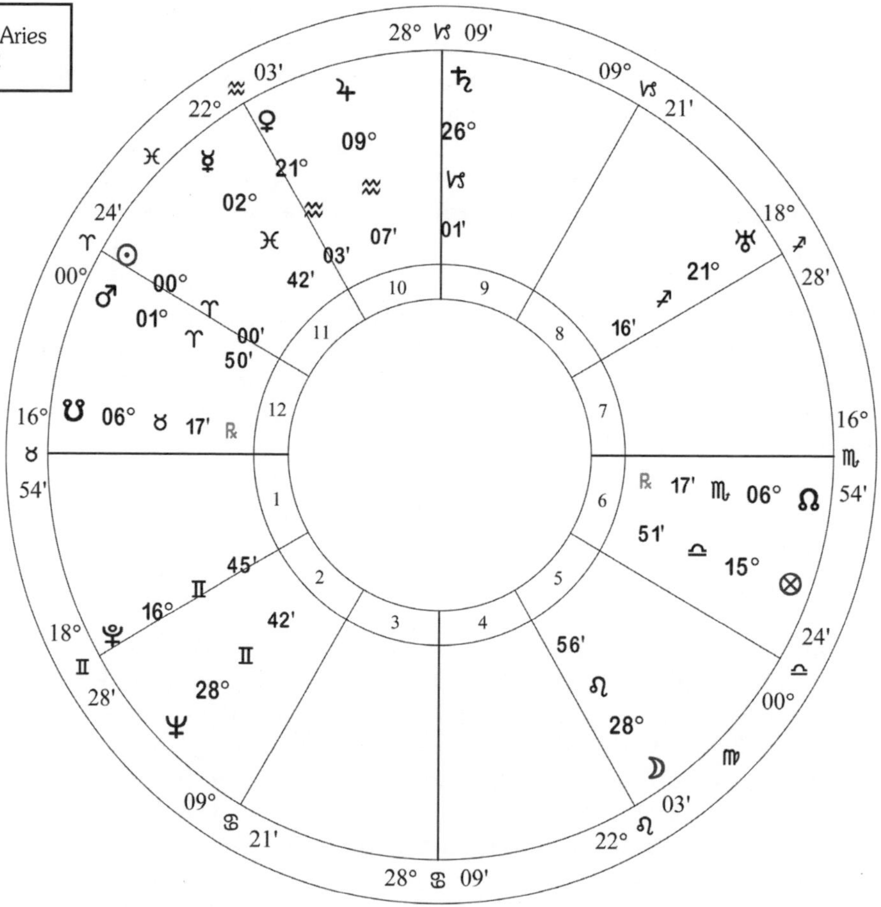

ESSENTIAL DIGNITIES (Dorothean)

Pl	Ruler	Exalt	Tripl	Term	Face	Detri	Fall	Score
☉	♂	☉ +	☉ +	♃	♂	♀	♄	+7
☽	☉	--	☉	♂	♂	♄	--	- 5 P
☿	♃	♀	♀	♀	♄	☿ -	☿ -	- 14 P
♀	♄	--	♄ m	♃	☽	☉	--	- 5 P
♂	♂ +	☉	☉	♃	♂ +	♀	♄	+6
♃	♄	--	♄	☿	♀	☉	--	- 5 P
♄	♄ +	♂	♀ m	♄ +	☉	☽	♃	+7
☊	♂	--	♀	♃	♂	♀	☽	--
⊗	♀	♄	♄	♃	♄	♂	☉	--
As	♀	☽	♀	♃	☽	♂	--	--
Mc	♄	♂	♀	♄	☉	☽	♃	--
☋	♀	☽	♀	♀	☿	♂	--	--

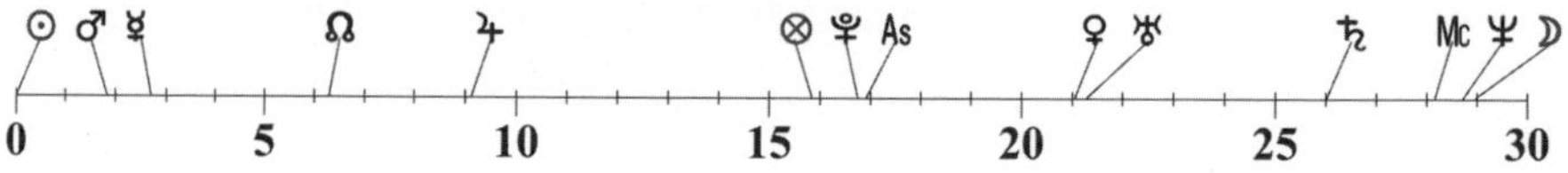

Pluto in Libra (1971-1984)

As I have already indicated, the conservation movement, which inspired the scientific work of the Pluto in Gemini period, was substantially different from the environmental movement of the period of Pluto in Virgo. Why had things changed so much?

One simple matter: the world population in 1900 was 1.6 billion: it was more than double that at 3.7 billion in 1970. It has taken roughly one hundred-fifty years to double the population from the 1900 mark: it would then take less than seventy years to double again. This kind of exponential growth is unsustainable in the long run, but in the shorter run, *when* critical mass is reached, is hard to predict. Although people in the developed world were not feeling the crunch, there is no question that substantial developments in energy use and transportation had to happen for this doubling to occur. However, to the end user in a developed country, this vast up-tick in infrastructure was invisible.

What allowed this infrastructural change was yet another of the quiet revolutions of Pluto in Virgo. It was the steadily increased usage of transistors and semiconductors. Discovered in 1947, the transistor utilizes semiconductors like germanium to mimic the activity of vacuum tubes. The transistor is much smaller, lasts longer, and uses much less electricity to run. The first computers used vacuum tubes – as did earlier radios. The number of vacuum tubes necessary to create useful computing "work" was enormous – and so the computers were gigantic and very temperamental, because a vacuum tube could blow at any time. They were also less robust in capability than many modern cell phones, let alone laptops. The average astrology program today is vastly superior to the software that NASA used to put men on the Moon.

In 1957 (think: Pluto in Virgo), the integrated circuit was invented. This allows multiple transistors to be designed directly on a single circuit board, again substantially reducing electricity and weight, while increasing performance and speed. These inventions saw mass development and distribution during the period of Pluto in Virgo. Growing up in this period, I remember *Danny Dunn and the Homework Machine*,[149] an early children's book about computers. In 1973, when I purchased my first electronic calculator, that handheld device was more powerful than Danny Dunn's behemoth.

Just as hardware was changing, so was software. The early coding of computers was exclusively at the hardware level, known as assembly language. In 1953, work began on FORTRAN, a compiled language that achieved commercial release in 1956, just as Pluto was changing signs.

Through the period of Pluto in Virgo, computers would go from expensive curiosities found only in advanced laboratories at AT&T, the government, and a few large universities, to machines common in most universities and mid-size companies. The personal computer was an invention of the period of Pluto in Libra, with the technology proliferating under Pluto in water sign Scorpio.

During Pluto in Virgo, once computer time was available for academics on a more regular basis, research programs could be established which utilized the number-crunching capabilities of these tools. Disciplines like meteorology began to develop modeling that was vastly more sophisticated than anything that had been remotely possible with hand computations. It was with this background that **systems theory** began to develop in earnest. Systems theory was applied in ecology early in the 20th century: it is an attempt to study complex systems. Ecologists were confronted with the problem of how species within an environment interact, and they attempted to build models for this, based on field observation. Later, it was realized that the same logic that was applied to ecosystems analysis could be utilized in many fields that were confronted with complex interrelationships. This work often generated cyclic theories, as in the kinds of population growth and crash models that we examined briefly in Chapter 2.

Thus, while many of the premises of systems theory, and its related term cybernetics, actually go back to the period of Pluto in Gemini, it wasn't until the period of Pluto in Libra that computing had hit the critical mass for these ideas to be applied in a meaningful way.

We can identify two Libran themes relating to the environment for this transit of Pluto. One is the theme of systems theory, and its specific application to the environment through the Club of Rome and *The Limits to Growth*. The second theme is that laws and administrative practices continued to emerge as a result of the political action associated with Earth Day and the nascent movement.

The Limits to Growth

We have seen that overpopulation was a significant theme of the environmental movement from the first. In these works on overpopulation, the line of argument generally followed Thomas Malthus: that population growth was growing geometrically (which was true), while agricultural production could *temporarily* grow geometrically because of inventions, but overall could only grow arithmetically. Even then, arithmetic growth of agriculture required additional land for either pasture or crop production, and it was becoming obvious that all the best land had already been taken. This was precisely the premise of the book, *Famine 1975!*

– a provocative title, but a very popular work of the period.[150] The authors' arguments are laid out very well in the section headings:

> *Part 1. Inevitability of Famine in the Hungry Nations*
>
> *Part 2. Nor Can the Resources and Talents of the Developed World Avert Famine from the Hungry Nations*
>
> *Part 3. Potential Role of the United States During the Time of Famines*

Part 1 presents a classical Malthusian argument: that between 1965 and 2000, the world's population will increase from 3 billion to 6 billion (pretty accurate, as the 6 billion mark was actually achieved in 1999), while the world's arable land would only increase by 5% (actually, this was optimistic).[151] So, their argument went, if there were already hungry nations, then hungry nations would turn into starving nations. Given that their two primary statistics – population growth and arable land – were both pretty accurate, then why wasn't there famine in 1975? Their chapter, *"'Something' Will Turn Up to Avert Famine – or Will it?"* turned out to be the key. Some of their supposed solutions read more like science fiction than anything which has been seriously applied in the last forty years. Yet they do hit upon a number of the factors which actually explain why their bottom line prediction didn't turn out right: changing agricultural practices, irrigation, and fertilizers. Still, they underestimated their impacts. They also missed the use of pesticides, fungicides, and changing distributions of food crops adapted for new conditions. Go out into a corn field today and it looks a lot different from one of forty years ago. Heavy intensity modern agriculture really has increased crop yields substantially. These were changes that, frankly, could never have been predicted by anyone in the authors' time period.

The authors were not statisticians. One was an agronomist; the other, a foreign service officer. While they were out in the field observing the signs that they reported on, others were beginning to model multiple factors together. The best known of these, which actually represented work bridging the transition between Pluto in Virgo and Pluto in Libra, was Donella Meadows' work, *The Limits to Growth; A Report for the Club of Rome's project on the predicament of mankind*, published in 1972.[152] In this work, a series of computer modeling experiments were performed that examined population growth, agricultural productivity, natural resource utilization, and pollution, and how any of those factors could become a limiting factor on the sustainability of the human race under the current patterns of growth and resource utilization. Many of these models predicted a future crash in population, because overstepping a limit could produce a catastrophic result.

This work was extremely influential and extremely controversial at the same time. For one, it spawned a whole series of response books, whether supporting, challenging, or analyzing further.[153] We will examine these concepts further, but let's look at Chart 22 for the Aries Ingress of 1972, to see what astrological patterns may enlighten this discussion.

What we see immediately is that this was the time of a Saturn-Pluto trine – and what better signature for the limits (Saturn) to growth (Pluto)! In the uproar over the release of this study many people missed one of the essential qualities of that trine. The authors were saying: our model may not be complete, there may be other factors, but eventually, this problem will bite us on the nose! Their intent was not to be missionaries of doom, but to allow people to make informed choices that could thereby prevent the catastrophic melt-downs that could happen. But the Saturn trine Pluto was not the only feature of this ingress. And of course, this book was hardly the only event for the year.

Meanwhile, the Vietnam War was still going on, Nixon was President and running successfully for reelection, and the Watergate break-in occurred. The massacre of Israeli athletes happened at the Munich Olympics. The last Apollo Moon landing was successful. The 10th house ruler, Saturn, has dignity, and so Nixon still made a strong showing that year. One would have to take the signature of Watergate to be the Sun in the 12th house, in a partile opposition to Pluto.

The chart for Washington was only a few degrees different on the angles than the chart for New York shown. However, while the New York chart had 2 Taurus on the Ascendant, thus becoming the only chart for the year, the Washington chart had 26 Aries. The Watergate break-in occurred before the Summer Solstice.

I have included the Aries Ingress for Munich shown as Chart 23. Here, a fixed sign is on the Ascendant, indicating this is the one chart for the year. Remember, by definition, all the planetary positions will be identical – it's the house placements and rulerships that vary by location. This year was a big one, by almost anyone's definition. What was it that made this year so major?

We can begin with the partile Sun-Pluto opposition. Of course, our cosmobiological friends would quite rightly note that this is the world axis. Classical does not explicitly mention zero of the cardinals as critical points: but then those are the very positions where the Sun's ingress is delineated. But how rare is it actually to have a ptolemaic hard aspect of the Sun and Pluto at the Aries Ingress? I went back to 1700 and forward to 2060, and the only other instance that I found was for 1915 – certainly another "big" year.

NATAL CHART
Sun enters Ari 3-20-1972
March 20, 1972
7:21:26 AM
New York, New York
40N42'51" 74W00'23"
Standard Time
Time Zone: 5 hours West
Tropical Regiomontanus

Chart 22. Sun enters Aries 1972, New York, NY and Washington, DC

Day of ☽	Hour of ♄
Last Hr ☽	- 18 mins
Next Hr ♃	+42 mins

FIXED STARS	
♀☌ Menkar	0°55's
☽☌ Aldebaran	0°14's
♄☌ Mirfak	0°02's
♂☌ Algol	0°09'a

Hs	Alm. (Dor)
1	♀
2	☿
3	☽
4	☽
5	☉
6	☿
7	♂
8	♃
9	♀♄
10	♂♄
11	♄
12	♃

ESSENTIAL DIGNITIES (Dorothean)

Pl	Ruler	Exalt	Tripl	Term	Face	Detri	Fall	Score
☉	♂	☉ +	☉ +	♃	♂	♀	♄	+7
☽	☿	☊	♄	♃	♃	♃	--	- 5 P
☿	♂	☉	☉	☿ +	☉	♀	♄	+2
♀	♀ +	☽	♀ +	☿	☽	♂	--	+8
♂	♀	☽	♀	♄	♄	♂ -	--	- 10 P
♃	♄	♂	♀	☿	♃ +	☽	♃ -	- 3
♄	☿	☊	♄ +	☿	♃	♃	--	+3
☊	♄	--	♄	♄	♀	☉	--	--
⊗	☽	♃	♀	♃	☿	♄	♂	--
As	♀	☽	♀	♀	☿	♂	--	--
Mc	♄	♂	♀	♃	♂	☽	♃	--
☋	☉	--	☉	♄	♄	♄	--	--

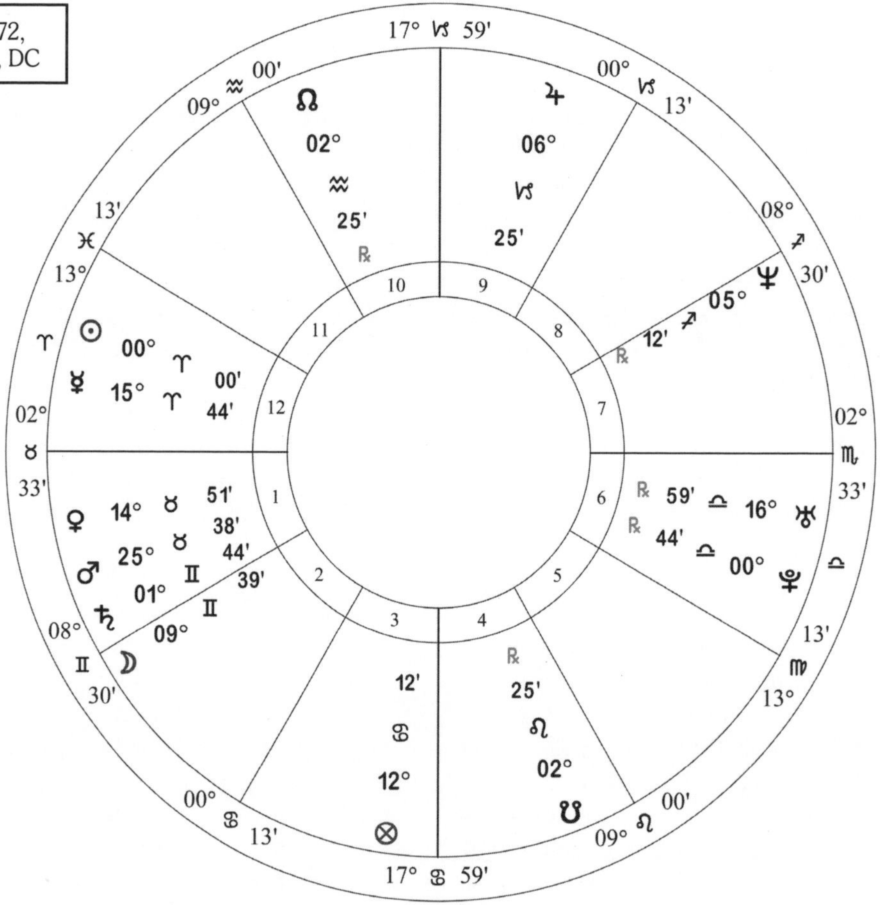

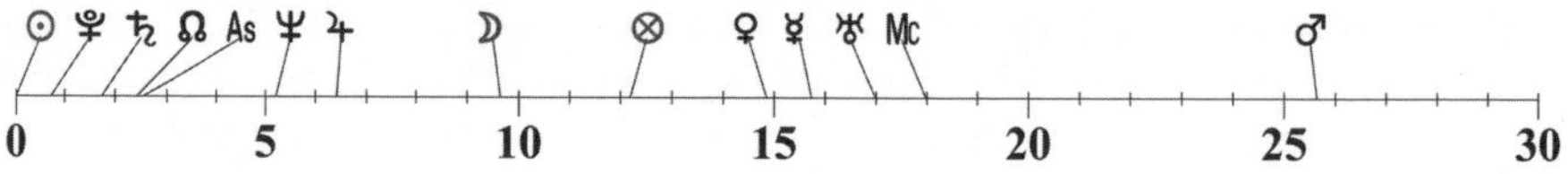

NATAL CHART
Sun enters Ari 3-20-1972
March 20, 1972
1:21:26 PM
Munich, Germany
48 N 08 11 E 34
Standard Time
Time Zone: 1 hours East
Tropical Regiomontanus

Chart 23. Sun enters Aries 1972, Munich, Germany

Day of ☽	Hour of ☿
Last Hr ♀	- 60 mins
Next Hr ☽	+ 0 mins

FIXED STARS	
♀☌ Menkar	0°55's
☽☌ Aldebaran	0°14's
♄☌ Mirfak	0°02's
♂☌ Algol	0°09'a

Hs	Alm. (Dor)
1	☉
2	☉
3	☿
4	♄
5	♂
6	♄
7	♄
8	♄
9	♀
10	☉
11	♀
12	♃

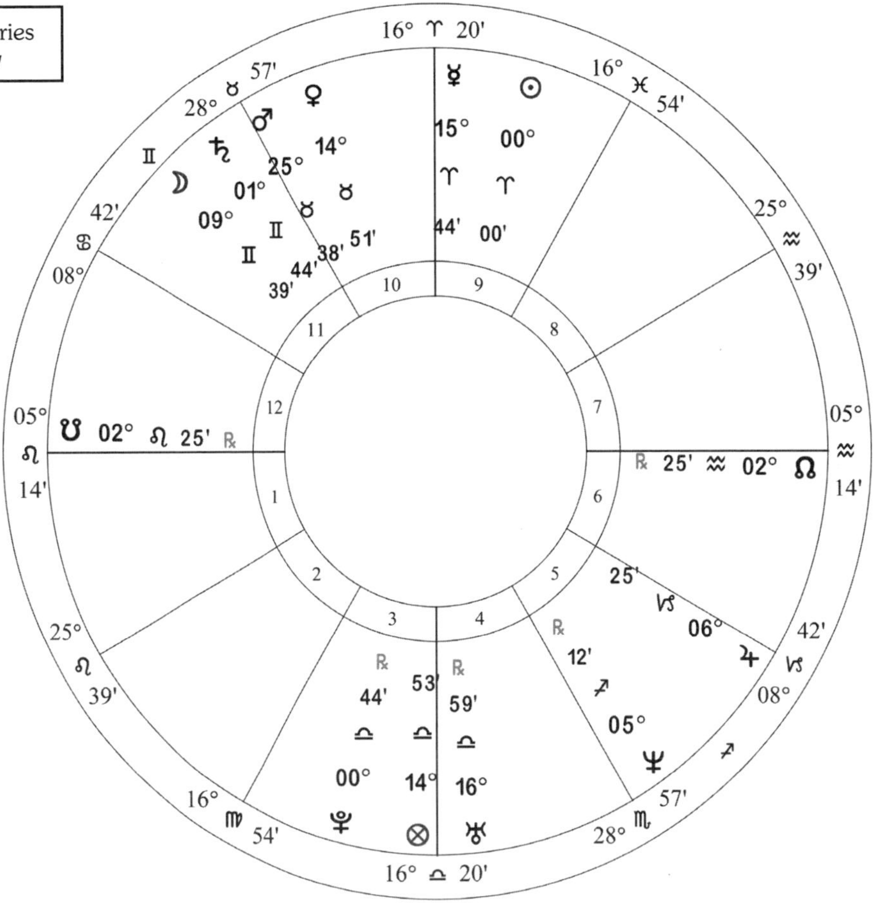

ESSENTIAL DIGNITIES (Dorothean)								
Pl	Ruler	Exalt	Tripl	Term	Face	Detri	Fall	Score
☉	♂	☉ +	☉ +	♃	♂	♀	♄	+7
☽	☿	☊	♄	♃	♃	♃	--	- 5 P
☿	♂	☉	☉	☿ +	☉	♀	♄	+2
♀	♀ +	☽	♀ +	☿	☽	♂	--	+8
♂	♀	☽	♀	♄	♄	♂ -	--	- 10 P
♃	♄	♂	♀	☿	♃ +	☽	♃ -	- 3
♄	☿	☊	♄ +	☿	♃	♃	--	+3
☊	♄	--	♄	♄	♀	☉	--	--
⊗	♀	♄	♄	♃	♄	♂	☉	--
As	☉	--	☉	♄	♄	♄	--	--
Mc	♂	☉	☉	☿	☉	♀	♄	--
☋	☉	--	☉	♄	♄	♄	--	--

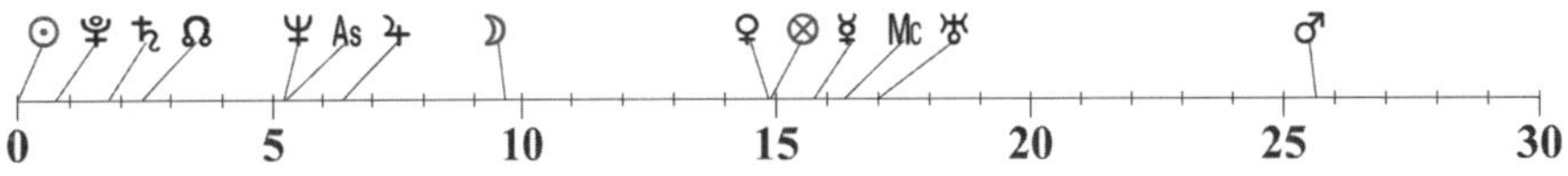

But that's not all. Mars was on Algol, one of the more nasty – and violent – fixed stars. Mars is the natural ruler of athletes – this is an unfortunate position, to say the least. And Mars ruled the 10th house in Munich – the reputation of the city and the Olympics resting on the athletes – which of course, it should. The violent nature of that particular placement took precedent over the games.

For Washington that year, Mars *and* Saturn were Co-Almutens of the 10th house cusp – and that was part of the problem. Mars in Detriment at Algol – that's way too vicious as an appropriate sign for a democratic leader – it's more the symbol of an arrogant autocrat. And Saturn coming to the opposition of Neptune? With the Sun in the 12th? There are some huge arguments for deception here – which we saw with Watergate.

However, there is still one more meaning for that Mars at Algol. Remember from Chapter 3 that Mars traditionally rules petroleum? The Arab oil embargo began in February 1973, still under the astrological year 1972. Recall that the Washington D.C. Aries Ingress had a cardinal sign rising, so all four ingress charts are needed to interpret the year. Therefore, to interpret the embargo, we need to examine the Capricorn Ingress for 1972, Chart 24.

In that ingress, Mars rules the Ascendant, and it is dignified, but in the 7th house. Recall the meaning of the ruler of a house in another house: Mars is controlled by the 7th here – the open enemies. Because of the U.S.A.'s support for Israel, the Arab countries tend to be seen as enemies, whether this should be true or not. So here is a stunning confirmation of the "promise" of trouble with the Mars conjunct strangling Algol in the Aries Ingress chart!

We may also note that Saturn, Ruler of the 10th, and thus President Nixon, was retrograde in Gemini: Saturn has Triplicity there, but the retrograde declares it to be imbecilic. That imbecility is not rendered. Further, with Jupiter in Fall also in the 10th house, this provides no support for Nixon's position, which is viewed as weak. The public is the Moon in Cancer, conjunct the South Node: the public is strong, but seriously debilitated, and placed at the 4th house cusp. This was a very up-front taste of limits – and people were pretty angry about it. Nixon declared the need for energy independence, and the Alaska oil pipeline was subsequently approved by Congress. But Nixon's weakness was played out primarily through the Watergate scandal.

But going back to *The Limits to Growth*, with all the political skulduggery going on, how did this study even make it through the chatter? Because make it through it did.[154] And suddenly, the expression "the limits to __" made it into the popular jargon, providing yet one more model of a scientific theory that was immediately transitioned into a metaphor for human activity, just as Blavatsky had applied evolution to spiritual growth, and expressions like "industrial ecology" became commonplace.

I believe it happened precisely because these conclusions fit with what people were seeing – the lens that was in place at this time. Of course, the Arab oil embargo brought resource limitation home to people at a very gut level. The concept of "limit" had become tenable – and even inevitable. But it would have been very easy for Americans to see this strictly as a foreign policy problem to be solved, not as a new reality which would require adjustments in one's thinking.

I believe that the Club of Rome study was in exactly the same relationship astrologically and sociologically as the theory of evolution was in the 19th century – and the furor was analogous. Consider –

NATAL CHART
Sun enters Cap 12-21-1972
December 21, 1972
1:12:55 PM
Washington, D.C.
38N53'42" 77W02'12"
Standard Time
Time Zone: 5 hours West
Tropical Regiomontanus

Chart 24. Sun enters Capricorn 1972, Washington, D.C.

Day of ♃	Hour of ♃
Last Hr ♄	- 20 mins
Next Hr ♂	+26 mins

FIXED STARS	
☿☌ Antares	0°47's
♂☌ Agena	0°32's
♃☌ Vega	0°30's
♄☌ Rigel	0°24's
Mc☌ Vega	0°21's
♃☌ Rukbat	0°49'a
Mc☌ Rukbat	0°58'a

Hs	Alm. (Dor)
1	☉
2	☿
3	☿
4	☽
5	☉
6	☿
7	♄
8	♃
9	♃
10	♂♄
11	♄
12	♀♃

ESSENTIAL DIGNITIES (Dorothean)

Pl	Ruler	Exalt	Tripl	Term	Face	Detri	Fall	Score
☉	♄	♂	♀ m	♀	♃	☽	♃	- 5 P
☽	☽ +	♃	♀	☿	☿ m	♄	♂	+5
☿	♃	☋	☉	♀	☽ m	☿ -	--	- 10 P
♀	♃	☋	☉ m	♃	☿	☿	--	- 5 P
♂	♂ +	--	♀	☿	♀	♀	☽	+5
♃	♄	♂	♀	♃ +	♂	☽	♃ -	- 2
♄	☿	☊	♄ +	♀	♂	♃	--	+3
☊	♄	♂	♀	♃	♂	☽	♃	--
⊗	♂	--	♀	♀	☉	♀	☽	--
As	♂	☉	☉	♄	♀	♀	♄	--
Mc	♄	♂	♀	♃	♂	☽	♃	--
☋	☽	♃	♀	☿	☿	♄	♂	--

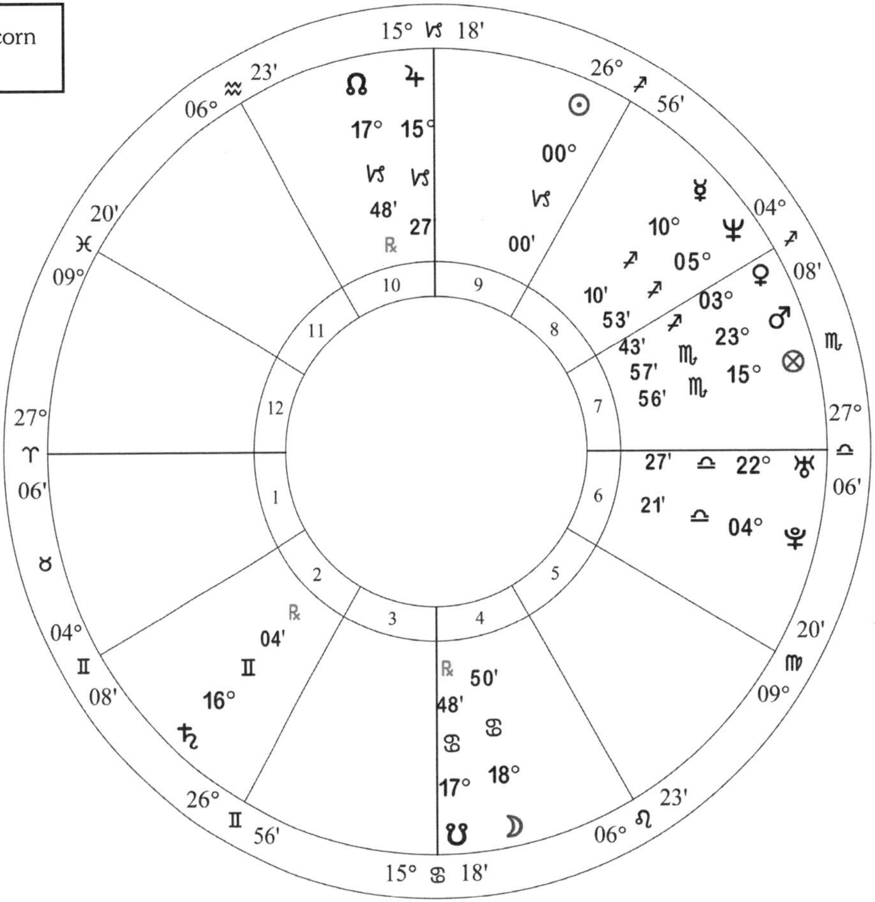

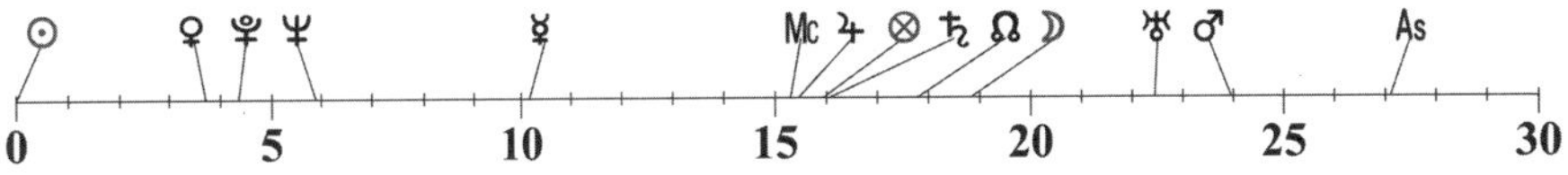

- In both cases, the research supporting the idea was amassed during an Earth Pluto cycle. And quite apart from the work which preceded the publication, the element of Pluto affects the kinds of ideas and ideals of any era. Neither Earth nor Air is especially religious in nature. The practicality of the Earth signs is definitely in the here and now: their interests are secular interests. The Air signs have often been called the social signs: their interests are within the human sphere. Theory and Justice – these are both Air concepts. A theory is not an absolute, but an attempt to model *reality*. It's an Air extension to an Earth construct. And Justice – while we can certainly talk about Divine Justice, I think most of us would prefer to see it in the here and now.

- In both cases, the scientific theory (although theory may be too strong a word for the Limits to Growth) runs right against conventional monotheistic dogma. Both are fundamental challenges to the prerogatives of an omnipotent God, or at least to the stories recounted in the sacred scripture of that God.

Darwin presented a view that did not require divine intervention to create the diversity of nature. It did not mesh with the creation story of Genesis, and most flagrantly, it suggested no special creation for Man. And yet, most mainstream Christian religions coped. However, the twin threats to literalism presented by evolution and textual criticism, arguably caused the division into mainstream and evangelical/ fundamentalist Protestant denominations in the U.S. The mainstream churches concluded that a literal interpretation of the Old Testament was not a necessary prerequisite to Christian faith, and the evangelicals and fundamentalists concluded otherwise.[155]

Darwin's theory came at roughly the same time that geologists were pushing back the age of the Earth – first by millions of years, then by billions. These were the greatest threats to religious precepts since Kepler, Galileo, and Copernicus. Yet, then, religion also adapted. But this has never been an easy process. And the difficulty can be seen through the fact that now virtually all Christians and Jews accept heliocentricism, but there are still many Christians, some Jews, and some Muslims who do not accept evolution. Before this begins to look like a serious roadblock to evolution, it's worth considering that while it's still possible to find new books being written to support the literal truth of geocentricism, the Catholic Church accepted it only in 1757 – roughly two hundred years after it was proposed. We have not yet lived two hundred years after Darwin's theory.

Then, along comes *The Limits to Growth*. Already, "Man's Special Place" in creation had been challenged. Man, after all, had been declared an animal. *The* Limits to Growth is mostly a much tamer religious challenge, except that it directly goes against that famous admonition in Genesis that I already referred to in Chapter 2 that commands man to be fruitful.

It's one thing to say that the story of creation is a myth or a story. It's another thing to come up against a specific admonition that has been stated as a quotation from God. This brings up the troubling question: is any command from God absolute for eternity? And if it's not, how do we determine when it no longer applies?

What was often lost in the reactions to *The Limits to Growth* was what the authors hoped to achieve by publishing their study. They were not pretending to have the final answer. They were simply stating that there are real constraints to our material existence, because we run up against material obstacles. Yes, we may be able to think our way around some of them. And yes, we may not know the contours or even the existence of all of them. And is it prudent in the long run to act as if we will always be able to find yet another solution? The Club of Rome report was intended to make us think about these limitations, and thereby make it easier to *make choices* about what we do about this. How Libran. This study was not meant to be depressing, but to show us what we are up against – and also to give us choices, by allowing people to conceptualize the problem before the brink occurs.

Ultimately, there are only so many atoms on earth, so many square miles or hectares of land, only so much water, so much soil, so much iron, so much oil, so much calcium. We know of no natural process that will increase these building blocks,[156] and we have no precedent for God intervening post-Creation and adding to the current stockpile. So there *are* absolute limits. What the Club of Rome study did was show that the *timeline* to those limits may not be so far away that we can act as if we don't have to care.

And once again, many people heard the call. This study was stated in a way which is highly appealing to a secular perspective, but also to a religious perspective that has only truly developed in the last few decades: one that takes the Genesis commandment and transforms it into a call for stewardship, not rulership.

In the U.S.A., the period of Pluto in Libra ran from the Presidency of Richard Nixon to the first term of Ronald Reagan, with the Presidencies of Gerald Ford and Jimmy Carter sandwiched in between. Throughout Nixon's presidency, after Earth Day, a whole series of environmental laws and policies was passed by Congress, and most were signed by Nixon and then Ford. These included the Federal Water Pollution Control Act, the Ocean Dumping Act, the Marine Mammal Protection Act, Toxic Substances Control Act, Endangered Species Act, the Safe Drinking Water Act, the Hazardous Waste Transportation Act, the Resource Conservation and Recovery Act, and the Federal Land Policy Management Act. From a legislative standpoint (Pluto in Libra again?) this certainly doesn't look like a slow-down in interest about things environmental – paralleling the developments during Pluto in Gemini.

This actually supports a belief that I have had for a long time: that conservation is a topic that actually may belong better among political conservatives than it does among liberals. Theodore Roosevelt was no wild-eyed liberal, despite how some Tea Partiers are choosing to see him. The idea of conservation is to *conserve* for the future: for our children, grandchildren, etc. This is also to say that the mere fact that we can ignore this is a matter of greed – and greed was one of the Seven Deadly Sins.

The passage of environmental laws under the Nixon and Ford Administrations illustrates this concept. It was not until Reagan that the Republican Party was realigned to the point that these old conservative interests became unwelcome amidst the newer, brasher, more evangelically-centered power base that took prosperity consciousness as a tenet of Christian faith, choosing to ignore Jesus's "eye of the needle" parable about wealth.[157]

Under Carter's presidency, environmental legislation and other activity continued. But the biggest environmental events during Carter's presidency were not positive ones: they were the Love Canal disaster, and Three Mile Island.

Love Canal and Three Mile Island

For Love Canal, I have shown the Cancer 1978 Ingress as Chart 25, because the Aries Ingress for 1978 had Libra Rising, and the story broke in the Summer of 1978. Here we see a T-square that is right on the angles, hence, a big story for sure. This T-square also activates the July 4, 1776 Sun. The land is given by the Ruler of the 4th, Saturn – which is in Detriment. There are two qualities of Saturn here that are especially important. First, there is the debility itself: the land is debilitated. Being in a fixed sign, the problem is one of long standing. Toxic dumping at the site had begun in the 1920s. The Moon (the people) in Detriment at the 4th house cusp square this Pluto gives an especially noxious quality to the problem.

Just as the news of the Love Canal was dying down, the next scare arrived: the nuclear accident at Three Mile Island, Chart 26. Coincidentally or not, just a couple weeks before Three Mile Island occurred, *The China Syndrome*, a movie about a nuclear meltdown was released. And then came Three Mile Island, just a few days after the Aries Ingress for 1979.

At first blush, this chart doesn't look as bad as the previous Cancer Ingress. The conditions here are completely different. Love Canal festered as a toxic dump for over thirty years, and then was exacerbated in the 1950s by knowingly building a school on top of it. Three Mile Island was the U.S.A.'s first exposure to the reality that no technology involving intrinsically dangerous materials can ever be considered 100% safe.

But this is still a dangerous chart. Observe the Sun at the Nadir. Again, how frequent is this? Taking an orb of 2 degrees, the answer is: not very. From 1700-2060, it has occurred or will occur four times: 1880, 1913, 1979, and 2012. These four charts are shown here. So our first question is: is the Sun at the Nadir a dangerous placement by itself? The answer is: possibly. Let's consider what happened in these years. The charts are shown in Chart 27.

1880 is certainly an interesting case. It was an election year, and the winner was James Garfield. Remember that these charts run from Aries to Aries: with the U.S. electoral system, the voting and the Inauguration *always* take place under the same Aries year. The 1880 chart presages a dangerous time for the president elected, with the Sun at the Nadir, Mercury ruling the 10th stationing retrograde, and Jupiter ruling the Ascendant, at the Nadir, and conjunct the fixed star Scheat – and Garfield was assassinated. Also notice the nodal axis across the 2nd-8th cusps of the chart. Mercury, ruler of the 10th in the 4th square the Moon in the 8th completes the nastiness of this ingress!

Our next example is 1913, which didn't turn out to be a horrible year – or even an *especially* memorable one. Wilson was inaugurated before this chart took effect. Here, Venus, Ruler of the President, is in Taurus, which looks a *lot* stronger! However, if we take into account that Wilson would ultimately suffer a debilitating disease *while in office*, perhaps this chart isn't so good after all. There was a fatal flood in Ohio right around the ingress that killed 400, so perhaps that is part of the story as well.

As for 2012, the angles are a precise repeat of 1880. 29 degrees on the MC does not always produce death in office. For the four assassinations, there has been at least one planet in the 8th house: a small sample, but suggestive. In 2012, there is no 8th house planet. But one other event of 1880 may be relevant: 1880 was the year that the U.S.A. signed a treaty with China restricting Chinese immigration. With both China and immigration reform in the news, either or both of those are certainly possibilities.

NATAL CHART
Sun enters Can 6-21-1978
June 21, 1978
2:09:35 PM
Washington, D.C.
38N53'42" 77W02'12"
Daylight Saving Time
Time Zone: 5 hours West
Tropical Regiomontanus

Chart 25. Sun enters Cancer 1978, Washington, D.C.

Day of ☿ Hour of ♀
Last Hr ☉ - 60 mins
Next Hr ☿ +14 mins

Hs	Alm. (Dor)
1	♄
2	♂
3	♃
4	♂ ♄
5	♀
6	♀
7	☉
8	♀
9	☿
10	☽
11	☿
12	☿

FIXED STARS	
Mc♂Sirius	0°02'a
♉♂Alhena	0°04'a
♃♂Sirius	0°09'a
♄♂Alphard	0°37'a
♅♂Alphecca	0°41'a
♆♂Rasalgethi	0°44'a
Mc♂Canopus	0°54'a

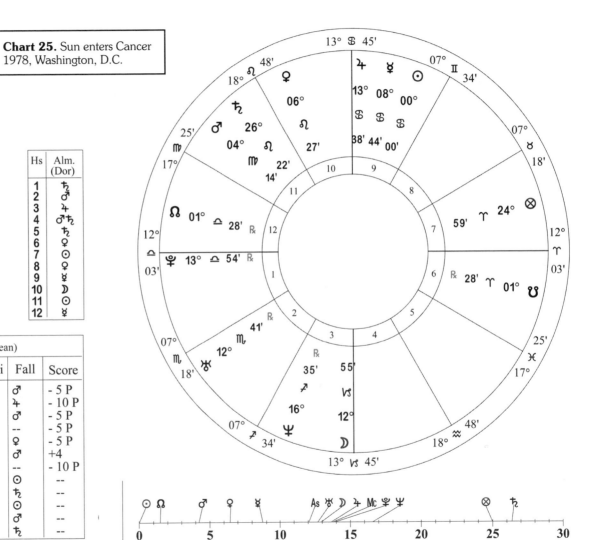

ESSENTIAL DIGNITIES (Dorothean)

Pl	Ruler	Exalt	Tripl	Term	Face	Detri	Fall	Score
☉	☽	♃	♀ m	♂	♀	♄	♂	- 5 P
☽	♄	♂	♀	♃	♂	☽ -	♃	- 10 P
☿	☽	♃	♀	♃ m	♀	♄	♂	- 5 P
♀	☉	--	☉ m	☿	♄	♄	--	- 5 P
♂	☿	☿	♀	♃ m	☿	♃	♂	- 5 P
♃	☽	♃ +	♀	☿	☿ m	♄	♂	+4
♄	☉	--	☉	♂	♂	♄ -	--	- 10 P
☊	♀	♄	♄	♄	☽	♂	☉	--
⊗	♂	☉	☉	♂	♀	♀	♄	--
As	♀	♄	♄	♃	♄	♂	☉	--
Mc	☽	♃	♀	☿	☿	♄	♂	--
☋	♂	☉	☉	♃	♂	♀	♄	--

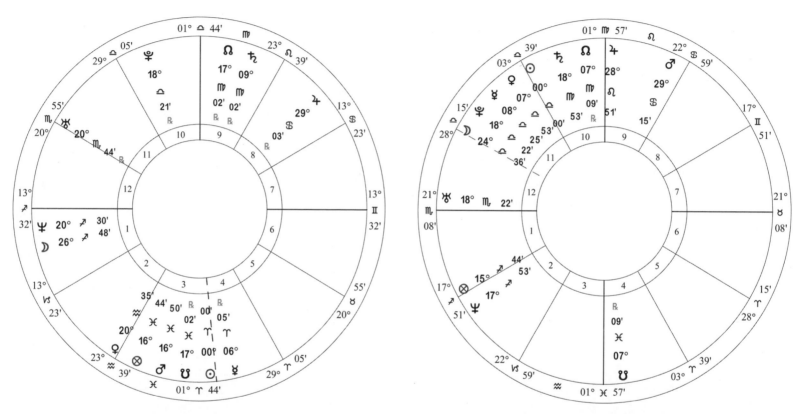

Sun enters Ari 3-21-1979
March 21, 1979
12:21:57 AM
Washington, D.C.
38N53'42" 77W02'12"
Standard Time
Time Zone: 5 hours West
Tropical Regiomontanus
NATAL CHART

Chart 26. Sun enters Aries and Libra 1979, Washington D.C.

Sun enters Lib 9-23-1979
September 23, 1979
11:16:25 AM
Washington, D.C.
38N53'42" 77W02'12"
Daylight Saving Time
Time Zone: 5 hours West
Tropical Regiomontanus
NATAL CHART

Immigration, it should be remembered *is* a sustainability issue. It has been noted for some time that immigration to the U.S. is a significant component of the U.S.'s population growth rate: and also, that fertility rates among immigrants exceed native-born citizens.[158]

But back to 1979. The President is not especially strong, being Venus in Aquarius – but he's not in physical danger either. Venus is partile square Uranus, right at the 12th house cusp. Something sudden can cause problems for the president. Combine with that the conjunction of Mars and South Node which is dangerous: two malefics conjunct is seldom a good thing. But is this Three Mile Island, or the taking of the U.S. embassy in Iran, which occurred in the second half of the year?

Pluto is generally given at least co-rulership of radioactivity. And so, here we have the first publicly disclosed leak of radioactivity on U.S. soil with Pluto in the 10th. But overall, this chart doesn't scream radioactivity. I think the more prominent picture is the complacency about being able to produce 100% containment of toxic materials when part of the means for doing so is boring and repetitive for the watchers: precisely the conditions that numb the mind and result in inattention, with Neptune Rising.

But really: how bad was this? Honestly, I have to say that this chart does not look as bad as the year before, at least from an environmental standpoint. Did the extensive coverage of Love Canal dull the impact of Three Mile Island? In a sense, it must have, because only a few years later, the Reagan administration was calling for an expansion of nuclear power – a proposal that would have been political suicide if the impact of Three Mile Island had been as serious as it seemed to many environmentalists at the time.

But we should also examine the Iranian hostage situation, because that grabbed all headlines once it occurred, and one would be on safe grounds to conclude that it cost Carter the presidency. Here, we need to examine both the Aries and the Libra Ingresses. The chart for the year does show danger, with the ruler of the Ascendant in the 8th house. Jupiter is imbecilic by retrogradation: stupid mistakes will be made. But where?

For mistakes, look to the malefics. Saturn is in the 9th: foreign policy, or foreign matters, or perhaps religion. Mars is opposite by sign but separating – but more importantly, applying to the South Node, the other malefic, in the 3rd house. Ouch. What else does Mars rule? Mars rules both the 4th and 5th houses. The 4th house is fairly straightforward: it's the sense of home. But the 5th? The 5th house rules ambassadors. This may be a fact mostly ignored, but this year is not a good one for ambassadors, and by extension, embassies.

This theme heats up in the Libra Ingress. Mars is again prominent: as Ascendant ruler, and now Mars has moved to the same degree where Jupiter was in the Aries Ingress. What for Jupiter is the sign of Exaltation is for Mars the sign of Fall – and also the ruler of the 5th house of ambassadors. The chart ruler in the 9th shows attention riveted on foreign affairs. That is what happened: foreign affairs consumed all else once this period hit.

It is ironic that the two major environmental disasters of the Pluto in Libra period occurred during the presidency of Jimmy Carter, who, of the four presidents of the Pluto in Libra period, was the most pro-environment. Of course, both were the product of decisions made and implemented years before.

Many political scientists as well as pundits have noted that Reagan's presidency marked a new era in American politics, but perhaps none so forcefully as Stephen Skowronek.[159] One

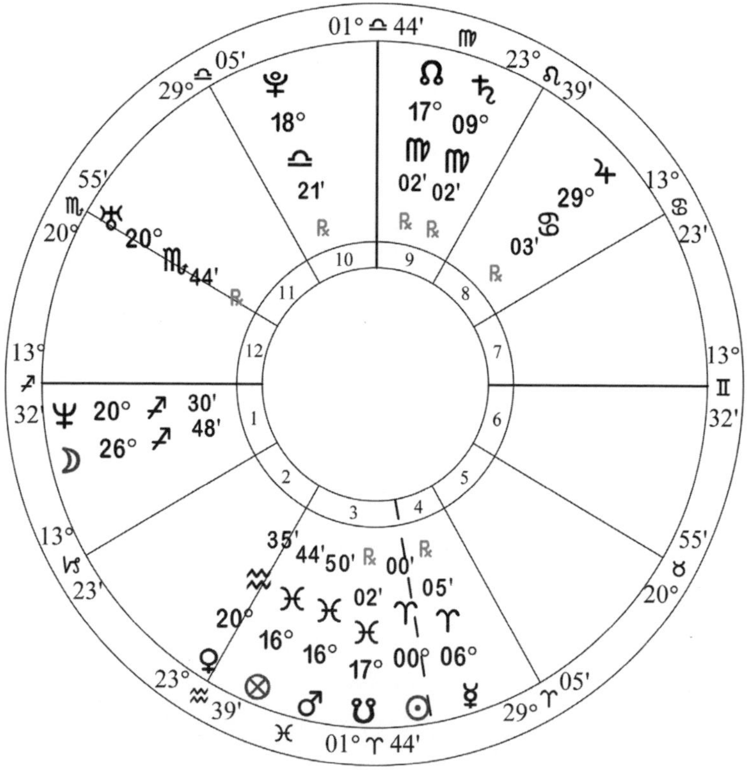

Chart 27. Sun enters Aries 1979, 1880, 1913 and 2012, Washington, D.C.

Sun enters Ari 3-21-1979
March 21, 1979 12:21:57 AM
Washington, D.C.
38N53'42" 77W02'12"
Standard Time
Time Zone: 5 hours West
Tropical Regiomontanus
NATAL CHART

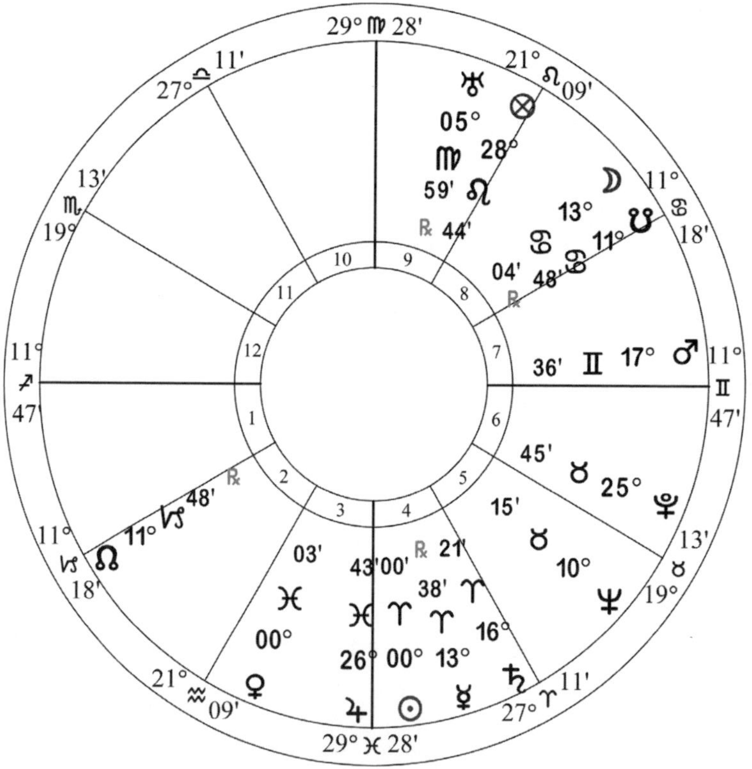

Sun enters Ari 3-20-1880
March 20, 1880 12:05:35 AM
Washington, D.C.
38N53'42" 77W02'12"
Local Mean Time
Time Zone: 0 hours West
Tropical Regiomontanus
NATAL CHART

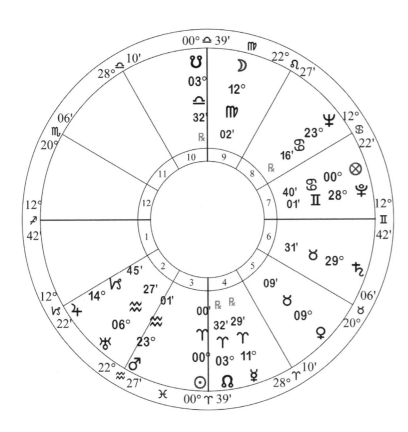

Sun enters Ari 3-21-1913
March 21, 1913 12:18:02 AM
Washington, D.C.
38N53'42" 77W02'12"
Standard Time
Time Zone: 5 hours West
Tropical Regiomontanus
NATAL CHART

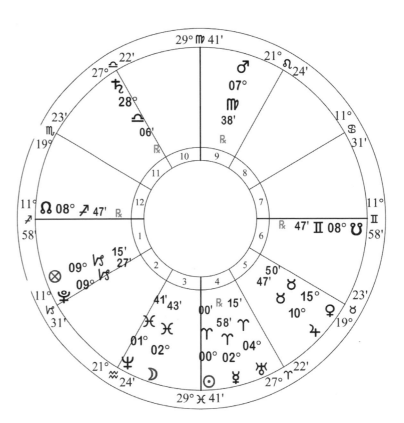

Sun enters Ari 3-20-2012
March 20, 2012 1:14:25 AM
Washington, D.C.
38N53'42" 77W02'12"
Daylight Saving Time
Time Zone: 5 hours West
Tropical Regiomontanus
NATAL CHART

could argue the case that this period from Nixon to Reagan actually represented the triumph of conservatism in American politics, as it encompassed the period of Nixon's so-called Southern Strategy. This fundamental realignment of U.S. politics involved convincing conservative Southern Democrats to move to the Republican Party and align with Western Republicans. In Nixon's own presidency, it was still not clear that this strategy would be successful, except temporarily. It was in the Reagan era that it became clear that it had worked. But what did this success mean in 1981, when Pluto was still in Libra? In 1984, Jack Kemp, who had been an early cheerleader for Reagan and the Republican victory at that time, published a compendium of his speeches from the late Seventies to the early Eighties, just as Pluto was moving into Scorpio. The first thing about the book that was fascinating was the title: *The American Idea: Ending Limits to Growth*. Embedded in this title was an implicit critique of the concept of the *Limits to Growth*.

What did Kemp actually say to refute this? Not much. He only said, "*The truth is, there are not absolute limits to growth except those obstacles government puts in the way. The human imagination is so fertile that no one can ever say all inventions have been invented, all resources have been discovered, all books have been written.*"[160] That's pretty thin as a refutation. The fact that he felt so strongly that he put this as a subtitle of the book shows how deeply the Club of Rome study had resonated. The rest of the book was stump speeches, primarily about the economy. Because, it is worth remembering, this was conservatism before religious conservatism got mixed in: that was a later era. This was the period when the "tax and spend liberal" was the conservative boggart.[161] Downsizing

government was the great priority of the Republican Party, which viewed big government as the major obstacle. Ironically, by the end of the Reagan presidency, the government had tripled in size.

From an environmental standpoint, both the Nixon and Carter presidencies represented considerable advances in governmental infrastructure – just as had been the case with Pluto in Gemini. While it was clear that Nixon was lukewarm on the environment as a priority, he nonetheless tended to appoint competent bureaucrats to run these new agencies. Carter was more likely to appoint enthusiasts. It was only under Reagan that anti-environmentalists were appointed to remove the teeth from the intent of the law: folks like James Watt.

Of course, the election of 1980 was not run on the basis of the environment. The Iranian hostages were the major news-grabber. We already saw the issue develop in 1979, and in 1980, there's still no relief in sight. Observe Chart 28.

The Aries Ingress has a mutable Ascendant, so the November election and the Inauguration fall under the Libra Ingress. But before we examine the election, let's see how the Aries Ingress matches up with the prior Libra Ingress, in order to see the flow of events. For the 1979 Libra Ingress, Uranus was conjunct the Ascendant, showing the disruption that affected the American people's outlook. Now, the Aries 1980 Sun itself is right on the Ascendant. This is the time for a new beginning. But are you going to get a new beginning in an election year when one person is running for *reelection*? Only if the other party wins! The last time the U.S. had experienced this aspect in an Aries Ingress was in 1947, when President Truman promulgated the Marshall Plan, which remade the face of Europe. Now the people wanted the same for the U.S.

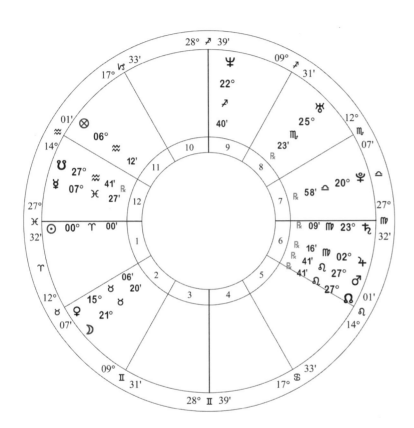

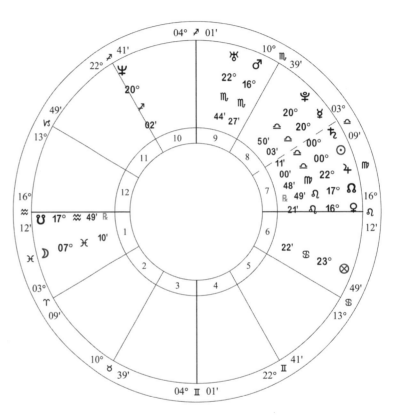

Sun enters Ari 3-20-1980
March 20, 1980
6:09:43 AM
Washington, D.C.
38N53'42" 77W02'12"
Standard Time
Time Zone: 5 hours West
Tropical Regiomontanus
NATAL CHART

Chart 28. Sun enters Aries and Libra 1980, Washington D.C.

Sun enters Lib 9-22-1980
September 22, 1980
5:08:42 PM
Washington, D.C.
38N53'42" 77W02'12"
Daylight Saving Time
Time Zone: 5 hours West
Tropical Regiomontanus
NATAL CHART

Carter is still showing as inept, with his Significator Jupiter cadent, retrograde and in Fall.

By Libra 1980, it's the South Node on the Ascendant. People were very upset. President Carter was still ruled by Jupiter in Virgo, in Detriment. He looked incompetent. Jupiter further was in the 7th house of enemies. The Libra Ingress had the Sun partile conjunct a very dignified Saturn. This was the image for the new era: reduction in government – Saturn eating its children. This image was completely out of touch with Carter. A new order was coming that would fulfill this symbol. And eat it did. Reagan's administration set about systematically cutting the size of the Environmental Protection Agency, as well as many other government departments with regulatory oversight. The lawyers and administrators who took over were charged with reducing the size and budget of their departments: not with actually providing the services of that department. Across-the-board cuts were made by administrators who often had no expertise at all in the specialty they were administering. This was actually part of a larger societal trend in management, in which the "generalist" – the manager with no special knowledge of the line being administered – was promoted as superior to the "engineer," who had line item experience. The generalist was said to be able to make better decisions by not being swayed by what had been done previously than experts in the field. In 1983, in the waning days of Pluto in Libra, Environmental Protection Agency head Anne Goresuch, who had no expertise in environmental issues whatsoever, would be forced from office, accused of having gutted the agency while she cut its size by over 20%. For the rest of her life, she showed no comprehension of how anyone could accuse her of doing anything wrong.

Endnotes: Chapter 5

126. Leopold, Aldo, and Charles Walsh Schwartz. *A Sand County Almanac. With Other Essays on Conservation from Round River*. [Enl. ed. New York,: Oxford University Press, 1966, p 183.

127. http//www.en.wikipedia.org/wiki/From_the_Earth_to_the_Moon

128. A good example of this idea is given in: Stent, Gunther Siegmund. *Paradoxes of Progress*. San Francisco: W. H. Freeman, 1978.

129. For an excellent work which covers this subject in great detail, see Gould, Stephen Jay. *The Mismeasure of Man*. 1st ed. New York: Norton, 1981.

130. Babylon 5, Season 1, Episode 105, "Believers."

131. Bonatti, Treatise 3, Chapter 7, p 211 in Dykes (2007).

132. Lilly's rules for ships at sea are in *Christian Astrology*, pp 157-161.

133. Lilly, p 158.

134. Lilly, p 159.

135. For a full grid of the parts of a ship, see either Lilly, p 158, or Lehman, J. L. (2002). *Martial Art of Horary Astrology*. Atglen, PA, Schiffer Pub., p 58

136. Lilly, p 158.

137. Lilly, p 159.

138. Lilly, pp 159-160.

139. Lilly, p 158.

140. Hays, Samuel P. *Conservation and the Gospel of Efficiency; The Progressive Conservation Movement, 1890-1920*. Harvard historical monographs, 40. Cambridge: Harvard University Press, 1959, Chapter 1.

141. Hays, Samuel P, p 9.

142. Turner, Frederick Jackson. *The Frontier in American History. [Essays.]*. 1920, p 297.

143. Kingsland, Sharon E. *The Evolution of American Ecology, 1890-2000*. Baltimore: Johns Hopkins University Press, 2005, pp 18-19.

144. Gauquelin, Michel. *Cosmic Influences on Human Behavior*. 2d ed. New York: ASI Publishers, 1978.

145. Kingsland, p 63.

146. Kingsland, p 68.

147. Kingsland, pp 63-64.

148. Kingsland, pp 68-69.

149. Williams, Jay, and Raymond Abrashkin. *Danny Dunn and the Homework Machine.* New York: Whittlesey House, 1958.

150. Paddock, William, and Paul Paddock. *Famine, 1975! America's Decision: Who Will Survive?* Boston: Little, Brown, 1967.

151. These statistics are compiled in many places, but here's one: *www. theglobaleducationproject.org/earth/food-and-soil.php*

152. Meadows, Donella H. *The Limits to Growth; A Report for the Club of Rome's Project on the Predicament of Mankind.* New York: Universe Books, 1972.

153. A few examples are these:
   • Boughey, Arthur S. *Strategy for Survival : An Exploration of the Limits to Further Population and Industrial Growth.* Menlo Park, Calif.: W.A. Benjamin, 1976.
   • Cole, H. S. D., and Unit University of Sussex. Science Policy Research. *Models of Doom; a Critique of the Limits to Growth.* New York: Universe Books, 1973.
   • Meadows, Dennis L. *Dynamics of Growth in a Finite World.* Cambridge, Mass.: Wright-Allen Press, 1974.
   • Mesarovic, Mihajlo D., Eduard Pestel, and Rome Club of. *Mankind at the Turning Point : The Second Report to the Club of Rome.* New York: Dutton, 1974.
   • Vacca, Roberto. *The Coming Dark Age.* Garden City, N.Y.: Doubleday, 1973.

154. Here's a sampling of some of the works which used these ideas as a starting point, and then either objected to, or extended the arguments into other fields.
   • Dobereiner, David. *The End of the Street: Sustainable Growth Within Natural Limits.* Montreal: Black Rose Books, 2006.
   • Hirsch, Fred. *Social Limits to Growth.* Cambridge, Mass: Harvard University Press, 1976.
   • Kemp, Jack. *The American idea: ending limits to growth.* Washington, DC: American Studies Center, 1984. .
   • Miles, Rufus E. *Awakening from the American Dream: The Social and Political Limits to Growth.* New York: Universe Books, 1976.
   • Stivers, Robert L. *Hunger, Technology & Limits to Growth: Christian Responsibility for Three Ethical Issues.* Minneapolis: Augsburg Pub. House, 1984.

155. For a good discussion of the impact of Biblical criticism on both Jewish and Christian thought, see Levenson, Jon Douglas. *The Hebrew Bible, the Old Testament, and Historical Criticism: Jews and Christians in Biblical Studies.* Louisville, Ky: Westminster/John Knox Press, 1993.

156. Except oil, which is a result of past natural life and decay processes – but the millions of years it would take is frankly not an option right now.

157. Mark 10:25.

158. See, for exmaple, Graham, Otis, Jr. "Immigration and America's Unchosen Future." *Negative Population Growth Forum Series* 117.October (2009): 8 pages.

159. Skowronek, Stephen, 1997.

160. Kemp, p xxiii.

161. See the Harry Potter series for this magical creature.

6

The Universal Solvent: Pluto in the Water Signs

There is always an easy solution to every human problem—neat, plausible, and wrong.

—H.L. Mencken,
The Divine Afflatus, 1917

THE CONSERVATION MOVEMENT AND NASCENT ECOLOGY DID NOT DIE WHEN PLUTO WENT INTO CANCER. It was simply reborn into a new phase. In the Hellenistic theories of four elements, earth and water together, being the two most dense elements, combined to form the Earth as we know it, because the denser elements would naturally settle down, while lighter air and still lighter fire would tend to rise.

Within this cosmological system, we see the importance of earth and water together in our ecology, our *oikos* or home. We also have seen in the history of the Pluto in Taurus and Gemini periods, how one of the factors that was most significant in developing land use strategies in the American West was the challenge of the much more arid climate, and how to adapt crops from moister regions to drier ones. We could obviously state that the same challenge of

arid conditions exists in large swaths of Canada, Russia, Alaska, Africa, the Middle East, India, and China, where crops can only be possible with irrigation: a front-and-center Water issue.

From an agricultural perspective, there are two kinds of irrigation. The most important kind of irrigation historically is diversion of river water. These practices were common in Mesopotamia, India, and China. Commonly, channels or canals are dug to divert river water to croplands. The result was much like the flooding of the Nile: these methods allowed the growth of crops in areas where the annual rainfall was either inadequate, or typically poorly timed for agriculture.

The second kind of irrigation has been mostly available since the industrial age: groundwater irrigation. While there are a few areas of the world where underground water erupts to the surface, in most cases, wells need to be dug. How deep? That depends on the water table: the depth at which all the spaces in the soil are filled with water. Above the **water table**, if you dig a hole, you'll mainly see soil, sand, or rocks. The soil is aerated to a certain degree, and if you see water, it's probably because of a recent rain. And this is

Cancer	Scorpio	Pisces
12 Sep – 19 Oct 1178	25 Dec 1243 – 13 Mar 1244	27 Mar – 10 Aug 1307
9 Jul – 30 Dec 1179	13 Oct 1244 – 4 Jan 1256	7 Feb 1308 – 23 Oct 1308
23 May 1180 – 19 Sep 1201	4 May – 1 Nov 1256	4 Dec 1308 – 8 Jun 1332
14 Dec 1201 – 23 Jul 1202		21 Jul 1332 – 7 Apr 1333
25 Feb – 26 May 1203		29 Sep 1333 – 23 Feb 1334
11 Aug 1423 – 22 Nov 1423	5 Nov 1490 – 19 May 1491	30 Mar – 4 Aug 1552
22 Jun 1424 – 19 Jan 1425	28 Aug 1491 – 31 Jan 1502	10 Feb – 15 Oct 1553
5 May 1425 – 11 Aug 1447	5 Apr – 19 Nov 1502	12 Dec 1553 – 4 May 1577
29 Jan – 20 Jun 1448	31 Jul – 23 Aug 1503	28 Aug 1577 – 19 Mar 1578
		27 Oct 1578 – 30 Jan 1579
24 Jul – 8 Dec 1668	5 Dec 1736 – 4 Apr 1737	11 Apr – 21 Jul 1797
8 Jun 1669 – 10 Feb 1670	1 Oct 1737 – 10 Dec 1748	17 Feb 1798 – 28 Sep 1798
13 Apr 1670 – 2 Sep 1692	8 Jun – 6 Oct 1749	26 Dec 1798 – 16 Apr 1822
30 Dec 1692 – 12 Jul 1693		
15 Mar – 8 May 1694		
10 Sep – 20 Oct 1912	5 Nov 1983 – 18 May 1984	9 Mar – 1 Sep 2043
9 Jul 1913 – 28 Dec 1913	28 Aug 1984 – 17 Jan 1995	19 Jan 2044 – 18 Jun 2066
26 May 1914 – 7 Oct 1937	21 Apr – 10 Nov 1995	10 Jul 2066 – 9 Apr 2067
25 Nov 1937 – 3 Aug 1938		27 Sep 2067 – 23 Feb 2068
7 Feb – 14 Jun 1939		

Table 6-1. Pluto Ingresses by Sign. Data from Michelsen, 1990, pp 63-64.

a good thing, because the roots of plants need air as well as water. When you continue to dig deeper and deeper, eventually you will come to a depth where your hole contains water all the time. This can be as little as a few feet, or as much as several hundred feet. Natural release of groundwater occurs at springs or seeps. Unless the water table is very close to the surface, pumping most likely will be required to pull the water up from the ground – and pumping requires energy. If the water use is occasional, as the old-time wells that many people had on their property, the pumping can be done by hand. But regular pumping for irrigation requires power – and the power required can be a significant factor if one compares the energy available in the food compared to energy used to *produce* the food.

Where does groundwater come from? Again, there are two main kinds. In areas with plentiful rainfall, say 1 meter or more per year (roughly 37") it's likely the rainfall is recharging the groundwater. However, there's also something called fossil groundwater. **Fossil groundwater** entered an area in a different geological time, presumably when rainfall was more plentiful in the region. Thus, even in a desert, there may well be water available if one drills down deep enough. Fossil groundwater can be present for millions of years.

However, once groundwater begins to be pumped out for irrigation or other uses, if there isn't sufficient rainwater recharging the groundwater, the water table will gradually drop. At first, this simply means that the wells have to be dug even deeper. But it is possible to completely use up an underground source of water. And this is not just idle theory: it's estimated that this kind of overpumping of groundwater is currently occurring in Saudi Arabia, China, the U.S. Great Plains, Yemen, India, Pakistan, Israel, Iran, and Mexico.[162] What this means on a long-term basis is that the farming practices of all these regions are not sustainable – because eventually, there will be drastic changes when the water runs out – as it will.

There's one more environmental impact that we have to consider before we return to the astrology: the long-term impact of irrigation on soil. Generally speaking, if irrigation is being done, one would presume that the soil otherwise would be dry. Both soil and water can contain salts. When the water evaporates, this can leave salt deposits behind in the soil. Under the right conditions, this salt can build up, eventually forming a crust on the surface of the soil, and leading to decreased crop yield, or even the abandonment of irrigated fields. This is especially a danger in desert and other arid regions, although excessive water use can produce the same effect elsewhere.

Pluto in Cancer
1912-1939

The period of Pluto in Cancer was transitional from 1912-1914, and then it lasted until the next transition to Leo in 1937-1939. The great transitional event between Gemini and Cancer was World War I, when "the Great War came upon us all."[163] This discussion also connects to my observation that the new sign of Pluto gets to clean up the excesses – or the logical outcomes – of the prior sign. So what is the changeover from Gemini to Cancer? Both are wet, but Gemini is hot and Cancer is cold. Later in this chapter, we will see a very parallel development when Pluto in Aquarius transitioned to Pluto in Pisces, with the advent of Napoleon's wars, followed by a much more peaceful world when Pluto had moved on to Aries.

So it may at first seem very strange that it was the period of Pluto in Pisces, not Pluto in Aries, when the wars were so prominent. And one could make a pretty good analogy to the alliance against Napoleon looking a lot like the alliances that featured so prominently in World War I. But consider: Mars and Venus are both triplicity rulers of the water signs. Both of these planets are very passionate, as we are so aware from natal astrology. Passion still happens in the mundane realm. All one has to do is to read the biographies of the people in the conspiracy that assassinated Archduke Franz Ferdinand to see that these men were passionate about Serbian independence, and firm in their belief that only acts of terror could accomplish their political ends. Similarly, Napoleon was passionate about the French Revolution before he rode it to Empire. Power evokes at least as much passion as sex.

Both the Water signs and the Earth signs share the same Triplicity rulers: they merely shift positions in terms of primary day, night, and mixed rulership. The Fire signs and Air signs share Jupiter and Saturn as Triplicity rulers. One can thus see that large social movements which are possible and probable under Fire and Air are going to manifest differently under Earth and Water. The assassination of the Archduke required both the political organization of the Serbian underground to recruit and transport the assassins, but also the assassins themselves, who were issued suicide pills along with their weapons.

Enter, then, our examination of the transition to Pluto in Cancer. If we examine the Aries Ingress for Sarajevo, where the assassination occurred (Chart 29), we observe several things:

- The cardinal sign rising means all four ingresses must be examined

- The Neptune rising looks ripe for a political conspiracy or clandestine activities: both of which were true

- The Part of Fortune conjunct the malefic fixed star Algol is something we will take up momentarily

- Pluto is in the 12th house of hidden enemies at 29 degrees Gemini

- The Sun is conjunct the 10th house cusp, which looks good for the king (in this case, of Bosnia-Herzegovina) – but Venus in detriment in the 10th gives an opposite meaning.

We have already noted that this chart "expired" with the advent of the Cancer Ingress. For comparison's sake, I am illustrating that chart done for Vienna, since the Archduke was the heir to the Austria-Hungarian throne. There is only a small shift in degrees: 2 on the MC, and one on the Ascendant. The only functional change is that the Vienna Part of Fortune is no longer conjunct Algol. These are shown in Chart 30.

When we examine the Cancer Ingress, we note that the Springtime angularity of Neptune and the Sun was no longer present in the Summer, and several other configurations have formed:

- Pluto has changed signs to Cancer. And it is in a partile conjunction with the Sun. This is a volatile combination, in the house of "friends," which might not be too much of a stretch to see as alliances.

Chart 29. Sun enters Aries 1914, Sarajevo, Bosnia

NATAL CHART
Sun enters Ari 3-21-1914
March 21, 1914
12:10:48 PM
Sarajevo, Bosnia
43 N 52 18 E 25
Standard Time
Time Zone: 1 hours East
Tropical Regiomontanus

Day of ♄	Hour of ☽
Last Hr ☿	- 17 mins
Next Hr ♄	+43 mins

FIXED STARS	
☽☌ Altair	0°57's
⊗☌Algol	0°51's
☊☌Ankaa	0°06's
☊☌Achernar	0°06'a
As☌Procyon	0°18'a
♂☌Sirius	0°26'a
♆☌Procyon	0°54'a

Hs	Alm. (Dor)
1	☽
2	☉
3	☿
4	♄
5	♂
6	♃
7	♂
8	♄
9	♀
10	☉
11	♀
12	☿

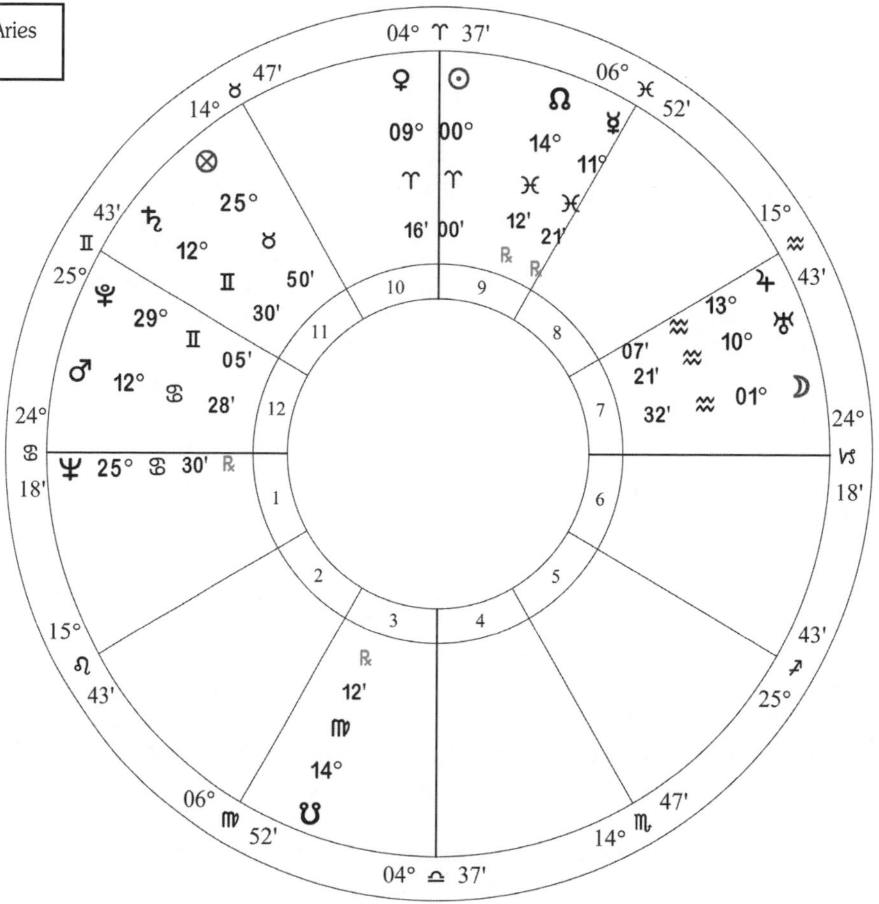

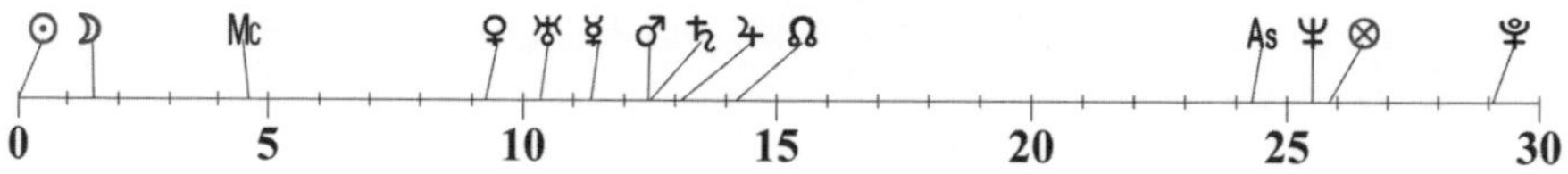

ESSENTIAL DIGNITIES (Dorothean)								
Pl	Ruler	Exalt	Tripl	Term	Face	Detri	Fall	Score
☉	♂	☉ +	☉ +	♃	♂	♀	♄	+7
☽	♄	--	♄	♄	♀	☉	--	- 5 P
☿	♃	♀	♀	♃	♃ m	☿ -	☿ -	- 14 P
♀	♂	☉	☉	♀ +	♂	♀ -	♄	- 3
♂	☽	♃	♀	♃	☿	♄	♂ -	- 9 P
♃	♄	--	♄	♀	☿ m	☉	--	- 5 P
♄	☿	☊	♄ +	♃	♂	♃	--	+3
☊	♃	♀	♀	☿	♃	☿	☿	--
⊗	♀	☽	♀	♄	♄	♂	--	--
As	☽	♃	♀	♀	☽	♄	♂	--
Mc	♂	☉	☉	♃	♂	♀	♄	--
☋	☿	☿	♀	♃	♀	♃	♀	--

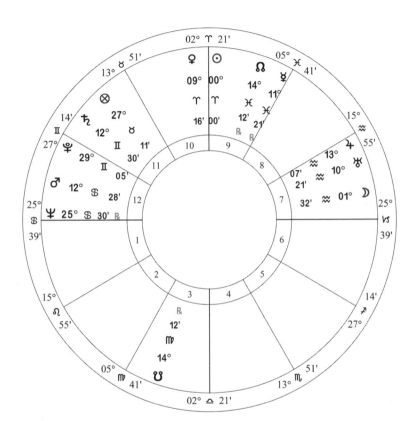

Sun enters Ari 3-21-1914
March 21, 1914
12:10:48 PM
Vienna, Austria
48 N 13 16 E 20
Standard Time
Time Zone: 1 hours East
Tropical Regiomontanus
NATAL CHART

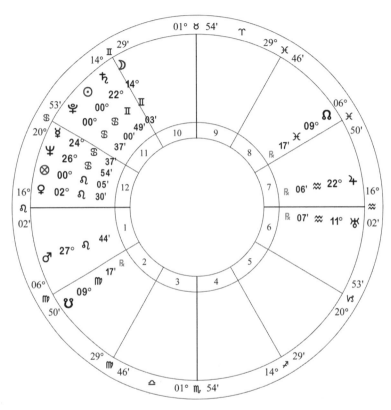

Sun enters Can 6-22-1914
June 22, 1914
7:55:07 AM
Vienna, Austria
48 N 13 16 E 20
Standard Time
Time Zone: 1 hours East
Tropical Regiomontanus
NATAL CHART

Chart 30. Sun enters Aries and Cancer 1914, Vienna, Austria

- Mars is in the 1st house, **separating** from an opposition to imbecilic Jupiter, which rules the 9th of foreign policy.

- The Moon is at the Bendings (*i.e.*, square the Nodes), and translating the light from Uranus to Saturn.

- Venus, ruling the 10th, squares the MC and was in the 12th – not a good thing for kings.

There is also a warning in this chart, because the Sun, ruling the Ascendant, and thus, Austria-Hungary, is much weaker than its enemies, given by Saturn, in Triplicity in the 11th. It was Austria-Hungary that declared war, thus beginning the conflict. Fixed signs on the angles are a traditional indicator that events under their rulership go slowly. And this war dragged into the horror show of the trenches and poison gas.

Thus, while the entire world was not at war at the beginning of Pluto in Cancer, things were leaning that way. The United States and Japan would join in, but not quite yet. Still, this seemingly sudden turn of events would dictate that other concerns took a back seat.

Chart 31 is the same Aries Ingress for 1914 set for the U.S. Notice here the juxtaposition of Pluto on the IC of the chart for Washington, DC. The U.S. was occupied by the opening of the Panama Canal, which also served to speed up transportation between the West and East Coasts of the U.S. The Army Corps of Engineers was beginning to investigate acid run-off from mines – a 4th house concern, and notice Mars in the 4th house – a double signature for *Army* Corps of *Engineers*.

But we cannot continue without noting that, by the beginning of the 20th century, war had become even more of an environmental disaster than it had been previously. The story of the Romans salting Carthage and destroying the fertility of the land may not have been typical, but historically, armies moving through your fields was a universal calamity for farmers. Visit a battlefield from the mid 19th century or earlier and observe that the land has recovered. All that pain and death is now under green fields – with the irony that the land may well have gotten better treatment being turned into parkland for a tourist attraction – or a graveyard. But as the 20th century proceeds, there is increasing possibility for poisoning the land – and of course, petroleum use, and the use of other resources mounts as weapons become high-tech. As future generations tally the wastefulness of our period, wars will surely be prominent on that list.

But how is a war different with Pluto in a water sign? It would be lovely were we to find that wars seemed fewer when Pluto transits a particular element – but sadly, there seems to be no let-up on war. Mars is a hard task master regardless of Pluto sign. But the Arabs noted that wars occur for dynasty or religion. Cancer could be said to contain both: its Moon rulership would make it more nationalistic than some signs, and Jupiter's exaltation there would favor religious concerns. What we have noted for World War I is that the transition from Air to Water was clearly a very rocky one. *All* Pluto sign transitions can be about a crumbling of a piece of the old order: sadly, war is one way that it can manifest.

NATAL CHART
Sun enters Ari 3-21-1914
March 21, 1914
6:10:48 AM
Washington, D.C.
38N53'42" 77W02'12"
Standard Time
Time Zone: 5 hours West
Tropical Regiomontanus

Chart 31. Sun enters Aries 1914, Washington, DC

Day of ♀	Hour of ☽
Last Hr ☿	- 55 mins
Next Hr ♄	+ 5 mins

FIXED STARS	
☽☌ Altair	0°57's
☊☌ Ankaa	0°06's
☊☌ Achernar	0°06'a
As☌ Scheat	0°13'a
♂☌ Sirius	0°26'a
♆☌ Procyon	0°54'a

Hs	Alm. (Dor)
1	♃
2	☽
3	☿
4	☿
5	☽
6	⊙
7	☿
8	♂
9	♃
10	♃
11	♂♄
12	♄

ESSENTIAL DIGNITIES (Dorothean)

Pl	Ruler	Exalt	Tripl	Term	Face	Detri	Fall	Score
⊙	♂	⊙ +	♃	♃	♂	♀	♄	+4
☽	♄	--	☿	♄	♀	⊙	--	- 5 P
☿	♃	♀	♂	♃	♃ m	☿ -	☿ -	- 14 P
♀	♂	⊙	♃	♀ +	♂	♀ -	♄	- 3
♂	☽	♃	♂ +	♃	☿	♄	♂ -	- 1
♃	♄	--	☿	♀	☿ m	⊙	--	- 5 P
♄	☿	☊	☿	♃	♂	♃	--	- 5 P
☊	♃	♀	♂	☿	♃	☿	☿	--
⊗	♀	☽	☽	♂	♄	♂	--	--
As	♃	♀	♂	♄	♂	☿	☿	--
Mc	♃	☋	♃	♂	♄	☿	--	--
☋	☿	☿	☽	♃	♀	♃	♀	--

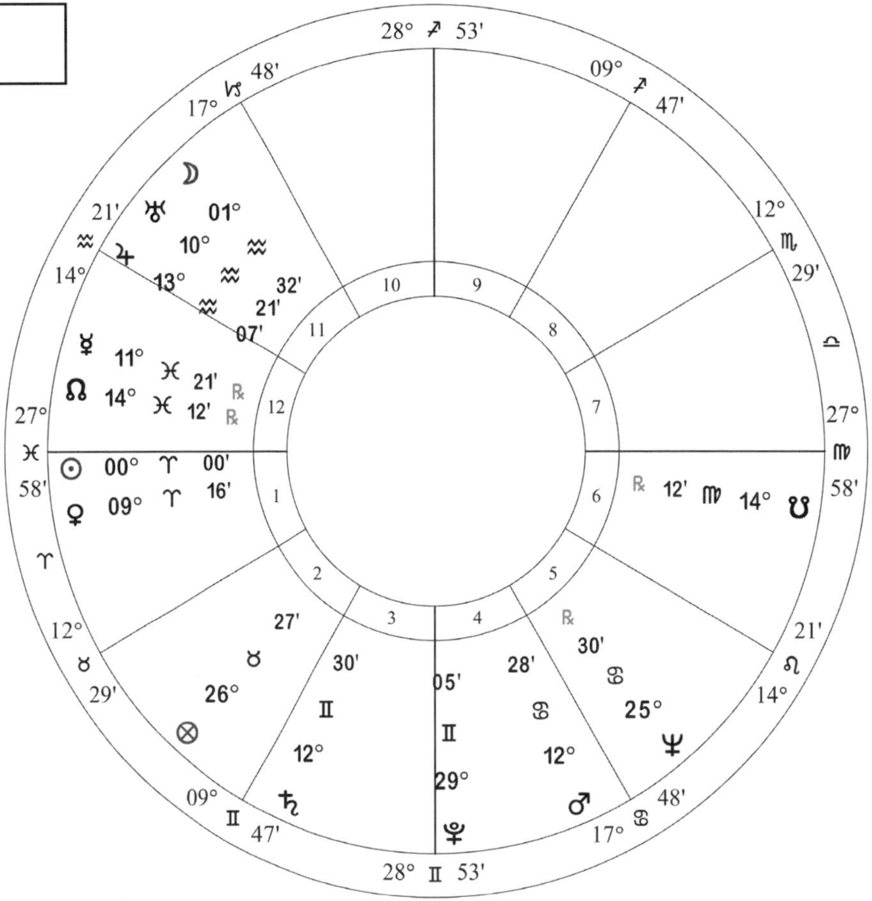

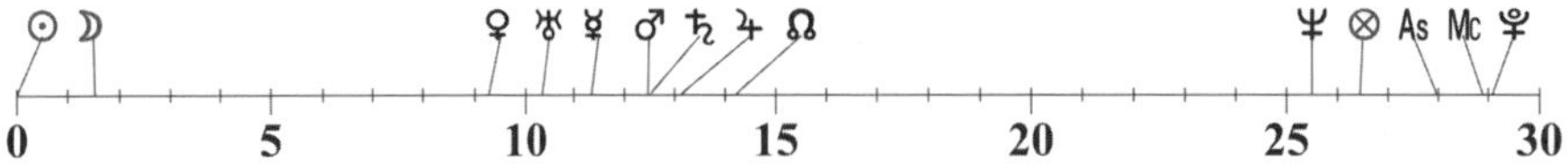

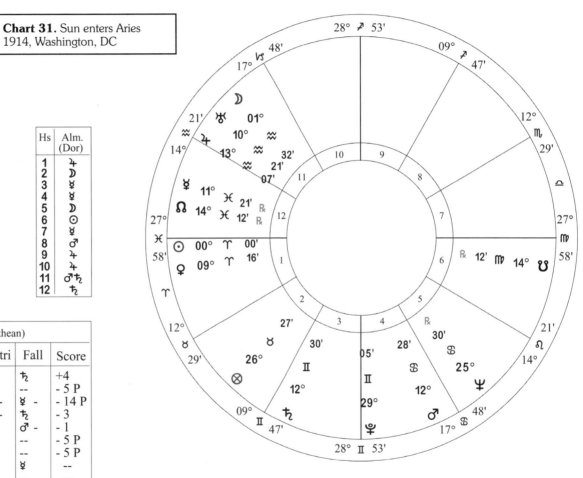

The Influenza Pandemic of 1918

If the image of war is not bad enough, the same period as the Great War also saw the worst pandemic since the Black Death in the Middle Ages: the 1918 influenza pandemic. If we first examine the Black Death itself – which killed a much larger proportion of the European population in 1348-1350 than the 1918 flu pandemic (although the actual numbers in 1918 were higher, because the world population itself was so much bigger) Pluto was in Aries, and Neptune was in Aquarius – neither near a sign ingress. So we will have to look further. But then, there was a classic definition: Saturn. The old demarcation of the two malefics Saturn and Mars was that Saturn was famine, drought and plagues; while Mars was violence, war, and fevers. So on this basis, the flu was definitely a pestilence (Saturn) – but with a high fever as well (Mars).

There is still some debate on the actual origin point of the 1918 flu epidemic, but what is clear is that possibly the most significant contributing factor to its conversion into a pandemic was that it attacked early in 1918 at the staging bases of the U.S. Army in preparation for sending the U.S. troops to Europe – and that it was the single-pointed efforts of staging an army with hugely overcrowded conditions in the camps and military censorship that allowed the disease to incubate out of control.[164] Accordingly, the epidemic started in 1917, although its dimensions did not become clear until 1918. Eventually, more people would die in the pandemic than would die in the war.

If we examine the Aries Ingress chart for 1917 for Washington, DC (Chart 32), we see immediately with Sagittarius Rising that this year will require analysis of the

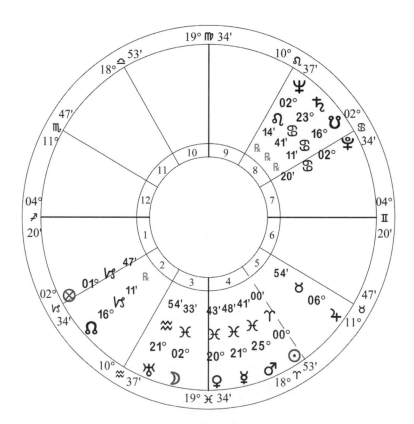

Sun enters Ari 3-21-1917
March 20, 1917
11:37:18 PM
Washington, D.C.
38N53'42" 77W02'12"
Standard Time
Time Zone: 5 hours West
Tropical Regiomontanus
NATAL CHART

Sun enters Lib 9-23-1917
September 23, 1917
10:00:13 AM
Washington, D.C.
38N53'42" 77W02'12"
Standard Time
Time Zone: 5 hours West
Tropical Regiomontanus
NATAL CHART

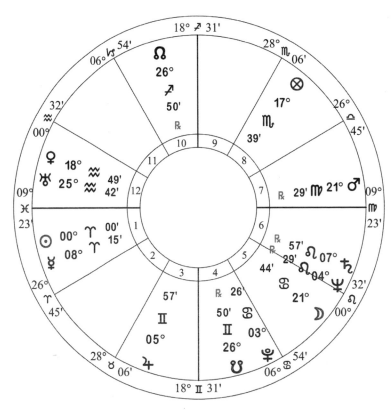

Sun enters Ari 3-21-1918
March 21, 1918
5:25:41 AM
Washington, D.C.
38N53'42" 77W02'12"
Standard Time
Time Zone: 5 hours West
Tropical Regiomontanus
NATAL CHART

Chart 32. Sun enters Aries 1917, Libra 1917, Aries 1918, Washington, DC

Libra Ingress as well. But already, this chart is ominous, with South Node, Saturn and Neptune already in the 8th house of death – and with Pluto partile conjunct the 8th house cusp in Regiomontanus. At this time, the U.S.A. was very near to declaring war on Germany, which happened on April 6th. So we were mobilizing at this point. The enemies of the U.S. were ruled by Mercury in Detriment in Pisces. Seemingly, our enemies didn't have teeth. But Jupiter, ruling the U.S.A., didn't have any dignity, so the U.S.A. doesn't look like it has the most penetrating vision either! And notice – President Wilson is ruled by the very same Mercury that ruled the enemies of the U.S.A. Does this mean that Wilson was in league with the enemy? Not necessarily, and I'm sure in this case, not true at all. What it means is that neither Wilson nor the Germans at this point had any clear vision.

The **Under Beams** part of the Mercury rulership is rather intriguing in this case, and the incident was called the Zimmerman telegram.[165] This secret telegram from Germany to Mexico called for Mexico to declare war against the U.S. in order to gain back the southwestern states, but, from Germany's perspective, to tie up the U.S. and keep it from entering the European campaign. Under Beams, like **Combustion**, is about secrecy. The British had cracked the German diplomatic code, and then shared the letter with Wilson, who publicized it, in order to build up U.S. support for the war. And perhaps more importantly for the interpretation of Under Beams, once Wilson presided over U.S. entry into the war, he suspended First Amendment freedom of speech and practiced the most comprehensive censorship the U.S. had ever experienced.

The focus on the 4th house in this chart describes the isolationist position of the U.S.A. leading up to this period, and the fact that the immediate focus was on getting the U.S. mobilized for war. Not knowing the outcome, one would be tempted to see the strong 8th house as presaging the loss of soldiers in battle.

But the Libra Ingress for 1917 shows a somewhat different picture. Here, we see Mars ruling the Ascendant – the people are converted to the idea of war. But what kind of war? Mars in Leo doesn't have dignity to begin with, but partile conjunct Neptune? Any realism associated with the horrors of modern warfare were being drowned in propaganda, another component of Neptune.

This chart shows the start of the pandemic. The Aries Ingress already has a pretty active 8th house, and it doesn't quit with the Libra chart. Here, we see an approaching South Node-Pluto conjunction in the 8th, with Jupiter in Detriment sitting at the cusp of the 8th, in the 5 degree zone. This chart raises a couple of points in interpretation. First, it is suggestive that the South Node-Pluto conjunction is still applying: while the virus surely had mutated into its pandemic form. By this time, it had not yet taken hold and produced its fatal effects yet. So this tracks.

But the question is what to do with the delineation of Jupiter. Jupiter is in Detriment – but it has Triplicity. And Jupiter's dispositor is highly dignified essentially, but retrograde and combust. How does one evaluate all of these factors together? Let's examine a table of the Detriments and Falls of the planets and whether the debilitated planet is also a Triplicity ruler of that sign. This is shown in Table 6-2.

Planet	Sign	Triplicity
Sun – Detriment	Aquarius	none
Sun – Fall	Libra	none
Moon – Detriment	Capricorn	night
Moon – Fall	Scorpio	mixed
Mercury – Detriment & Fall	Pisces	none
Mercury – Detriment	Sagittarius	none
Venus – Detriment	Scorpio	day
Venus – Detriment	Aries	none
Venus – Fall	Virgo	day
Mars – Detriment	Libra	none
Mars – Detriment	Taurus	mixed
Mars – Fall	Cancer	night
Jupiter – Detriment	Gemini	mixed
Jupiter – Detriment	Virgo	none
Saturn – Detriment	Cancer	none
Saturn – Detriment	Leo	mixed
Saturn – Fall	Aries	mixed

Table 6-2. Relationship of Detriment, Fall and Triplicity.

Summarizing our result, there are seventeen different cases of Detriments and Falls – and in just over half, namely nine cases, the planet in debility is a Triplicity ruler of that same sign. So in these cases, the effect of the debility is not so much muted, as variable, since *both* the debility *and* the dignity can occur at the same time.

This Jupiter rules the 2nd and 5th houses. While one doesn't usually think of diseases in terms of their financial toll (2nd house), that is true as well. One is obviously tempted to see Jupiter in its expansive state here as high death – but one can carry this even further. It's a human sign (the air signs) on the cusp of the 8th, which also plays in to the theme we see building.

And we definitely need to implicate the Mars-Saturn-Neptune in the 9th. The military had moved all these soldiers to very cramped quarters prior to moving them overseas – a 9th house trip. It was precisely the overcrowding of soldiers in the staging camps that provided such a fertile ground for the rampaging of the virus – combined with the military's tight schedule for getting the troops overseas, and then not wanting to isolate troop ships later on when they landed in U.S. ports with infected soldiers. This policy expedited the contagion of the disease through the general population. And all this is showing as the disease was setting up – in other words, *before the general public had the slightest clue that this deadly process was developing.* The chart that shows the rampage is 1917, when the conditions which allowed its spread were being set up – not so much in the chart for the year where the pandemic actually occurred. Is this what Fate looks like: the horror is shown while the catastrophe is developing, and the inevitable result almost looks like a letdown? This is the Fate of Greek tragedy, or of Wagner's Ring Cycle, where a series of seemingly rational or even trivial decisions and actions sets up the avalanche – and the astrology shows the developing avalanche.

But how do we distinguish between a developing avalanche, and the genuine tragedy in the moment that such a chart can also show? We examined the development of the Spanish-American War and showed how the war could not have occurred before it did. In that case, the ingresses were showing the events, not the development of future events. The answer is: at this time, we don't know, because these sorts of questions have not been seriously discussed.

When we examine the Aries Ingress for 1918, when the death toll mounted alarmingly in the U.S.A., we have several choices of suspects. Is it the out of sign opposition of Sun and Mars? Probably not – it's a large orb, and it's doubly separating. Plus, there's that obvious point that the U.S. was at war, and Mars is the planet of war in the house of the enemy – and the U.S. was fighting on foreign soil. Mars' position at the Bendings makes Mars even more prominent.

What else? How about Saturn conjunct Neptune, in the 6th house of disease? That, I can begin to get behind. Saturn is the traditional planet of plagues, here in the sign of its detriment, and conjunct a planet that has the properties of confusion and contagion which allowed the pandemic to develop in the absence of common sense in dealing with it. That this was trine the 1st house Sun and Mercury just made the process easier rather than better. And speaking of the Sun-Mercury conjunction, the major problem with the spread of the pandemic was censorship – the unwillingness to share or provide information – symbolized by the Combust configuration.

So world-wide distractions of the first few years of Pluto in Cancer certainly kept the attention away from matters we might associate with the environment, even if public health does represent a degree of overlap. Nonetheless, there were some early signs of the change. We would reasonably expect, therefore, that the environmental issues of Pluto in Cancer relate to water: either its presence, or its absence. The year of the transition, 1914, showed an up-tick in the duties of the Army Corps of Engineers, which began a pollution survey of *streams and harbors*. The Ascendant for Washington, DC was 27 Pisces – another water sign! Pluto was right on the IC, and certainly, the redesign of riverbeds could be construed to be plutonic in nature. It was also the year of the extinction of the passenger pigeon, a much larger bird than our present pigeons, but present in the millions when European humans colonized the New World and destroyed them – a story of mismanagement of natural resources that belied the early establishment of conservation during Pluto in Gemini – always as being for the benefit of *man*.

And our 1918 chart for the flu pandemic? 1918 was also the year when *Scientific American* reported on the blend of alcohol and gasoline to solve engine knocking. This idea would be abandoned only seven years later with the adoption of leaded fuels, first developed by General Motors in 1921, and implemented without health testing despite evidence suggesting its toxicity.[166] The League of Nations had adopted a ban on white-lead interior paint in 1922, but curiously, the U.S. refused to adopt the same ban.

We now know this as gasohol. The traditional ruler of alcohol would be the Moon, for all liquids, but the modern experience is Neptune. The 1918 chart supports Neptune, because it is not associated with Mars (traditional ruler of petroleum, and hence, gas), and only in semisextile to Pluto. If the idea had been adopted, then surely it would have been that highly dignified Moon in Cancer driving its acceptance. Instead, the idea would wait for decades.

It was during the 1920s that, according to Kingsland, "*ecology acquired disciplinary coherence.*"[167] What does that mean? It means that it was in this period that ecology had enough of a common basis among its practitioners that allowed for a commonality of vision and method. And what may be the most surprising, an ecologist emerged in this time period with an idea about how the earth worked that would prefigure Lovelock's Gaia hypothesis: Frederic Edward Clements. In Kingsland's description:

> Clements argued that the organization and self-equilibrating properties of plant associations made it legitimate to consider them to be a special type of organism. The 'complex organism' was not therefore a figure of speech but a term denoting a new class of organism. But like the individual organism, it had a definite developmental sequence, Clements imagined that it evolved over time in a direction that could be predicted.[168]

Here we have an idea which is really a metaphor – that it is useful to think of associations of living creatures as being like an organism, or literally *being* an organism – this is a style of thinking that we can easily classify as wet in nature, very appropriate for Pluto in Cancer. Clements was an extremely influential ecologist of his day, so this theory was not peripheral at all, even if it was not advocated by all ecologists.

And the problem with leaded gasoline did not go away, as we can see with Chart 33. On October 24, 1924, about a year and a half after tetraethyl lead gasoline first went on sale, five workers at a plant manufacturing it died in an industrial accident – and at least seventeen workers would die in its manufacture within the next two years. Lead is ruled by Saturn, a unanimous attribution, both ancient and modern. But lead was recognized as causing poisoning many centuries ago: and when I looked up lead poisoning in classical 17th century sources, what did I find but the Moon as ruler.[169] In terms of classical logic, this makes sense. If lead is Saturn, then its antagonist is the Moon or Sun,

the planets ruling the signs opposite it. Medicine at this time was seen primarily as antipathic – a substance cured that which was opposite in quality to that which caused the disease. So the Moon makes sense. But consider this odd idea: Pluto transiting the sign of lead poisoning results in the adoption of leaded gasoline, which massively increases the population of people exposed to lead – and all of this, in spite of scientific knowledge at the time of lead's harmful side effects! If there were no choices, it would be one thing, but an alternative technology existed, namely gasohol. Amazing.

The Aries Ingress for 1924 was Virgo Rising, so the Libra Ingress is also necessary. The Mars-Pluto opposition in Spring highlights petroleum as one of the possible indicators, as these are the co-rulers of this substance. In astrological shorthand, the people are imbecilic: the Ascendant ruler is combust, and in detriment as well. In the Libra Ingress, Uranus is in the 8th, indicating some prominent fatal accident. With the Sun sitting partile conjunct the 8th house cusp in the Spring, the fatal accident of the Fall is already set up. Also, the Springtime Mars went from being in Exaltation, but in Saturn's sign, to being in Saturn's other sign, where it has only minor dignity. Mars' placement conjoins the South Node, with the two bracketing the **Portals of Death**. To recapture a bit of Hellenistic terminology, the Ascendant itself is the Portals of Life, thus, the Descendant is the Portals of Death. In fact there does seem to be a correlation of death specifically with the Descendant (*i.e.*, not the rest of the 7th house), which is metaphorically the death of the Sun, being sundown. Mars and Saturn are in mutual reception, or, as I am tempted to say, mutual deception, because neither planet has any major dignity in the sign they are in. However, Mars has Term, so Mars itself is not peregrine. To add to the Mars-Saturn theme, they are also

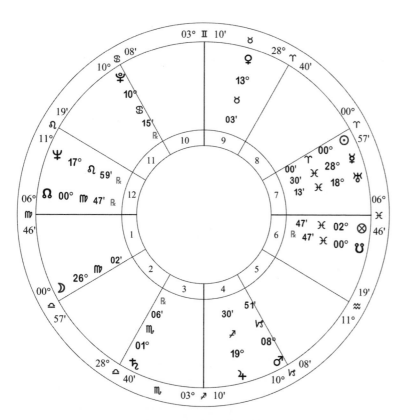

Sun enters Ari 3-20-1924
March 20, 1924
4:20:10 PM
Washington, D.C.
38N53'42" 77W02'12"
Standard Time
Time Zone: 5 hours West
Tropical Regiomontanus
NATAL CHART

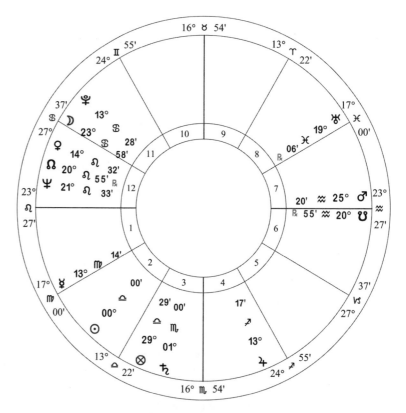

Sun enters Lib 9-23-1924
September 23, 1924
2:58:19 AM
Washington, D.C.
38N53'42" 77W02'12"
Standard Time
Time Zone: 5 hours West
Tropical Regiomontanus
NATAL CHART

Chart 33. Sun enters Aries and Libra 1924, Washington, DC

in a wide **antiscial** relationship. Saturn rules the workers – 6th house.

This shadow side of the development of the auto industry during the period of Pluto in Cancer is the seldom recorded flip side of the transformation of American culture by the automobile. While the development of the Transcontinental Railroad was celebrated in the 19th century, the advent of automobile culture in the 20th century, with its promise of individual mobility, created a new image of the American Dream: visiting anywhere in the U.S.A., without having to rely on "dirty" or "crowded" public transportation. And that, sadly, is the American attitude toward public transportation: that it's for the poor. Fostered by brilliant marketing in the early 20th century, every household had to have a car – and the more they could do with it, the better. The tetraethyl lead story became an environmental time bomb that could not be defused.

Dams

But it was not the only one. We have already seen that the Army Corps of Engineers was expanding its activities in river and waterway surveying. In 1927, the River and Harbor Act again increased their mandate for planning changes to the entire system of inland navigation. But large waterway engineering projects were not limited to the Army Corps. Municipalities also engaged in significant engineering projects, and they seldom had the expertise for major projects of this magnitude. In 1928, the St. Francis Dam, designed as part of Los Angeles' water reservoir system, collapsed upon first filling, resulting in what has been called the greatest engineering disaster in the U.S.A. of the 20th century.[170]

The actual time of the disaster is shown, and the Moon is applying to conjunction with Saturn through the South Node, with the Moon just rising, an especially dangerous configuration. In electional astrology, the Moon conjunct the Ascendant is considered unfortunate, for the simple reason that the Moon always represents change, and the usual purpose of electional is to create a lasting edifice. If we compare the actual chart with postmortems on the disaster, there are certain issues we can see.[171] The conclusion now is that engineering methods of the time were incapable of accounting for a number of stress factors. In addition, the site for the dam was the site of a paleo-landslide – in other words, a landslide in geological time. This tells you that the land was unstable to begin with. The conglomerate rock underlying part of the dam structure was unstable. But there were also factors that contemporaries could have identified, the most glaring being that twice during the design of the dam, an additional height of ten feet had been added, without increasing the dimensions of the base – an absolute no-no in engineering. From this, we understand the 1st house configuration in the chart. Also, Pluto in the 8th signifies the 420-500 deaths – no exact number can be applied *because the bodies were swept out to sea.* But why this day? That's always one of the problems in examining disaster charts. I'm afraid part of the answer is non-astrological: this was the first day that they had filled the dam as high as they did. Pressure gauges suggest that the dam began leaking sometime around 8 P.M., but the dam actually blew when both Lights arrived at angles – a fact that, while reasonably common, does not occur *every* day. If the dam was going to fail this day, then this was a "good" time.

But as we have seen, the problem with event charts is that they are not predictive – they are explanatory. And speaking

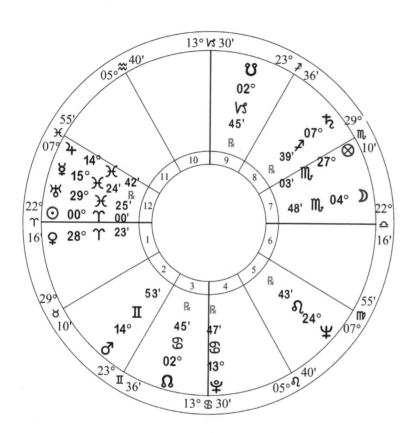

Sun enters Ari 3-21-1927
March 21, 1927 6:59:07 AM
Los Angeles, California
34N03'08" 118W14'34"
Standard Time
Time Zone: 8 hours West
Tropical Regiomontanus
NATAL CHART

Chart 34. Sun enters Aries and Capricorn 1927, Aries 1928, Los Angeles, CA; and St. Francis Dam collapse

Sun enters Cap 12-22-1927
December 22, 1927 12:18:31 PM
Los Angeles, California
34N03'08" 118W14'34"
Standard Time
Time Zone: 8 hours West
Tropical Regiomontanus
NATAL CHART

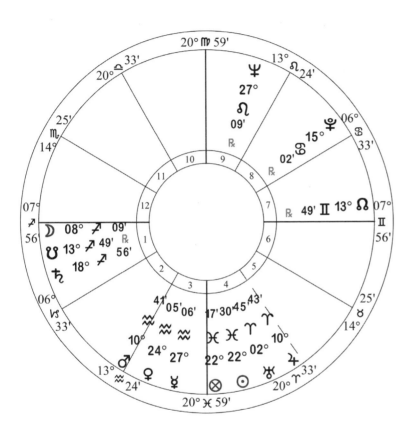

St Francis Dam collapse
March 12, 1928 11:57 PM
Santa Clarita, California
34 N 03 118 W 14
Standard Time
Time Zone: 8 hours West
Tropical Regiomontanus
NATAL CHART

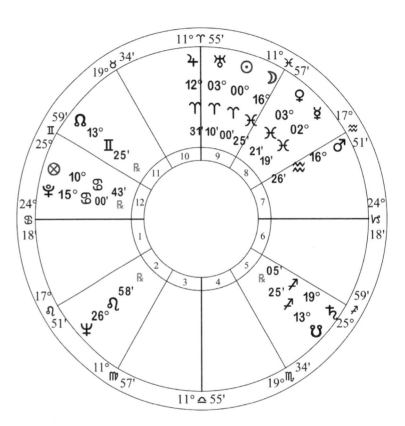

Sun enters Ari 3-20-1928
March 20, 1928 12:44:17 PM
Los Angeles, California
34N03'08" 118W14'34"
Standard Time
Time Zone: 8 hours West
Tropical Regiomontanus
NATAL CHART

of explanatory: how about this? What do we do with the Part of Fortune conjunct the IC conjunct the Sun? The issue here is that the house position of the Part of Fortune is *always* a function of the angular separation of the Sun and Moon – that is how it's defined, after all. Its position here is because the Sun and the Moon are themselves located on angles. But the Part of Fortune can be read through its principal dispositors – the Almuten being also the sign ruler, Jupiter. Jupiter is in the 4th House, the in sect Triplicity ruler of Aries – dignified, but applying by square to that 8th house Pluto. What do we make of this? Vale and Campanella describe the four stages of disaster recovery that is typical in cities – and after the initial clean-up, the rebuilding process often spurs a local economic boom.[172] It is entirely likely that this is Jupiter's involvement – but this idea comes from reasoning out consequences, not merely from reading the chart.

Perhaps the better question astrologically is whether this disaster was predictable – or at least, whether something of its nature was predictable. And this one also is good for addressing a common observation of astrologers who deal with the more personal version of revolutions: solar returns. Astrologers (including myself) often comment on how there are certain intimations of the coming solar return which *seem* to happen before the current solar return is past. Here, we have an event in early March of 1928. This puts the collapse in the final phase of the 1927 solar year. And it also means that much of the clean-up of the disaster would fall in 1928. Which ingress shows the problem?

I calculated the 1927 Ingress for Los Angeles because the dam was being created by the City of Los Angeles for their benefit – so it should fall within the fate of the city. First, we observe that the 1927 Aries Ingress had a cardinal Ascendant, so the dam burst fell under the Capricorn Ingress, which we shall examine next. But for the Aries Ingress itself, Pluto partile conjunct the IC is already a pretty strong warning sign of a problem relating to the land. As we are aware by now, water is not too terribly divorced from land, and it's even showing up through the sign Cancer on the IC. The Moon itself, disposing that IC, is in its Fall in Scorpio. The water sign Part of Fortune conjunct the 8th house cusp – financial benefit from death, as we saw all too clearly with Vale and Campanella. And Uranus is conjunct the Sun in the 12th house from a water sign – they never saw it coming. So the Aries Ingress of 1927 is showing the problem pretty clearly.

When we turn to the Capricorn Ingress of 1927, we see even more. Uranus at 29 degrees Pisces was square the Sun at the MC: a high-profile accident. The Moon was approaching the South Node – a scary prefiguration of the chart of the event itself. Pluto was in the 4th, in an exact contra-antiscial relationship to that Moon.

Contrast this with the Aries Ingress of 1928, not even two weeks after the disaster. Here, the focus is on the 9th, with both Lights there and the Moon applying to square Saturn. The authorities called in university geology professors to figure out what went wrong: and they did come up with part of the picture. Some of the principles known today only emerged from examining dam failures – this, and subsequent ones. One immediate result of the disaster was that the federal government moved in to take a larger role in reviewing the geology of such proposed projects. This raises the question: how do you see the Feds in a chart for a city? I'm tempted to say the 12th, with Pluto and the Part of Fortune there.

Enter the 1930s

It would be entirely justifiable to see the 1930s as the rise of Fascism, running as it did from Nazi gains in the 1930 election through to the outbreak of World War II. But this would also be misleading, because the antecedents to the virulent Anti-semitism of the Nazi Party were already well entrenched in Europe of the 19th century, and in Germany and Austria-Hungary in particular. The crash of 1929 is arguably as great a factor in the growth of Fascism as the remnants of the war reparations still left over from the Great War. The 1930s was a world that still operated under the illusion that there could not be another major war, and where many economies were turned inward, seeking to deal with the economic challenges of the time.

The 1933 election of Franklin Roosevelt as President arguably could have been won by a chimpanzee against the Republican Hoover, who was blamed for the Depression. And speaking of the Depression, what were the astrological indicators for the 1929 crash? In March 1929, Saturn moved from Sagittarius to Capricorn. We have recently seen how many astrologers predicted at least some of the components of what is now called the Great Recession in 2008 based on Pluto's Ingress into Capricorn. Pluto, in the classical sense, doesn't have rulership in any sign: but Saturn does. So the exuberance of Sagittarius (Jupiter's sign) hitting the brick wall of Capricorn (Saturn's sign) was true in this case – except for two added wrinkles. In general, we expect the sign ingresses of Saturn to be less traumatic than those of Pluto, because Pluto spends more time in a sign, and thus, there is more to get used to and then to shake up. But secondly, while Saturn is in rulership in Capricorn, it has mixed Triplicity in Sagittarius – so Saturn is not so out of sorts in Jupiter's day-sign as one might think. Saturn's

Ingress into Capricorn is not enough to explain the 1929 stock market crash and the subsequent Great Depression. As if to support the Saturn theme even further, the other sign ingress that year was Neptune, going from expansionary Leo to penurious Virgo.

Just as we have been discussing the signs of Pluto and their impact on the environment, environmental policy, and politics; Stan Barker did an analogous exercise for the signs of Neptune called *The Signs of the Times: The Neptune Factor and America's Destiny*.[173] Barker talked about the Roaring Twenties specifically as a function of Neptune in Leo – with the party then coming to a crashing halt when Neptune entered Virgo. Playtime and consumption gave way to production and economics – and it hurt! The 1920s stock bubble shared with the 2000s real estate bubble the belief – even kept alive by dubious statistics – that each was part of a permanent (or at least long-term) up-tick. Both times shared the belief that positive feedback could operate without a crash at the end. Both were wrong.

But what is the difference between such a cycle based on Neptune vs. Pluto? Neptune is glamor and fashion – and what was more fashionable than fast cars and a flapper? Pluto is what you do obsessively – whether you actually *want* to do it or not. Hitler rode a wave of anxiety about the future with an economic plan that was shallow and unworkable, but which featured scapegoats, so that the average German could blame somebody else for his or her difficulties.

So what was the Pluto water wave doing as it shifted to accommodate the Virgoan Neptune wave? With the 1933 election, Roosevelt set many plans in motion, all designed to energize the economy into jump-starting, even if the exact means by which this would work were unknown. One of these early programs founded in 1933 was the Civilian Conservation Corps, which funded not only massive tree planting, but also road, fire tower and bridge building. They also funded a number of ecological studies. But as it turned out, this work was too little, too late, because it wasn't big enough to address the less famous reason that the Great Depression lasted as long as it did: the weather.

The Dust Bowl

Recall that in the period of Pluto in Gemini, a great deal of research was begun in the Western U.S. to develop dry farming methods that would be better adapted to the low rainfall conditions of the West. In the 1920s, with Pluto in Cancer, farmers first developed the capability of doing groundwater irrigation. This style of irrigation – the only choice today in many parts of the world – relies on fossil fuel-based pumping to bring groundwater to the surface. You might recall that it was this water-pumping technology that was utilized during Pluto in Taurus to adapt to pumping oil to the surface. By the 1920s, there were irrigation wells with electric or diesel motors that farmers could install to drill deeper than had previously been feasible. With these wells, farmers were not completely dependent on rainfall in order to grow crops. But the technology was only beginning, and these wells were not yet very deep – deep well technology was not available to farmers until the end of Pluto in Cancer. So most farmers remained dependent upon rainfall. And this became a problem.

In 1930 and 1931, drought came to the Eastern U.S. In 1934, drought conditions occurred in 80% of the U.S., recurring in 1936, 1939, and 1940. For farmers dependent upon rainfall – and rainfall at the right time of year to harvest crops at all – this was disastrous. But even more ruinous, when crops couldn't grow, topsoil was exposed – and topsoil could simply blow away. The 1929 crash had devastated the stock market, banks had been hit and many were insolvent – and then the weather didn't cooperate, leaving the farmers dependent on banks that couldn't handle it... the cycle goes on.

We can see the issues building through Chart 35, those three years of drought. 1930 has Venus in Aries in a partile conjunction to Uranus ruling the 4th house cusp. The land is hot and dry, and the Moon is also in a fire sign. The ruler of the 4th is in the 2nd, along with the Sun, focusing on prices. The ruler of the 2nd is in detriment.

In 1931, the 4th house cusp itself is a fire sign, with the disposing Sun also fire by definition, and the Moon in a fire sign as well. Hot and dry all around, with Uranus, Mercury, and the North Node also hot and dry.

Finally, in 1934, Venus ruling the 4th is at least not in fire, but partile conjunct the North Node, with the nodal axis across the 2nd – 8th axis of the chart. The Sun and Mars are conjunct. The South Node in fire is at the 8th house cusp, and the Moon is in a barren sign.

But under these weather conditions, Roosevelt's Civilian Conservation Corps looks a lot more progressive, because what they were doing was building windbreaks which would slow down soil erosion. Unfortunately, these efforts were not enough. Dust storms began to be seen in the Great Plains and the Midwest as early as 1932, but, at first, they were localized. Everything came to a head on Black Sunday, April 14, 1935. On that day, life simply came to a halt because the amount of dust in the atmosphere with 60 mph winds created impassable conditions. This was a hurricane of soil, not rain. It was the visual evidence of over one hundred million acres partially or completed denuded of topsoil. The name Dust Bowl appeared in the Associated Press on April 15, 1935.

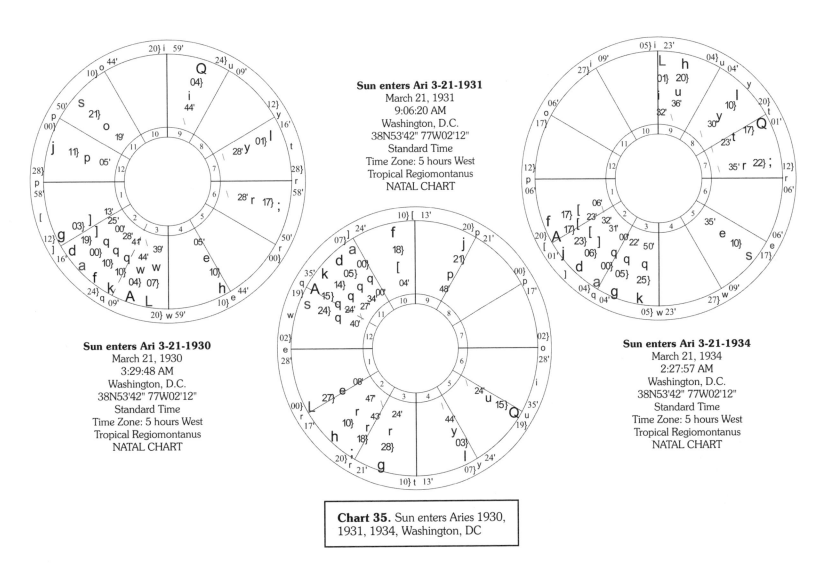

Sun enters Ari 3-21-1931
March 21, 1931
9:06:20 AM
Washington, D.C.
38N53'42" 77W02'12"
Standard Time
Time Zone: 5 hours West
Tropical Regiomontanus
NATAL CHART

Sun enters Ari 3-21-1930
March 21, 1930
3:29:48 AM
Washington, D.C.
38N53'42" 77W02'12"
Standard Time
Time Zone: 5 hours West
Tropical Regiomontanus
NATAL CHART

Sun enters Ari 3-21-1934
March 21, 1934
2:27:57 AM
Washington, D.C.
38N53'42" 77W02'12"
Standard Time
Time Zone: 5 hours West
Tropical Regiomontanus
NATAL CHART

Chart 35. Sun enters Aries 1930, 1931, 1934, Washington, DC

This dramatic catastrophe propelled a technological thrust for improved drilling and groundwater irrigation as farmers said – never again! The scientists who studied the region discovered the Ogallala Aquifer – a huge underground water cache underlying states from Nebraska to New Mexico. But drilling that deep required hydraulic rigs that could no longer be run by wind power; they needed petroleum. So farmers invested in drilling equipment and drove the technology toward dependence on fossil water. And some banks were smart enough to see the benefit of lending money for this purpose. Energy independence of the farms disappeared as farmers worked to become drought independent. This also drove the acquisition of larger farms – relatively easy, since so many had simply abandoned the land when the Dust Bowl hit. The greater financial and power requirements of drilling and groundwater *mining* (because that's what we should call it, as it is the extraction of a non-renewable resource) made the family-farm obsolete as the optimal farm size. The bigger farms mandated by the water requirements in turn necessitated bigger tractors and more machinery and still more energy dependence on fossil fuels.[174]

When we examine a chart for the Dust Bowl, it is certainly striking. The Aries Ingress for Washington, DC, for 1935, Chart 36, has a very unusual configuration: the South Node partile conjunct the 4th house cusp. What better symbol for the destruction of the country's land?

In the middle of a depression, the Pisces Mercury in Detriment (and Fall) and conjunct Saturn makes sense as a 2nd house ruler. So does Venus, Ruler of the Ascendant in Detriment and in the 12th house conjunct Uranus, at the Bendings. What is interesting was that Venus, no matter how afflicted, was at the Northern Bendings, not the Southern one. The problem associated with the Northern Bendings is being ahead of one's time. This may well indicate the leap of faith that farmers made at this time in choosing to invest in the future through technological upgrades. While it was horrendous getting there, one has to grant that this was by far the best choice for the time.

While my comments about "mining water" may have seemed a little harsh, the fact is that, seventy five years later, the water tables under the Great Plains have dropped by 100 feet. The Ogallala Aquifer was estimated to be between 150-300 feet thick. A little math suggests that therefore, it is entirely possible that between one-third and two-thirds of the water in that aquifer has already been used. And it doesn't take much more math at all to realize that it would take a lot less than eighty years to use up the rest. What happens at that time? Does the entire Great Plains return to dependence on rainfall? What impact would that have on U.S. farming production? Will they then attempt to drain the Great Lakes?

The problem with "it seemed like a good idea at the time" as a working principle is that one's successors forget that today's "business as usual" is yesterday's "it seemed like a good idea at the time." Midwest farmers today don't have to think about the size of the aquifer, because they never had to face farming without one. Because of this, it's hard to mobilize people to act in advance of the next crisis. Which, in relation to fossil groundwater, I would predict will fall by the time Pluto is in Pisces, or even Aquarius – unless we start pro-acting about it. This change in utilization of groundwater has a major impact on land use in the U.S.A., as agriculture moved West when water ceased to be a limiting resource. There was a marked abandonment of farms in the Eastern part of the U.S. – the very area least dependent on irrigation.[175]

Just as Pluto in Cancer started with World War I, Pluto leaves Cancer with World War II. But we shall defer the discussion of that war until we reach the fire signs.

NATAL CHART
Sun enters Ari 3-21-1935
March 21, 1935
8:17:47 AM
Washington, D.C.
38N53'42" 77W02'12"
Standard Time
Time Zone: 5 hours West
Tropical Regiomontanus

Chart 36. Sun enters Aries 1935, Washington, DC

Day of ♃	Hour of ☉
Last Hr ♂	- 2 mins
Next Hr ♀	+58 mins

FIXED STARS	
☿☌ Sadalmelik	0°39's
♀☌ Alrischa	0°27's
☿☌ Fomalhaut	0°09's
♅☌ Mirach	0°09's
♃☌ Agena	0°12'a
♄☌ Deneb Adige	0°17'a
♀☌ Mirach	0°35'a

Hs	Alm. (Dor)
1	♀
2	☿
3	♃
4	☽
5	☉
6	♄
7	♂
8	♃
9	♄
10	♄
11	♄
12	☉

ESSENTIAL DIGNITIES (Dorothean)

Pl	Ruler	Exalt	Tripl	Term	Face	Detri	Fall	Score
☉	♂	☉ +	☉ +	♃	♂	♀	♄	+7
☽	♀	♄	♄	♃	♄	♂	☉	- 5 P
☿	♃	♀	♀	♀	♄	☿ -	☿ -	- 14 P
♀	♂ m	☉	☉	♄ m	♀ +	♀ -	♄	+1
♂	♀ m	♄	♄	☿	♃	♂ -	☉	- 5 P
♃	♂	--	♀	☿	♀	♀	☽	- 5 P
♄	♃	♀	♀	♀ m	♄ +	☿	☿	+1
☊	♄	♂	♀	♄	☉	☽	♃	--
⊗	♃	☋ +	☉	♃	☿	☿	--	--
As	♀	☽	♀	♃	☽	♂	--	--
Mc	♄	♂	♀	♄	☉	☽	♃	--
☋	☽	♃	♀	♄	☽	♄	♂	--

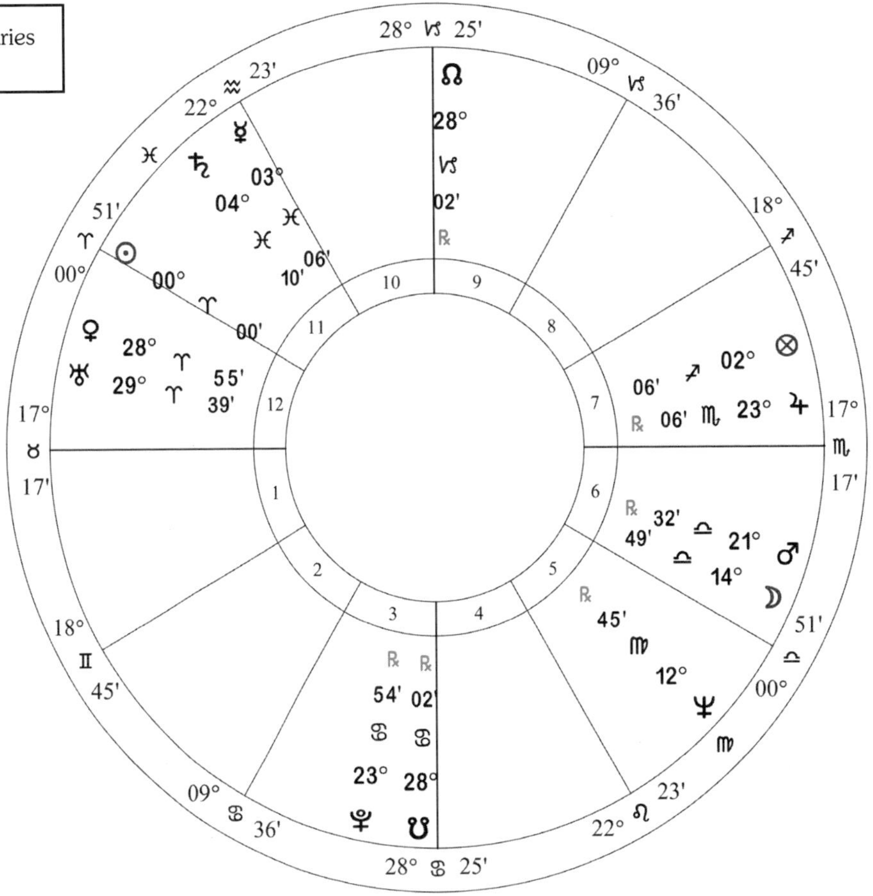

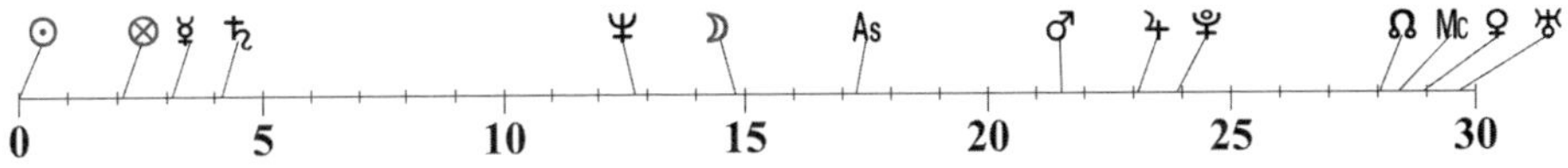

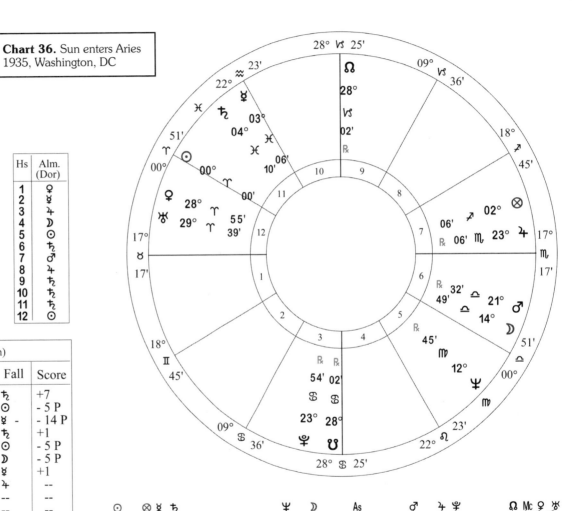

Pluto in Scorpio
1983 – 1995

The transition to Pluto in Scorpio occurred in the U.S.A. during the 1st term of Ronald Reagan's presidency. It was clear from the beginning that the Reagan White House put no priority whatsoever on environmental issues. The Republican reaction to environmental problems – to the extent that they were acknowledged at all – was to presume that good ol' American know-how could be applied to fix any problem.

It's worth stopping to consider this idea. Was this position really far-fetched? The answer has to be: no, it wasn't. As Peter Ho has said quite bluntly:

> *Although initially successful, the increasingly catastrophic predictions and environmental doomsaying of the green movement during the 1960s and 1970s proved self-defeating in the end. For one thing, Neo-Malthusianism was surprisingly resilient as an explanatory philosophy in the face of ever-expanding – and yet still surviving – Spaceship Earth..... The juggling of statistics by green activists to support their cause incited fierce criticism of the Limits-to-Growth approach. According to Maddux (1972:2) "the doomsday cause would be more telling if it were more securely grounded in fact," while Simon declared the work of the Club of Rome to be a "fascinating example of how scientific work can be outrageously bad and yet be very influential" (Simon, 1981: 286). The result of garbled data on sustainability had been the emergence of a countercurrent in environmental thinking.*[176]

Jimmy Carter had tried to view energy policy as a realist – and he was immensely unpopular in this quest. The reason? Probably because Americans did not want to think about real limits to anything. Environmentalists had only to look at the figures for population growth, which was exponential, to be completely alarmed. The party had to end *sometime*, but when? Others either saw the population problem as being much further out in time, or they assumed that there would come a technical fix. After all, the "solution" to the Dust Bowl is a perfect example of this – didn't scientific study discover the aquifers, while engineering provided the means to exploit them?

The argument then devolved into two rigid sides. Environmentalists (pessimists) would respond by saying, "Yes! That time, there was a solution – but how many times will this continue to be true?" And then the other side (optimists) would respond by saying, "Where there's a will (and enough funding) there's a way." Both sides were pretty frozen in position by the time of Pluto in Scorpio, and the period opened with the Optimists at the helm of government, and the pessimists camped out in academia.

And it didn't hurt that Pluto in Scorpio opened in a business expansionary period that lasted until 1990. The economy appeared to be cooperating with Reagan's vision. So it is probably not surprising that the first three major salvos of environmental issues with Pluto in Scorpio occurred outside U.S. boundaries.

Bhopal

The first, in 1984, involved the toxic release of gas from a manufacturing plant in India owned by a U.S. company.

From this point, the name Bhopal would refer not to a city, but a tragedy. Many astrologers examined and published on this disaster. Re-examining the chart now, well after the fact, allows us to raise again some of the issues related to event interpretation. Perusing a source like Wikipedia reveals a chronology of the disaster, but also points out an essential characteristic of it: several steps happened, any one of which was necessary to the eventual gas leak: but what is the moment of the event?[177] That is always the question so important in event astrology. Most astrologers would probably say that the correct time to use was the actual moment for when the gas was released into the atmosphere: that is the time I am using here. But 90 minutes before, operations to clean the pipes leading to the methyl isocyanate tank began. Thirty minutes before the release, water entered that tank, beginning the reactions to produce the gas. Years before, the safety equipment for the methyl isocyanate had stopped working. One might even go so far as to say that the accident was set up by Union Carbide (now part of Dow Chemical) choosing to site this dangerous operation outside the U.S.A., in a location where safety regulations and inspections were less intense.

But here in Chart 37, the release of toxic gas is the point where something bad has occurred. Were I to believe this time were perfectly accurate, then I might be highly impressed by the presence of the shipwreck star Scheat right at the 8th house cusp: Scheat's interpretation is very close to the English four letter expletive that has a similar pronunciation. With the Moon in the 8th and its dispositor Mars in the 6th, casualties are going to happen. The Ascendant, 2nd, and 10th house ruler, Mercury, is partile conjunct Neptune. The 10th ruler would be Union Carbide, as the owner of the company. Union Carbide claimed that sabotage was the cause of the accident, not negligence on their part. Does this chart support this idea? By charging sabotage, we do have to decide who would want to sabotage it? Enemies of the state? Of Union Carbide? The workers, out for revenge?

We have already seen how it may be possible to use the rules for theft to apply to other criminal acts. If we do this, then the first thing we note is that the angular peregrine planets are Mercury and the Sun. Mercury rules the 10th, the 1st, and the 2nd, but not the 6th. The 10th would be management; the 6th would be workers, the 4th would be enemies of the 10th. Because Mercury does *not* rule the 6th, this was not sabotage by workers. The only obvious party implicated by Mercury is management. The Sun, conjunct the 4th house cusp, rules the 12th of secret enemies and applies to a sextile of Mars in the 6th house of illness. The prominence of Mercury suggests that it was mistakes by management, not the workers, that set up this tragedy.

If we want to look at the prediction of the disaster, then we have to examine the Aries Ingress for 1984 in India, shown here as Chart 38. The translation of the light between Pluto and Saturn in Scorpio, by debilitated Moon in Scorpio, is a very notable signature for this ingress. The Midheaven of this chart is close to Algol, a fixed star we have already seen as being of a dangerous character. Mars is at the IC – and very strong. Actually, three malefics are in the 4th house, and that is not a good sign. The Sun is in the 8th house of death. The fixed angles and late ascending degree may also suggest that this problem was long in the making – as it surely was.

NATAL CHART
Bhopal disaster
December 2, 1984
11:30 PM
Bhopal, India
23 N 16 77 E 24
Standard Time
Time Zone: 5 hr 30 min East
Tropical Regiomontanus

Chart 37. Bhopal disaster

Day of ☉	Hour of ☽
Last Hr ☿	- 27 mins
Next Hr ♄	+40 mins

FIXED STARS	
♃☌Vega	0°11'a
Mc☌Mirfak	0°35'a
☊☌Algol	0°44'a

Hs	Alm. (Dor)
1	☿
2	☿
3	♀
4	♃
5	♄
6	♄
7	♀
8	♃
9	♂
10	☿
11	☽
12	☉

ESSENTIAL DIGNITIES (Dorothean)

Pl	Ruler	Exalt	Tripl	Term	Face	Detri	Fall	Score
☉	♃	☋	♃	♀	☽	☿	--	- 5 P
☽	♂	☉	♃ m	♀	♂	♀	♄	- 5 P
☿	♄	♂	☽	♀	♃	☽	♃	- 5 P
♀	♄	♂	☽	♂ m	☉	☽	♃	- 5 P
♂	♄ m	--	☿	♀ m	☿	☉	--	+0 P
♃	♄	♂	☽ m	♃ +	♂	☽	♃ -	- 2
♄	♂ m	--	♂	☿	♀	♀	☽	+0 P
☊	♀	☽	☽	♂	♄	♂	--	--
⊗	♀	☽	☽	♀	☿	♂	--	--
As	☿	☿	☽	☿	☉	♃	♀	--
Mc	☿	☊	☿	☿	♃	♃	--	--
☋	♂	--	♂	☿	♀	♀	☽	--

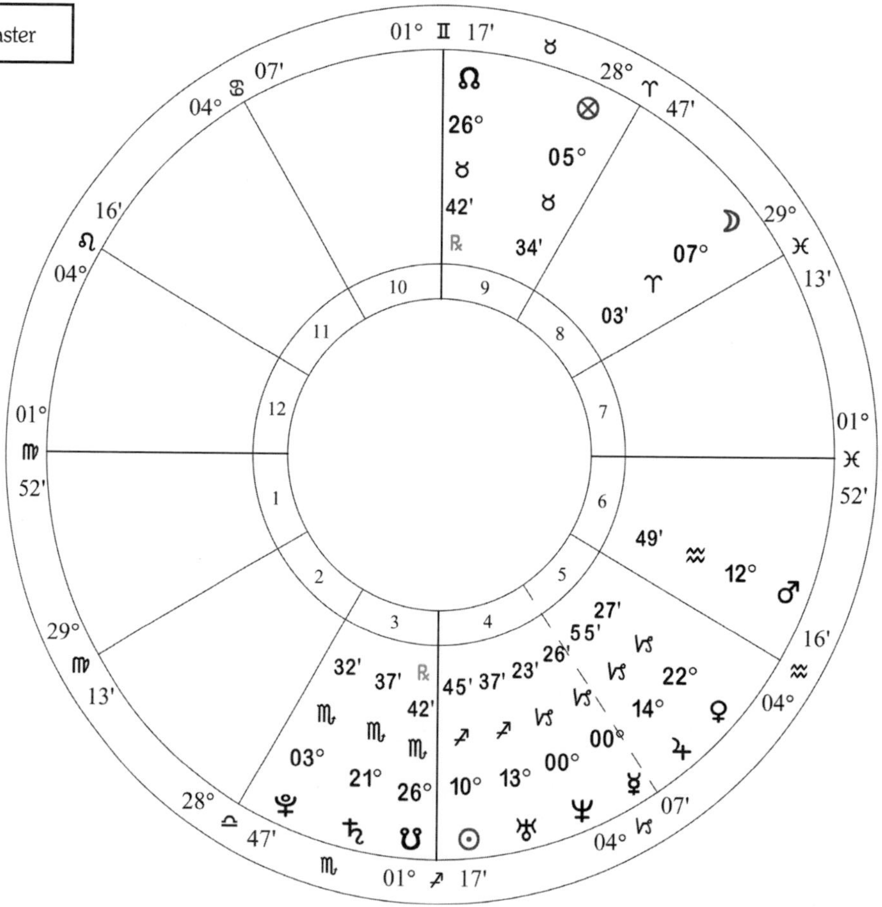

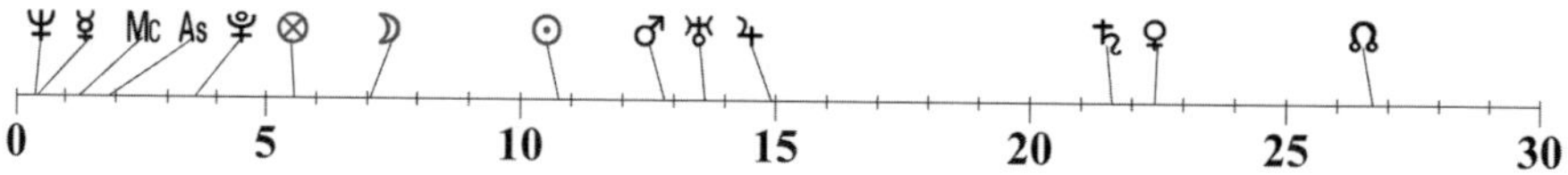

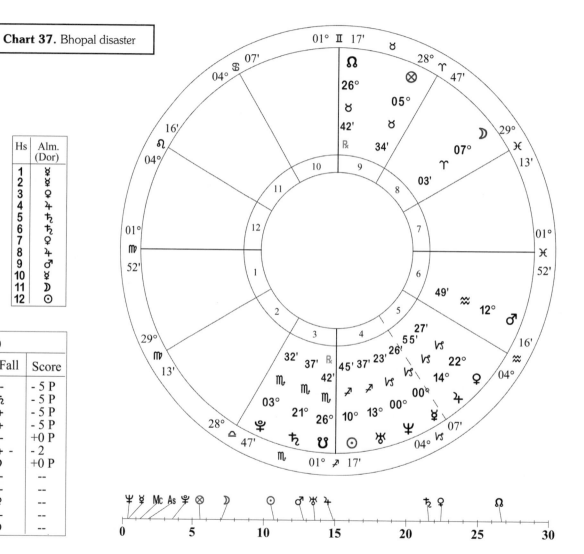

NATAL CHART
Sun enters Ari 3-20-1984
March 20, 1984
3:54:21 PM
New Delhi, India
28 N 36 77 E 12
Standard Time
Time Zone: 5 hr 30 min East
Tropical Regiomontanus

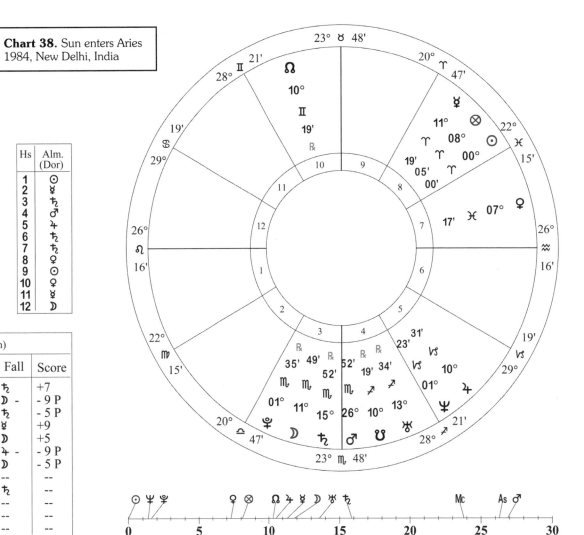

Chart 38. Sun enters Aries 1984, New Delhi, India

Day of ♂	Hour of ♀
Last Hr ☉	- 26 mins
Next Hr ☿	+34 mins

FIXED STARS	
☉☌Scheat	0°51's
☽☌ Acrux	0°10's
Mc☌Capulus	0°10'a
☽☌ Alphecca	0°15'a
☊☌Aldebaran	0°45'a
As☌Alphard	0°47'a

Hs	Alm. (Dor)
1	☉
2	☿
3	♄
4	♂
5	♃
6	♄
7	♄
8	♀
9	☉
10	♀
11	☿
12	☽

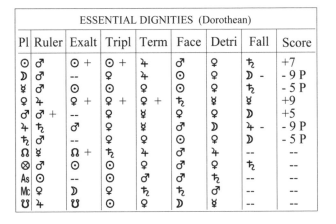

ESSENTIAL DIGNITIES (Dorothean)

Pl	Ruler	Exalt	Tripl	Term	Face	Detri	Fall	Score
☉	♂	☉ +	☉ +	♃	♂	♀	♄	+7
☽	♂	--	♀	♃	☉	♀	☽ -	- 9 P
☿	♂	☉	☉	♀	☉	♀	♄	- 5 P
♀	♃	♀ +	♀ +	♀ +	♄	☿	☿	+9
♂	♂ +	--	♀	☿	♀	♀	☽	+5
♃	♄	♂	♀	☿	♂	☽	♃ -	- 9 P
♄	♂	--	♀	♀	☉	♀	☽	- 5 P
☊	☿	☊ +	♄	♃	♂	♃	--	--
⊗	♂	☉	☉	♀	♂	♀	♄	--
As	☉	--	☉	♂	♂	♄	--	--
Mc	♀	☽	♀	♄	♄	♂	--	--
☋	♃	☋	☉	♀	☽	☿	--	--

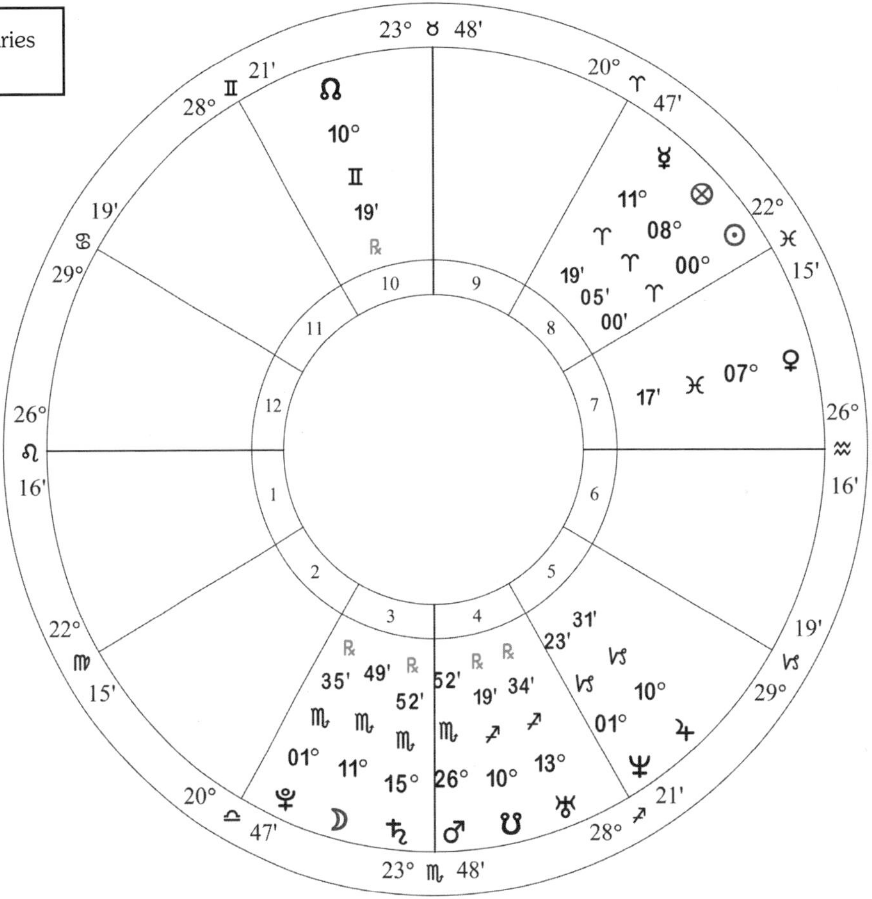

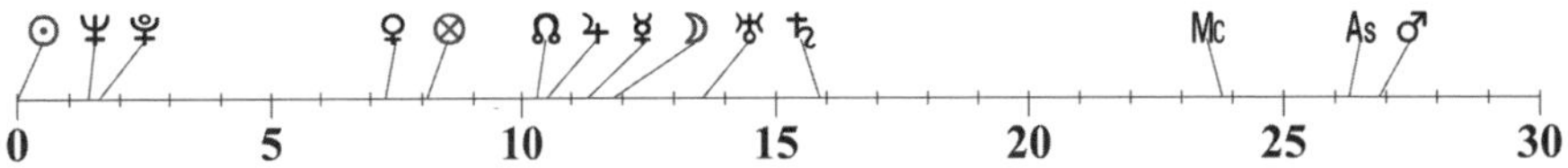

1985: The Ozone Hole and The Rainbow Warrior

The very next year, the ozone hole was discovered over Antarctica. Once the existence was confirmed, and the cause was traced to fluorocarbons, eventually, legislation banning them was passed at the international level as well as within the U.S.A.

The ozone hole may have been caused by human activity – but no one set out to deliberately create it. The same cannot be said of the second environmental news story of 1985: the deliberate sinking of the *Rainbow Warrior*, a ship owned by Greenpeace. As it was subsequently established, the French government had ordered its secret service to destroy the *Rainbow Warrior* in a misguided attempt to cut off protests against the continued nuclear weapons testing by France at Moruroa Atoll in the Pacific Ocean. France's atomic weapons program was a child of Pluto in Virgo, where their first test sites were located in the Sahara Desert. After 1966, they relocated to the Pacific. By the time of this relocation, only France and China were doing atmospheric testing. Despite the bad publicity, the French government did not abandon testing until Pluto was barely into Sagittarius.

In 1985, the French got more than they bargained for, because the destruction of the *Rainbow Warrior* produced still more protest and especially bad publicity, once the French government had been identified as the perpetrator.[178]

As we did with the sinking of the *Maine*, we examine William Lilly's section on ships at sea (Appendix D). Here's a more detailed description of his considerations for Chart 39.

- The Ascendant and the Moon rule the ship

- The Ruler of the Ascendant is the crew

- Connection between Ascendant and 8th can indicate death

- Shipwreck is given by the Ruler of the Ascendant in the 8th, or in a malefic relation to the Ruler of the 8th, 4th, 6th or 12th; or a malefic in the 1st and disposing the 8th; or the Moon combust or under the earth

- If the Ruler of the Ascendant is fortunate but the Moon and the ascending degree are afflicted, the crew is safe, but the ship is wrecked.[179]

In this event for the bombing, the Ruler of the 1st and the 8th are the same: just as occurred with the sinking of the *Maine* that we examined in Chapter 4. Mars, Ruler of the 1st is combust. The Moon under the Earth is another argument that the ship is lost – just like the *Maine*![180]

Like the *Maine*, we know the ship exploded. Again, like the *Maine*, we have Mars in the 4th – malefics in angular houses are a danger to the ship.[181] The South Node is in the 8th house, dangerous in the sign that rules where the crewmen are lodged. Now this is especially fascinating, because the one death that resulted from the bombing was of a photographer who went back to his quarters, presumably to get his camera, and then was trapped there and drowned. Lilly says: *"If the unfortunate Signes (viz., those which are afflicted by the presence of Saturn, Mars or South Node) be those which signifie the bottom of that*

NATAL CHART
Rainbow Warrior bombing
July 10, 1985
11:38 PM
Auckland, New Zealand
36 S 52 174 E 46
Standard Time
Time Zone: 12 hours East
Tropical Regiomontanus

Chart 39. *Rainbow Warrior* bombing

Day of ☿	Hour of ♃
Last Hr ♄	- 24 mins
Next Hr ♂	+48 mins

FIXED STARS	
☿☌ Acubens	0°57's
♂☌ Castor	0°26's
☊☌ Menkar	0°57'a

Hs	Alm. (Dor)
1	♂
2	☽♀
3	☿
4	♃
5	☉
6	☿
7	♀
8	♂
9	♃
10	♄
11	☿
12	♃

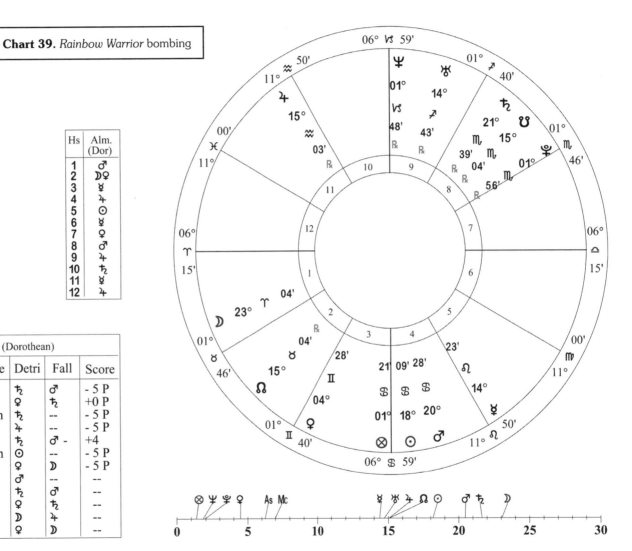

ESSENTIAL DIGNITIES (Dorothean)

Pl	Ruler	Exalt	Tripl	Term	Face	Detri	Fall	Score
☉	☽	♃	♂	☿	☿	♄	♂	- 5 P
☽	♂ m	☉	♃	♂	♀	♀	♄	+0 P
☿	☉	--	♃ m	♀ m	♃ m	♄	--	- 5 P
♀	☿	☊	☿	☿ m	♃	♃	--	- 5 P
♂	☽ m	♃	♂ +	♀	☽	♄	♂ -	+4
♃	♄	--	☿ m	♀	☿ m	☉	--	- 5 P
♄	♂	--	♂	☿	♀	♀	☽	- 5 P
☊	♀	☽	☽	♃	☽	♂	--	--
⊗	☽	♃	♂	♂	♀	♄	♂	--
As	♂	☉	♃	♀	♂	♀	♄	--
Mc	♄	♂	☽	☿	♃	☽	♃	--
☋	♂	--	♂	♀	☉	♀	☽	--

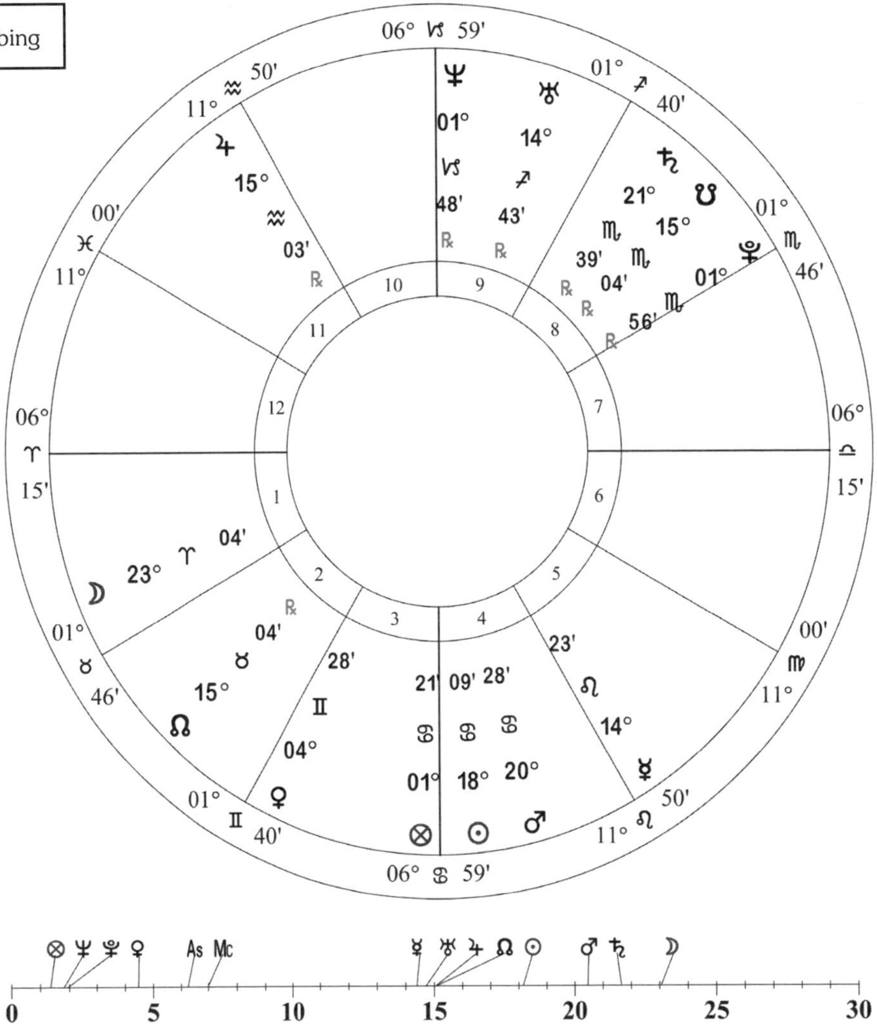

part of the Ship which is under Water, it's an argument of the breaking and drowning thereof, or receiving some dangerous Leak..."[182] Here, we have Mars in Cancer – the sign of the bottom of the ship – in the 4th house.[183]

Unlike the situation with the *Maine*, we know this was sabotage and we know who did it. But can we see anything else about this in the chart? The interpretation is going to be different, because here the contenders are a nonprofit political action organization and a sovereign government – and Greenpeace is not a French organization. This is not a usual pairing, and that makes it more difficult to assign houses.

First, I was struck by Pluto sitting right on the 8th house cusp. The whole reason that Greenpeace was there in the first place – and why the French bombed them – was because of protests against the continuing French nuclear testing program. Many astrologers have associated Pluto with nuclear power, and I can see many good reasons to do so, too. The Part of Fortune in a partile trine to that Pluto from the 4th suggests that Greenpeace's actions actually did help to further their goal of stopping the nuclear tests – and the opposition to Neptune does suggest the sneakiness of the French operation – and how its uncovering actually gave Greenpeace far more publicity than they ever could have achieved without the loss of their vessel.

One could perhaps argue for France here as being the 7th house since they're the "enemy" of the ship. Although this is not a government-to-government confrontation, Greenpeace already was in an action against France. As such, the ship's enemy is Venus, peregrine and cadent. France may have succeeded in the bombing, but they lost very publicly when their actions were exposed.

In Chart 40, I present here a comparison of the sinking of the *Maine* and the bombing of the *Rainbow Warrior* because there really are some stunning similarities.

Among the similarities are:

• Ruler of 1st and 8th is the same planet

• Ruler of 1st (and 8th) is combust

• The Moon is under the earth

• Each has an angular malefic Mars in the 4th

• Each has an affliction in the sign of Cancer, which rules the bottom of the ship.

We shouldn't leave the *Rainbow Warrior* without also examining Chart 41, the Aries Ingress, which is done for Auckland, New Zealand, as the site of the bombing. And this raises yet another question: does one use the Aries Ingress as the start of the year in the Southern Hemisphere or should the Libra Ingress be used? My initial hypothesis would be that the use of the Aries Ingress has a strong resonance with beginning of the year that developed in the cultures that later "discovered," settled and exploited the Southern Hemisphere. On that basis, the Aries Ingress is more a calendar statement than just a seasonal one, and so it should stand. However, since I have not exhaustively tested this hypothesis, I am open to the possibility that perhaps the Libra Ingress should be used in its stead.

As we already discussed, part of what makes it hard to determine the house rulerships is the non-governmental status of

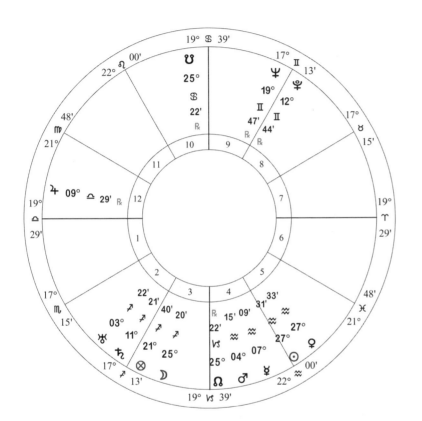

Sinking of the Maine
February 15, 1898
9:40 PM
Havana, Cuba
23 N 08 82 W 22
Standard Time
Time Zone: 5 hr 30 min West
Tropical Regiomontanus
NATAL CHART

Chart 40. Sinking of the *Maine* and *Rainbow Warrior* bombing

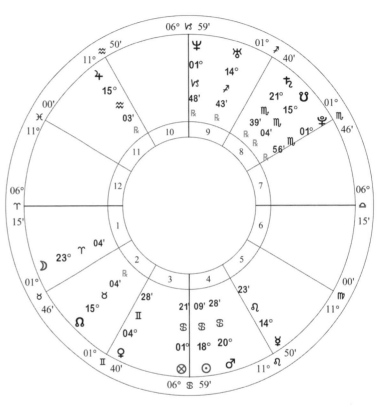

Rainbow Warrior bombing
July 10, 1985
11:38 PM
Auckland, New Zealand
36 S 52 174 E 46
Standard Time
Time Zone: 12 hours East
Tropical Regiomontanus
NATAL CHART

NATAL CHART
Sun enters Ari 3-20-1985
March 21, 1985
4:13:45 AM
Auckland, New Zealand
36 S 52 174 E 46
Standard Time
Time Zone: 12 hours East
Tropical Regiomontanus

Chart 41. Sun enters Aries 1985, Auckland, New Zealand

Day of ☿	Hour of ☿
Last Hr ♀	- 45 mins
Next Hr ☽	+15 mins

FIXED STARS	
☉☌Scheat	0°50's
As☌Sadalmelik	0°42'a
Mc☌Toliman	0°43'a

Hs	Alm. (Dor)
1	♀
2	♃
3	♂
4	☽
5	☽
6	☉
7	☿
8	☿
9	♀
10	♂
11	♄
12	☿♄

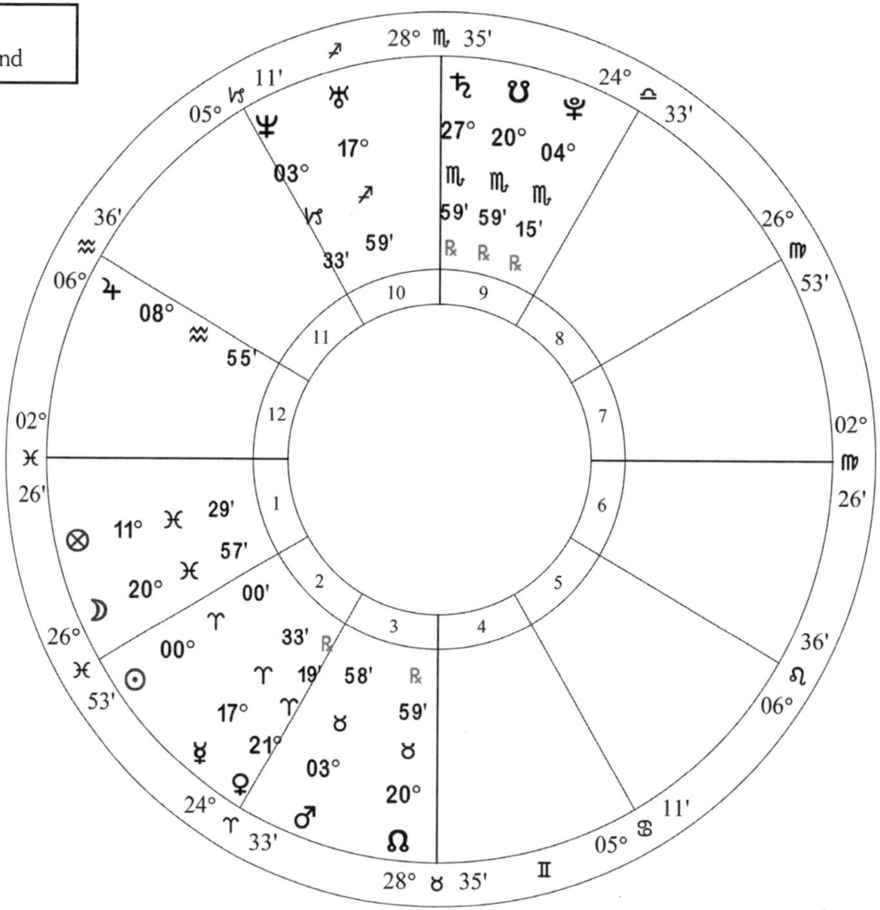

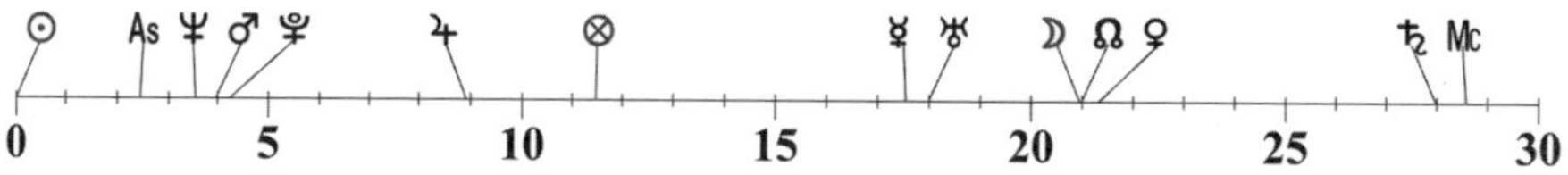

ESSENTIAL DIGNITIES (Dorothean)								
Pl	Ruler	Exalt	Tripl	Term	Face	Detri	Fall	Score
☉	♂	☉ +	♃	♃	♂	♀	♄	+4
☽	♃	♀	♂ m	☿	♂	☿	☿	- 5 P
☿	♂	☉	♃ m	☿ +	☉	♀	♄	+2
♀	♂ m	☉	♃	♂ m	♀ +	♀ -	♄	+1
♂	♀ m	☽	☽ m	♀ m	☿	♂ -	--	- 5 P
♃	♄	--	☿ m	☿	♀	☉	--	- 5 P
♄	♂	--	♂	♄ +	♀	♀	☽	+2
☊	♀	☽	☽	♃	♄	♂	--	--
⊗	♃	♀	♂	♃	♃	☿	☿	--
As	♃	♀	♂	♀	♄	☿	☿	--
Mc	♂	--	♂	♄	♀	♀	☽	--
☋	♂	--	♂	♀	♀	♀	☽	--

Greenpeace. Drawn for Auckland, Greenpeace could probably be seen as 11th house – an association. With Neptune there, it's not clear whether the deception is on the part of the organization – or applied to it. This could also be idealism, but it could also represent spying by the French government on Greenpeace itself. But Saturn ruled the 11th – the organization, and it was conjunct the Midheaven – publicity comes to the organization – but under unfortunate circumstances.

The South Node and Pluto are in the 9th. New Zealand, like many of the oceanic states, considered the nuclear testing that France (a 9th house entity) was doing to be unsafe. The Mars-Pluto opposition for this chart suggests that these profound differences in viewpoint were coming to a head.

Chernobyl

If the sinking of the *Rainbow Warrior* highlighted issues relating to radioactivity, then the nuclear accident at Chernobyl the following year prevented anyone from forgetting about it for very long.

The accident at Chernobyl remains the largest nuclear power accident ever, contaminating vast tracts of the Soviet Union and Europe, releasing four hundred times more fallout than the bombings of Hiroshima and Nagasaki. The accident occurred at the end of an experiment, when coolant rods lowered into the reactor failed to stop the reaction before coolant had boiled off, with the result that two explosions occurred.

Chart 42 for the 1:23 A.M. power spike that resulted in the explosion of the core shows Uranus rising, which is as dramatic as could be for an accident. We have a poisoning event with the Moon in Scorpio, in this case, ruling the 8th. The Sun was in a partile opposition to Pluto, and that opposition fell in angular houses. The South Node at the MC shows the very public nature of the disaster. In fact, this chart has a lot of angularity, which emphasizes its impact beyond the immediate area of the region. Mars and Neptune in the 1st show the explosion: and probably confusion related to the end of the experiment, and most certainly, the slowness of understanding the developing catastrophe.

Looking at the Aries Ingress for Moscow for 1986 (Chart 43), I have to say that the chart is not as compelling as some: but still suggestive. Saturn is conjunct the Ascendant. The Moon so dignified in the 8th unfortunately denotes the deaths – although the immediate number of deaths was not reported as high as Bhopal. Like the accident chart, there is a lot of angularity here: Mars, Saturn, and Uranus in the 1st, with debilitated Venus in the 4th, and Sun conjunct the IC.

For comparison, I also present the Aries Ingress for Kiev. At the time of the accident, the Ukraine was part of the USSR, so Moscow was the legal capital, and thus Kiev was a regional capital. We can see that the chart was very similar, except that the Sun was in the 4th, not just conjunct the IC from the 3rd, as it was in Moscow. The Kiev IC was the degree of the fixed star Scheat, that we found active at Bhopal. The Sun applied to square Neptune, which may be a good indicator of the confusion at the time about coolant temperature in the reactor.

NATAL CHART
Chernobyl accident
April 26, 1986
1:23 AM
Chernobyl, Kijev, Ukraine
51 N 17 30 E 15
Daylight Saving Time
Time Zone: 3 hours East
Tropical Regiomontanus

Chart 42. Chernobyl accident

Day of ♀	Hour of ♄
Last Hr ☽	- 15 mins
Next Hr ♃	+34 mins

Hs	Alm. (Dor)
1	♃
2	♄
3	♃
4	♂
5	☽
6	☿
7	☿
8	☽
9	☿
10	♀
11	♂
12	♃

FIXED STARS	
♄☌ Antares	0°59's
☽☌ Agena	0°50's
As☌ Rasalhague	0°34's
☊☌ Mirach	0°29's
♅☌ Rasalhague	0°14's
☊☌ Alrischa	0°33'a
♃☌ Achernar	0°44'a
♀☌ Alcyone	0°55'a
♃☌ Ankaa	0°55'a

ESSENTIAL DIGNITIES (Dorothean)

Pl	Ruler	Exalt	Tripl	Term	Face	Detri	Fall	Score
☉	♀	☽	☽	♀	☿ m	♂	--	- 5 P
☽	♂	--	♂ m	☿	♀	♀	☽ -	- 9 P
☿	♂	☉	♃	♀	☉ m	♀	♄	- 5 P
♀	♀ +	☽	☽	♂	♄	♂	--	+5
♂	♄	♂ +	☽ m	♃	♂ +	☽	♃	+5
♃	♃ +	♀	♂	☿	♃ +	☿	☿	+6
♄	♃	☋	♃	♀	☿	☿	--	- 5 P
☊	♂	☉	♃	♄	♀	♀	♄	--
⊗	☿	☊	☿	☿	♃	♃	--	--
As	♃	☋	♃	♄	♄	☿	--	--
Mc	♀	♄	☿	♂	♃	♂	☉	--
☋	♀	♄	☿	♂	♃	♂	☉	--

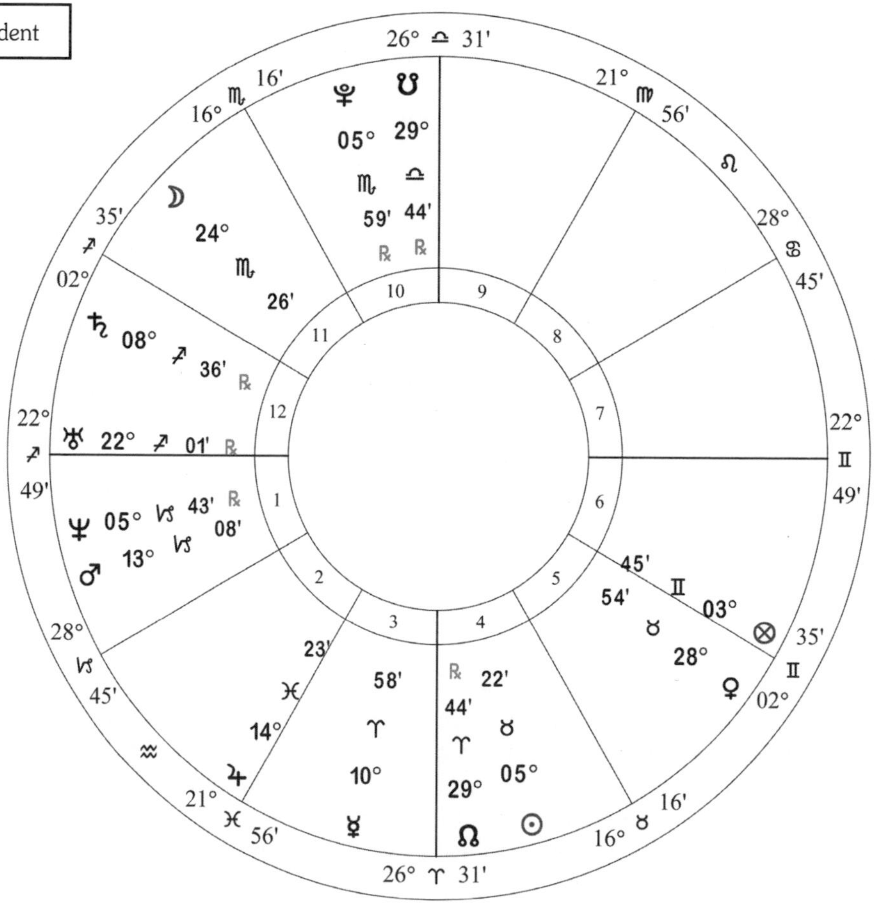

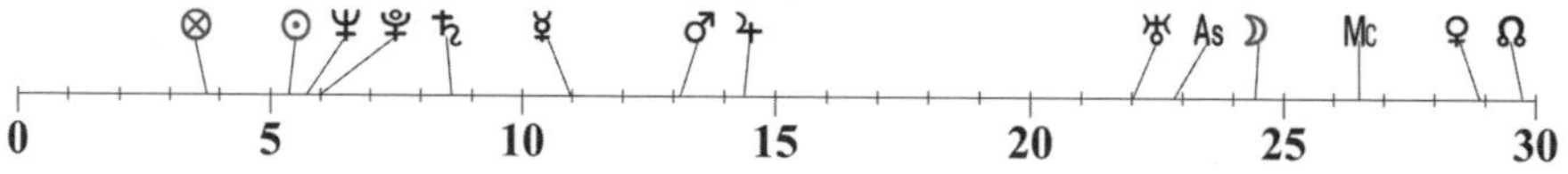

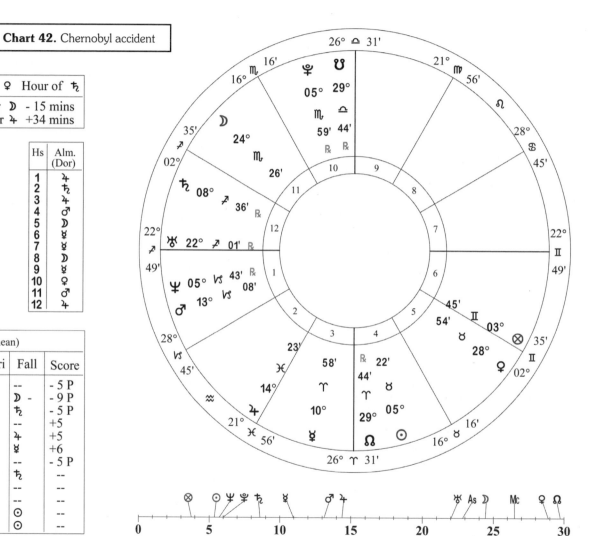

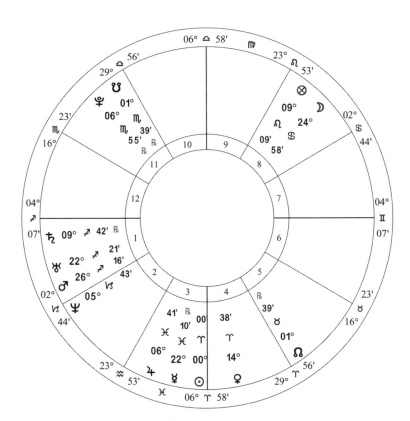

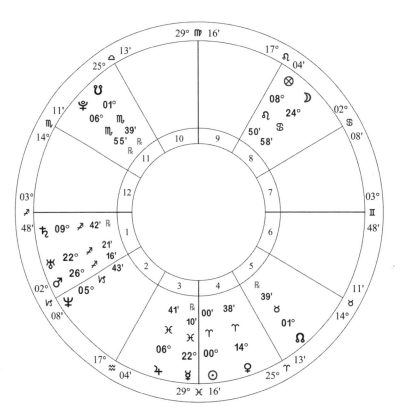

Chart 43. Sun enters Aries
1986, Moscow and Kiev, USSR

Sun enters Ari 3-20-1986
March 21, 1986
1:02:43 AM
Moscow, Moskva, Russia
55 N 45 37 E 35
Standard Time
Time Zone: 3 hours East
Tropical Regiomontanus
NATAL CHART

Sun enters Ari 3-20-1986
March 21, 1986
1:02:43 AM
Kiev, Kijev, Ukraine
50 N 26 30 E 31
Standard Time
Time Zone: 3 hours East
Tropical Regiomontanus
NATAL CHART

The Wreck of the Exxon Valdez

Unfortunately, we have not yet exhausted our inventory of environmental disasters for Pluto in Scorpio. Next was the oil spill caused by the shipwreck of the *Exxon Valdez* in 1989. This is shown in Chart 44.

I admit to more than the usual interest in that particular disaster, because I had a computer job in the early 1980s installing and programming computers on oil tankers that plied the Valdez – Central America route – where the tankers dropped off their oil on the West Coast, to be transported to the Gulf by either the Panama Canal or pipelines. As a result, I had personal experience with seeing the docks of Valdez – not to mention the otter families who lived there. That also meant I had seen the merchant marine's alcohol culture up close and personal – for which reason, I knew that it was only a matter of time before there was some disaster like the *Exxon Valdez*.

At the time of the event, astrologers rushed to get information on the time of the accident. But Mr. Lilly would have worked from the time the voyage began. Both times are well documented. We have already examined shipwreck charts before, and we see many of the same configurations here with the *Exxon Valdez* that we saw with the *Maine* and the *Rainbow Warrior*:

- The Ruler of the 1st and 8th is the same planet

- The Ruler of the Ascendant is in Detriment

- The Ruler of the Ascendant is Combust

We might also mention the Moon rising, which we have already seen was not considered a good placement for the Moon in electional astrology. And Pluto was sitting right on the 2nd house cusp – a big financial black eye for Exxon.

By the time of the collision, the Ascendant had moved to Scorpio, and Mercury, co-Almuten of the 1st in the voyage chart, in Detriment in Pisces, had now moved to the 4th house cusp. I suspect that Mercury represented the crew who had not had proper rest before the start of the trip. Having watched some of this process during my time at sea, I can tell you: the First Mate and the Boson generally worked a twenty-four hour or more shift to get the cargo loaded, while the rest of the crew went ashore to the bars, with the exception of those few who didn't find those particular entertainments to their liking. Mostly, I was glad that my work ended in Valdez, and that I was on a plane out of there to Anchorage!

If we examine the Aries Ingress for 1989, Chart 45, we see a familiar configuration: the South Node conjunct the IC. It's not so tight as it was for 1935 and the Dust Bowl, but, once again, we see a configuration that does not bode well for the land. Mercury, Ruler of the IC, is in Detriment – as you can see, this was just a couple of days before the *Exxon Valdez* spill, so the planetary configurations look very similar. And Mars and Jupiter are at the Southern Bending, while the Part of Fortune is at the Northern one. This is a very dangerous configuration. It was the period of the Saturn-Uranus-Neptune conjunctions: the year of the fall of the Berlin Wall and much of hard-line Communism, not to mention Tiananmen Square: a very busy year! But the consequences of the oil spill are easy to see in the 4th house of the Aries Ingress.

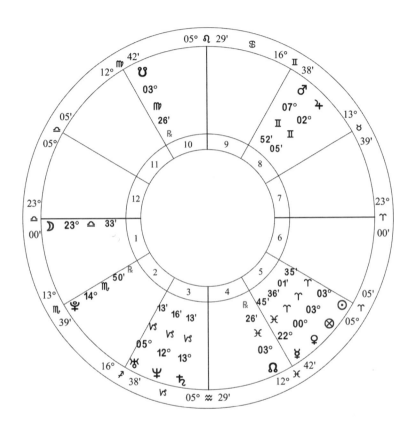

Exxon Valdez leaves port
March 23, 1989
9:10 PM
Valdez, Alaska
61N07'51" 146W20'54"
Standard Time
Time Zone: 9 hours West
Tropical Regiomontanus
NATAL CHART

Chart 44. *Exxon Valdez* leaves port and *Exxon Valdez* collision

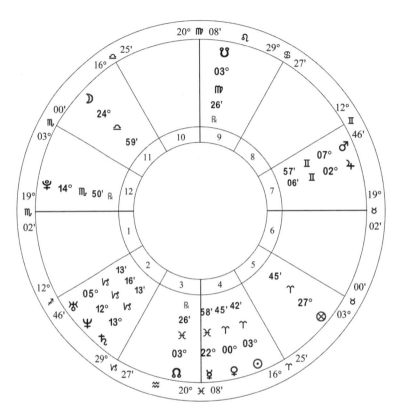

Exxon Valdez collision
March 24, 1989
12:04 AM
Bligh Reef, Alaska
60N50'26" 146W52'48"
Standard Time
Time Zone: 9 hours West
Tropical Regiomontanus
NATAL CHART

NATAL CHART
Sun enters Ari 3-20-1989
March 20, 1989
10:28:16 AM
Washington, D.C.
38N53'42" 77W02'12"
Standard Time
Time Zone: 5 hours West
Tropical Regiomontanus

Chart 45. Sun enters Aries
1989, Washington, DC

Day of ☽ Hour of ☉

Last Hr ♂	- 12 mins
Next Hr ♀	+48 mins

Hs	Alm. (Dor)
1	☿ ♄
2	☽
3	☉
4	☿
5	♄
6	♂
7	♃ ♄
8	♂ ♄
9	♄
10	♀
11	☉
12	♀

FIXED STARS

♅♂ Ankaa	0°57's	
☉♂ Scheat	0°46's	
As♂ Alnilam	0°43's	
☊♂ Fomalhaut	0°05's	
♇♂ S Scale	0°03's	
☽♂ Zosma	0°21'a	
☊♂ Sadalmelik	0°25'a	
♃♂ Mirfak	0°28'a	

ESSENTIAL DIGNITIES (Dorothean)

Pl	Ruler	Exalt	Tripl	Term	Face	Detri	Fall	Score
☉	♂	☉ +	☉ +	♃	♂	♀	♄	+7
☽	☿	♀	♀	♀	♀	♃	♀	- 5 P
☿	♃ m	♀	♀ +	☿ +	♃	☿ -	☿ -	- 2
♀	♃	♀ +	♀ +	♀	♄	☿	☿	+7
♂	☿	☊	♄	☿	♃	♃	--	- 5 P
♃	☿ m	☊	♄	☿	♃ +	♃ -	+1	
♄	♄ +	♂	♀	♃	♂	☽	♃	+5
☊	♃	♀	♀	♀	♄	☿	--	
⊗	♃	☊ +	☉	♃	☿	☿	--	
As	☿	☊	♄	♄	☉	♃	--	
Mc	♀	♀	♀	♀	♄	☿	--	
☋	☿	☿	♀	♀	☉	♃	♀	--

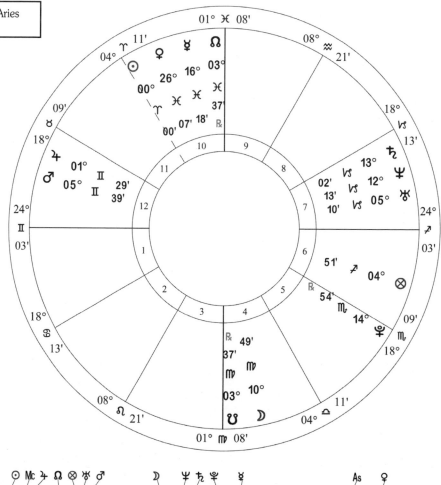

A Tale of Two Countries

Now I would like to examine one other matter relating to 1989 – in part as a beautiful example of both the Law of Unintended Consequences, and of how seemingly unconnected events really do connect.

I already mentioned that 1989 marked the fall of Communism after the Berlin Wall came down. One might expect therefore to go into a discussion of the Saturn-Neptune conjunction, Communism in general, and how these factors contributed to the demise of the Eastern Bloc. However, it's worth noting that it was *Soviet* Communism that failed, not all of Communism. China had the stress of Tiananmen Square – but no meltdown. I would like to address two smaller Communist states: and how the challenge of the Soviet meltdown impacted them. In a sense, it's a Tale of Two Cities. And as a story or a metaphor, I am not so much going to follow the exact sequence of events through charts, as to show the 1989 Aries Ingress, and how it set up each country's path through the next few years.

North Korea and Cuba are both Communist states, and in 1989, both were heavily subsidized by the Soviet Union, through petroleum imports, food aid, and other subsidies.[184]

Korea is a relatively small peninsula off the Chinese mainland. While most of its history has been as an independent country, living so close to such a superpower has meant that Korea is constantly shaped by its relations with the Chinese. During World War II, the Japanese had already been occupying Korea for close to 50 years. When Japan was defeated in the war, the Koreans broke free, and then a struggle ensued for the country which resulted in its partition as a Communist

zone and a supposedly democratic zone. (South Korea hardly followed the rules of fair elections for the first few decades of its existence.) However, it was the Soviets who held sway in North Korea, not the Chinese. The northern part of the now-divided country has less agricultural potential than the southern part. What the North has is coal and hydroelectric potential, but only poor soils. With oil and food subsidies from the USSR, North Korea embarked on still more industrialization, as well as heavily petroleum-subsidized agriculture: heavy use of artificial fertilizers, irrigation, and mechanization.

Meanwhile, in much more tropical Cuba, Castro's revolution had kicked out a corrupt government that had been completely enmeshed with U.S. economic ties, resulting in extremes of wealth inequalities. Castro's brand of Communism educated the people (96% literacy, the highest in Latin America), dismantled the U.S.-backed plantation economy, collectivized agriculture, but it was still heavily dependent upon sugar and tobacco production. Like North Korea, Cuba was heavily dependent upon Soviet food and fuel subsidies.

While the Fall of the Berlin Wall was a profound event that occupied great attention in Europe and North America, the fall of the USSR and the chaos engendered was not necessarily easy for her people in the short run. But for client states like North Korea and Cuba it was catastrophic. The subsidies they had been receiving evaporated: and each one became a possible laboratory for what it looks like when there is a sudden and unexpected decline in petroleum availability: a much more profound test than any Arab Oil Embargo.

Here in Chart 46, we see the Aries Ingress for 1989 for both countries' capitals, as road maps for how they both dealt with the almost identical challenges of loss of energy. It is certainly

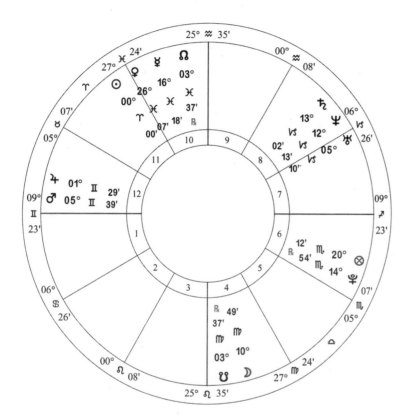

Sun enters Ari 3-20-1989
March 20, 1989
11:28:16 AM
Havana, Cuba
23 N 08 82 W 22
Daylight Saving Time
Time Zone: 5 hours West
Tropical Regiomontanus
NATAL CHART

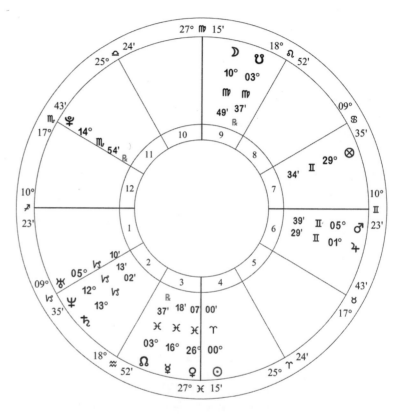

Sun enters Ari 3-20-1989
March 21, 1989
12:28:16 AM
P'yonggang, SE, N.Korea
38 N 26 127 E 16
Standard Time
Time Zone: 9 hours East
Tropical Regiomontanus
NATAL CHART

Chart 46. Sun enters Aries 1989, Cuba and North Korea

striking that their Ascendants are precisely 180 degrees apart! Furthermore, the Ascendant for Cuba – the Descendant for North Korea – is the fixed star Aldebaran: the eye of the bull, a royal star. Blindness and acuity of sight: the twin issues of an eye star, are here in evidence. Both countries suffered severe food shortages, as well as other major national dislocations when the shortages hit. But the difference in the two countries' approaches is evident in these two charts.

The chart for Cuba is not wildly different from the U.S. Aries Ingress chart: while the Ascendants are further separated, the longitude difference between Havana and Washington results in only six degrees difference on the MC/IC axis. Both show devastation to the land. Washington lacks Aldebaran. The Saturn-Neptune is in the 8th in Cuba, and the 7th in Washington. The 8th house focus in Cuba shows the deaths that resulted from the loss of the food subsidies. Pluto close to the 6th in Washington may be the signature for the devastation of birds and smaller mammals (otters?), whereas in Cuba, the fauna was unaffected by the events.

What is truly amazing is how well Cuba responded to the crisis: and here, the dignified Saturn ruling the 9th of education makes a lot of sense. Both top down and from the bottom up, Cuba set about retooling their agriculture. The loss of fossil fuel translated to a commitment to converting their agriculture to completely organic – not dependent on artificial fertilizers, or even much farm equipment. They broke the size of acreage farmed by families into smaller, more manageable units. They created incentives for cooperation and the sharing of what equipment there was. They encouraged local markets, to cut down on transportation use of fossil fuels. And spontaneously, the urban population began growing food, creating their own equivalent of victory gardens on vacant land to such an extent that the government had to invent a department to expedite the marketing of the excess produce.

The crisis had caused a decline of per capita caloric intake of nearly 40%. That decline has been almost totally reversed: and Cuban agriculture is now Green. People are moving back to the land from the cities, because they see the future on the land. The 4th house shows both the devastation and the hope: the South Node so close to the IC, but the Moon in Virgo – so like the technocratic revolution that took the U.S. to the Moon, here applied to the land. Cuba had many agricultural research stations before the crisis: these kicked into overdrive to help solve the problems.

We can see this through the Moon in Virgo in the 4th: taking a complicated set of circumstances, and breaking it down into manageable chunks. Smaller is better. The people are ruled by the Moon.

Unfortunately, the story line for North Korea was not so encouraging. Part of the reason is undoubtedly the far greater challenge of agriculture above the 39th parallel. While in the same latitude as portions of the U.S.A., the climate in North Korea is much harsher.

But North Korea was constantly reacting to the South: the military was the favored organ of state – a much more profound consideration than Cuba experienced, as an island. At the time of partition, it might have seemed that North Korea's industrial base was advantageous. But North Korean leadership let their industrial facilities age, without addressing infrastructure. By 1989, aging factories and power plants were not easily convertible to anything less inefficient – and there was no money for capital improvement. Earlier debt default meant that Korea had no international credit, so the loss of Soviet subsidy was absolutely disastrous.

Here, the focus on the 2nd house for the Saturn-Neptune, not to mention catastrophic Uranus right on the cusp of the 2nd, shows the picture too well: North Korea went from subsidized to broke and in debt overnight. Here it is the Sun highlighting the 4th house, and the MC ruled by a cadent Mercury in Detriment. Korea's leadership completely failed, continuing to focus on their paranoid fears of the South (Mars conjunct the Descendant). The people, ruled by Jupiter in Gemini as the ruler of the 1st, in Detriment , were hostages of the war machine. Here, the Moon in the 9th continues to show the focus on foreign, not domestic, affairs. People starved, and, like Cuba, the people suffered a massive drop in per capita caloric consumption. But unlike Cuba, the North Koreans have still not recovered from this disaster over twenty years later.

Interestingly, viewing the people from the placement of the Moon, I judge them willing – and creative as well. But with the Moon placed in the 12th from the 10th, the leadership could not see them, and many good ideas died.

Pluto in Pisces

Pluto will not arrive in Pisces until 2043. That is still some time in the future as I write this. I will have some general comments about some possible contours when we reach Chapter 8. But for now, it's back to the past. We will look a bit at Pluto in Pisces to set the table for our discussion about Pluto in Aries in the next chapter. Then we will return to Pluto in Pisces in Chapter 8.

To late 18th century Europeans, the American Revolutionary War was comparatively a blip – it was a colonial insurrection –

successful, which was still unusual, but hardly something which represented a major power shift. We discussed its astrology in Chapter 1. It was the French Revolution which impacted the politics of Europe well into the 19th century, both because that revolution actually took place on European soil, and because it resulted in not only the fall, but the execution of a European monarch. This had not been seen since the 17th century in England – and it wasn't considered a pretty picture then either. What followed the first phase of the French Revolution was the Terror – a time when the revolution went much further than probably the vast majority of the French people wanted – but some of the revolutionary committees were determined to re-make France from the bottom up, seemingly no matter the cost.

When the violent excesses of the Terror were replaced by Napoleon's Empire, Europe reacted again, this time to his invading armies. Napoleon got as far as Egypt and Russia, whose climate as much as her people finally defeated his army. Napoleon was defeated by a coalition of allies: Britain, Austria, Russia, Prussia, Sweden, and Portugal in 1814, and exiled to Elba. In 1815, he escaped, returned to France, raised his standard again, beginning the "Hundred Days" of his returned empire. He was defeated by the British and Prussians at Waterloo in 1815, when he was permanently deposed. During this same period, Britain wrapped up its war with the U.S.A., resulting in a territorial stalemate at the Treaty of Ghent signed in 1814.

Thus, in the final few years of Pluto in Pisces, Europe achieved a new beginning, as far as geopolitical boundaries were concerned. But peruse a map of Europe from this period and you will not see the same country boundaries as today. Germany was not a yet a unified country, but a series of smaller kingdoms, principalities, and lesser states; most of the countries of Eastern Europe didn't exist, Prussia and Austria were major powers, Italy was not united, and the Balkans were different. But a scant ten years before, Napoleon controlled half of Spain, most of Germany apart from Prussia, and most of Italy.

The 19ᵗʰ century opened with Pluto in Pisces – and one of the early technological innovations of the century was the development of canals and other artificial waterways: in the U.S., the Erie Canal was proposed in 1808, when Pluto was in the middle degrees of Pisces, with construction beginning in 1817. This first great artificial waterway of the U.S. allowed for moving crops much more efficiently from the farming regions to the cities. At almost the same time, France was also developing its canal system.

And unfortunately, one of the less savory "firsts" with Pluto in Pisces was that cholera, the great water-borne disease, jumped from being endemic to India to pandemic status throughout Europe and America. At least five cholera pandemics occurred in this century, often lasting for years, and only separated by a few years in between. And sadly, just as Pluto went into Taurus in 1854, evidence was presented that cholera was caused by contaminated water – but nothing was done about this for over fifty years.[185]

The Year Without a Summer

It's very satisfying to think of the build-up of canals and waterways as a symbol of Pluto in Pisces and Neptune in Scorpio. But water also affects the weather, and Pisces is a winter sign in the northern hemisphere. In 1815, a volcano erupted in Indonesia which resulted in 1816 being dubbed the "Year without a Summer." According to tradition, the Aries Ingress should show something of the weather for this period of time. But what can we say in this case, because a specific event in 1815 caused an entire hemisphere to have unusual weather the following year? I think a technique such as the ingress chart cannot be expected to bring home the goods in 1816, because the effect in that year was too universal to show in charts that are drawn for particular locations. However, the question is whether we can see something special in Indonesia, the site of the explosion, in 1816 when the eruption that would disrupt weather actually occurred.

When we examine the Aries Ingress in 1815 for Jakarta, we see the same South Node conjunct the IC configuration that we already saw for the U.S. Dust Bowl. That doesn't immediately identify the problem as being volcanic, but, following the symbolism, it is a disaster for agriculture. Jupiter is at the Bendings, and on the Ascendant, in a partile square to the MC/IC axis. With Pluto as mythological Lord of the Underworld, we might expect it to be strong in an eruption chart: here it's cadent, and not especially impressive, except that, by the date of the eruption (10 April 1815) the Mercury has gone direct, and is in a partile conjunction with it.

The Aries Ingress for 1816 has the Sun at the IC: but this does not prove to be as consistently problematic as the placement of the South Node there. Indonesia may have been the epicenter of volcano action in the prior year – but the damage to the atmosphere already had been done. It was no longer any worse here than anyplace else. But are there aspects in the 1816 Ingress that show the weather disaster in a way independent from the house placements? The two outer planet aspects for the year were Jupiter square Saturn, and Neptune square Pluto. The only other

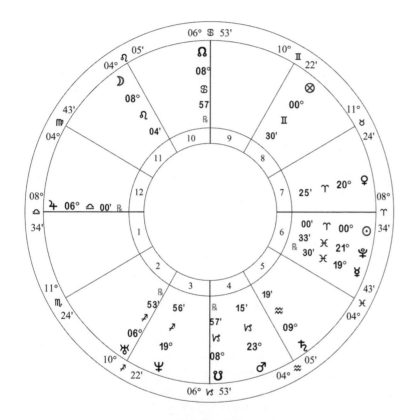

Sun enters Ari 3-21-1815
March 21, 1815
6:37:34 PM
Jakarta, Indonesia
6 S 10 106 E 48
Local Mean Time
Time Zone: 0 hours West
Tropical Regiomontanus
NATAL CHART

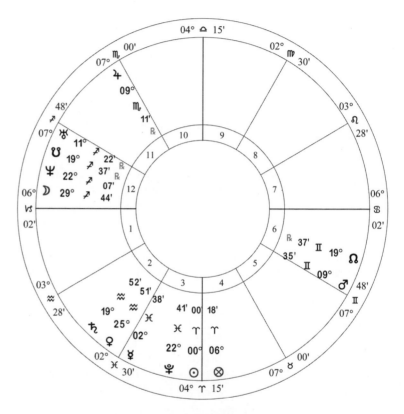

Sun enters Ari 3-20-1816
March 21, 1816
12:23:09 AM
Jakarta, Indonesia
6 S 10 106 E 48
Local Mean Time
Time Zone: 0 hours West
Tropical Regiomontanus
NATAL CHART

Chart 47. Sun enters Aries
1815, 1816, Jakarta, Indonesia

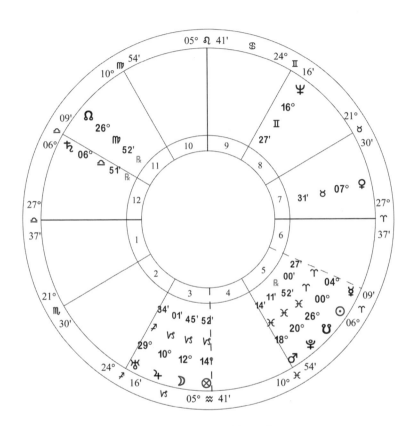

Sun enters Ari 3-20-1569
March 20, 1569
8:39:59 PM
Paris, France
48 N 52 2 E 20
Local Mean Time
Time Zone: 0 hours West
Tropical Regiomontanus
NATAL CHART

Chart 48. Sun enters
Aries 1569, Paris, and
Sun enters Aries 1816,
Jakarta

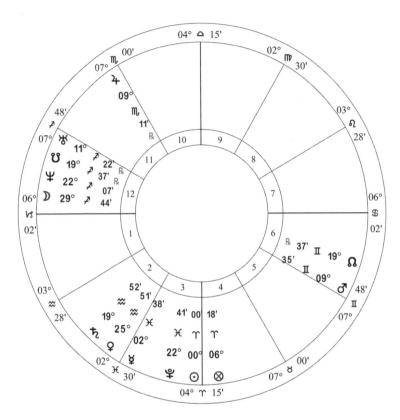

Sun enters Ari 3-20-1816
March 21, 1816
12:23:09 AM
Jakarta, Indonesia
6 S 10 106 E 48
Local Mean Time
Time Zone: 0 hours West
Tropical Regiomontanus
NATAL CHART

occurrence of this combination since 600 c.e. Was 1569, shown in Chart 48.

Interestingly, 1569 also had Pluto in Pisces – but no worldwide wintry conditions. Besides the two outer planet aspects, Neptune is in the opposite sign, and both also have hard aspects of Pluto with the Nodes, and Saturn dignified. Evidently, these outer planet configurations are not predictive of the extreme weather. It would appear that the consecutive hits of the South Node and then Sun to the 4th house cusp in these two sequential ingresses may say more, as well as the Sun-Jupiter opposition in 1815 at the Bendings.

1815 had no outer planet hard aspects – a not terrifically unusual condition. So in either case, this unusual weather is not shown at all in the 1816 charts, and the outer planets don't show the issue in 1815 either, at least by hard aspect. And 1815 of course was also the final defeat of Napoleon – a truly significant event by itself as well.

As we prepare to leave Pluto in Pisces, the final defeat of Napoleon and the triumph of the coalition brought an economic boom fueled on speculation which lasted until 1820 – still under Pluto in Pisces. Like Sagittarius, Pisces is a Jupiter-ruled sign, so, in a sense, this final run-up under Pluto in Pisces bears a certain resemblance to the speculative run-up in Sagittarius in 2008.

But world systems don't turn on a dime. Economic speculation can shoot up immediately, but Europe was in the same place after Napoleon as before – except now, there had been the additional casualties and cost of the war, plus a power vacuum where Napoleon had been.

We shall continue this story in the next chapter, as Pluto moved into Aries.

Endntoes: Chpater 6

162. Brown, Lester, pp 38-41.

163. A quotation from Babylon 5, Episode 201, "Points of Departure," but equally descriptive here.

164. For a comprehensive account of the development of the pandemic, please see: Barry, John M. *The Great Influenza : The Epic Story of the Deadliest Plague in History*. New York: Viking, 2004.

165. A very good read on this subject was Tuchman, Barbara Wertheim. *The Zimmermann Telegram*. [New ed. New York,: Macmillan, 1966.

166. See, for example, Warren, Christian. *Brush with Death : A Social History of Lead Poisoning*. Baltimore, MD: Johns Hopkins University Press, 2000, pp 115-128.

167. Kingsland, p 125.

168. Kingsland, p 144.

169. For example, Lilly, page 81; Saunders, Richard. *The Astrological Judgment and Practice of Physick, Deduced from the Position of the Heavens at the Decumbiture of the Sick Person, &C*. London: Thomas Sawbridge, 1677, p 100.

170. Nichols, John. *St. Francis Dam Disaster*. Images of America. Chicago, Ill.: Arcadia Pub., 2002, p 7.

171. For an excellent Powerpoint on this disaster, see Roger, J. David. *Reassessment of the St. Francis Dam Failure*, web.mst.edu/~rogersda/st_francis_dam/reassessment_of_st_francis_dam_failure.pdf

172. Vale, Lawrence J., and Thomas J. Campanella. *The Resilient City : How Modern Cities Recover from Disaster*. New York: Oxford University Press, 2005, pp 335-355, cited in Svensen, Henrik. *The End Is Nigh : A History of Natural Disasters*. London: Reaktion, 2009 p87.

173. Barker, Stan. *The Signs of the Times : The Neptune Factor and America's Destiny*. Llewellyn's Popular Astrology Series. 1st ed. St. Paul, Minn., U.S.A.: Llewellyn Publications, 1984.

174. Some really good diagrams of the aquifer, and a timeline of these issues relating to the Dust Bowl can be found at*www.livinghistoryfarm.org/farminginthe30s/farminginthe1930s.html*.

175. Drummond, Mark A., and Thomas R. Loveland. "Land-Use Pressure and a Transition to Forest-Cover Loss in the Eastern United States." *Bioscience* 60.4 (2010): 286-98.

176. Ho, Peter, Trajectories for Greening China," Chapter 1 in Ho, Peter, and E. B. Vermeer. *China's Limits to Growth : Greening State and Society*. Development and Change Book Series. Malden, MA, U.S.A.: Blackwell, 2006.

177. *www.en.wikipedia.org/wiki/Bhopal_disaster*

178. A full account of the bombing is given at Greenpeace's site, *www.greenpeace.org/international/about/history/the-bombing-of-the-rainbow-war*.

179. Lilly, p157.

180. Lilly's rules for ships at sea are in *Christian Astrology*, pp 157-161.

181. Lilly, p 158.

182. Lilly, p 159.

183. For a full grid of the parts of a ship, see either Lilly, p 158, or Lehman, 2002, p 58

184. The work that has documented the energy issues of these two countries is: Pfeiffer, Dale Allen. *Eating Fossil Fuels : Oil, Food and the Coming Crisis in Agriculture*. Gabriola Island, BC: New Society Publishers, 2006, Chapters 6 and 7.

185. For a full discussion on the history of these epidemics, see Hays, Jo N. *Epidemics and Pandemics: Their Impacts on Human History*..ABC-CLIO, 2005. See Chapter 25 for a discussion of the evidence about water contamination.

7

The Long Twilight Struggle: Pluto in Fire Signs

Now the trumpet summons us again – not as a call to bear arms, though arms we need; not as a call to battle, though embattled we are – but a call to bear the burden of a long twilight struggle, year in and year out, "rejoicing in hope, patient in tribulation" – a struggle against the common enemies of man: tyranny, poverty, disease, and war itself.

—John F. Kennedy,
Inaugural Address,
20 January 1961

IF YOU HAVE GOTTEN THE IDEA THAT I HAD BEEN VERY INFLUENCED BY STAN BARKER'S BOOK ON NEPTUNE THROUGH THE SIGNS, YOU WOULD BE RIGHT! It was the section on Aries and savage warfare that got me. War is horrid in the best of times, but Barker picked out times when the degree of bloodthirstiness definitely seemed to increase. Aries was therefore the sign to use to test the question: how similar was transiting Neptune in Aries compared to transiting Pluto in Aries. Strangely, or not so strangely, the answer may well be: not as similar as you might think.

One way of conceptualizing this is to think about the difference between psyche and power. Neptune may set the ethos or the tone for a period, but Pluto is more about deeds than words or thoughts. Here's a good example of this difference. Contrast Neptune in Virgo (1928/9 – 1942/3) with Pluto in Virgo (1956/8 – 1971/2). Barker referred to Neptune in Virgo as the "common thread." Among the components that he mentioned were economic declines and also the assertion of the rights of the "common man." The pass of Neptune in Virgo began with the stock market roaring, then the 1929 stock market crash, followed by the Great Depression, ultimately ending during World War II.

What Barker focused on here is how the period began with a virtually worshipful attitude toward big business. When the Depression hit, President Hoover's response looked like the forerunner of President Reagan's "trickle-down" economics in that only big business and the rich were aided by the government, under the theory that aiding the workers directly would somehow undermine the system. This attempt at proto-trickle-down didn't work – and many of the "common men" became really angry –

Aries	Leo	Sagittarius
8 May 23 Aug 1088	19 Sep – 14 Dec 1201	4 Jan – 4 May 1256
22 Mar – 20 Oct 1089	23 Jul 1202 – 25 Feb 1203	1 Nov 1256 – 31 Dec 1269
4 Feb 1090 – 21 Jun 1118	26 May 1203 – 23 Oct 1218	18 Jul – 1 Nov 1270
11 Sep 1118 – 2 May 1119	12 Jan – Aug 19 1219	
6 Nov 1119 – 20 Mar 1120	15 Apr – 5 Jun 1220	
8 Jun – 21 Jul 1332	11 Aug 1447 – 29 Jan 1448	31 Jan – 5 Apr 1502
7 Apr – 29 Sep 1333	20 Jun 1448 – 18 Oct 1464	19 Nov 1502 – 31 Jul 1503
23 Feb 1334 – 20 June 1362	17 Jan – 16 Aug 1465	23 Aug 1503 – 2 Jan 1516
9 Sep 1362 – 1 May 1363	21 Apr – 31 May 1466	18 Jul – 2 Nov 1516
5 Nov 1363 – 20 Mar 1364		
4 May – 28 Aug 1577	2 Sep – 30 Dec 1692	10 Dec 1748 – 8 Jun 1749
19 Mar – 27 Oct 1578	12 Jul 1693 – 15 Mar 1694	6 Oct 1749 – 7 Jan 1762
30 Jan 1579 – 7 Jul 1606	8 May 1694 – 17 Oct 1710	8 Jul – 9 Nov 1762
22 Aug 1606 – 10 May 1607	19 Jan – 17 Aug 1711	
26 Oct 1607 – 28 Mar 1608	Apr 19 – 1 Jun 1712	
16 Apr – 19 Sep 1822	7 Oct – 25 Nov 1937	17 Jan – 21 Apr 1995
3 Mar 1823 – 20 May 1851	3 Aug 1938 – 7 Feb 1939	10 Nov 1995 – 26 Jan 2008
14 Oct 1851 – 7 Apr 1852	14 Jun 1939 – 20 Oct 1956	14 Jun – 27 Nov 2008
12 Dec 1852 – 14 Feb 1853	15 Jan – 19 Aug 1957	
	11 April – 10 Jun 1958	

Table 7-1. Pluto Ingresses by Sign. Data from Michelsen, 1990, pp 63-64.

and radicalized. This resulted in rapid growth of membership in such organizations as the Communist Party – a fact that would haunt the American psyche twenty years later with the scourge of McCarthyism.

Barker did not follow the parallel examples outside the U.S., but the Thirties also marked the rise of Fascism, not just Communism. One entirely analogous idea with respect to Germany was that the German military and a number of politicians severely underestimated Hitler – in part because he *was* a common man, meaning: from the worker class. They encouraged and facilitated Hitler's rise to power, expecting to use him for their own ends – and ending up subservient instead. Hitler's story all too clearly illustrated how even in the era of the "common man," there is no decrease in Alpha males!

By contrast, when Pluto went into Virgo, all the ideologies of the period were already set. However, there are still similarities: in the U.S.A., both periods began with a Republican President, with the Democrats winning the next election, and holding on to the Presidency until the end of the Virgo period. Also, both periods were marked at the beginning by a Depression or Recession, although the recession of 1957-1958 was much less severe. Pluto in Virgo was the Space Race. The engineering side seemed more significant with Pluto than the political side when Neptune was in Virgo. However, both threads were there. Pluto in Virgo included the political process of student unrest of the 1960s, while we have already seen how in the 1930s Neptune in Virgo era, the engineering developments leading to exploitation of fossil water began through advances in drilling technology.

Shortly, we shall examine how these multiple themes of a sign can have different priorities when we examine Pluto in Aries

and compare it to Neptune in Aries. But before we examine Aries in detail, let's consider a couple of details about the fire signs in general. Let's review the sequence of signs as we have presented them here. These are presented in Table 7-2.

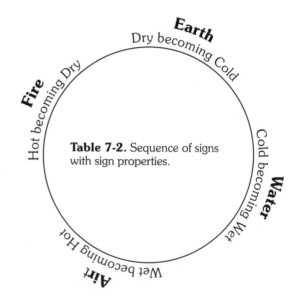

Table 7-2. Sequence of signs with sign properties.

The transitions between Earth to Air, and Water to Fire, would seem to be the most problematic, because these transitions involved signs with no properties in common. By contrast, the transition from Air to Water involves signs that are wet, while the transition from Fire to Earth involves signs that are dry. One might also note that this is the way that the elements are also grouped in Jungian astrology as the element pairs that cluster together, as shown in Table 7-3.[186]

Thinking (Air) and Feeling (Water) are both rational/judging	Sensation (Earth) and Intuition (Fire) are both irrational/perceptive

Table 7-3. Jungian elemental grouping, from Hamaker-Zondag, 1994, p 20.

The transition from Earth to Air did not seem to be especially problematic, because it seemed to work out as going from an engineering approach, to a theoretical one. The earth sign went out and got dirty with hands-on, and then the air sign crunched the data and decided what it meant. The transition from water to fire can be volatile, but the essence of the fire sign periods could be summed up simply: living the dream.

Pluto in Aries
(1822-1853)

As we saw in the last chapter, the beginning of the 19th century, with Pluto in Pisces, saw the map of Europe re-written at least twice. Something new came to Europe in the 19th century – and that process was mostly set up with Pluto in Aries. As I alluded to in the Preface, one of the "jobs" of Pluto in each sign is cleaning up the excesses of Pluto in the previous sign. Pluto in Pisces included Napoleon and his conquest of much of Europe and Egypt. While this did result in positive developments, such as the adoption of the Napoleonic Code of Law and greater emphasis on technical education, the idea of most of Europe falling under a single dictator was scary indeed. The victory against Napoleon, which was accomplished by a military alliance, demonstrated to those European states the value of alliances as a way to promote stability within Europe. Understand – this desire for peace had nothing to do with benefiting the people – it was for the convenience of the monarchs. In fact, that was one of the most notable effects of the reaction to the "problem" of France – extreme reactionary politics on the part of most of the European royal families – and even Parliament in Britain. What arose out of a desire to prevent another Napoleon was first, a period known as the Age of Metternich, named after Prince Klemens Wenzel von Metternich of Austria, which is usually dated from 1815-1848, encompassing most of Pluto in Aries.

Chronologies for the 1820s seem to show that a level of business as usual developed in the wake of Napoleon's exit from the world stage. The European leaders who engineered his exit continued to meet, and reintegrated France into the mix in 1818. By 1819, the U.S.A. was experiencing the first financial panic of its existence. The last meeting of the five super-powers took place in 1825 – in the early years of Pluto in Aries. The "universal solvent" properties of Pluto in water allowed for the union of nations to defeat a common enemy. As this great danger receded, the powers split into two rival factions that dominated the next part of the 19th century. Thus, although historians may date the Age of Metternich to 1815, the coalition and balance of power alignments for which he was known, actually date more specifically to Pluto in Aries.

While there were disputes during the Pluto in Aries period, it was a comparatively peaceful time, at least as far as European conflicts. There were conflicts between European powers and non-European powers, such as India and China. The next major conflict was the Crimean War in 1854 – in the Pluto in Taurus era. If this Aries sojourn of Pluto wasn't the era of savage warfare as Barker had found for Neptune in Aries, what was going on?

During the transition from Pluto in Pisces to Aries, increasingly, colonies were breaking away from their mother countries. And then in 1822, the year of the Pluto Ingress, the Greeks declared independence from the Ottoman Empire, instigating a seven year struggle for independence. In 1823, in the wake of all the Western Hemisphere separations, the Monroe Doctrine was promulgated by the United States, warning European powers not to interfere in the affairs of the hemisphere. And in that year, a decade-long economic recovery began.

With Pluto in Aries, some of the most important inventions in agriculture involved replacing iron tools with steel: the McCormick reaper was patented in 1834, and John Lane began to manufacture plows that featured steel saw blades. In 1837 John Deere and Leonard Angus began manufacturing steel plows. John Deere equipment is still manufactured today. Even with the greater efficiency in machinery, the farm population was still 69% of the total U.S. population.[187]

The expansion in steel production massively affected transportation: the first modern railway opened in 1825 in Europe, in the same year as the Erie Canal opened in the U.S.A. Neither of these would have been possible without steel. This is hardly surprising, given that the ruling planet of Aries is Mars, and Mars is the natural ruler of iron, the principal component of steel.

Canals

The development of the canal system in the U.S. is something that we can see as a transitional issue of Pluto in Pisces to Pluto in Aries. And sure enough, the Erie Canal was proposed in 1808, and construction began in 1817 under Pluto in Pisces, although it wasn't completed until Pluto in Aries.[188]

Since the Erie Canal was not financed by the federal government, I chose to compute the Aries Ingress not for Washington, DC, but for the New York State capital. This has a further use, because one of the impacts of the opening of the Canal was on New York City, which became a much more prominent port as a result of the traffic generated by the Canal.

Chart 49, the Aries Ingress for 1817 shows the difficulty of building the canal, something we cannot even begin to imagine today. The 29 degrees on the angles means nothing is going to be easy: but also that something major is going to happen, since the Sun is conjunct that Descendant. The Erie Canal was dug using human and animal power: a ditch four feet deep and forty feet wide, over 300 miles long mostly through territory that was wilderness. The only difference in methodology with ancient times was that they had blasting powder at their disposal. Hence, perhaps, the Moon square Mars in fixed signs! Mercury, the chart Ruler, in Detriment is yet one more indication that this was done the hard way. As I have said previously, absence of dignity does not deny: the effect is more that of starting a few steps behind the pace. The Moon in Taurus in the 8th house with Venus also there shows the financial promise of the Canal – and it completely exceeded expectations once it was in operation.

We have to look at the mutable angles as indicating that projects started under this configuration proceed apace: not especially quickly, not especially slowly. And it is interesting that one of the major concepts that Barker emphasized in his discussion of Neptune in Virgo was that Virgo represents the "common man." As a mundane statement, this is certainly backed up in this chart, not for the Neptune sign itself, but for the Virgo Ascendant, because the Commissioners who oversaw the construction of the Canal chose to hire local people to do the digging, rather than major

NATAL CHART
Sun enters Ari 3-20-1817
March 20, 1817
6:05:30 PM
Albany, New York
42N39'09" 73W45'24"
Local Mean Time
Time Zone: 0 hours West
Tropical Regiomontanus

Chart 49. Sun enters Aries 1817, Albany, NY

Day of ♃	Hour of ☿
Last Hr ♀	- 58 mins
Next Hr ☽	+ 2 mins

FIXED STARS	
♄☌ Sadalmelik	0°21'a
☊☌ Mirfak	0°44'a
♄☌ Fomalhaut	0°50'a

Hs	Alm. (Dor)
1	☿
2	♄
3	♂
4	♃
5	♄
6	♀
7	♀
8	☉♂
9	♀
10	☿
11	☉
12	☿

ESSENTIAL DIGNITIES (Dorothean)

Pl	Ruler	Exalt	Tripl	Term	Face	Detri	Fall	Score
☉	♂	☉ +	☉ +	♃	♂	♀	♄	+7
☽	♀	☽ +	♀	♀	☿	♂	--	+4
☿	♃	♀	♀	♀	♄	☿ -	☿ -	- 14 P
♀	♀ +	☽	♀ +	♃ m	☽	♂	--	+8
♂	♄	--	♄	☿	☿	☉	--	- 5 P
♃	♃ +	☋	☉	♀ m	☽	☿	--	+5
♄	♃	♀	♀	♀	♄ +	☿	☿	+1
☊	☿	☊ +	♄	☿	♃	♃	--	--
⊗	♂	--	♀	♂	♂	♀	☽	--
As	☿	☿	♀	♂	☿	♃	♀	--
Mc	☿	☊	♄	♂	☉	♃	--	--
☋	♃	☋	☉	♃	☿	☿	--	--

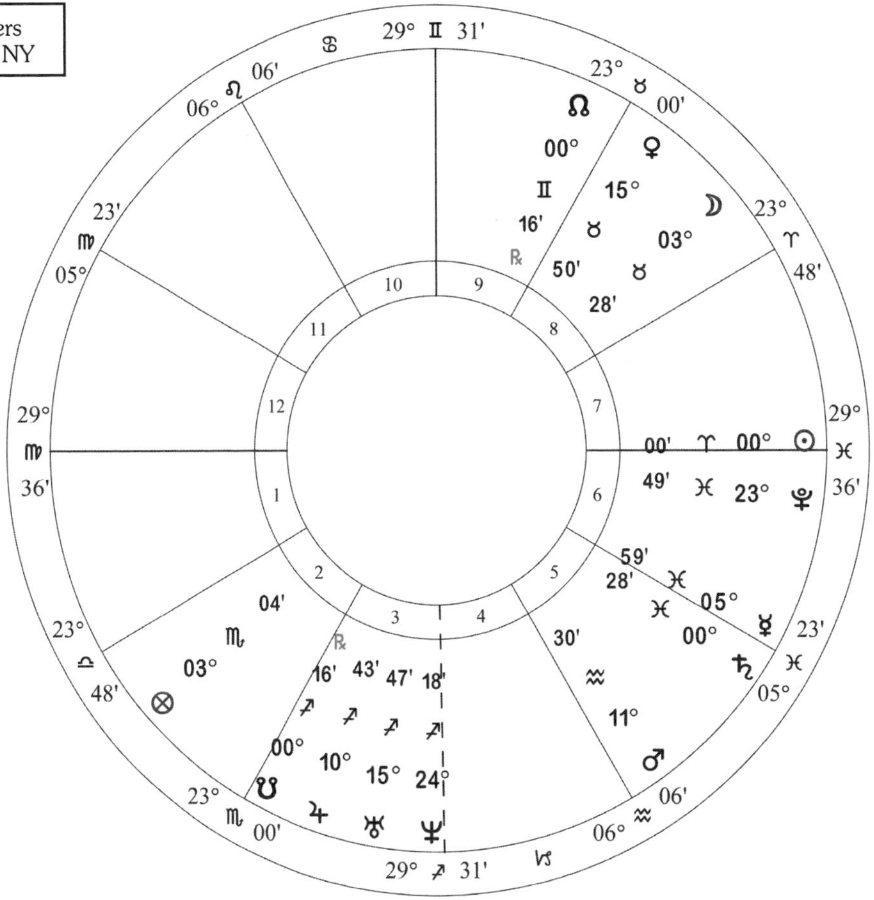

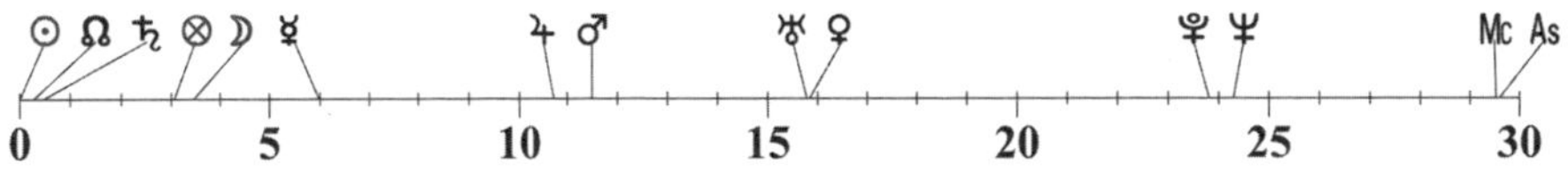

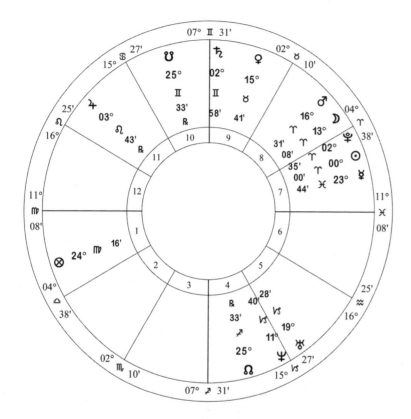

Sun enters Ari 3-20-1825
March 20, 1825
4:30:27 PM
Albany, New York
42N39'09" 73W45'24"
Local Mean Time
Time Zone: 0 hours West
Tropical Regiomontanus
NATAL CHART

Chart 50. Sun enters Aries
and Libra 1825, Albany, NY

Sun enters Lib 9-23-1825
September 23, 1825
3:36:30 AM
Albany, New York
42N39'09" 73W45'24"
Local Mean Time
Time Zone: 0 hours West
Tropical Regiomontanus
NATAL CHART

contractors, under the presumption that local people would best know the terrain. These workers devised a number of engineering inventions for felling trees and uprooting stumps, not to mention digging the canal itself, that utilized the steel technology that they had access to, wheels and horse-drawn plows, all allowing the size of the project to be broken down into simpler steps.[189] They were the "Steely-eyed Missile-men" of their day – but they came by their skills by trial and error, not through education. They did it the hard way, in other words – but their inventions changed the nature of canal building.

What rules a canal? I have not found an ancient reference. Lilly said that Pisces ruled watermills,[190] but that a water-work is co-ruled by the Moon and Saturn.[191] When the canal was started, Saturn had just moved into Pisces, and was partile at the Bendings. This makes sense, because, while Saturn had dignity only by Face, Saturn in a water sign described the process of creating the canal. DeWitt Clinton, who was running the Commission, had wanted the Canal finished in 1824, when Saturn was still in Taurus. It wasn't ready – and recall my comment about the mutable Ascendant for the year 1817 showing that the project would be completed in an average time, not a speedy one. Clinton's timetable was based on the 1824 election cycle, not one related to the Canal itself. Sections of the canal had opened to traffic as early as 1820. It wasn't until Saturn passed into the sign of its Triplicity, Gemini, that the Canal opened: October 26, 1825.

So the astrological picture emerges: building a canal (Pisces) through trail-blazing virgin forest (Aries) on a massive scale (Pluto). In Chart 49, we see the overlap of signs clearly. Now we are ready to examine the charts for 1825, when the canal was completed, Chart 50. First, we find we must defer the delineation to the Libra Ingress, since the Canal opened in October, and the Aries Ingress

has Virgo Rising. In the Aries Ingress chart for 1825, we see many of the same themes as 1817, with Mercury in Pisces ruling the Ascendant, but now the Sun and Pluto are conjunct in the 7th, although just over the line diurnally from the 8th. The 8th house has a Moon-Mars conjunction, with the Mars highly dignified. But between the Aries and the Libra charts, we see that the Ascendant ruler Mercury has moved from being in Detriment in Pisces to being in Sign and exaltation in Virgo, although retrograde.

Religious Revivals

The religious dimension from Pisces' rulership by Jupiter did not go away when Pluto moved into Aries, because the first great religious movement that jumped from Pluto in Pisces to Pluto in Aries was temperance.[192] This is hardly surprising, since Jupiter is the nighttime Triplicity ruler of the fire signs – so Jupiter is still a dispositor of Pluto. The United States became the site of early temperance activity because alcohol consumption during the Revolutionary War had evidently gotten completely out of hand. Benjamin Rush, the Scottish doctor who had emigrated to Philadelphia, where he became extremely influential in developing early public health, had observed and declared on the health problems of excess alcohol.

The original temperance movement was actually about temperance – curtailing consumption, not abstinence. According to Armstrong, the first such group in the U.S.A. formed in 1808 – well during Pluto in Pisces. Chart 51 for 1825 in Boston, where the group formed (the date was February 13, 1826, but this puts it under the prior year's charts), are not significantly different than they were for Albany: about 2 degrees on the angles. We do run into a tricky problem here: what rules temperance? Rush believed

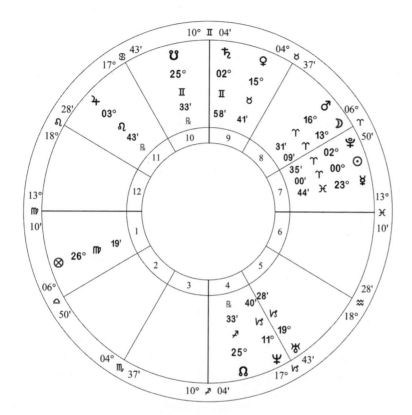

Sun enters Ari 3-20-1825
March 20, 1825
4:41:15 PM
Boston, Massachusetts
42N21'30" 71W03'37"
Local Mean Time
Time Zone: 0 hours West
Tropical Regiomontanus
NATAL CHART

Chart 51. Sun enters Aries
and Libra 1825, Boston, MA

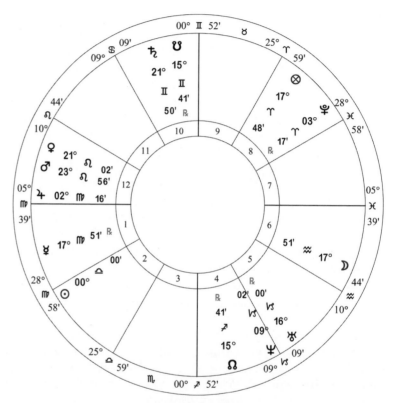

Sun enters Lib 9-23-1825
September 23, 1825
3:47:18 AM
Boston, Massachusetts
42N21'30" 71W03'37"
Local Mean Time
Time Zone: 0 hours West
Tropical Regiomontanus
NATAL CHART

that alcohol consumption was a health problem, but according to Armstrong, he approached a minister to do something about it. So is this 1st-6th (health) or 9th (religious) – or should we use the 11th house, since this chart was for forming an organization? The American Temperance Society was hugely successful, generating 1.5 million members within ten years who had "taken the pledge." For the population size at the time, these numbers are staggering.

I have to say, I like the idea of the Moon in Saturn's sign for something involving abstinence – or at least limitation! In these early years of Pluto in Aries, by definition, the ingresses have a hard Sun-Pluto aspect; in the Libra Ingress, it's the opposition. This really throws down the gauntlet, so to speak! The opposition is sitting in the 2nd and the 8th. This was a time of slow economic recovery. The 2nd-8th cusps in terms of this issue was surely the financial ruin – not to mention, danger of early death – which could destroy families of the men who overimbibed. And yet, the justification and the verbiage favored the religious dimension. In this time period, addiction as a biological phenomenon was not understood at all, and so the drive within the movement from cutting down consumption to total abstinence was mostly a religious effect. So where is the religion?

To answer that question, we have to understand that the contours of 19th century religion were much different than those of the 20th century One of the biggest differences was in the role of men: not just as priests, ministers, and spokesmen, but as the driving force within a religious congregation. Many of us in the 20th century grew up with the sense that women are often the driving force within the fabric of a congregation, but the 19th century was the era of the "manly man" in religion.

Not only that, but the 20th century impression of evangelicalism and Fundamentalism (at least by white Americans) is a socially conservative force. But in the 19th century, evangelicalism was a progressive, even liberal force, as seen in the overlap of the Temperance, Abolitionist, and early Feminist movements. Here, we have Mars in Leo in the 12th ruling the 9th house. The Mars had dignity by Face, and this makes sense – after all, fear tactics were being used to encourage (primarily) men to take the pledge.

Jupiter in Virgo, its Detriment but a barren sign, conjunct the Ascendant also makes sense, as oaths are often a religious matter, and Jupiter, the planet of organized religion, dominates this chart from its position. Mercury itself is at the Bendings, also prominent as the 1st house ruler in the 1st, in dignity but retrograde. Here, the retrogradation may actually be descriptive, and one interpretation of the retrograde is a change of state. How can we know how permanent was the change? I don't have any figures, but with Mercury in a mutable sign (and being Mercury anyway), I have to wonder.

The age of Pluto in Aries included many utopian movements which formed communes or settlements. Again, I can see an Aries argument for this, because these were not just books about utopia – these were people willing to actually *do* it. One of the most important movements that surfaced at this time was American Transcendentalism. Transcendentalism had its roots in the 18th century clashes between the rationalists and the naturalists: a clash that has some relevance for our theme of the environment. These points of view, as we saw in Chapter 3, are sometimes called by other names, such as Apollonian and Dionysian. We should stop and say that environmentalism, like any great (meaning large) idea, has elements of both. The

French Revolution had been perceived, rightly or wrongly, as a child of the Enlightenment (Apollonian), which was the rationalist perspective. That meant that, in the wake of Napoleon's defeat, Romanticism, the Dionysian movement of the late 18th century, held much greater currency going into the period of Pluto in Aries. Transcendentalism shared with its older sibling a love of nature, a love which reverberates down through pretty much all conservationist movements from this time forward. Nature in its wilderness aspect was also a scary proposition – something that comes across clearly in the descriptions of the building of the Erie Canal.

But love of nature had not yet acquired a religious dimension, as Christianity had a history of believing that God had created the world for the benefit of man. This position would be challenged directly when a different religious source became available in the West: the Indian Vedas. In 1830, the first translation of the Rig Veda became available – in Latin.[193] The Rig Veda, born to the period historians of religion now call the **Axial Age**, presents a completely different viewpoint to the Christian one – and the Transcendentalists were hooked. This early translation lacked the scholarship of the later works of Max Müller, but it was enough to give Westerners a hint of Indian perennial wisdom. It's worth remembering that the element fire has long been associated with spirit – and Transcendentalism produced a more complete package that viewed nature multi-dimensionally. The value of the inner mystical experience took on new meaning in the West. Through the works of Emerson and Thoreau especially, the conservation movement that would develop had the first of its sacred texts.

Emerson's essay "Nature," published in 1836 is considered the clarion call of this movement. The Aries Ingress for 1836 for Boston (Chart 52) has a couple of features that do suggest this movement. The close conjunction of the Moon and Venus in Taurus, where both are strongly dignified, actually illustrates the strong place of women in this movement – some time before such a thing was politically correct. Margaret Fuller was a prominent person within Transcendentalism. This conjunction was square Neptune and opposite Saturn. To some of their contemporaries, the Transcendentalists were considered a bit crazy – New Agers of their own time period. Neptune in the 9th but conjunct the MC illustrates the prominence and influence that this movement will have.

The spiritual influence of this period should not be underrated. For example, in 1832, the American painter *George Catlin* (1796-1872), who was doing for Native Americans what Audubon was simultaneously doing for flora and fauna, proposed the idea of the national park system. We have already seen how a couple of specific attempts at establishing national parks were tried with Pluto in Taurus, but it was the period of Pluto in Gemini where the idea really took hold.

It was also a time of economic extremes. The period we have just been discussing, from 1834-1837, was a speculative bubble that burst with the Panic of 1837, followed by a five year depression. These sorts of economic booms and busts were common in the 19th century, proving the point that connecting the currency to actual bullion as it was in the 19th century does *not* produce economic stability.

It was also a time of great inventions, such as the photograph (1826), the Babbage forerunner to the computer (1834), anesthesia

NATAL CHART
Sun enters Ari 3-20-1836
March 20, 1836
8:54:45 AM
Boston, Massachusetts
42N21'30" 71W03'37"
Local Mean Time
Time Zone: 0 hours West
Tropical Regiomontanus

Chart 52. Sun enters Aries 1836, Boston, MA

Day of ☉	Hour of ☿
Last Hr ♀	- 47 mins
Next Hr ☽	+13 mins

FIXED STARS	
☿☌ Fomalhaut	0°43's
♅☌ Fomalhaut	0°36's
⊗☌ Sirius	0°05's
♃☌ Alhena	0°23'a
⊗☌ Canopus	0°47'a
☿☌ Deneb Adige	0°48'a
☊☌ Capulus	0°52'a
♅☌ Deneb Adige	0°55'a

Hs	Alm. (Dor)
1	☿
2	☽
3	☽
4	☉
5	☿
6	♄
7	♃
8	♀♄
9	♂
10	♄
11	♀
12	☉

ESSENTIAL DIGNITIES (Dorothean)

Pl	Ruler	Exalt	Tripl	Term	Face	Detri	Fall	Score
☉	♂	☉ +	☉ +	♃	♂	♀	♄	+7
☽	♀	☽ +	♀	♀	☿	♂	--	+4
☿	♃	♀	♀	♀ m	♄	☿ -	☿ -	- 14 P
♀	♀ +	☽	♀ +	☿ m	☿	♂	--	+8
♂	♃	♀	♀	♃	♄ m	☿	☿	- 5 P
♃	☽	♃ +	♀	♃ +	♀	♄	♂	+6
♄	♂	--	♀	♂	♂ m	♀	☽	- 5 P
☊	♀	☽	♀	♄	♄	♂	--	--
⊗	☽	♃	♀	♃	☿	♄	♂	--
As	☿	☊	♄	☿	♃	♃	--	--
Mc	♄	--	♄	☿	♀	☉	--	--
☋	♂	--	♀	☿	♀	♀	☽	--

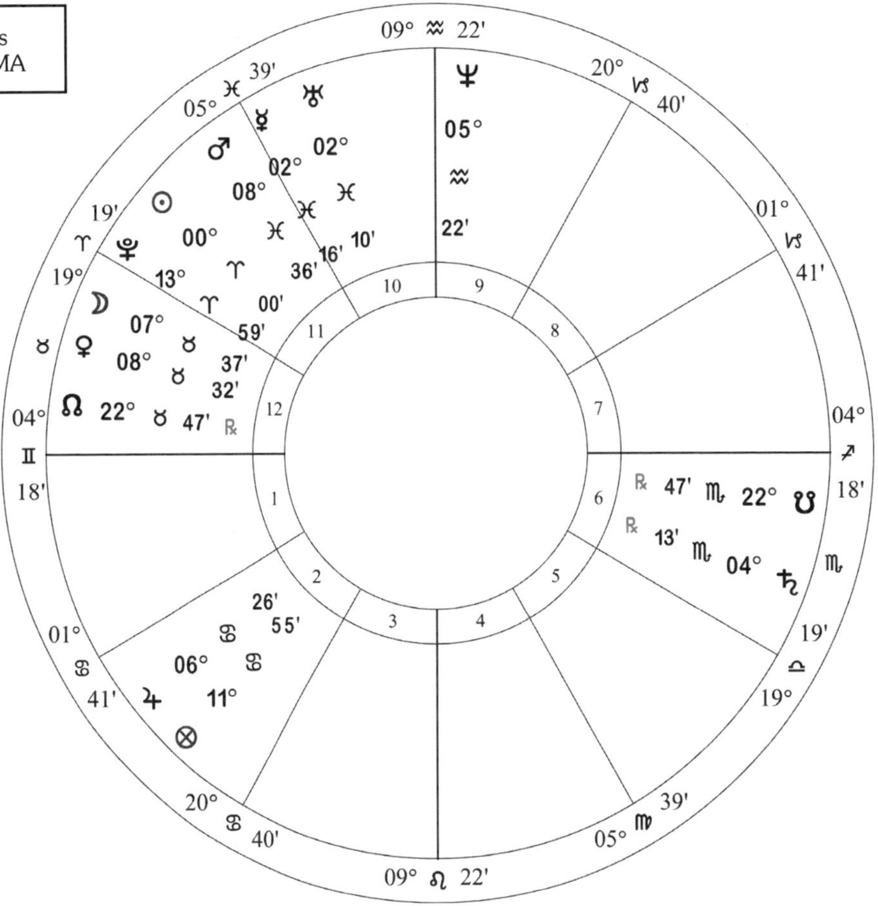

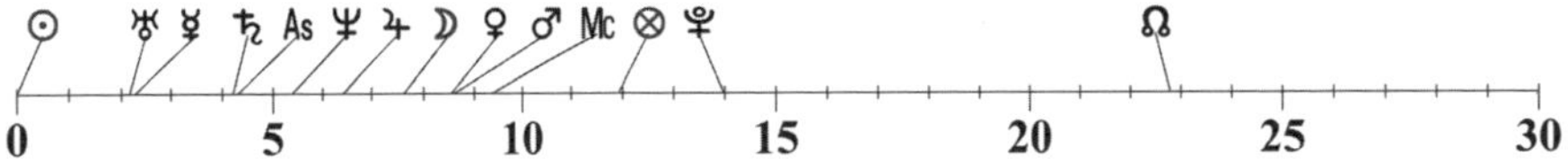

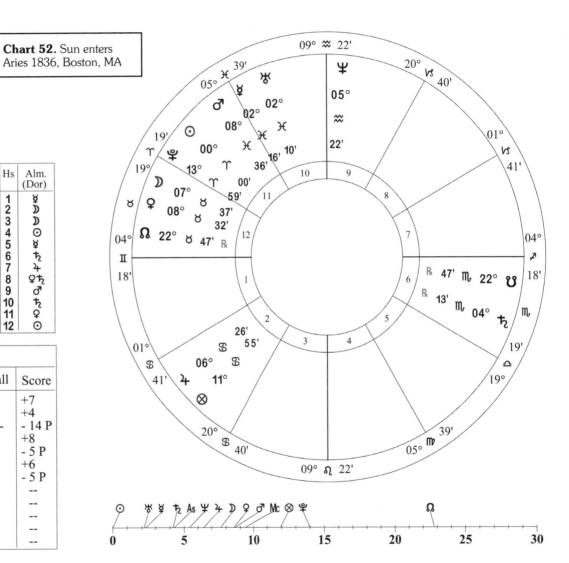

(1842), and the telegraph (1844). Darwin's voyage on the *H.M.S. Beagle* took place from 1831-1836: this was the foundation for the evidence that eventually found its way to the surface during the Pluto in Taurus era when Darwin finally published the theory of evolution.

The Irish Potato Famine

The second half of the 1840s, the third decanate of Pluto in Aries, proved to be as volatile as the third decanate of Pluto in Pisces in the 1810s. It began with the Potato Famine in Ireland in 1846, which resulted in massive emigration from Ireland.[194] The potato was a plant of the Americas that was exported to the Old World. It was perfect for subsistence farming in Ireland, because a family farm could produce enough to live on. The potato was so successful that it virtually became the only crop – and that was the downfall, because sooner or later, *any one* crop will fail in a year.

What made this period so difficult? Biologically, the answer was the potato blight – a parasite that periodically ravages potato crops, but especially so in any area – like Ireland – where the potato was grown so extensively that the mold causing the disease could propagate easily. Politically, Ireland was a land of extreme poverty, exacerbated by centuries of restrictions of landholding by Catholics that had reduced the Catholic majority to abject poverty and exploitation by absent English landlords. In 1845 half of the potato crop of Ireland was destroyed, followed by three-quarters in 1846. The 1846 loss was so severe that there were no seed potatoes saved, and starvation began. Through starvation and emigration which followed, Ireland lost 20% of its population by 1851.[195]

We can see these effects in Chart 53. The Aries Ingress for 1845 shows the South Node in the 9th – an interesting signature for destruction from overseas. The Moon-Neptune opposition at the Bendings didn't help: it was easier to look for scapegoats than do anything about the underlying causes, namely poverty and subsistence farming. Mercury, ruling the Ascendant and MC, is conjunct Scheat, a shipwreck star. Jupiter at the 8th house cusp exactly does appear very dangerous as well.

There are indications of problems – but this was not the tipping point. A single bad harvest is a problem, but not a disaster. The disaster came in 1846. In the Aries Ingress for 1846, quite apart from its location in any one place, there was a Mars square Saturn, with Saturn dignified, and Mars in Detriment. Already, this is a difficult combination. Adding to that, Mars is conjunct Alcyone, the brightest star of the Pleiades, a location long associated with disaster. Jupiter is conjunct the South Node. The 4th house (the country's land) has Uranus there to add to the volatility, with that angry Mars conjunct the 7th house cusp. And the land itself is ruled by Jupiter – in the toilet, as my partner Maggie Meister has characterized conjunctions to the South Node.

Starvation and emigration: the great themes of 1847-1848. The Aries Ingress has always been viewed as the harbinger of the year's agricultural productivity, whether it is the only chart used for the year or not. Jupiter, the 4th house ruler in 1846 conjunct the South Node – there is the astrological indication of the destruction of the seed potatoes. For those of you who don't think like a farmer, seed, or seed potatoes in this case, is the portion of the harvest held back to be able to plant in the Spring. Whenever the next year's seed supply has to be eaten to make it through winter, you are forfeiting your crop for the following year, and thus opening the door to future starvation by attempting to prevent it in the moment. The 1847 Aries Ingress shows Saturn, the planet of famine, in Pisces in the 1st house, in dignity only by Face (fear and anxiety), and in a contra-antiscial relationship to Pluto, a relationship you might remember as having the nature of the opposition. This is a huge stellium in the 1st, and famine is walking the land, with Mercury, ruler of the 4th besieged between Uranus and the South Node.

By 1848, the chart is not as severe, but the hole already dug is massive. The Aries Ingress fell just after a Full Moon, it's an eclipse, with the Sun in a partile conjunction with the South Node. The land, ruled by Mercury in Detriment, Fall and also retrograde, has still not recovered. The exalted Jupiter at the Ascendant gives the survivors at least some hope that they have survived the worst. With the Moon in the 4th, the flight from the land toward the sea occurs with the Ascendant in a water sign, the ruler of the IC in a water sign, and the dispositor of the Moon in the 9th.

Any crop failure is a potential environmental problem – and it certainly was in this case, being an early example of what is called **monoculture**: the exclusive or near-exclusive cultivation of a single plant species. This is exactly the sort of practice that produces unstable ecosystems. Agriculture produces much simpler ecosystems than the natural vegetation of a particular region. Even so, agriculture in a region almost always has featured multiple crops, if only because farms produced first for themselves, and only secondarily for sale. People seldom thrive on a single crop. In natural ecosystems, there are no examples of a single plant species, except under the most harsh, unstable, and extreme conditions. Monoculture is an extreme example of the adage, "putting all of your eggs in one basket." In fact, the Irish Potato Famine became the signature piece warning of the perils of this approach to agriculture.

As we wrap up Pluto in Aries, what can we extract from this that is relevant to our core issue of sustainability? We have one literary movement, Transcendentalism, which can be considered ancestral to an environmental perspective. There were people who had developed a Romantic interest in Nature – but this was often more by way of contrasting what they saw as natural purity with the corruption of so-called civilized life. In the U.S.A. especially, this translated into utopian movements forming isolated colonies where adherents could attempt to live their ideals. At least at this pass of Pluto in Aries, the possibly belligerent qualities of Aries were trumped by the explorational aspects.

Pluto in Leo
(1937-1958)

If Pluto in Aries ended with the Crimean War, Pluto in Leo began with another war. And if Pluto in Aries was too early to really examine how Pluto in a Fire Sign interfaced with sustainability, Pluto in Leo wasn't. Ecology was already in place as a discipline, as we saw with Pluto in Cancer. And Pluto in Leo is often our astrological parlance for the Baby Boom generation, a watershed in population issues which drove concern about changing demographic profiles long before there was a major shift in consciousness about overpopulation.

Before we get to the development of ecology, conservation, and environmentalism under Pluto in Leo, we do have to address one aspect of World War II: the development of the atomic bomb. While modern astrologers almost universally attribute radioactivity to Pluto, this attribution doesn't fall out of anything so obvious as the discovery of radioactivity corresponding to the discovery of

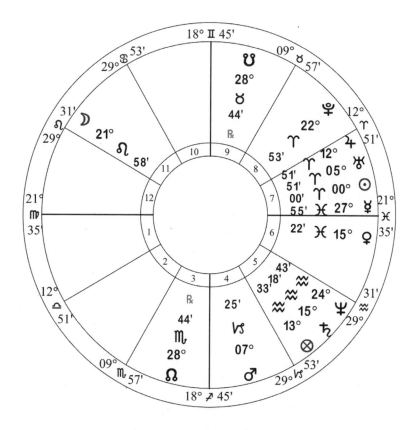

Sun enters Ari 3-20-1845
March 20, 1845 5:18:36 PM
Dublin, Ireland
53 N 20 6 W 15
Local Mean Time
Time Zone: 0 hours West
Tropical Regiomontanus
NATAL CHART

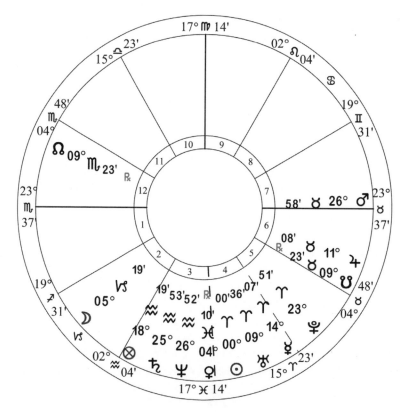

Sun enters Ari 3-20-1846
March 20, 1846 11:20:33 PM
Dublin, Ireland
53 N 20 6 W 15
Local Mean Time
Time Zone: 0 hours West
Tropical Regiomontanus
NATAL CHART

Chart 53. Sun enters Aries
1845-1848, Dublin, Ireland

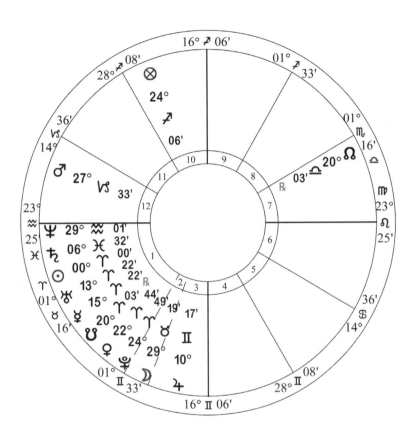

Sun enters Ari 3-21-1847
March 21, 1847 5:07:07 AM
Dublin, Ireland
53 N 20 6 W 15
Local Mean Time
Time Zone: 0 hours West
Tropical Regiomontanus
NATAL CHART

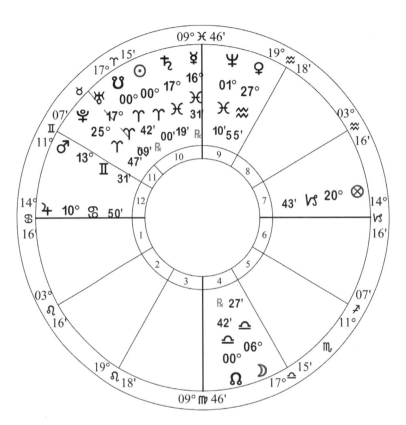

Sun enters Ari 3-20-1848
March 20, 1848 10:52:49 AM
Dublin, Ireland
53 N 20 6 W 15
Local Mean Time
Time Zone: 0 hours West
Tropical Regiomontanus
NATAL CHART

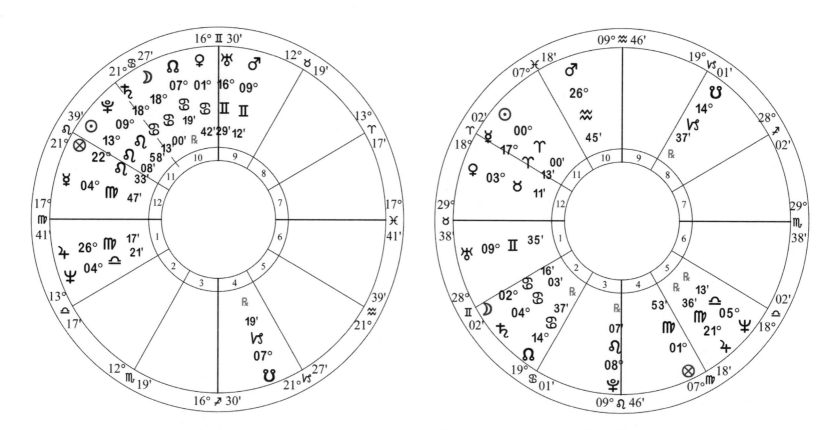

Bombing of Hiroshima
August 6, 1945 8:15 AM
Hiroshima, Japan
34 N 24 132 E 27
Standard Time
Time Zone: 9 hours East
Tropical Regiomontanus
NATAL CHART

Chart 54. Bombing of Hiroshima; Sun enters Aries 1945, Washington, DC and Tokio, Japan; Sun enters Cancer 1945, Washington, DC

Sun enters Ari 3-20-1945
March 21, 1945 8:37:14 AM
Tokyo, Japan
35 N 42 139 E 46
Standard Time
Time Zone: 9 hours East
Tropical Regiomontanus
NATAL CHART

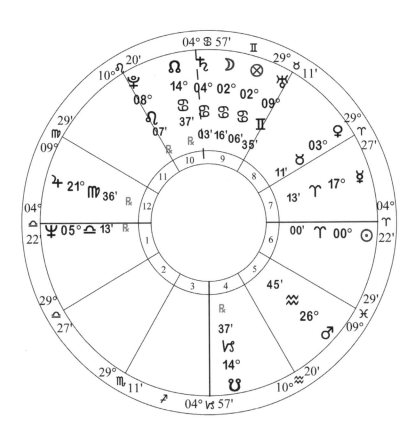

Sun enters Ari 3-20-1945
March 20, 1945 7:37:14 PM
Washington, D.C.
38N53'42" 77W02'12"
War Time
Time Zone: 5 hours West
Tropical Regiomontanus
NATAL CHART

Sun enters Can 6-21-1945
June 21, 1945 2:52:05 PM
Washington, D.C.
38N53'42" 77W02'12"
War Time
Time Zone: 5 hours West
Tropical Regiomontanus
NATAL CHART

Pluto. Radioactivity was studied under the name Becquerel rays beginning in 1896 (Pluto in Gemini) following its discovery by – you guessed it! – Henri Becquerel. Marie and Pierre Curie were also early researchers. By 1934, *i.e.*, just a few years after Pluto's discovery, Frédéric Joliot discovered that some elements could be made radioactive by bombardment with hydrogen atoms. In 1938, just as the lead-up to the war was occurring, Otto Hahn and Fritz Strassmann reported on experiments that produced fission of uranium; their former colleague Lise Meitner, who had been forced to flee to Sweden because she was a Jew, recognized, along with her nephew Otto Fritsch, that this process could be used to build an atomic bomb. They communicated this information to colleagues in the U.S.A., from whom it reached Fermi and Szilard, who began working on the physics of fission. At this point, there were a great many physicists researching this topic, but it became part of *the* war effort both for Germany and the Allies as greater evidence accumulated that this knowledge could be used to create an atomic bomb. There are three events that have generally been used for astrology of the atomic bomb. The first was the first nuclear chain reaction, 2 December 1942 3:25 P.M. CST, Chicago, IL. The second was the first atomic explosion, 16 July 1945, 5:29:51 A.M. MWT, Alamogordo, NM. The third was the time that the bomb was dropped at Hiroshima, 6 August 1945, 8:15 A.M., Hiroshima, Japan.[196]

So we will examine this event in part to see whether Pluto does in fact seem to have anything to do with it. Examine Chart 54. We begin with the bombing chart itself. The first question is: how do we understand what we are even looking at? The bomb killed 80,000 people immediately; the casualties totaled somewhere between 30 – 40% of both Hiroshima and Nagasaki. These were civilians. Now that many U.S. World War II records have been declassified, there is considerable evidence to suggest that the U.S. government prolonged the war for several months in order to drop the bombs, both to avoid post-war criticism about developing a weapon and not using it (this had happened after World War I), and because Secretary of State Byrnes believed that having the bomb would increase concessions from the Soviets (that didn't work).[197] So are we viewing a "battle," or mass murder, if not genocide?

I'm not sure the chart actually gives us any answers to this. The partile Moon-Saturn conjunction, with the North Node, and a dignified Venus all in the 10th, does suggest the successful mission – and the emphasis on Cancer may even invoke the fact that the pilot decided to name the plane after his mother! Uranus conjunct the MC may show something of the suddenness of both the casualties and Japan's rapid capitulation. The state of the 7th house ruler, being in its Detriment and in the 1st house, surely shows the resulting surrender, since the 1st house must be given to the U.S.A. as the initiator of the bombing.

The three major outer planets' aspects for the year 1945 were Jupiter square Saturn, Jupiter conjunct Neptune, and Saturn square Neptune. None were in force at the time of the bombing. Other years which shared these patterns were: 1191, 1280, 1370 (which also had Uranus square Pluto), and 1766. In two of those years, 1191 and 1370, significant war campaigns did end – but obviously, not like this at all!

Examining the Aries Ingress at Tokyo has the Pleiades (Alcyone) rising – a sure sign of something truly awful. Mars representing the U.S.A. (7th house ruler) is square that Ascendant – and all of this in fixed signs shows the high casualties and difficulties of the last few months of the war. The fixed signs might also be evidence for the apparent stubbornness of the U.S.A. in prolonging the war. Pluto at the IC can surely be unfortunate, and the sign of the fighting on their homeland, if not total destruction of it. And frankly, this is our first argument of some relationship between Pluto and radioactivity – because Pluto wasn't actually that active at all when the bomb was dropped.

The chart for the Aries Ingress for Washington is pretty busy – but Hiroshima will fall under the Cancer Ingress. The Aries Ingress does cover the death of Franklin Roosevelt on April 12th, the death of Hitler on April 30th, and the surrender of Germany on May 7th. Here, the Moon-Saturn is at the 10th: the death of the President. And Neptune is rising! Whereas there are some conspiracy theories around Roosevelt's death, he had been a sick man for a long time, and so I choose not to speculate about that. This could well be the initiation of the State Department cover-up of Japan's attempts to surrender. This Neptune, after all, is squared by the Moon (10th house ruler) which rules Truman coming into office just as surely as Roosevelt going out of office. The South Node in the 4th is probably descriptive of Hitler's death – the 10th (leader) from the 7th (enemy) being the radical 4th – and his destruction there.

For the Cancer Ingress for Washington, the Ascendant-Descendant axis rulers are conjunct at the 8th house cusp: "*Now I am become Death, the Destroyer of Worlds,*" as J. Robert Oppenheimer quoted from the *Bhagavad-Gita* after the July 16th Trinity test.[198] The Moon in Scorpio roughly opposite this conjunction also shows this is perhaps not in good faith. Here, Pluto is in the 10th: the public demonstration of an awesome weapon of destruction. The presence of so much activity in the 9th – where foreign relations lies – shows this was less about the war than its aftermath. However, embassies and ambassadors are ruled by the 5th. Saturn ruling the 5th is in the 9th – nice symbolism, were this not Saturn in Detriment. The ploy wouldn't work.

Aldo Leopold: The Soul of Emerging Wildlife Management

If the nature of Pluto in Leo isn't entirely clear in the chart for dropping the atomic bomb, it has a quite literal meaning in environmental developments. To begin to understand how Pluto in Leo affected the course of environmentalism and consciousness about the earth and its resources, one has to understand the career of Aldo Leopold. Leopold went to the Yale Forest School during Pluto in Gemini, worked for the Forest Service and as a Professor of Game Management during all of Pluto in Cancer. He then purchased eighty acres of deserted land in Wisconsin which he managed, with the experience becoming the basis for *A Sand County Almanac*, published posthumously in 1949. Recalling that sequence, the environmental ethic of the Pluto in Gemini period was to create national parks to preserve certain aspects of wilderness, but to apply science to agricultural and range problems, primarily in the West. Environmental science was tied to development, and was designed to facilitate it by studying new approaches to dry farming.

In the period of Pluto in Cancer, the Army Corps of Engineers worked overtime with the Civilian Conservation Corps to manage the waterways, and then to develop water conservation and irrigation systems. Focus moved away from the Southwest, as the droughts of the 1930s forced farmers around the country to redesign their agriculture around irrigation. With the shift East, one of the areas of ecology that developed very strongly was what is called **old field succession**. This was an idea prized by Frederic Clements, to whom I referred in the last chapter. It posits that if a mature ecosystem is damaged by fire, logging, or other means, there is a recognizable and predictable pattern of regrowth, which will eventually result in a new mature ecosystem after a period of time, which could be a century, or could be less. The exact nature of the succession will vary from place to place for exactly the same reasons as different climates and geologies produce different mature ecosystems in the first place.

So when Leopold was assigned by the Forest Service to jobs in Arizona and New Mexico beginning in 1901, he was following the epicenter of ecological research. One of his early jobs was hunting wolves and other top carnivores, because they were seen as competitive with ranchers – and thus unacceptable, in this vision of land managed for the benefit of man. In his essay, "Thinking Like a Mountain,"[199] Leopold describes his reaction to the death of a she-wolf, and the extinction of her spirit, as a life-altering experience. It would percolate through his consciousness for decades, emerging on the other end as he developed his land ethic. Even so, almost immediately, he began to question the wisdom of eliminating top predators as violating principles of good ecosystem management. It took decades for wildlife biologists to come to grips with the environmental damage they inflicted in the form of population explosions and crashes in ecosystems when the predators were removed.

Leopold also witnessed the workings and damage created by the second great management disaster of ecosystem engineering of the 20th century – and the one that would only be understood as such once Pluto got into Leo: fire control.[200] Heretofore, it had been the policy of the Forest Service to suppress fire, but ecologists of the 1950s were seeing that this was driving a process of succession that was completely unintended. They also became aware that the attempt to suppress fire resulted in a lot of flammable undergrowth, which meant that when a fire finally did occur, it was catastrophic. Even though the documentation on these points has become overwhelming, management by controlled burning remains controversial even today among homeowners in dry forested regions. There are those who object to the aesthetic of partly burned scenery, seemingly unaware of the potentially catastrophic danger to themselves and property when a wildfire becomes too large to control.[201] Leopold himself lost his life from a heart attack which occurred while he was helping a neighbor to fight a grass fire.

By the time of Pluto in Leo, wildlife biologists and ecologists could begin to comprehensively examine man's influence on the environment. Human population growth was making it absurd to attempt to separate an increasingly scarce pristine nature from human activity, whether from urbanization, highway growth, agricultural growth, or pollution of all kinds.

Perusing the abstracts of the conference convened by Carl Sauer in 1955, the topics could have been presented at any Earth Day event in 1970 – or many environmental conferences thereafter.[202] So the obvious question is: why didn't these ideas take off *then*? The drag, then as now, is that accepting these ideas affects direct lifestyle choices that people make.

And not only were the children born of Pluto in Leo the Baby Boomers, but the period of the Fifties was an odd mix: a driving desire for a normal family life following the horrors of the Second World War, an anti-Communist crusade that brought paranoia to the national stage, an expansion of consumerism on a scale never seen before, and an urban sprawl into suburbia. Environmentalism brings an awareness of limits; people didn't *want* limits. And yet all this frenzied normality was in the midst of the first generation to live with The Bomb – and the reality that life on earth could be ended instantly.

Smog at Mid-Century

Yet, all the signs of environmental degradation were there. Smog, as a result of coal burning had been known for centuries. By the 1930s, chemical smog was beginning to happen. The term "greenhouse gas" was coined in 1937, just as Pluto was first going into Leo.[203] One of the most prominent examples was in Donora, PA, October 27, 1948. Here, a killer smog developed as a result of a temperature inversion and sulfur dioxide and other emissions from the Donora Zinc Works and the American Steel & Wire plant. Twenty people died, and several thousand were affected. U.S. Steel, the parent company, tried to evade legal responsibility by claiming that it was an Act of God. Nonetheless, U.S. Steel settled.

This incident was crucial in the process of teaching people about the danger of air pollution, as well as industrial culpability, at least under certain conditions.

Chart 55, the Aries Ingress for Donora is very close to that of Washington: the Washington angles are 13 Cancer Rising and 24 Pisces culminating. This starts out as a good year if one sees the Moon in Cancer ruling the Ascendant, with Venus in Taurus in the 11th conjunct the North Node. The 2nd house is problematic: this is a triple conjunction (remember, they are all in the same decanate) with Saturn in Detriment – and everybody retrograde, to add to the imbecilic quality. The triple conjunction was at the Bendings, which simply stepped up that likelihood that this wasn't something trivial. Pluto was square the Part of Fortune – leading one to the conclusion that whatever it was going to be, it was likely expensive. The cardinal Ascendant reveals that the Libra Ingress will be necessary to track the events of October 27th.

The Libra Ingress has Uranus in the 1st house and square the Sun. Mars and Pluto were part of the triple conjunction in the Spring: now they are square, and Mars rules the 6th house of illness from its dignity in Scorpio. Saturn is now partile conjunct the 4th house cusp. Partile or even close conjunctions to the 4th house in event charts or ingresses are seldom a good thing! A planet conjunct the IC, which symbolizes *Terra firma*, upsets the status quo.. Here both Saturn and Uranus have moved into new signs, bringing a level of instability to the whole equation.

So where's the air? This, after all is considered the birth of U.S. awareness about *air* pollution – and having Sun, Mercury, and Neptune in Libra may be more convincing than no air – but it's hardly a big focus. The answer is – what *caused* the problem? It was mining operations. Traditionally, mining is a saturnian affair, but mythologically, Pluto makes sense as well. What is the nature of mining and processing? Fire and earth – smelting applied to minerals and rocks. The air was passive – it was merely the substrate for the problem to be transmitted, so to speak.

We can also examine this question using London's killer fog of 1952. On 2-5 December, an inversion resulted in the trapping of coal smoke from residential burning: it was a very cold month. While London had a history of noxious fogs, this was considerably worse, and the government attributed 3,000 deaths to the fog. However, Bell and Davis note that the death toll for that period was actually considerably elevated, but the government chose to blame an influenza outbreak for the rest of the deaths. Reassessing the data, Bell and David concluded the actual death toll from the killer fog was 12,000.[204]

Chart 56, the Aries Ingress had a mutable Ascendant, so the Libra Ingress will apply. We do see a warning with the Aries Ingress, though, with the Sun conjunct the 8th house cusp and the Moon

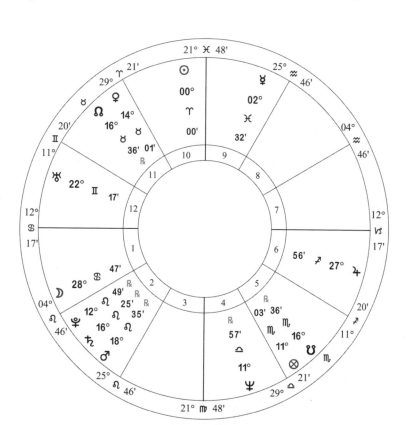

Sun enters Ari 3-20-1948
March 20, 1948
11:56:48 AM
Donora, Pennsylvania
40N10'24" 79W51'28"
Standard Time
Time Zone: 5 hours West
Tropical Regiomontanus
NATAL CHART

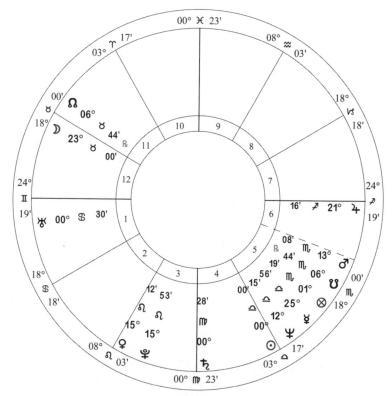

Sun enters Lib 9-23-1948
September 22, 1948
11:21:43 PM
Donora, Pennsylvania
40N10'24" 79W51'28"
Daylight Saving Time
Time Zone: 5 hours West
Tropical Regiomontanus
NATAL CHART

Chart 55. Sun enters Aries
and Libra, 1948, Donora, PA

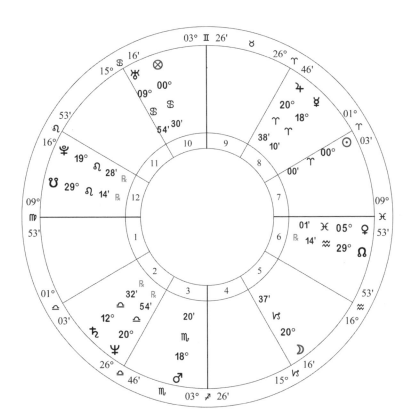

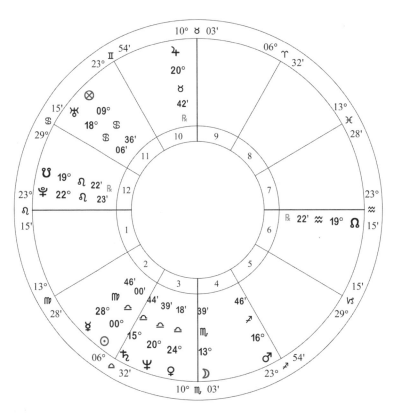

Sun enters Ari 3-20-1952
March 20, 1952
4:13:47 PM
London, England
51 N 30 0 W 10
Standard Time
Time Zone: 0 hours West
Tropical Regiomontanus
NATAL CHART

Chart 56. Sun enters Aries and Libra, 1952, London

Sun enters Lib 9-23-1952
September 23, 1952
3:23:42 AM
London, England
51 N 30 0 W 10
Daylight Saving Time
Time Zone: 0 hours West
Tropical Regiomontanus
NATAL CHART

square Jupiter, ruler of the 4th in the 8th conjunct Mercury, Ruler of the 1st, also in the 8th. This configuration is a partile T-square of Moon, Jupiter and Neptune. The Libra Ingress has Jupiter as the ruler of the 8th at the Bendings, imbecilic by retrogradation. In addition, the South Node is just past Pluto, which itself is conjunct the Ascendant, although in the 12th house. The 6th is ruled by Saturn: appropriate, since Lilly, Ramesey, and Partridge are unanimous in attributing coal mines to Saturn (they classify the place, but not the coal itself).[205] Notably, the Moon in Scorpio is at the IC – and we have already seen lots of examples where a malefic at the IC causes trouble.

The UK would enact the Clean Air Act in 1956, in part as a result of this event, but not without another killer smog that same year – fortunately, of lesser magnitude.

Industrial Fallout of the Late Pluto in Leo Period

Before we end our survey of Pluto in Leo, we have two incidents to consider in 1956 – the year Pluto first entered Virgo. You will recall that the early part of Pluto in Leo – the war part – showed an acceleration of work relating to practical applications of radioactivity. Bomb-making, which culminated in dropping the bombs on Hiroshima and Nagasaki, followed a few years later by the development of the hydrogen bomb. By 1953, the USSR also had the hydrogen bomb. The two emerging superpowers spent the Fifties developing the missile technology that could deliver those bombs – the same missile technology that would be utilized by the space program with Pluto in Virgo. The missile technology came right out of the Nazi

rocket development program during World War II – another Pluto in Leo development.

In the wake of the war, there were people like Glenn Seaborg, who were determined to develop peaceful uses of the atom. They dreamed of producing electrical power so cheap that it wouldn't be metered.

In England, the first nuclear power plant opened at Sellafield on 31 March 1956. Unfortunately, the line between civilian and military uses was more fictitious than real – while the plant did produce power, it was also designed to produce plutonium for Britain's weapons. Yet it was also the first commercial nuclear reactor for civilian power use.

Both power and weapons have a Mars rulership – and we can add Pluto, if we accept that designation for radioactivity. The Aries Ingress (Chart 57) shows the Moon opposite Mars configuration is probably a great signature for the peaceful (for the people, Moon) versus the military (Mars) uses – and they are not only opposite, they are both strong by dignity. Both players are at the table. Meanwhile, Pluto is in the 12th, but conjunct the Ascendant – behind closed doors, so to speak – which is odd, considering that this was a very public unveiling. It was public for only part of the program. The Ascendant was zero Virgo – and its ruler Mercury in Detriment was at the Bendings.

Barely a month later, there was another incident we need to consider. On May 1, Hajime Hosokawa writes up what he calls "Minamata disease" because it was affecting residents of the Japanese towns of Kumamoto and Minamata. Hosokawa was immediately suspicious of the fish diets of the residents. He was able to identify the disease as mercury poisoning as a result of dumping by Chisso Corporation. Mercury poisoning was an old occupational disease: the Mad Hatter in *Alice in Wonderland* suffered from classic Mercury poisoning, which was a known issue

NATAL CHART
Sun enters Ari 3-20-1956
March 20, 1956
3:20:19 PM
London, England
51 N 30 0 W 10
Standard Time
Time Zone: 0 hours West
Tropical Regiomontanus

Chart 57. Sun enters Aries 1956, London

Hs	Alm. (Dor)
1	♀
2	♅
3	♄
4	♂ ♀
5	♀ ♄
6	♄
7	♀
8	♀
9	♂
10	♀
11	☽
12	☉

Day of ♂ Hour of ♀

Last Hr ☉ - 12 mins
Next Hr ☿ +48 mins

FIXED STARS		
♀♂ Menkar	0°36's	
♅♂ Achernar	0°16's	
♅♂ Ankaa	0°05's	
♇♂ Alphard	0°04's	

ESSENTIAL DIGNITIES (Dorothean)							
Pl	Ruler	Exalt	Tripl	Term	Face	Detri	Fall	Score
☉	♂	☉ +	☉ +	♃	♂	♀	♄	+7
☽	☽ +	♃	♀	♃	☿	♄	♂	+5
☿	♃	♀	♀	☿ +	♃	☿ -	☿ -	-7
♀	♀ +	☽	♀ +	☿	☽	♂	--	+8
♂	♄	♂ +	♀	♃	♂ +	☽	♃	+5
♃	☉	--	☉	♃ +	♂	♄	--	+2
♄	♃	☋	☉	♃	♀	☽	--	-5 P
☊	♃	☉	☉	♀	☽	--	--	--
⊗	♃	☋ +	☉	☿	☽	--	--	--
As	☿	☿	♀	☿	♃	♃	♀	--
Mc	☿	☽	♀	♃	☉	♃	♂	--
☋	☿	☊	♄	♃	♂	--	--	--

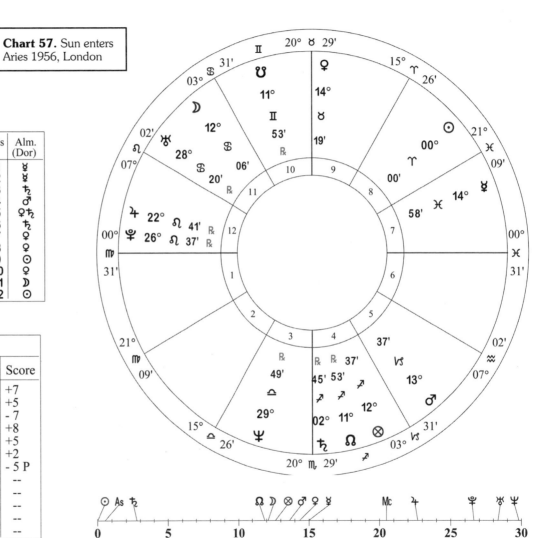

NATAL CHART
Sun enters Ari 3-20-1956
March 21, 1956
12:20:19 AM
Tokio, Japan
35 N 42 139 E 46
Standard Time
Time Zone: 9 hours East
Tropical Regiomontanus

Chart 58. Sun enters Aries 1956, Tokio, Japan

Day of ♂	Hour of ☽
Last Hr ☿	- 32 mins
Next Hr ♄	+28 mins

FIXED STARS	
♀☌ Menkar	0°36's
Mc☌ Diadem	0°20's
☿☌ Achernar	0°16's
☿☌ Ankaa	0°05's
♇☌ Alphard	0°04's
Mc☌ Vindemiatrix	0°39'a
As☌ Rasalhague	0°56'a

Hs	Alm. (Dor)
1	♃
2	♂
3	♀
4	♂
5	☽♀
6	☽
7	☿
8	☽
9	☿
10	♀
11	♂
12	♂

ESSENTIAL DIGNITIES (Dorothean)

Pl	Ruler	Exalt	Tripl	Term	Face	Detri	Fall	Score
☉	♂	☉ +	♃	♃	♂	♀	♄	+4
☽	☽ +	♃	♂ m	♃	☿	♄	♂	+5
☿	♃	♀	♂	☿ +	♃	☿ -	☿ -	- 7
♀	♀ +	☽	☽	☿	☽	♂	--	+5
♂	♄	♂ +	☽ m	♃	♂ +	☽	♃	+5
♃	☉	--	♃ +	♃ +	♂	♄	--	+5
♄	♃	☋	♃	♃	☿	☿	--	- 5 P
☊	♃	☋	♃	♀	☽	☿	--	--
⊗	☿	☿	☽	♀	☉	♃	♀	--
As	♃	☋	♃	♄	♄	☿	--	--
Mc	♀	♄	☿	♀	☽	♂	☉	--
☋	☿	☊	☿	♃	♂	♃	--	--

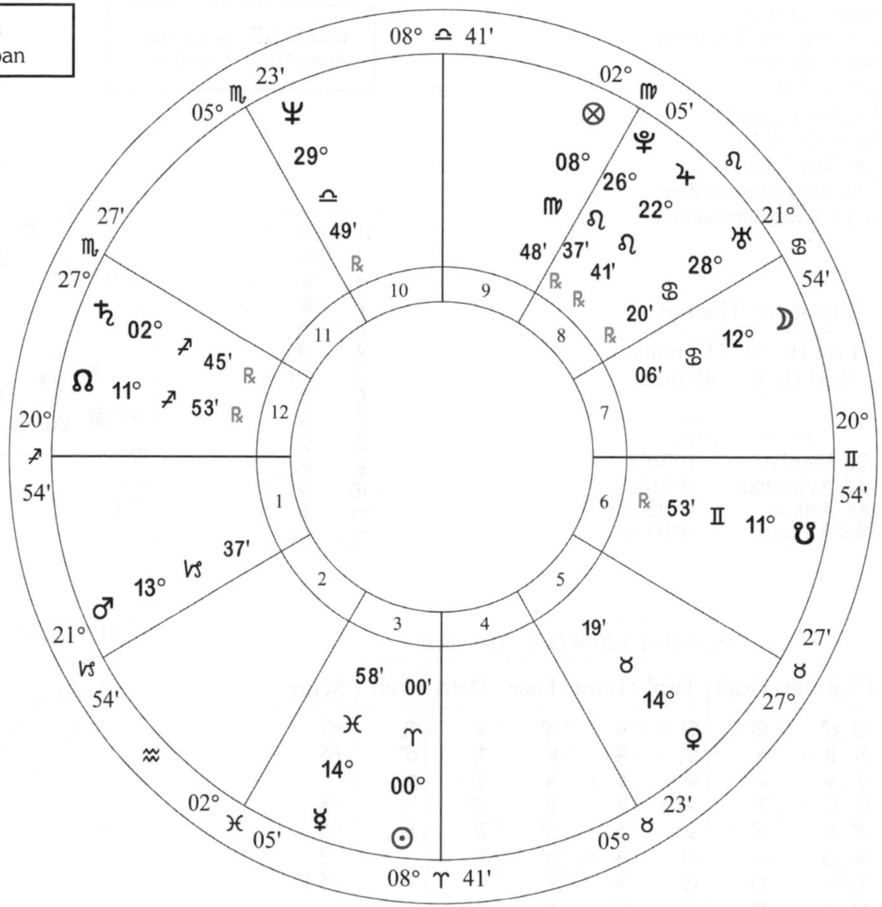

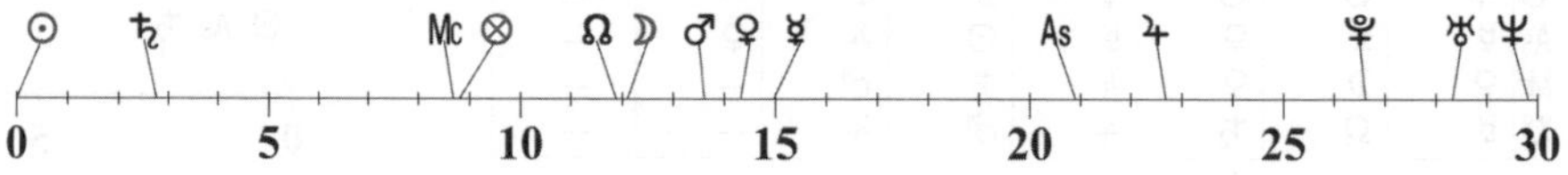

for hatters, who encountered the mercury because it was used in the felting process.

In Chart 58, we are now looking at the same ingress we just did for London. What rules mercury? Could it be: Mercury? Well, yes! Also historically known as quicksilver! And here we see Mercury in Detriment, at the Bendings, with the Moon coming to trine Mercury – which is probably why Hosokawa found the answer to the problem so readily. The Mercury-ruled South Node was in the 6th, which is surely the disease itself. Like the 1952 killer fog, the Ruler of the 1st was in the 8th. One other point: observe the fixed star Vindemiatrix on the MC. This star is also known as the widow's star. Metaphorically, an event which produces widows (or widowers) is a typical signature event.

Minamata was yet one more instance where it became clear that industry in proximity to residential areas was becoming extremely dangerous. And population densities were beginning to dictate the fact that there was no choice about people and chemicals residing cheek by jowl. Sadly, these incidents would only increase in frequency in the coming years.

While enthusiasts for the atom dreamed their dreams of unlimited power, the ecologists of the day realized that perhaps the most extreme impacts of humans on the landscape was as a result of war.[206] Ecologists were not so easily taken in by the hype about both the safety and the unlimited potential of nuclear power. After the thermonuclear testing that produced the hydrogen bomb at about the time of the Saturn-Neptune conjunction of 1952-1953, U.S. weather forecasts attempted to present radioactive debris in the atmosphere as "harmless."[207] Ecologists had been shifting their activities into studying ecosystems, but this work did not bear fruit in terms of understanding the effects of atmospheric radioactive testing until the period of Pluto in Virgo.[208]

Pluto In Sagittarius
(1995-2008)

It is exceptionally hard to discuss an historical period which has just ended, because we lack the objectivity to see the important themes. And we are barely out of Pluto in Sagittarius, which ended in 2008. What an end! Instead of a transition by war, there was an economic meltdown: not the worst that the world has ever seen, but the extent of it globally reemphasized that national economies are tied together globally as they have never been before.

For now, I simply want to highlight some of the important environmental issues of the period of Pluto in Sagittarius (and Neptune in Aquarius). We will discuss them within a different context in the next chapter.

As the period opened, Greenpeace was highlighting nuclear issues, the United Nations Intergovernmental Panel on Climate Change had already issued a report on global warming[209], and there was a moratorium on toxic waste incineration within the United States. The ozone hole was still expanding, but the chemicals that had been identified as the cause – chlorofluorocarbons (CFCs) – were declining. In the first pass into Sagittarius, the Congress which took office had a Republican majority for the first time in decades: and dismantling environmental regulations was a high priority for them. However, with a Democratic president, this wasn't going to be easy, except that they could block environmentally progressive legislation at will.

To examine these events in Washington, we need to go to the prior Aries Ingress in 1994, shown in Chart 59. My presidential election studies have shown that the Aries Ingress is not the best chart for predicting the outcome of the election. And we cannot

NATAL CHART
Sun enters Ari 3-20-1994
March 20, 1994
3:28:01 PM
Washington, D.C.
38N53'42" 77W02'12"
Standard Time
Time Zone: 5 hours West
Tropical Regiomontanus

Day of ☉	Hour of ☿
Last Hr ♀	- 12 mins
Next Hr ☽	+48 mins

FIXED STARS	
♃☌S Scale	1°00's
♀☌ Alpheratz	0°59's
⊗☌Toliman	0°54's
♄☌Deneb Adige	0°50's
☉☌Scheat	0°42's
As☌Alphard	0°50'a
☿☌ Sadalmelik	0°52'a

Chart 59. Sun enters Aries 1994, Washington, DC

Hs	Alm. (Dor)
1	☉
2	☿
3	♄
4	♂
5	♃
6	♄
7	♄
8	♀
9	☉
10	♀
11	☿
12	☉

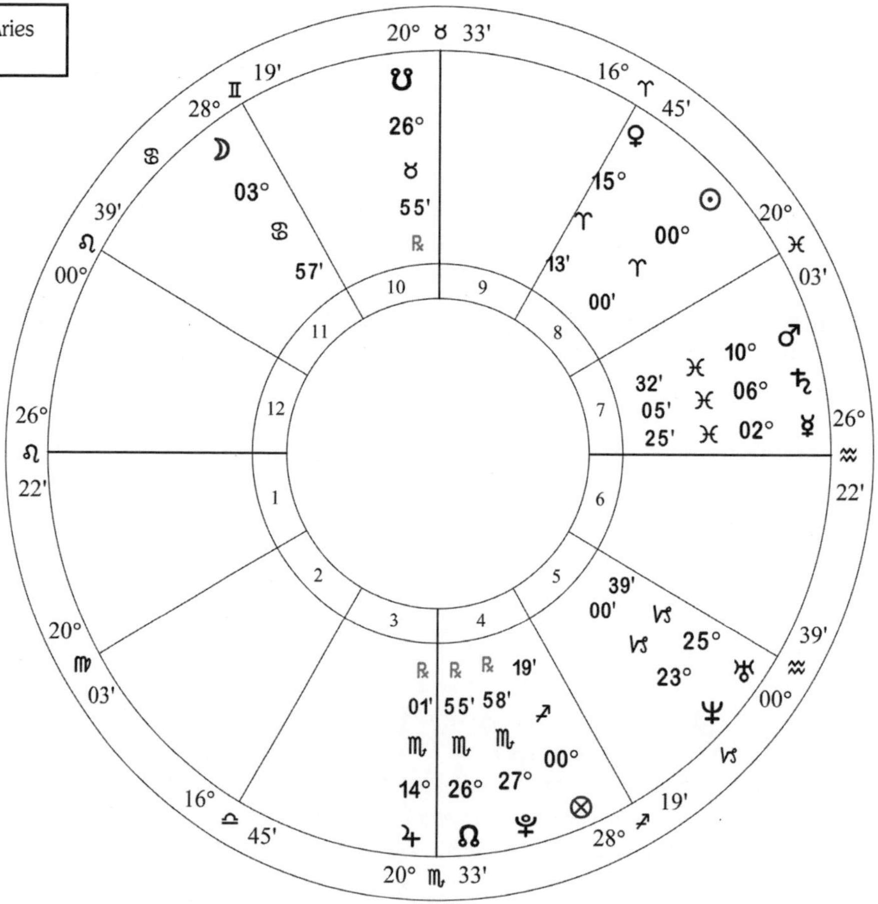

ESSENTIAL DIGNITIES (Dorothean)								
Pl	Ruler	Exalt	Tripl	Term	Face	Detri	Fall	Score
☉	♂	☉ +	☉ +	♃	♂	♀	♄	+7
☽	☽ +	♃	♀	♂	♀	♄	♂	+5
☿	♃	♀	♀	♀ m	♄	☿ -	☿ -	- 14 P
♀	♂	☉	☉	☿ m	☉	♀ -	♄	- 10 P
♂	♃ m	♀	♀	♃	♃	☿	☿	+0 P
♃	♂ m	--	♀	♀	☉	♀	☽	+0 P
♄	♃	♀	♀	♀	♄ +	☿	☿	+1
☊	♂	--	♀	☿	♀	♀	☽	--
⊗	♃	☋ +	☉	♃	☿	☿	--	--
As	☉	--	☉	♂	♂	♄	--	--
Mc	♀	☽	♀	♃	♄	♂	--	--
☋	♀	☽	♀	♂	♄	♂	--	--

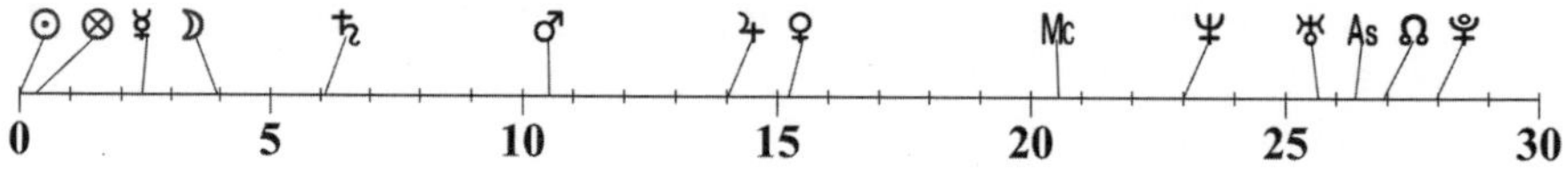

assume that fixed signs on the angles has anything to do with whether the party in power remains the party in power.

The major circumstance that we see is a beleaguered President Clinton, shown by the South Node in the 10th house., and reasonably near the MC itself. Venus, ruling the 10th was in Aries – hardly a strong position, except for showing a combative nature. Congress is ruled by the 11th, and the Moon in Cancer is there, showing a change of focus – but mixed effectiveness, with Mercury in Pisces ruling the 11th, and applying to Saturn. This was true – Clinton was accused of sexual harassment while he was a governor in May 1995.

By now, it is abundantly clear that much of the impetus for environmental progress was coming from outside the United States, as the Republican-controlled Congress worried about restoring logging in old growth forests. The Kyoto Protocol, adopted in 1997 by almost every country except the United States (the Clinton administration supported the treaty, but the Congress rejected it) was designed to address global warming through the control of carbon dioxide emissions – inadequately, according to most environmentalists. It went into effect in 2005. The Green Party was developing in Europe, with no counterpart in the U.S.A.

The Environmental Disaster of Mining

Environmental awareness doesn't always happen in a vacuum. And our current era is no exception: environmental disasters are waiting to happen everyday. Historically, one could make a case for the mining industry having the worst environmental impact. Even in Roman times, it was known that slaves sent to work mines were effectively being given a death sentence, since the working conditions were so bad. The first works on occupational illness were

all devoted to mining. The problem is obvious: mining attempts to extract minerals that are present in a fairly low concentration. So even under the best conditions, there are huge quantities of rock to be moved. Part of that rock becomes pulverized as it's removed – and the miners breathe it. A lot of the tailings (the waste rock) gets exposed to the air, and pollutes the water.

The justification for mining has always been that its "fruits" are valuable, and it is done far away from areas of population, to provide as little danger as possible. The problem is: there is no longer a large separation between mines and population centers. As human population on the globe has increased, there simply aren't that many areas left with no population density to speak of – forgetting for the moment, the question of the effect of ecosystem devastation on all populations, human and animal, downwind and downstream.

As the original veins of mineral have been depleted by mining, and the demand has continued to grow, mining techniques to extract far lower densities of mineral have become economically viable. One of the worst from an environmental standpoint is the use of cyanide to extract gold. And this point was proved in February 2000 near Baia Mare, Romania, when a chemical spill of cyanide slurry devastated animals and fish downriver, and threatened the drinking water of four European countries in what was called "*a catastrophe of European dimensions.*"[210]

The Aries Ingress for 1999, Chart 60, has Capricorn Rising, so all four ingress charts for 1999 are needed. The event took place in February 2000, so it falls under the Capricorn Ingress for 1999. Both charts show a late Capricorn Rising, with Neptune quite close to the Ascendant. I think the Neptune rising was a large part of the signature for this event. In the Capricorn Ingress, the Ascendant itself is 29 degrees, making the message that much

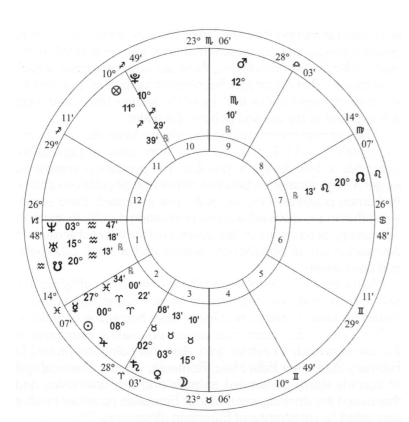

Sun enters Ari 3-21-1999
March 21, 1999
3:45:50 AM
Bucharest, Romania
44 N 26 26 E 06
Standard Time
Time Zone: 2 hours East
Tropical Regiomontanus
NATAL CHART

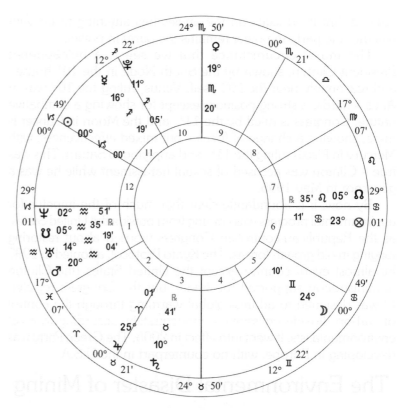

Sun enters Cap 12-22-1999
December 22, 1999
9:43:49 AM
Bucharest, Romania
44 N 26 26 E 06
Standard Time
Time Zone: 2 hours East
Tropical Regiomontanus
NATAL CHART

Chart 60. Sun enters Aries and
Capricorn 1999, Bucharest, Romania

more dramatic. Saturn, ruling both the Ascendant and the Sun, was square Neptune. The IC for these charts is pretty close to the degree of the vicious star Algol. Mines are given by the 4th house. In the Capricorn Ingress, the IC ruler Venus is in Detriment, and square the 1st house malefic Mars.

But, is there any tie-in to the Pluto in Sagittarius? I think the Neptune speaks to carelessness, and poison as well. Pluto in the Aries Ingress is conjunct Fortuna and trine the 2nd house ruler, suggesting the focus on profit – loss. In the Capricorn Ingress, Pluto was still disposed by Jupiter, also ruler of the 2nd house as in the Aries Ingress, and square Fortuna. The 4th house cusp is close to Algol, another argument of destruction of the land. The problem with too large a focus on profit is simple: everything else takes a back seat, including safety. If we read this chart in the style of the shipwreck charts we have already examined several times, then Aquarius rules the captain[211] – and with Neptune, Uranus and the South Node there in both Aries and Libra Ingresses, and also Mars in the Libra Ingress, one might suggest supervisor error, given the malefic quotient in the sign. But is the Pluto in Sagittarius an argument that nobody was taking seriously the possibility of error? Fire, after all, tends toward being long on confidence, short on contingency planning.

The real damage is shown in the Aries Ingress that followed. While dead fish were everywhere after the event, the damage to the rivers downstream was so extensive that estimates for recovery stated that it would take at least five years. This is not the case as with other disasters where the rebuilding afterward actually sparks a housing or other economic boom. Here, the effects were entirely negative.

In Chart 62, the chart is just after a Full Moon: the event has already occurred, and everyone is dealing with the aftermath. Pluto is sitting right on the Descendant – and this is actually the signature of the disaster, and how it did not go away. Jupiter in Taurus was Almuten of the 2nd – and in the 12th, at the Bendings, having squared Neptune, and coming to conjoin Saturn. Remember that fixed signs mean that the activities associated with the chart take longer to come to fruition: in this case, the economic impact of the spill will take years to unfold.

Mining is one of the most difficult environmental problems. Here, the mine where the disaster occurred was co-owned by an Australian mining company, and the Romanian government. So who is at fault? Who pays? The fact is, no government is taxing mining companies in a way that could actually pay for an environmental disaster of this magnitude. And yet, governments generally get stuck with the payment costs. Until mining clean-up costs are factored into the cost of doing business globally and taxed appropriately, I'm afraid we will continue to see disasters of this magnitude – and worse.

And sadly, mining disasters weren't done for the year 2000. Maybe it was the number of outer planet squares: there were squares of Jupiter and Uranus, Jupiter and Neptune, and Saturn and Uranus that year. On October 11, 2000 somewhere over 300 million gallons of coal slurry sludge was released when an impoundment dam collapsed near Inez, Kentucky. What followed was a mess. The spill occurred late in the Clinton Administration, which meant that the investigation and clean-up fell during the Bush Administration. The investigation was assigned to the Department of Labor, headed by Elaine Chao, the wife of Republican Senator Mitch McConnell, himself the recipient of more campaign contributions from coal companies than any other senator. She appointed industry executives to be in charge of the investigation.

NATAL CHART
Sun enters Ari 3-20-2000
March 20, 2000
9:35:15 AM
Bucharest, Romania
44 N 26 26 E 06
Standard Time
Time Zone: 2 hours East
Tropical Regiomontanus

Chart 61. Sun enters Aries 2000, Bucharest, Romania

Day of ☽	Hour of ♂
Last Hr ♃	- 12 mins
Next Hr ☉	+48 mins

FIXED STARS

☿☌ Sadalmelik	0°49's
☉☌ Scheat	0°37's
☿☌ Fomalhaut	0°18's
♄☌ Menkar	0°06'a

Hs	Alm. (Dor)
1	☿
2	♃
3	☽
4	☉
5	☿
6	♂
7	♃
8	♄
9	♄
10	♄
11	♃
12	♀

ESSENTIAL DIGNITIES (Dorothean)

Pl	Ruler	Exalt	Tripl	Term	Face	Detri	Fall	Score
☉	♂	☉ +	☉ +	♃	♂	♀	♄	+7
☽	♀	♄ m	♄	♄	☽ +	♂	☉	+5
☿	♃	♀	♀	♀	♄	☿ -	☿ -	- 14 P
♀	♃ m	♀ +	♀ +	♃ m	♄	☿	☿	+12
♂	♂ +	☉	☉	♄	♀	♀	♄	+5
♃	♀ m	☽	♀	♀ m	☿	♂	--	+0 P
♄	♀	☽ m	♀	☿	☽	♂	--	- 1 P
☊	☉	--	☉	♄	♄	♄	--	--
⊗	♃	☋ +	☉	☿	☽	☿	--	--
As	☿	☊	♄	♃	♂	♃	--	--
Mc	♄	--	♄	♀	☿	☉	--	--
☋	♄	--	♄	♄	♀	☉	--	--

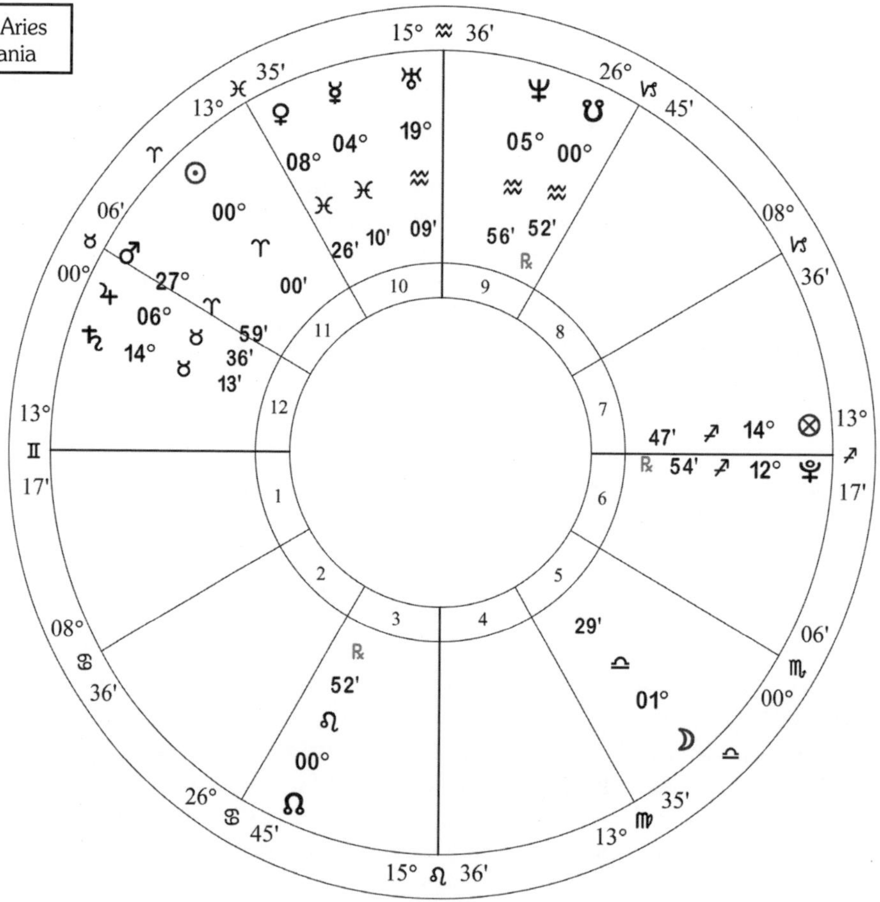

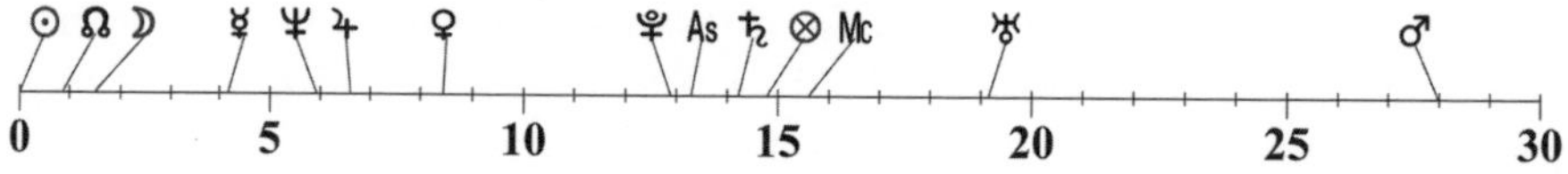

We have already examined that Aries Ingress for Romania. In Washington, Chart 62, all four ingress charts will be needed for the year. The Neptune-South Node conjunction falls in the 1st house, showing that lies and deception would be the theme for this election year.

The Libra Ingress shows the period when the disaster (and the election) actually occurred. Here, Mars ruled the 4th of mining, square to Saturn. The square is suggestive, but it is clear that this was not the lead story for this period – and it wasn't. The coverage tended to get lost in the election.

The Capricorn Ingress not only shows the result of the investigation, but the Inauguration of Bush's presidency. With the South Node right on the Ascendant, the people's interests will not be served. Saturn is in the house of mining, retrograde, and conjunct Algol. That Saturn rules the 2nd house – money. Guess who pays?

The Moon in Scorpio in the 10th (the President) is square Venus, Ruler of the 4th house. The Administration will not be good for the land. But as the Moon is also the people in a mundane chart, in this case, Bush was not acting against the people's wishes. The Ruler of the Ascendant was at Algol in the 4th. There was far more interest in development than land conservation.

The Bush Administration's environmental policy was to increase energy production. Rarely, this would be considered environmentally progressive, such as tax credits for wind power production in 2002. They allowed mountaintop removal mining, de-fanged the Clean Air Act, and diluted the enforcement of endangered species biology – and that was all in his first term. The rest of the world found that it had to act without the cooperation of the United States, symbolized by Kenyan environmentalist Wangari Maathai winning the Nobel Peace Prize in 2004, the first African woman to win the prize. In 2005, the European Union banned phthalates, highly carcinogenic compounds used in many plastics. The U.S.A. has not followed suit. In 2006, the Indian state of Kerala banned the production and sale of both Coca Cola and Pepsi products because of a report of high pesticide levels in each.

By 2007, a report by the UN Environmental Program estimated that 2% of the world's energy is being produced by renewable sources., while accounting for 18% of new investment. In the U.S.A., Bush and Senate Republicans blocked the recension of a tax break to oil companies that would have financed renewable energy. And in an ironic environmental end to the Bush Administration, a still larger coal sludge dam spill occurred in Kinsport, TN on 22 December, 2008, just after Pluto had moved back into Capricorn.

If it seems that I am Republican-bashing here: it may be true, but not because I believe the Republican Party is permanently anti-environment. Since Ronald Reagan, the Republican administrations have generally had abysmal records on environmentalism. Conservatism itself *should* be (or at least *could* be) conservative of resource. The current poor record of the Republican Party on environmental issues reflects the current dominance of major corporations driving that party that benefit from environmental indifference. One may only hope that this will change in the future.

In the next chapter, we slice the pie differently. Now, instead of looking at similar themes within elements, we are going to look at a series of sequential signs: Sagittarius, Capricorn, Aquarius and Pisces, so we can more clearly see transitions, and how each sign both solves the problems left by the old sign, while creating problems for the next one to solve in turn. Why are these problems? The answer is: if something really works, it simply gets incorporated

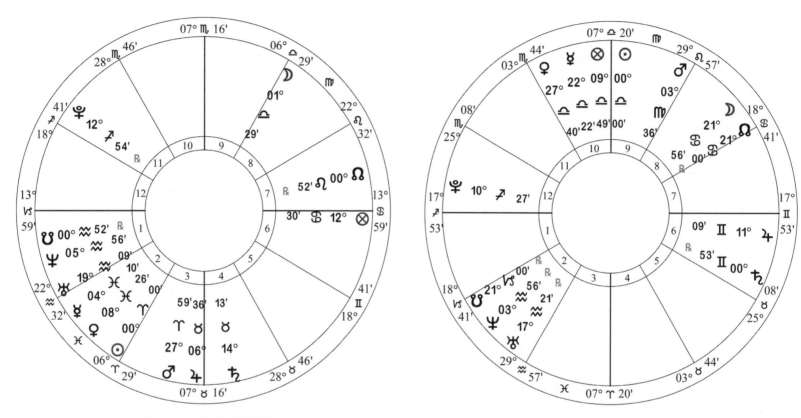

Sun enters Ari 3-20-2000
March 20, 2000
2:35:15 AM
Washington, D.C.
38N53'42" 77W02'12"
Standard Time
Time Zone: 5 hours West
Tropical Regiomontanus
NATAL CHART

Chart 62. Sun enters Aries, Libra, Capricorn 2000, Washington, DC

Sun enters Lib 9-22-2000
September 22, 2000
1:27:36 PM
Washington, D.C. 38N53'42" 77W02'12"
Daylight Saving Time
Time Zone: 5 hours West
Tropical Regiomontanus
NATAL CHART

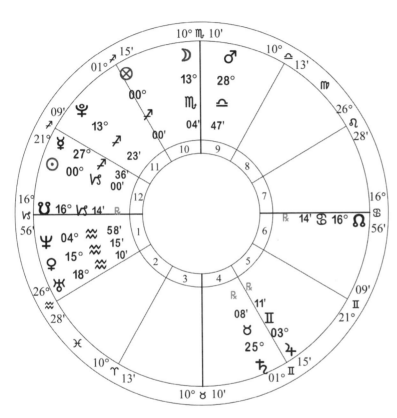

Sun enters Cap 12-21-2000
December 21, 2000
8:37:26 AM
Washington, D.C.
38N53'42" 77W02'12"
Standard Time
Time Zone: 5 hours West
Tropical Regiomontanus
NATAL CHART

into How-Things-Are. When they don't work, they tend to get deferred until they break down entirely. The human race is not historically good at preventative maintenance.

Endnotes: Chapter 7

186. See, for example, Hamaker-Zondag, Karen. *Foundations of Personality : Combining Elements, Crosses, and Houses with Jungian Psychological Concepts in Horoscope Interpretation.* York Beach, Me.: S. Weiser, 1994, pp 19-21.

187. United States. Dept. of Agriculture. Economic Research, Service. *A History of American Agriculture, 1607-2000.* Vol. ERS-POST-12. Washington, DC: U.S. Dept. of Agriculture, Economic Research Service., 2000.

188. For a full description of the circumstances surrounding the building of the canal, please see Bernstein, Peter L. *Wedding of the Waters: The Erie Canal and the Making of a Great Nation.* New York: W.W. Norton, 2005.

189. See, for example, Bernstein, pp 208-211.

190. Lilly, *Christian Astrology*, p 99.

191. Lilly, *Christian Astrology*, p 214.

192. Armstrong, Lebbeus. The Temperance Reformation: Its History. Gardners Books, 2007, pp 18-21.

193. Rosen, Friedrich. Rig-Vedæ Specimen. Edit F. Rosen. Sansk. & Lat. 1830.

194. For an excellent discussion of the rationale behind the potato famine, see Pollan, Michael. *The Botany of Desire: A Plant's Eye View of the World.* New York: Random House, 2001.

195. For a good discussion of the history surrounding this tragedy, see Donnelly, James S. *The Great Irish Potato Famine.* Thrupp, Stroud, Gloucestershire: Sutton, 2001.

196. There has been some controversy over whether the chart for the nuclear chain reaction should be scored as CST or CWT, as War Time was observed.

The University of Chicago clocks were all on standard time. However, all three of these times are verified by Troinski, E.H. *Das Horoskop Des Atom-Zeitalters*. Hannover: Baumgartner-Verlag, 1956, pp 40, 91-98; with reproductions of letters from government officials.

197. Alperovitz, Gar, and Sanho Tree. *The Decision to Use the Atomic Bomb and the Architecture of an American Myth*. New York: Knopf, 1995.

198. Bird, Kai, and Martin J. Sherwin. *American Prometheus : The Triumph and Tragedy of J. Robert Oppenheimer*. 1st ed. New York: A.A. Knopf, 2005, p579.

199. Leopold, Aldo, and Charles Walsh Schwartz. *A Sand County Almanac. With Other Essays on Conservation from Round River*. [Enl. ed. New York,: Oxford University Press, 1966, pp 129-132.

200. Kingsland, p 167.

201. For a modern discussion, see Diamond, Chapter 1.

202. Thomas, William Leroy. *Man's Role in Changing the Face of the Earth*. Chicago,: Published for the Wenner-Gren Foundation for Anthropological Research and the National Science Foundation by the University of Chicago Press, 1956.

203. Trewartha, Glenn Thomas. *An Introduction to Weather and Climate*. Mcgraw-Hill Series in Geography. 1st ed. New York, London,: McGraw-Hill Book Company, inc., 1937. Page 29 in the 1943 edition.

204. Bell M H, Davis, D L. "Reassessment of the Lethal London Fog of 1952: Novel Indicators of Acute and Chronic Consequences of Acute Exposure to Air Pollution." *Environ Health Perspect*. 109(Suppl 3).June (2001): 389–94.

205. Lilly, p 60; Ramesey, p 51; Partridge, p 11)

206. Kingsland, p 180.

207. Kingsland, pp 180-181.

208. Kingsland, pp 187-200.

209. Intergovernmental Panel on Climate Change. *Potential Impacts of Climate Change: Report*. [Geneva]: World Meteorological Organization/United Nations Environment Programme [Intergovernmental Panel on Climate Change], 1990.

210. For an account of the event, see *www.wsws.org/articles/2000/feb2000/cyan-f15.shtml*.

211. Lilly, p 158.

8

Pluto from Sagittarius to Pisces

WE HAVE NOW EXAMINED PLUTO IN ALL FOUR ELEMENTS, AND WE HAVE OBSERVED CERTAIN TRENDS. These include:

- The traditional rulerships of things work. So, if Pluto is in Aries, and Mars rules iron, then we may see technological improvements relating to iron or steel accelerate in these times. But *which* Mars-ruled themes dominate may vary from transit to transit.

- The earth and water signs have the closest approximation to what we talk about as the earth or globe, speaking from a planetary point of view. This makes sense, because agricultural fertility requires not only fertile soil but rainfall in the right quantity and temporal frequency.

- The earth and water periods are characterized more by engineering, whereas the air and fire periods conceptualize more. The activities of the Army Corps of Engineers during

Pluto in Cancer might at first be seen as looking more like earth activities – but the medium was water. The process of learning how to utilize ground-water irrigation in the late 1930s was every bit as much engineer-driven as the Race to the Moon in the 1960s.

- Literal qualities of the signs are likely to apply. For example, the development of rocketry (fire) with Pluto in Leo was necessary to have the engineering developments leading to the lunar expeditions (Pluto in Virgo).

- Major themes like economics, agriculture, or warfare are less likely to be domains of separate signs as much as that *each* sign shows something of how that theme will be experienced. For example, religion is not something expressed in any one sign, but each sign has a different means of demonstrating its religious convictions – or lack of them.

- Each sign brings gifts or opportunities to the human race – but also each sign leaves debris from its failed ideas and achievements.

- Accordingly, each sign is always "picking up" after the previous sign, as well as expressing its own priorities.

- Outer planet aspect patterns may not be as important in defining a period as many astrologers have assumed, both because the duration of influence is relatively short, and because there are almost always overlapping aspect patterns in effect. But there are definitely significant effects (such as the Saturn-Neptune signature for the fall of Communism[212]) which seem to be characteristic of them. We will return to the outer planet aspect cycles in the next chapter, proposing a slight twist on them which may serve to clarify their effects.

- Even when the Aries Ingress is not the operative Ingress chart for an event, it often shows intimations of the problem of later quarters.

Outer Planet Considerations and Constraints

Let's begin here by considering the issue of outer planet aspects more fully. In Chapter 4, I compared the outer planet aspect patterns between the 1960s and the 2010s, concluding that there were some considerable similarities, and yet obvious differences between a Mercury-ruled Pluto sign (Virgo) and a Saturn-ruled one (Capricorn). The obvious conclusion is that, while the patterns may be similar, the malefic nature of Saturn will not make this passage through Capricorn as easy (if easy it was). However, there is some mitigation of this conclusion for a piece of that time, because Saturn is the exaltation ruler of Libra (Saturn's placement until October 2012), and then Saturn is a Triplicity ruler of the fire signs for Saturn's transit of Sagittarius (December 2014 – December 2017, with a retrograde period in Scorpio), and then Saturn has sign rulership in Capricorn and Aquarius (December 2017 – March 2023). This means that for almost the entire period when Pluto is in Capricorn, its dispositor Saturn is actually dignified, making it less malefic. However that one stretch in Scorpio (October 2012 – September 2015, not including retrogrades), is likely to show us the true nature of Pluto in Capricorn without that help from Saturn, and then the transit of Pluto through Aquarius will lack a dignified Saturn except for the time of Saturn in Gemini (June 2030 – July 2032, except for retrograde periods). This alone argues that the period of Pluto in Capricorn will be easier on us mere mortals than the period of Pluto in Aquarius.

To help us understand this more clearly, I want to examine not only the last two passes of Pluto in Capricorn, but Pluto through that slice of the zodiac from Sagittarius to Pisces. However, as we examine earlier periods, we need to remember always that astrology acts within the matrix of the society of the time. What a pass of Pluto in a sign can bring is dependent upon the resources of that society, whether economic, technological, environmental, or spiritual.

But why this slice of the zodiac, apart from the obvious point that we are in it as I write this? We saw in Chapter 3, there is a 3:2 relationship between the orbital periods of Neptune and Pluto, and Uranus isn't far off a 2:1 relationship with the orbit of Neptune. These simple astronomical facts impose a higher order on the interpretation of how these three bodies will work in long-term time. Essentially, these relationships mandate that:

- Each pass of Neptune in a sign has almost the same Uranus sign relationship as the last pass of Neptune in the same sign.

- Every other pass of Pluto in a sign has a remarkably similar line-up of Pluto, Neptune and Uranus.

We seldom talk about astronomical constraints and how they affect astrological interpretation. Most of the ones we consider relate to the inferior planets, Mercury and Venus. We geocentrists cannot have Sun opposite Mercury, for example (although heliocentric Mercury opposite Earth is completely reasonable).

With the outer planets, these constraints by sign tell us that, a little less than every five hundred years, we go through roughly the same challenges, imposed yet one more time upon the matrix of our civilization such as it is. Five hundred years is a time range unfathomable to humans unless they study their history. It is not a unit of time we can easily digest, given our own life expectancies. But as astrologers, comprehend it we must in order to understand what our true challenges are as a collective within any time period.

Within psychological and spiritual astrology, there has been much discussion about whether it is even possible to interpret the outer planets from historical periods prior to their discovery. According to this theory, when a new body is discovered, an advance of consciousness occurs – or recently has occurred – bringing this planetary meaning up from the unconsciousness into a conscious place. Yet, virtually all astrologers who have treated these planets in a mundane capacity have looked at the outer

planets through hundreds, if not thousands, of years of historical time. This implies that the operation of these planets is no different for a society, discovered or not.

I would merely indicate that a false dichotomy has been implied by some concerning these two statements, which are both equally true. To say that the bodies "work" does not actually speak to whether they *can* be worked consciously. The rules of calculus work just fine whether I know them or not.

But back to our question: why the emphasis on where the Outers are now, apart from our own immediate concern for them? The answer actually lies in an interesting symmetry that is embedded in classical astrological theory. To understand this, please examine Table 8-1.

Sagittarius	Capricorn	Aquarius	Pisces
Jupiter	Saturn	Saturn	Jupiter
Day	Night	Day	Night

Table 8-1. Successive signs and their rulers, Sagittarius through Pisces

An examination of the traditional rulerships reveals a symmetry: beginning with (this is a circle after all, so one can begin wherever one likes) the two signs of Saturn, Capricorn and Aquarius. Expanding out one sign in either direction gives the two signs of Jupiter, Sagittarius and Pisces; then the two signs of Mars, Scorpio and Aries; then the two signs of Venus, Libra and Taurus; then the two signs of Mercury, Virgo and Gemini; until one gets to the two lights, which only rule one sign each, Leo and Cancer.

Therefore, there is a symmetry to rulerships. Jupiter and Saturn have very different properties. In certain respects, they are the antithesis of each other, just as Venus and Mars are the opposite of each other. But Venus and Mars grace the opposite houses: if Venus rules the Ascendant, then Mars *must* rule the Descendant, and vice versa. But Jupiter and Saturn do not face each other across a chart angle: they succeed each other. The transition from Capricorn to Aquarius is the *only time* that there is the same ruler of two successive signs. But the interrelationship between these two rulers is even deeper. In Sagittarius, Saturn is a Triplicity Ruler. So the transition from Sagittarius to Capricorn brings Saturn from a background player to a foreground player. And since Jupiter rules the first Face of Capricorn, the transition runs both ways for the first ten degrees of Capricorn, although the Face is a much weaker dignity. I had observed in *Essential Dignities* that one of the primary manifestations of the Face rulership was fear and anxiety: on a mundane level, this can mean scapegoating that which has gone before.

Jupiter has no strong dignity in Capricorn: in fact, it is in its Fall there. But in Aquarius, Jupiter regains strong dignity as the participating Triplicity ruler. In Pisces, Saturn has no strong ruler, but it owns the first Face of Pisces. So, analogous to the transition from Sagittarius to Capricorn, the transition from Aquarius to Pisces not only involves the loss of dignity for Saturn, but the tendency to scapegoat it.

This is a remarkable sequence of four signs with such intricate interrelationships. In many respects, this sequence of Pluto through these signs represents a very meaningful arc, whether it is considered the "beginning" of this outer planet cycle or not. Charles Harvey, in his posthumously published work, *Anima Mundi*, discussed the significance of the four phases of cycles, based on the archetypal agricultural cycles that have been used to discuss the astrology of the seasons, not to mention the lunation cycle. He says:

The archetypal cycle has a moment of seeding – a beginning at midnight, midwinter, and the dark of the Moon – when everything seems to be reduced to its bare bones, its skeleton. This is Capricorn... Everything is absolutely minimal. All the non-essentials have been stripped away. The process of decay, beginning with the autumn equinox in Libra, leads to everything gradually being broken down, and we get to the bare bones.[213]

Whatever is said here for Capricorn can be equally said of Aquarius. Traditional farming and herding societies in the higher latitudes knew that Winter was the time of rationing, because no more food would be produced until Spring. Even the animals had to live on hay harvested the prior year. But it is also in this time of year that germination occurs underground. Charles spoke for the idea of cycles beginning at this time, because he equated Spring with birth – the point being, that without gestation, there is no birth.

These long-term cycles may not map exactly to the shorter agricultural cycles. But there is a value to considering the bare bones as an important phase of the cycle. And it is interesting that it is Jupiter's raiment that is last removed, and the first added back, once we humans pass through the discovery of essence in Saturn's phase.

Pass One: The Early Modern Period 1502-1577

As our period opens, Leonardo da Vinci has just started the *Mona Lisa*, although he will not finish it for a few years. The Americas have already been discovered. In the 15th century, the Portuguese and Spanish Empires are the great world powers. The Treaty of Tordesillas in 1494 had split the world between them. Every Christian in Europe is a Catholic – there have been occasional rebellions, but none of them have been successful, and most have been ruthlessly suppressed. Michaelangelo's *David* had just been publicly installed in Florence.

From the standpoint of exploration, the period of Pluto in Sagittarius from 1502-1516 marked the time of the devastation of populations in the Americas: through environmental destruction, slavery, and deliberate policies of genocide.[214] It was also the time of the introduction of New World plants and animals, such as turkeys, tomatoes, potatoes, sugar, and corn into Europe. Columbus's last voyage to the Americas was in 1502. And lest one think that all the bad stuff was happening in the New World, a riot in Lisbon in 1506 resulted in the massacre of at least 2,000 *Conversos* – converted Jews.

If I hadn't said that Pluto in Sagittarius began in 1502, chances are, many astrologers would have assumed that Pluto was in Sagittarius for the discovery of America for several reasons: the long voyage, the sense of adventure through travel, the idea of discovery – these all seem more fiery than watery. But then – it was about crossing the *ocean*, right? Actually, it was Neptune that was in Sagittarius – late Sagittarius, to be sure. Neptune moved into Capricorn in December 1492.

Pluto in Sagittarius brings religious intolerance and genocide. Ferdinand and Isabella came to power in an era of general religious toleration in the Iberian Peninsula. Political factions rarely divided out easily along religious lines – until after they united Castile and Aragon to create Spain. At their crowning, their regalia recognized the diversity of their kingdoms, a diversity that cruelly evaporated shortly thereafter.[215] Genocide for religious reasons sounds an awful lot like the dark side of Pluto in Sagittarius.

The idea that Pluto in Sagittarius marked such a tremendous expansion in knowledge about the world is not so surprising.

And here, Neptune's transit of Sagittarius for the actual discovery seems to be the harbinger of the future expansion in knowledge when Pluto arrives in that sign. What may not at first seem so obvious is that this massive increase in awareness of the rest of the globe had *absolutely no discernible impact* on anyone's religious faith, philosophy, or political leanings in Europe. Instead, the conquistadors walked side-by-side with the friars, who saw the discovery of new peoples only as an opportunity to expand the Faith. And all the while, back in Europe, serious Christians were questioning the wealth, avarice, and sexual improprieties of the Catholic clergy – matters that would shortly come to a boiling point as Pluto changed signs.

Considering the title of this book, it might seem strange that I have gone back to an era before we can easily trace such an ecological ethic – at least in the West. This fact is something that has given me pause in presenting this chapter for this time period at all. But I decided that it was necessary to illustrate certain facets of the Neptune-Pluto pairings. Also, we do need to understand the genesis of the difficulty in accepting not merely the environmental perspective as being necessary, but as being urgent.

Our period also opens with the starting point of Keith Thomas's book: *Man and the Natural World : Changing Attitudes in England 1500-1800*.[216] In this work, Thomas traces the beginning of the ideas which would ultimately allow what we might call an ecological ethic. When this pass opens with Pluto in Sagittarius in 1503, the prevailing attitude toward flora and fauna alike was completely encased in the Christian viewpoint that all animals and all plants were on Earth for no reason other than to serve Man's needs. This idea had resulted from a fusion of Genesis 1:27 with Aristotle's tripartite soul: plant, animal, and human.[217] As such, Man was so much higher than any other form of life that there was absolutely no point thinking about the welfare of an animal. The conquest of an animal was merely a metaphor for the superiority of the man who accomplished it.[218] This in turn set up the attitude that the man who had a horse was superior to the man who didn't – part of social standing in the Old World that became especially significant in the New World, that lacked not only horses, but large cattle generally (at least in Central and South America: North America had the bison). The many uses of "beast" as an expression for uncivilized man illustrates this position. With this attitude, it is no surprise that the main reaction to the discovery of the New World, with *both* its novel human and animal resources, was primarily one which invited conquest and exploitation. It also explains any difficulty we may encounter in trying to find a period parallel for our modern ecological interests: such a concern for the Earth and its creatures is simply not a mainstream component of the Aristotelian-Christian synthesis.

Nobody believed that animals have souls, rational behavior, or even the ability to feel pain. England had been ramping up its meat production to become the highest per capita meat consumer in the world, while maintaining that a heavy meat diet is a healthy diet.[219] Anything that smacked of animal nature was to be shunned. Yet, at the same time, the structure of the long house, in use in different parts especially of Northern Europe, meant that humans and animals literally lived under one roof. The low status of wild animals was enshrined in Medieval law as *ferae naturae* – wild animals could not even be considered property at all in England. The people considered this reason enough that they had the right to kill and eat wild animals whenever they wanted – despite attempts to reserve certain animals for the pleasure and use of the aristocracy.[220]

A crucial piece of this Medieval attitude toward living things is that all animals and plants were even classified according to their use for man: edible, functional, or medical.[221] This issue of functionality is something that I touched upon from an astrological standpoint in *Essential Dignities*, in demonstrating that plant rulerships were overwhelmingly assigned according to medical use, rather than any other criterion.[222] It was only toward the end of this pass, with Pluto in Pisces, that the Flemish botanist Mathias l'Obel (Matthaeus Lobelius in Latin), published *Stirpium adversaria nova* in 1570, for the first time classifying plants not by use, but by the structure of the leaves. This, followed rapidly by other works, introduced the concept that plants or animals might have relationships quite apart from its relationship with man, a truly revolutionary concept.[223] The idea would be so revolutionary that it continued to be ignored. This simple separation of plant and animal properties from human wants and needs would completely change human thinking about the living world, in the form of the theory of evolution in the mid 19th century.

But back to this pass. To illustrate the difference in world view, one could not even have a pet in the sense that so many people today do, where one might have a beloved dog, cat, ferret, or some type more exotic. In the 15th century, one could have a dog – but the dog would perform work, whether hunting, guarding, or spit-turning. The 16th century seems to be the approximate dividing line, before which, dogs were seen primarily to possess negative qualities like greed and filthiness, and afterward, positive qualities like loyalty. This is when pets are seen as existing for their own sake.[224] It is only after pets become common that there seems to be any awareness of the possible intelligence or good character of animals.[225]

At this beginning of the early modern era, it is estimated that 80% of England has already been deforested. This led to an increase in the use of coal as a heating fuel, but it primarily reflects the conversion of the land to agriculture and pasture. Increased iron production will at first drive even more forests out of existence, but iron production needs charcoal, and this eventually led to deliberate cultivation of trees for this very purpose. Woods were fine – on land not easily farmed, and with the trees planted like a crop and harvested regularly. What we now call virgin forest was wild, probably evil, and dangerous, as the refuge of outlaws and other primitives.[226] This attitude explains much of the dismay of European colonists to the New World upon seeing the expanse of forests. Clearing land for farming, especially grubbing stumps, was hard work, but necessary both for survival and for civilization.

Table 8-2 shows us the sign distribution of the planets from Saturn out for the period of Pluto in each of the four signs of interest. The reason that I have not included Jupiter in this table is simple: for every sign of Pluto except Scorpio, Jupiter travels through all twelve signs.

The reason we consider this now is that Saturn is the one planet on this list that has essential dignity – and so its dignity tells us something about how well Saturn is performing – and specifically, whether it is acting malefic (normal), *very* malefic (in Detriment and Fall), or close to neutral verging on benefic (in dignity). I summarize these relationships in Table 8-3.

Aries	Participating Triplicity; Fall
Taurus	
Gemini	Daytime Triplicity
Cancer	Detriment
Leo	Participating Triplicity; Detriment
Virgo	
Libra	Daytime Triplicity; Exaltation
Scorpio	
Sagittarius	Participating Triplicity
Capricorn	Rulership
Aquarius	Daytime Triplicity; Rulership
Pisces	

Table 8-3. Saturn's major dignity by sign, Dorothean triplicities.

What this table tells us is that there is considerable disparity in the distribution of rulership when one considers a series of sequential signs. And if, with the typical pass of Pluto in a sign, Saturn goes through half or somewhat more than half the signs, the

Pluto	Sagittarius	Capricorn	Aquarius	Pisces
Neptune	Capricorn – Aquarius	Aquarius – Pisces	Pisces – Taurus	Taurus – Cancer
Uranus	Pisces – Taurus	Taurus – Cancer	Cancer – Libra	Libra – Aquarius
Saturn	Gemini – Sagittarius	Sagittarius – Cancer	Cancer – Aquarius	Pisces – Capricorn

Table 8-2. Outer Planet signs: First pass, 1502-1577.

disparity can be significant. The best five sequential signs of Saturn to have in a particular Pluto sign passage is Libra through Aquarius: there, Saturn has major dignity in all signs except Scorpio. This is precisely the sequence we have now, in the current pass of Pluto in Capricorn. In this first pass we are examining, this "good" run of Saturn was split between Pluto in Sagittarius and Capricorn. What does this mean in operation? When Saturn has dignity, one expects fewer obstacles. One doesn't have as many roadblocks. That is not to say there are *no* roadblocks! Other factors in the chart can conspire to produce delays and denials.

We can create a similar table for Jupiter, shown as Table 8-4.

Aries	Nighttime Triplicity
Taurus	
Gemini	Participating Triplicity; Detriment
Cancer	Exaltation
Leo	Nighttime Triplicity
Virgo	Detriment
Libra	Participating Triplicity
Scorpio	
Sagittarius	Rulership; Nighttime Triplicity
Capricorn	Fall
Aquarius	Participating Triplicity
Pisces	

Table 8-4. Jupiter's major dignity by sign, Dorothean triplicities.

But what about aspects? Consider 1504. Just following the Jupiter-Saturn conjunction in Cancer, we see that this is a triple conjunction with Mars, again weaving in and out of the same decanates. What happened? Drought in Spain. Notice here the Mars-Saturn, which is considered the start of the Mars-Saturn sequence. In Chapter 1, we referred to this beginning conjunction as being notable, for having both planets in debility. This cannot bode well for the period.

Here is Chart 63, the Aries Ingress for 1504 for Madrid, and immediately, we see the problem. Having the malefic Saturn, extra strongly malefic, sitting exactly on the Portals of Death, the 7th house cusp, is quite a harbinger of excess death. You may observe that the Jupiter-Saturn conjunction for 1504, which was a one-pass conjunction at 16 Cancer, was not technically a triple conjunction with Mars, because Mars did not make its conjunctions in the same Face. However, I seriously doubt that a contemporary astrologer would not have noted it. And this actually clarifies a conundrum about dignity and debility, at least in this year.

Remember that the classical idea with an aspect or conjunction was to examine which planet had the greater degree of dignity, and that planet then is said to rule the aspect. Here: is Jupiter exalted (+4) "stronger" than Saturn in Detriment (-5)? The answer is in part what you think of the concept of negative numbers. A modern mathematician would answer that +4 is greater on a scale that would run +4, +3, +2, +1, 0, -1, -2, -3, -4, -5. But that's not the system in which these astrological ideas developed. What is pretty clear is that the plus and minus were simply conventions to denote good and bad, not strong or weak. Both +5 and -5 have 5 as their absolute value, and this is what the system of dignity points originally meant. When you examine Lilly's Table of Fortitudes and Debilities of the planets, he lists the fortitudes on one side, and

NATAL CHART
Sun enters Ari 3-21-1504
March 21, 1504
2:19:05 AM
Madrid, Spain
40 N 24 3 W 41
Local Mean Time
Time Zone: 0 hours West
Tropical Regiomontanus

Chart 63. Sun enters Aries 1504, Madrid, Spain

Day of ☉	Hour of ♂
Last Hr ♃	- 12 mins
Next Hr ☉	+48 mins

FIXED STARS	
As☌Rukbat	0°56's
♆☌Altair	0°48's
⊗☌Markab	0°44's
Mc☌Acrux	0°07's
Mc☌Alphecca	0°10'a

Hs	Alm. (Dor)
1	♂♄
2	♄
3	♂
4	☽♀
5	☽
6	☿
7	♃
8	☉
9	♄
10	♂
11	♂
12	♃

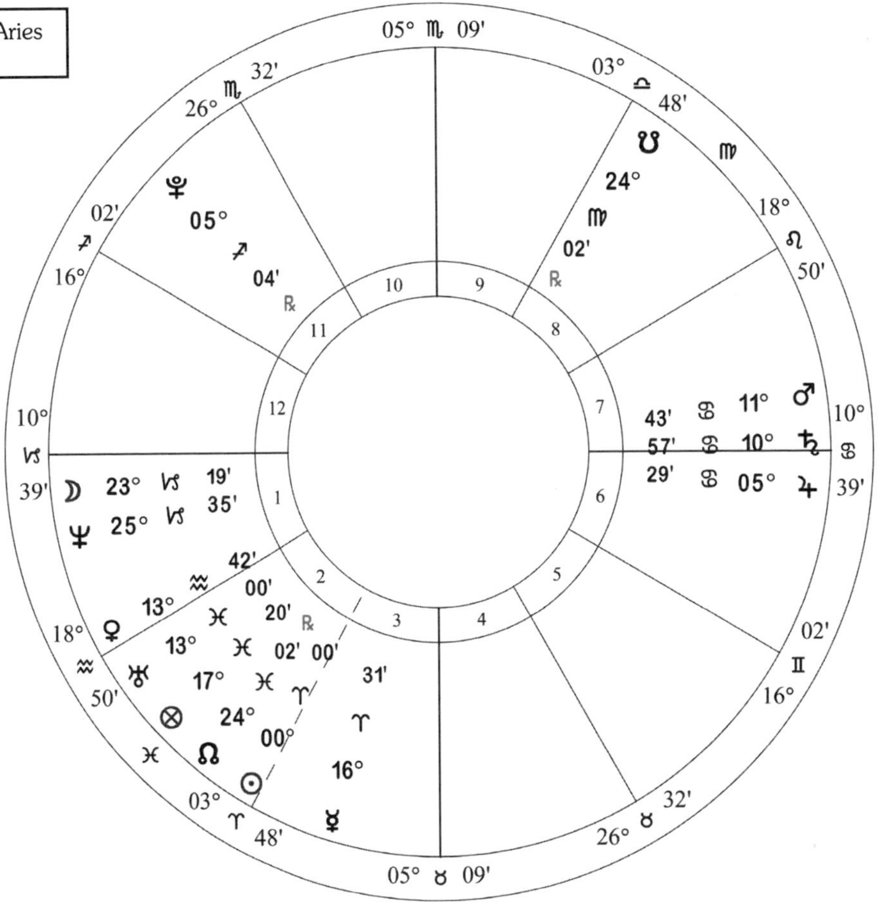

ESSENTIAL DIGNITIES (Dorothean)

Pl	Ruler	Exalt	Tripl	Term	Face	Detri	Fall	Score
☉	♂	☉ +	♃	♃	♂	♀	♄	+4
☽	♄ m	♂	☽ +	♂	☉	☽ -	♃	+3
☿	♂	☉	♃	☿ +	☉	♀	♄	+2
♀	♄	--	☿	♀ +	☿	☉	--	+2
♂	☽	♃	♂ +	♃ m	☿	♄	♂ -	- 1
♃	☽	♃ +	♂	♂ m	♀	♄	♂	+4
♄	☽ m	♃	♂	♃	☿	♄ -	♂	- 5 P
☊	♃	♀	♂	♂	♂	☿	☿	--
⊗	♃	♀	♂	☿	♃	☿	☿	--
As	♄	♂	☽	☿	♂	☽	♃	--
Mc	♂	--	♂	♂	♂	♀	☽	--
☋	☿	☿	☽	♂	☿	♃	♀	--

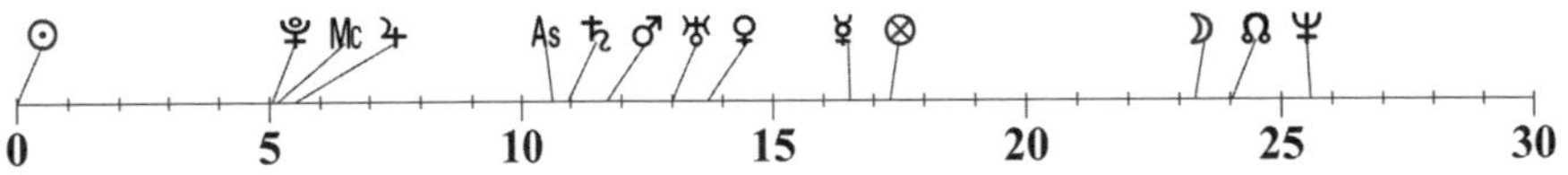

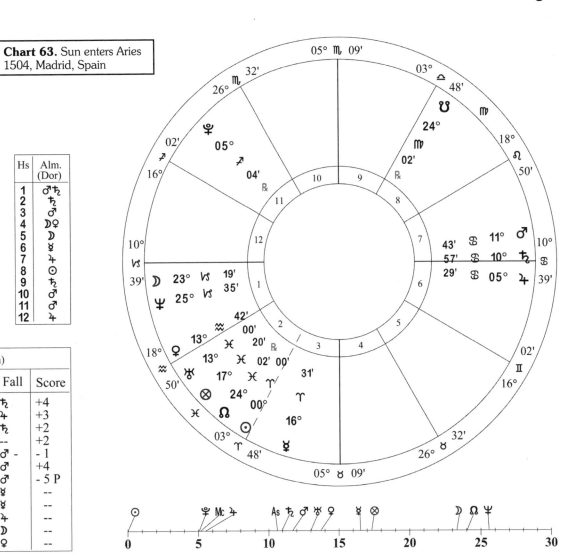

the debilities on the other.[227] So in this system, Detriment (-5) is stronger than exaltation (+4).

This makes Saturn the ruler of this Jupiter-Saturn conjunction, not Jupiter. And Mars weaving in and out seals the deal – this is a malefic triple conjunction, and one which is capable of producing death for the country of Spain.

Looking ahead through the aspects for this period, one is struck by 1507, with the Saturn-Pluto square, occurring Virgo to Sagittarius. It was a big year for the wrong reason: the first smallpox epidemic of the New World, decimating the Taino Native American population of Hispaniola (modern-day Haiti and the Dominican Republic) – the first disease calamity to affect the first tribe who will be completely annihilated by the Spaniards.

The Aries Ingress for 1507 for Santo Domingo, Dominican Republic, Chart 64, shows a nasty configuration which may account for this. The Ascendant ruler is in the 8th, conjunct the malefic Mars. Uranus is there, showing the surprise effect of death. The ruler of the 6th is in the 1st, both in Detriment and retrograde. Algol is on the MC. We can see the Neptune in the 6th as showing the complete lack of immunity by the Native Americans, although this is a modern interpretation.

1509 is the next year to stand out, with Sun conjunct Uranus, Chart 65. This lasted for roughly two years, roughly the same amount of time as the plague that ravaged London. The Aries Ingress for 1509 in London has a Jupiter-North Node-Pluto conjunction in the 8th house, with the void Moon in Scorpio in the 7th. Jupiter, being ruler of the 8th and in the 8th dignified is strong – and relating to exactly the wrong thing, namely death. Mercury, Ruler of the 6th, opposite Saturn in the 6t from the 12th and debilitated is yet another indicator of the disease picture. Pluto was stationary.

In the midst of the usual wars, deaths of kings, invasions, and either good or bad harvests, can we see any patterns emerging from this period of Pluto in Sagittarius? Certainly, people's experience of the world (from a Eurocentric perspective) was expanding. The great ocean voyages that produced the discovery of the New World occurred in Scorpio, but it was with Pluto in Sagittarius that the New World began to be exploited, and also began to be recognized for what it was, and not the westward passage to India and China.

Exploitation took the form of slavery, whether it was called that or not. The way that the Spaniards treated the Native Americans (and I am simply picking out the Spaniards because of the time period, not because the other European nations didn't do the same later) was radically different from how they might have treated English or Dutch prisoners of war. The massively superior technology that the Europeans possessed became a basis for bullying and the assertion of absolute superiority.[228]

It's very easy to be morally righteous about slavery in this period, seeing moral arrogance and hypocrisy everywhere. But the fact is: the great civilizations of the New World relied on slave labor just as much as the Old World. A large percentage of so-called civilizations have relied on slave labor, whether full-time or in forms such as the corvée, a time of service owed to the king by every (male) citizen. A major difference between the slave labor that was to develop in this period and carry over into the 19th century was that "traditional" slaves, both in the Americas and much of the Mediterranean world were prisoners of war – they were your vanquished enemies, not put into camps, but into forced labor. This was probably way better than prison, and lest we feel so superior, consider! We have used fossil fuel, a disappearing resource, to accomplish much of what older civilizations did more sustainably with slave labor. It is rather presumptuous of us to complain about others employing slaves to

NATAL CHART
Sun enters Ari 3-21-1507
March 21, 1507
3:11:05 PM
Santo Domingo, Domin.Rep.
18 N 28 69 W 54
Local Mean Time
Time Zone: 0 hours West
Tropical Regiomontanus

Chart 64. Sun enters Aries 1507, Santo Domingo

Day of ♃	Hour of ☉
Last Hr ♂	- 3 mins
Next Hr ♀	+57 mins

FIXED STARS	
Mc☌Capulus	0°57's
☽☌ Achernar	0°31's
☽☌ Ankaa	0°16's
♄☌Regulus	0°30'a
Mc☌Algol	1°00'a

Hs	Alm. (Dor)
1	☉
2	☿
3	♄
4	♂
5	♃
6	♂
7	♄
8	♀
9	☉
10	♀
11	☿
12	☽

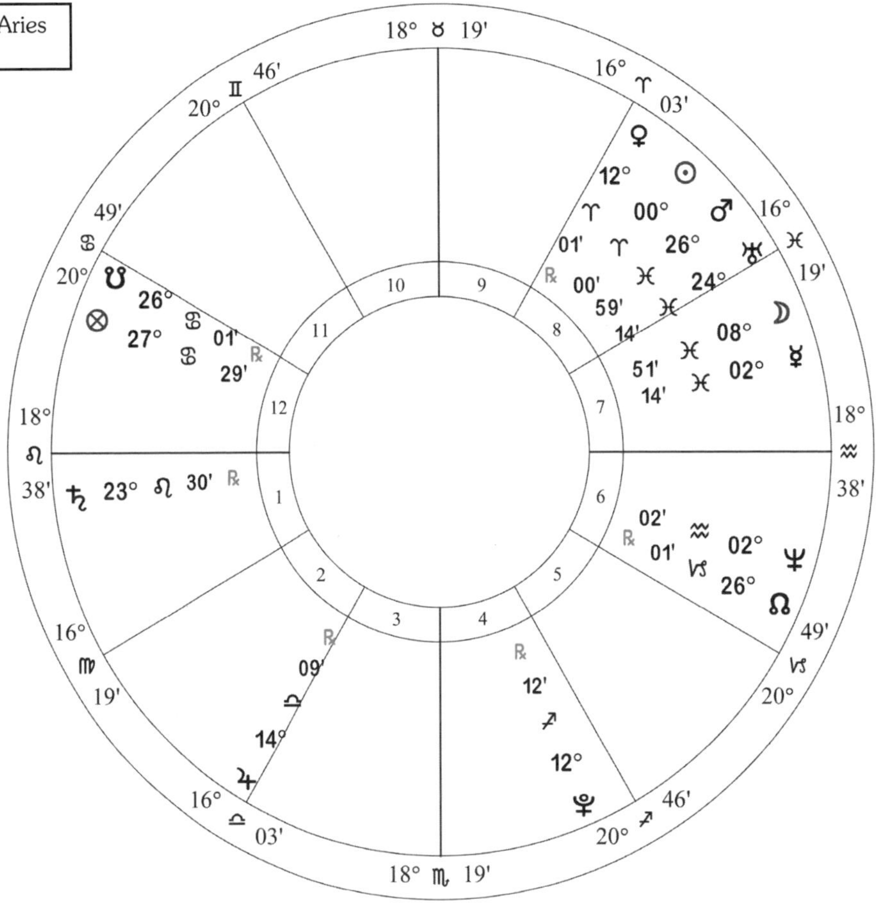

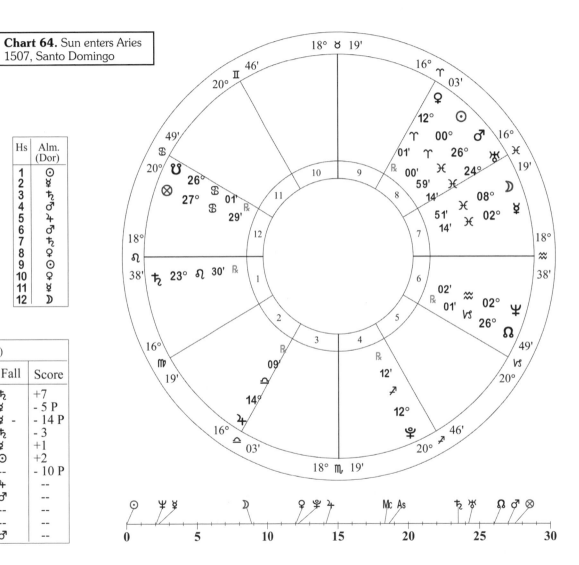

ESSENTIAL DIGNITIES (Dorothean)

Pl	Ruler	Exalt	Tripl	Term	Face	Detri	Fall	Score
☉	♂	☉ +	☉ +	♃	♂	♀	♄	+7
☽	♃	♀	♀	♃	♄	☿	☿	- 5 P
☿	♃	♀	♀	♀	♄	☿ -	☿ -	- 14 P
♀	♂	☉	☉	♀ +	☉	♀ -	♄	- 3
♂	♃	♀	♀	♄	♂ +	☿	☿	+1
♃	♀	♄	♄	♃ +	♄	♂	☉	+2
♄	☉	--	☉	♃	♂	♄ -	--	- 10 P
☊	♄	♂	♀	♄	☉	☽	♃	--
⊗	☽	♃	♀	♄	☽	♄	♂	--
As	☉	--	☉	♀	♃	♄	--	--
Mc	♀	☽	♀	♃	☽	♂	--	--
☋	☽	♃	♀	♀	☽	♄	♂	--

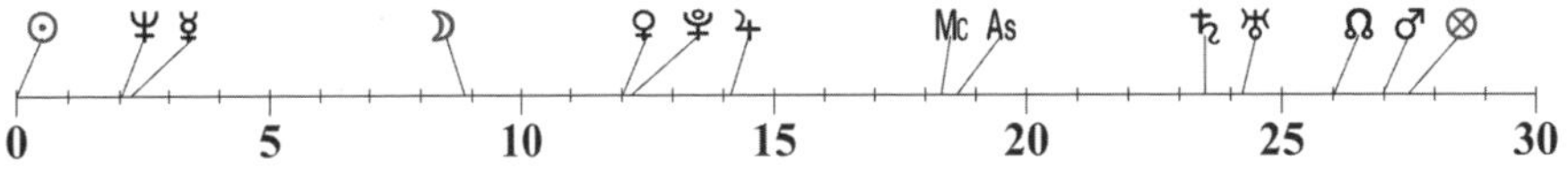

NATAL CHART
Sun enters Ari 3-21-1509
March 21, 1509
7:20:09 AM
London, England
51 N 30 0 W 10
Local Mean Time
Time Zone: 0 hours West
Tropical Regiomontanus

Chart 65. Sun enters Aries 1509, London

Day of ☉	Hour of ♀
Last Hr ☉	- 12 mins
Next Hr ☿	+48 mins

FIXED STARS	
☊☌Aculeus	0°38's
♃☌Aculeus	0°32's
⊗☌Vega	0°15'a

Hs	Alm. (Dor)
1	♀
2	☿
3	☽
4	☽
5	☉
6	☿
7	♂
8	♃
9	♀♄
10	♂♄
11	♄
12	♀

ESSENTIAL DIGNITIES (Dorothean)

Pl	Ruler	Exalt	Tripl	Term	Face	Detri	Fall	Score
☉	♂	☉ +	☉ +	♃	♂ m	♀	♄	+7
☽	♂	--	♀	♄	♀ m	♀	☽ -	- 9 P
☿	♃	♀	♀	☿ +	♂	☿ -	☿ -	- 7
♀	♄	--	♄ m	♃	☽ m	☉	--	- 5 P
♂	♂ +	☉	☉	♀	☉ m	♀	♄	+5
♃	♃ +	☋	☉	☿	☽	☿	--	+5
♄	☿	☿	♀ m	♄ +	☿	♃	♀	+2
☊	♃	☋	☉	☿	☽	☿	--	--
⊗	♄	♂	♀	☿	♃	☽	♃	--
As	♀	☽	♀	☿	☽	♂	--	--
Mc	♄	♂	♀	♃	♂	☽	♃	--
☋	☿	☊	♄	♀	♂	♃	--	--

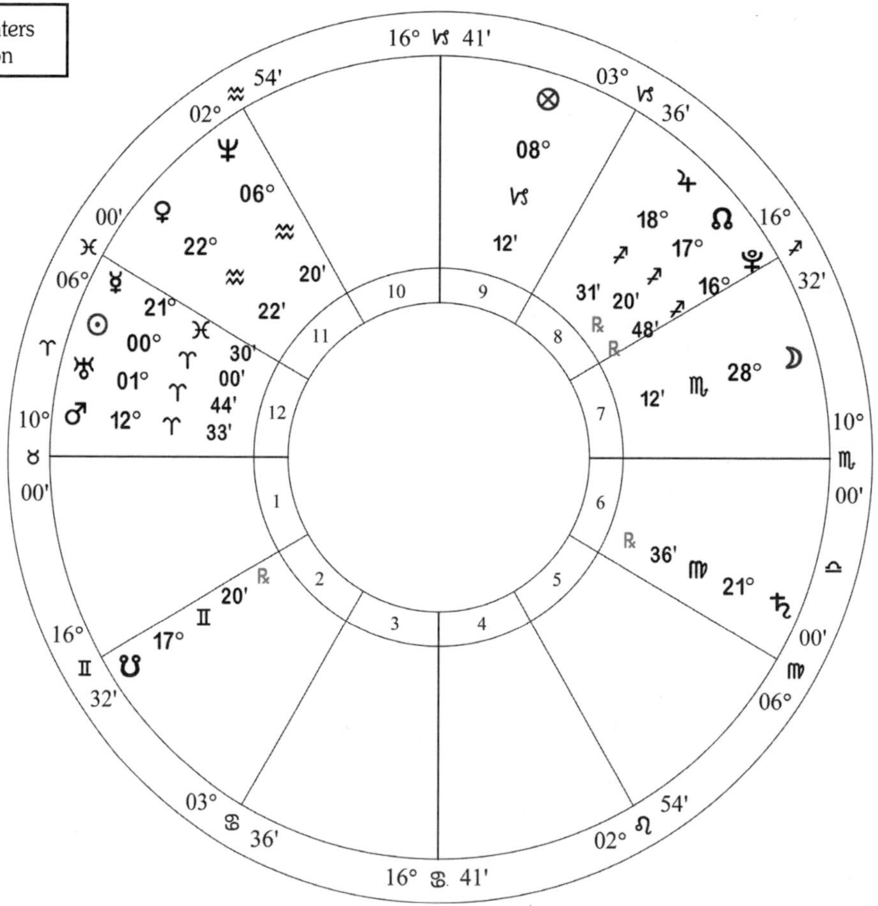

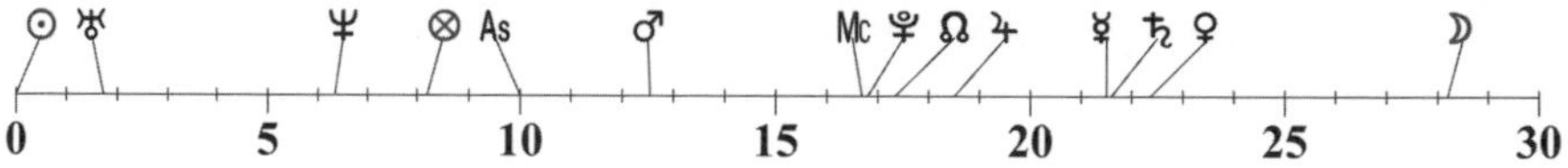

clean their clothes, when we are using up oil and coal to do the same.[229] I am not nostalgic about slavery! I'm merely pointing out that our own moral blindness should have limits.

I maintain the image in my mind of Stan Barker's descriptions of the bloodthirstiness of Neptune in Aries – and I am tempted to conclude that Pluto in Sagittarius, as a fire sign, may be a time for treating others not as individuals, but as members of a larger group, who are treated well or poorly according to one's own prejudices. One is reminded of the treatment of Muslims in the U.S.A. after 9-11: the way they were stripped of all identity *except* for being Muslims. One is tempted to see the treatment of Jews, Gypsies, and homosexuals under the Nazis (again, most of the atrocities performed under Pluto in Leo) as another manifestation of this prejudice. Ethnic cleansing is a horrible price to pay for someone else's righteousness.

Another factor I might extract out is not listening. One could easily derive this idea from the positive qualities of the Fire and Air signs – that, being outwardly directed, they will tend to broadcast more and listen less. Introspection is not part of the package. It is the job of Fire to seek, not to listen quietly. I mentioned earlier the curious observation that all this exposure to different civilizations seemed to have absolutely no impact on anyone's beliefs. Ideas and attitudes were unquestioned.

Should we be surprised? For nine centuries, Christian Europe had traded and fought with civilizations more technologically advanced, namely the Islamic Empires and India. At various points over seven hundred years, the Europeans barely stopped an Islamic invasion of Europe, both from Spain, and from the Ottoman Empire to the East. Yet, none of this made them question their Christian faith. How could God fail to protect them? So now, when they were the superior force, wasn't this vindication of these beliefs?

While in this Early Modern period, all the change that resulted from territories explored, the experience of the younger sons who were sent off to carve up the New World, new species of plants introduced to European agriculture, didn't seem to affect anybody's beliefs much. The discovery of new continents was an accounting matter, not a challenge to belief.

Pluto in Capricorn

The first smallpox pandemic in Cuba began in 1516, just as Pluto was moving into Capricorn, and it jumped from there to the rest of emerging Hispanola. These major epidemics had run their courses by the end of Pluto in Capricorn.

I would add that cluelessness is a general characteristic of a period with a change in outer planet sign: the people who have benefited from the Old Regime often are slow to notice that the rules have changed.

Consider the metaphor. During Pluto in Sagittarius, Catholicism had the chance to grow, to encompass the religious beliefs and practices of the New World. It didn't. The discovery of all these "new" people also didn't trigger a serious discussion of how a just and good God could have allowed all these generations of people to forgo the possibility of Paradise, because they were born outside the Christian zone, which alone had the keys to Heaven.

The movement of Pluto into Capricorn meant that the party was over for the ability of religious movements to do whatever was expedient. Saturn's continued presence there, however, made it next to impossible for the Old Guard not to try to go to the well one more time. In 1517, the Pope announced that indulgences would be sold, with the profits to be used to rebuild St. Peter's Basilica. This was done with no awareness by the Pope that the idea of so brazenly selling the promise of Heaven could be an offensive concept. In the Age of Capricorn, this would seem like Heaven was a profit center, not the reward for a holy life.

This idea of "going to the well one too many times" is probably another good description of the changeover of sign of an outer planet, but especially Neptune or Pluto. The fact is, people learn what works. Once they establish such a pattern, it's very difficult to convince anyone that the means should change. They've worked before, why shouldn't they work now? Especially when one has had more than a decade to observe the effect, as is true with Neptune and Pluto sign changes.

One can make a good case for the birth of Protestantism being a Pluto in Capricorn affair. Pluto flirted with Capricorn in 1516, then stayed there in 1517. Luther nailed the 95 Theses to the Church door October 31st, 1517, the beginning of the (successful) birth of Protestantism. But why did this critique of the Catholic Church succeed when previous ones failed – and what has this got to do with Pluto in Capricorn? One could argue that materialism was a huge factor in both Luther's objections and why they caught on. But one could equally argue that Luther was reacting to excesses of the Pluto in Sagittarius period. The corruption that Luther attacked had been present in the Church for a long time. What that Church couldn't anticipate is how the winds of change were blowing in a new direction, once Pluto changed signs.

Luther – at least at first – was acting as a reformer, not attempting to create a new institution. Pope Leo X didn't excommunicate Luther until 1520, and on 10 December 1520, Luther publicly burned the letter of excommunication. But once his positions were demarcated by the Church as outside its boundaries, some of the German princes saw an advantage – a material advantage – to being outside of Catholicism, beginning with the freedom from tithe that went from every Catholic church to Rome.

We actually have a time for when he burned the Bull of Excommunication, because Luther put it into a letter, shown as Chart 66.[230]

Before we interpret this chart, it's best to think about what the chart actually is. When Luther posted his Theses in 1517 he was operating within the rules of the Church – by posting his message the way he did, he was opening his premises to discussion and debate. And debate there was! Even in 1520, when Leo issued the Bull of Excommunication, there was still a sixty day clause for Luther to reply after he received it. This burning of the Bull on 10 December (20 December NS calendar) was Luther's response. It was not until then that he declared himself outside the power of the Church. Images of him for this period between 1517-1520 show him tonsured, in clerical garb. So while the 1516 event was necessary to the beginning of this process, the burning of the Bull should actually be taken as the birth of Protestantism, or at least Lutheranism.

Pluto partile conjunct the Ascendant is a good start. This event took place right after a New Moon, which is also descriptive. We have just seen that Pluto in Sagittarius didn't do much for questioning religious orthodoxy. And perhaps that is the point. Certainly, Luther was neither the first nor the last German prelate who was offended by the opulence of Rome. Luther was not the only theologian to speak out against the practice of selling indulgences – what were essentially "Get out of Jail Free" cards for Purgatory.

The 3rd – 9th axis is where we would look for the religion itself, and with the North Node in the 3rd, and South Node in the 9th, the heresy (from Catholicism's standpoint) is shown as growing, while

NATAL CHART
Luther burns Bull
December 20, 1520
9:00 AM
Wittenberg, Germany
51 N 52 12 E 39
Local Mean Time
Time Zone: 0 hours West
Tropical Regiomontanus

Chart 66. Luther burns Bull

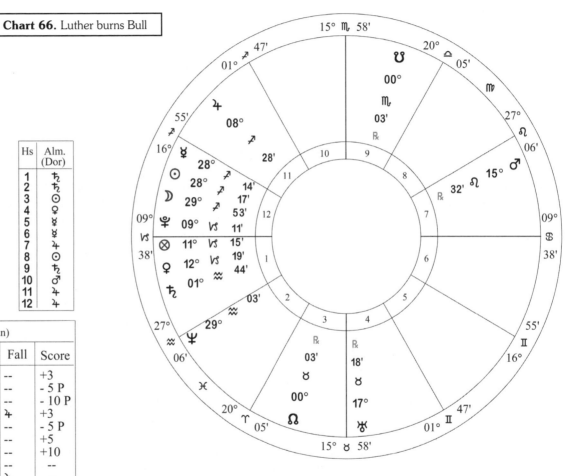

Day of ☽ Hour of ♄
Last Hr ☽ - 9 mins
Next Hr ♃ +28 mins

Hs	Alm. (Dor)
1	♄
2	♄
3	☉
4	☉
5	♀
6	☿
7	♃
8	☉ ♄
9	♄ ♃
10	♄ ♃
11	♃
12	♃

FIXED STARS	
☊♂Hamal	0°55's
♀♂Vega	0°35's
♆♂Deneb Adige	0°18's
♅♂Capulus	0°14's
As♂Rukbat	0°19'a
♀♂Rukbat	0°46'a
♃♂Rasalgethi	1°00'a

ESSENTIAL DIGNITIES (Dorothean)							
Pl	Ruler	Exalt	Tripl	Term	Face	Detri	Fall	Score
☉	♃	☋	☉ +	♂	♄	☿	--	+3
☽	♃	☋	☉	♂	♄	☿	--	- 5 P
☿	♃	☋	☉	♂	♄	☿ -	--	- 10 P
♀	♄	♂	♀ +	♃ m	♂	☽	♃	+3
♂	☉	--	☉	♀	♃	♄	--	- 5 P
♃	♃ +	☋	☉	♀ m	☿	☿	--	+5
♄	♄ +	--	♄ +	♄ +	♀	☉	--	+10
☊	♃	♀	♀	♀	♄	♂	--	--
⊗	♂	♂	♀	♀	♂	♀	♃	--
As	♄	♂	♀	♀	♃	☽	♃	--
Mc	♂	--	♀	♀	☉	♀	☽	--
☋	♂	--	♀	♂	♂	♀	☽	--

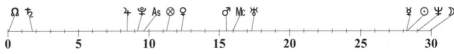

the established church is declining. Saturn in the 1st house, at the Bendings, shows the restructuring of religion in Western Europe that resulted. This is truly a fascinating chart.

To understand how things arrived at this point, we have to go back to the few years prior. Let's look at 1517 first, Chart 67. The Aries Ingress in Wittenberg was 29 Aries rising – this triggers the Libra Ingress for our purposes, but one has to see that affairs are coming to a head, in the 29th degree of a sign. Uranus so close to the Ascendant in a fixed sign trine Pluto in the 9th indicates the immediacy of a break with the past – and being in a fixed sign, such a break will be experienced as wrenching indeed.

The fact that Mercury, ruler of the 3rd house of heresies, is in Aries, in mutual reception with Mars, heightens the religious tension, showing a real confrontational aspect. Jupiter, representing conventional Catholicism (and how appropriate!) has nighttime Triplicity, but is retrograde. This demonstrates some of the callousness of the high Catholic officials, in completely missing the rage of many Catholics over objections to their positions – these officials could not see the storm brewing.

The Libra Ingress shows the period of the actual event of Luther's posting of the 95 Theses. The traditional date given is October 31st, although there is some uncertainty about this. The Moon in Virgo rules the 3rd, and there is some appropriateness to this, because Luther's objections were technical, and what his procedure at this time initiated was a public debate. The Moon is trine Uranus, again giving the theme of change and disruption.

Saturn ruled the 9th, in the sign of Sagittarius, where it has participating Triplicity. Now this is interesting. The Moon is in sect, whereas Saturn is in what we might call the lesser Triplicity. Furthermore, Saturn is angular, while Mercury is succedent,

suggesting that it's a real toss-up as to which is stronger. We have the additional factor that Saturn was transiting the sign that Pluto had just left. I think that when a less ponderous planet (hard to think of Saturn that way!) transits a sign that a more ponderous planet has just left, it gives the opportunity for the loose ends from the prior sign transit to surface, be recycled, be resolved, or remain, whether "solved," or waiting for the next opportunity on center stage.

So we are right back to where we started with Pluto in Capricorn: with a religious theme. Surely, the largest theme for this period *is* religious, first with the expansion of missionary work in the New World with Pluto in Sagittarius, followed by a breakdown in the unity of the Church with Pluto in Capricorn. But this fissure did not reduce Christian faith.

This religious fracture may also have contributed to the changes in people's attitudes toward their environment. During this pass of Pluto in Capricorn, the idea of cultivating flowers that did *not* have medicinal or food value becomes prominent. Throughout the Middle Ages and even earlier, herb gardens were a common fixture of many houses and communities. Plants that we now consider ornamental, like roses and primroses, were cultivated either as medicine (the roses), or as food (primroses were used in salads). But now, in this period, flowers were bred and cultivated for their scent, or for their appearance, especially in flower beds and borders, leading to what a little later in the Elizabethan Era would be called "gardens of delight." This would ultimately lead to importation of exotics on a massive scale, but this development belongs to a later historical period.[231, 232] At first, this may seem an odd development for utilitarian Pluto. I think the basic element of earth trumps the utilitarianism this time.

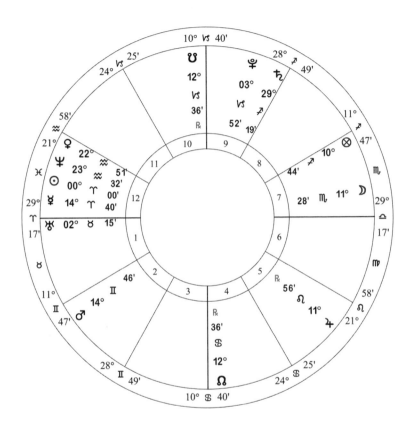

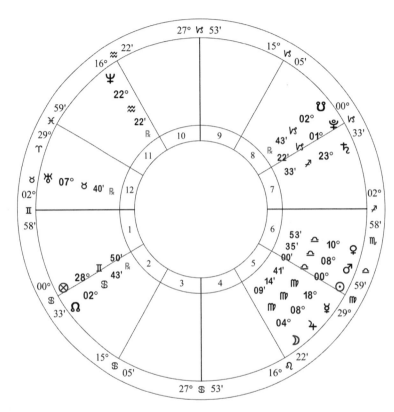

Sun enters Ari 3-21-1517
March 21, 1517
6:54:11 AM
Wittenburg, Germany
53 N 31 11 E 04
Local Mean Time
Time Zone: 0 hours West
Tropical Regiomontanus
NATAL CHART

Chart 67. Sun enters
Aries and Libra 1517

Sun enters Lib 9-23-1517
September 23, 1517
7:52:14 PM
Wittenburg, Germany
53 N 31 11 E 04
Local Mean Time
Time Zone: 0 hours West
Tropical Regiomontanus
NATAL CHART

Pluto in Aquarius

Pluto passed into Aquarius in 1532, and Neptune entered Aries in 1533. Just as Pluto was transitioning to Aquarius, Henry VIII removed the Church of England from being under the Church of Rome, and declared himself head of the Church of England.

But a new day had dawned. Aquarius is classified astrologically as a human sign. One literal rendering of this concept was that bestiality itself became illegal in England in 1534.[233] On a somewhat less extreme note, artistic license on the topic of human-animal metamorphosis were generally condemned as immoral, although several Pluto signs later, Shakespeare would revive the genre with *A Midsummer's Night Dream*. It is perhaps worth noting that the word "inhumane," a word now often applied to cruel treatment of animals, in this period meant "inhuman," and meant behavior to be condemned as being unworthy of a human. Forget about how one treated the beast! To call someone a beast in this period, as Henry VIII did of the commoners of Lincolnshire, was a much more extreme insult than we could even imagine today. It virtually meant calling them soulless.[234] For humans to act like beasts was to both invite and justify slavery. Eventually, this logic would reverse, and the opponents of slavery would label the confusion of any human with an animal to be demeaning to all humans, regardless of rank.

In 1545, the Council of Trent began. Lasting until 1563, it began as an answer to the objections raised by Protestants, and also was the last major Catholic Church council until Vatican II in the 1960s. But it also began with Pluto in Aquarius, and ended with Pluto in Pisces. In the early phase, under Pluto in Aquarius, Protestants planned to speak and attend – and did. But after it reconvened under a new Pope with Pluto in Pisces, the agenda had changed completely to a strong condemnation of Protestantism. In other words, it went from being ecumenical to parochial.

Pluto in Pisces

Pluto had moved into Pisces in 1552, while Neptune moved into Gemini in 1560. Even before the Council of Trent ended, the killing had begun in France. By 1562, skirmishes and killings had begun, and would last for 36 years. Curiously, at the same time over in India, the Mughal Emperor Akbar was reducing religious tension by marrying a Hindu princess. In 1563, plague broke out in England, resulting in over 80,000 deaths.

On the political front, just after Pluto began moving into Pisces in 1552, Mary I of England (reigned 1553-1558) returned that country to Catholicism until her successor Elizabeth I changed it back to Protestantism. While Mary executed enough of the Protestant hierarchy to be nicknamed Bloody Mary, the amount of bloodshed hardly amounted to as much as even a typical peasant's revolt. The ascension of Elizabeth I in England in 1558 (Pluto in early Pisces) marked the English Renaissance, which lasted throughout her reign, ending in 1603, just in time for the Great Mutation of the Jupiter-Saturn cycle to renew itself in the fire element, and marking the end of the Tudor dynasty. In the meantime, Pluto had gone from Pisces to Aries, beginning in 1577.

One important point that modern astrologers miss by using the modern rulerships is certain tendencies of the sign Pisces. Thus, initially, it probably sounds extremely odd to think of warfare and violence increasing when Pluto went into Pisces. But classical astrologers see this more simply: water sign Triplicity rulers are Venus, Mars and the Moon. When Mars is a Triplicity ruler, violence is possible, and the Venus-Mars coupling always produces sparks. Under Pisces and other water signs, belief can be a terrible thing, especially when the believer cannot accept that it is possible to believe otherwise, as is sadly often the case. The empathy which can be such a mark of positive water turns into scorn and vengeance.

Notice the sequencing. Sagittarius is a fire sign, but there is no Mars major dignity in the fire signs, apart from Aries. Capricorn has Mars' Exaltation, and also Mars is the mixed Triplicity ruler there. The Exaltation is often where a planet is best behaved. The mixed Triplicity seems to operate in a somewhat weaker fashion than the Day and Night Triplicity rulers. In Capricorn, with the birth of Protestantism, there was enough militancy – and there was violence. But the major thrust seemed to be much more pragmatic. Aquarius, an Air sign, lacks Mars as any major ruler. But now along comes Pisces. Mars and Jupiter together – the threat of a religious militancy: always a bad idea!

But not only religious, because Jupiter also is associated with judges and magistrates. By the 1570s, struggle was afoot in Russia, between the massacres of Ivan the Terrible and the sacking of Moscow by the Crimean Tatars. The Holy League decimated the Ottoman navy at the decisive Battle of Lepanto in 1571. In 1572, the infamous St. Bartholomew's Day massacre in France instigated by Catherine de' Medici decimated the French Huguenots. The Dutch and the Spanish were also at war since 1568: this was both a religious war and a war of independence. This changeover in conflict in 1568 seems to correspond to the beginning of the exact Neptune-Pluto square, which went in and out of exactitude, with the last pass in 1572. In 1573, Neptune began to move into Cancer.

Pass 2: The Enlightenment Era (1748-1822)

Our period opens with Neptune in Cancer, shortly moving into Leo in 1751. In this pass, unlike the one before, the major sign occupation of Neptune in each Pluto sign is in the same Triplicity: thus, Neptune was in Leo for most of the time Pluto was in Sagittarius, Neptune was in Virgo for most of the time Pluto was in Capricorn, Neptune was in Libra for most of the time Pluto was in Aquarius, and Neptune was mainly in Scorpio when Pluto was in Pisces. This elemental overlap provides the pass of Pluto through these signs with less cognitive dissonance. (This arrangement doesn't hold for the whole time of the Pluto sequence, but it manages here because in these Pluto signs, the length of stay of Pluto in each sign is not so far different from Neptune's that the two planets have started to "slip" out of this relationship.) But the essence is the same: we are still examining the time when what is now the old cycle is achieving its maximum reach, or most extreme development, before settling into its metaphorical winter, where it gets stripped down to its essence, before being reclothed in a new philosophy, before being sent out as a new cycle with Pluto in Aries. In this type of pass, Neptune and Pluto reinforce each other by sharing Triplicity; in the alternate passes, Neptune's presence in a sign a couple decades before Pluto gets there acts as an early warning system: the problems are laid out, and then, if not adequately addressed, Pluto will make the problem even more obvious.

Table 8-5 shows the sign distribution of the planets from Saturn out for the period of Pluto in each of the four signs of interest. Unlike our last pass, Saturn does not split out so simply into a distribution with a lot of dignity in any particular Pluto sign. Pluto in Capricorn begins with Saturn in its detriment, and Pluto in Aquarius begins with Saturn in a sign where it is mostly peregrine – Scorpio. When Pluto entered Sagittarius this time, Neptune was in Cancer, giving Jupiter strong dignity in both of their placements. For the later phase of Pluto in Pisces, Neptune was in the sign of Jupiter's detriment. For a while with Pluto in Aquarius and Neptune in

Pluto	Sagittarius	Capricorn	Aquarius	Pisces
Neptune	Cancer – Leo	Leo – Virgo	Virgo – Scorpio	Scorpio – Capricorn
Uranus	Aquarius – Aries	Aries – Gemini	Gemini – Virgo	Virgo – Capricorn
Saturn	Scorpio – Aries	Aries – Scorpio	Scorpio – Gemini	Gemini – Pisces

Table 8-5. Outer Planet signs: Second pass, 1748-1822.

Libra, Saturn strongly ruled both planets, Neptune being ruled from Saturn's Exaltation in Libra. For most of that time, namely 1779-1788, Saturn was in Sagittarius, Capricorn and Aquarius, three signs where Saturn has strong dignity. Thus, that period would be especially strong in a positive saturnine sense. But Saturn's ingress into Pisces after so long with dignity is generally quite a jolt. This time, that jolt is seen in the French Revolution.

Since we left civilization in 1577, colonization has continued. But so has industrialization. And colonies have completely shifted in their function for the mother country: no longer a source of gold and silver, they are a source of raw materials for the mills of the mother country and an outlet for the finished products of those same mills. This economic scheme, which separates raw material and industrial capacity, proved as politically destabilizing then as it is proving wasteful of fossil fuels now.

Mercantilism

The Age of Discovery had settled in to create the beginnings of a global economy, but one very different from the global economy today. The Age of Feudalism had defined wealth as land. The new economic system, mercantilism, defined wealth as cash, which was essentially bullion. Within this system, new wealth could only be created by mining additional gold and silver. While this continued to occur, the system mostly treated the amount of cash/bullion as if it were fixed. When the Spanish acquired massive amounts of gold from the New World in the early 1500s in our last pass, the only result could be hyperinflation. In that early period of the gradual transition to mercantilism (there was no mercantile revolution which suddenly changed the economic system overnight), the normal economic assumption of fixed total cash was wildly distorted, so all gold was temporarily devalued to allow the economy to swallow the Incan elephant, so to speak. Trade became important, because what I can produce, you could buy. Money didn't just sit in a counting house somewhere. The development of mercantilism paralleled the development of nationalism, and so the successful state exported more than it imported. As colonies counted as part of a nation, successful integration of the colonies into the mother country's economy meant a much bigger economic pie that hopefully resulted in few imports, and greater exports.

Historians of economics rate mercantilism peaking around 1650: right around the time of the Neptune-Pluto conjunction in Gemini. How perfect a symbol, given that Mercury is the planet of commerce! Where mercantilism eventually got a little frayed was its definition of wealth as *only* bullion: later, capitalism would decouple that pairing and replace bullion with production.

Views of Nature

Another major shift that has occurred in the interim since our last period is a radical rethink of nature. The early modern view of nature for man's use made what we might appropriately call the slavery of animals completely justifiable. During the time of the last pass of Pluto through Sagittarius to Pisces, this idea was breaking down, as animals began to been seen as creatures in their own right. By now, the cultivation of plants for their aesthetic qualities which first surfaced during the last pass of Pluto in Capricorn is not only well established, but the Dutch Tulip Craze bubble (1636-1637) had come and gone. Seeds are easy to transport around the globe, and gardeners were always happy to try new varieties. Gardening is well established as both a profession and an honored avocation. The gardens produced are seldom anything like a natural environment, however they do have the effect of making many more people sympathetic to natural delights.

This change in focus away from dominion over other living creatures did not improve the status of nature at all. Far from it. The measure of benefit for man had not completely disappeared. The divine clockmaker had become the popular metaphor that served as a description of a remote Deity who left the day-to-day running of the *Cosmos* to natural law. This meant that animals and plants – and Nature herself – were merely machines created by God, not Man. The great philosopher Immanuel Kant in 1790 stated that Man could not logically conclude that he was the final creation, as Christians had long maintained. Gone was Man at the center of *Cosmos*.[235]

While the status of nature had not necessarily improved, the greater amount of data amassed by biologists and geologists was challenging biblical literalism as it had never been challenged before. But really – biblical literalism had not been the norm in Christianity for most of its existence. The Catholic Church had not emphasized this viewpoint at all. The Protestant and Catholic Churches had survived the transition to heliocentricism which had started with Copernicus in 1543 (Pluto in Aquarius, in our last pass), and continued into the 17th century, without a loss of Christian belief when such passages as Joshua making the Sun stand still had to be understood metaphorically. But throughout this second pass, more and more geological information was accumulating, resulting in geologists accepting an Earth much older than the assumed biblical age of less than 10,000 years. This shift in focus was complete by 1820, just as Pluto in Pisces was about to give way to Pluto in Aries.[236]

God had withdrawn to a more distant place. As Stephen Jay Gould tells it, the growth of scientific knowledge about the Earth that occurred during this period that we are identifying as the second pass, results in the development of what Gould calls Non-Overlapping Magisteria (NOMA): the mutually agreed upon (by scientists and theologians) idea that theories about nature should be left to scientists, while ideas about God and morality should be left to religion.[237] However satisfying this distinction may be to the modern mind, in practice, it decoupled the nascent stewardship theme that had run through the dominion argument in the first pass. Now, people were *really* free to exploit nature as it had never been done before.

As our period opens in Sagittarius, Frederick the Great has been King of Prussia since 1740. We encountered his civil engineering projects in Chapter 2. Societal changes, quite apart from the usual dynastic and political wars, were also taking place. Just as Frederick's changes – and those wrought by his contemporaries – resulted in population increases for his country, so too industrialization was driving people to the cities from the country. It is estimated that in 1800, the number of people living in larger towns had doubled since the last century.[238] The towns went from being the harbingers of civilization – rustics always having a bad name – to sites of pollution, from coal, or from industries, whether tanning, metal-working, slaughtering, or dyeing; not to speak of human sewage. Disease was worse in town, as seen a century earlier in Lilly's removal horaries that related to whether it was better to leave for the countryside to escape the plague.

By the time that Pluto had moved into Capricorn, fashion had dictated that the ideal vacation was to either mountains or wilderness, whether the Scottish Lake District or Switzerland.[239] Landscape sculpting and cultivation continued, but the prejudice against wildness, and specifically mountains, began to break down.

Revolutions

The U.S. Revolutionary War seems to stand as the great event for Pluto at the end of its period in Capricorn in the 1760-1770s, as the Protestant rebellion against Rome did in the 1510-1520s. One a religious event, the other a political one – and yet religion and politics mingled in each case. There is a certain symmetry there.

There also is an astrological explanation for the distinctions between the American and French Revolutions most famously made by Hannah Arendt.[240] She said that the American Revolution should be seen as in its earlier meaning, as with the Glorious Revolution of William and Mary – *a return* to a better time. It is in *this* sense of "return" that we understand the use of the word "revolution" as a synonym for "solar *return*." Arendt pointed out that the colonial Americans did not see themselves as creating an entirely new system of government, but as re-establishing classical ideals, especially those of Athenian democracy. That ideal is enshrined in the neo-classical architecture of the early federal buildings of Washington, DC, or Jefferson's Monticello – a hope for a perfect melding of the best of Greek and Roman architecture and politics. By contrast, Arendt pointed out that the French revolutionists rapidly went beyond a more participatory democracy to a deliberate reconstruction of society from the ground up, eliminating not only the Crown, the aristocracy, but much of the Church as well. This New World Order had *nothing* in common with the old regime – and it was the French Revolution, not the American one, that changed the meaning of the word "revolution" to meaning a break with the past, rather than a cyclic re-establishment of Things-as-They-Should-Be. The stark contrast in France between the old and the new terrified the rest of Europe, leading to an upswing of conservatism that itself was only toppled beginning with the revolutions of 1848 – a time of Pluto in late Aries.

We can also reflect on Charles Harvey's comment about Capricorn stripping things down to their essence. The American Revolution resulted from the awareness of the colonies that their status would always be second class. By rebelling, they challenged the economic system that made them so useful to England. They did not challenge the English monarchy, or anything about the structure of the English government. And ironically, through the 19th century, mercantilism would be pursued vigorously by the U.S.A. after it was being rejected as a system in Europe, being replaced by capitalism. The stripping here of the sign of Capricorn was challenging an economic system that had *developed in the prior cycle of Pluto*.

By contrast, the French Revolution demolished the very idea of monarchy. If Pluto in Capricorn strips off some of the obsolete or dysfunctional systems in place, Pluto in Aquarius then can take matters even further. The day sign of Saturn has both the sign and Triplicity rulerships, after all.

The period of Pluto in Aquarius ran from 1777 to 1797, which encompasses the build-up to, and then much of, the French Revolution. The wars of the French monarchs leading up to this period had left a huge debt, and had stripped France of valuable colonies. Remember that this is under the period of mercantilism, so it was not so easy to go into debt without extreme consequences. Louis XVI was forced to call an Estates General in 1789 in order to get financial reform.

The commoners were one of the three parts of the Estates General. When the Third Estate (*i.e.*, the commoners) stepped out of the Estates General to form the National Assembly (and then were joined by most of the clergy and some of the nobles), they swore an oath that they would meet until they had a constitution in place. Debate proceeded, abolishing all hereditary office except the kingship, with the goal of producing a constitutional monarchy. When the constitution was finally created, Louis swore an oath to protect and defend it in September 1791. Once the new Assembly was convened, he vetoed key legislation, creating a constitutional crisis from which the Terror emerged.

The French Revolution was a social process that lasted for years, and went through several distinct phases. What we may note was that up until the first part of 1792, Neptune had been in Libra. The cry of the Revolution to this point? Liberty, Equality, Fraternity! How Libran! It wasn't until Neptune got into Scorpio that you got war – and Terror!

The actual Reign of Terror was comparatively short: 1793-1794, when as many as 40,000 were executed by guillotine, many more were summarily executed in the streets, and probably more than that in the country. None of this solved any of the economic problems that set up the revolution in the first place. There followed the Directorate, a corrupt holding action, where the fiscally bankrupt legislature was dependent upon the army, which needed war – foreign or civil – to maintain its income and power. It was out of that quagmire that Napoleon staged a coup in 1799 – with the coming of Pluto into Pisces.

The Enlightenment

But this second pass of Pluto in Sagittarius and Capricorn was not just about Revolution. Because this era marked the period known as the Enlightenment, and there were major philosophical, as well as religious, changes. Jean-Jacques Rousseau, while not the original author of the phrase "Noble Savage," nonetheless upended the Christian concept of original sin by positing that Natural Man was the one with the morals – that civilization had degraded us morally. He laid out his ideas in the period from 1754 to 1762[241] – when Pluto was transiting from roughly 12 Sagittarius to 1 Capricorn. Rousseau's Pluto in Capricorn work, *Social Contract,* has the look and feel of Pluto in Saturn's sign!

We can see that in both the 16th and the 18th century passes of Pluto in Capricorn, that there is a mix of religion and politics. If it seems that the 16th century pass was primarily religious, while the 18th century pass was primarily political, think again. Because 1776 also marked the death of David Hume, the first philosopher who can truly be called an atheist within the modern definition of the term. Until the 18th century, atheism was a derisive term, but nobody could actually believe it possible to *not* believe in God. Hume's philosophy, promulgated under Pluto in Sagittarius and Capricorn, did not require a God, Demiurge, or Clockmaker. This represented a radical departure in Western thinking. So here, the period of Pluto in Sagittarius saw the introduction of the flip side of belief: atheism. Later, this seed germinated, and in the 19th century, atheism became one major theme in European intellectual discourse.[242]

The Enlightenment is every bit as much a religion as Christianity is. As such, the whole idea of the Enlightenment is up for re-examination as Pluto passes through Capricorn. The very idea of reform and restructure which Capricorn brings is then codified. Finding a moment for the beginning of the Enlightenment is impossible. Everyone agrees on the end point: the French Revolution. One of the most important philosophical ideas within Enlightenment thinking is the idea of progress proposed by Condorcet toward the end of the Pluto in Aquarius period.

We took up the meaning of Pisces in this time period in Chapter 6 to explain how things worked when Pluto moved into Aries. By 1797, when Pluto had made it to Pisces (Neptune was already in Scorpio), Napoleon was already winning battles for revolutionary France – but he hadn't declared himself Emperor yet. George Washington was just finishing his second term in office, and John Adams was inaugurated as the second American president.

The Rise of Quantitative Thought

From an environmental standpoint, possibly the most significant philosopher of this pass was Thomas Malthus. As we saw in Chapter 2, Malthus published *An Essay on the Principle of Population* in 1798. It was promptly ignored or ridiculed. It would have won a sleeper award, because it turns out to have been one of the most influential books of the period, but it was definitely before its time. We should broaden our discussion to put Malthus in the context of the new field of learning that he represented: what was then called political arithmetic, but which then became subsumed under statistics.[243] Amidst the carnage of the French Revolution, there were some significant steps forward. French technical and mathematical education was massively improved

with the foundation of the *École Polytechnique* in 1794. The emphasis on mathematics and engineering which was so important for Napoleon and his military enterprise also served to move higher education away from the traditional liberal arts curriculum toward something more scientifically and mathematically based.

In fact, viewing social problems more from a quantitative standpoint had really begun under Frederick the Great, moved to industrializing England, and from there to progressive France. It is not difficult to see its genesis in the development of the concept of insurance, because much of the early work related to demographics, life expectancy, and the development of census data. Malthus could not have formulated his ideas in the absence of this kind of basic background information. So while it seemed that Malthus had suddenly gone in a new direction, he had simply been bolder at concluding what the data available to all actually meant.

As quantitative models had come into vogue, some of the old Christian utilitarianism had died. By the end of this period, no one was still advocating the idea that animals had been created only for man's purposes. Gradually, the grip which had viewed all things through the eyes of the Book of Genesis was loosening.[244]

Summary of Passes One and Two

As Pass One opened with Pluto in Sagittarius, we saw how the Europeans expanded their territories, if not their mental horizons. Of all the elements, Fire is the most exuberant, ever-curious, always asking the question of what's out there. The question will always hinge upon what this exuberance is tied to. In the early 1480s, with nothing more to go on than an amazing imagination, Leonardo da Vinci made a diagram of a helicopter: sometime around a Uranus-Neptune conjunction in Sagittarius. In 1907, Paul Cornu flew the first free flight of a helicopter – with a Uranus-Neptune opposition between Capricorn and Cancer. Earth makes a great engineer for Fire's ideas.

But this also means that Earth cleans up after Fire's messes. In the Chinese system, Earth is the ash left over from Fire's burn – and this image is true enough. Sadly, with derivatives, we've just seen how financially creative Sagittarius/Fire can be – and one could say that indulgences were financially creative in the same way 500 years ago.

With Pluto in Capricorn, Luther was willing to try to scrape Christianity back to its essence, although one clearly might quibble about exactly what that essence should be. Two hundred fifty years later, the American colonists were ready to challenge the creative taxation of the Mother Country, being willing to strip their lives back to the bare bones, having concluded that relations with the U.K. were permanently unfavorable. Pluto went into Aquarius in 1777, and Neptune went into Libra in 1778, well before the end of the war in 1783. An abortive attempt at governance under the Articles of Confederation was part of the U.S. learning curve for producing a workable government. The U.S. didn't adopt the Constitution until 1787 – well into the Pluto in Aquarius period. Thinking of Neptune in Libra, the crafting of the Constitution, with its checks and balances and establishment of the rule of law, one understands why later the French delegates were so eager to create a constitution: they were still in the same Neptune-Pluto phase where the idea of this kind of system of law was so appealing. The previous pass of this combination of Neptune and Pluto had occurred during the reign of Edward I of England, whose most notable accomplishment was legal reform.

So what part of this theme is the Pluto in Aquarius, and what part the Neptune in Libra? We did not see a huge interest in this kind of legal reform in the 1530s, so that gives a hint. I think that part of the process with this two planet combination is that Pluto in Aquarius, like Pluto in Capricorn, is still that Winter strip-to-the-essence Saturn theme, but this time, in the area of ideas, and possibly also specifically relating to the human condition. In Edward I's case, one of the things he did was to completely challenge the Barons' historical privileges, requiring them to produce the actual documentation of their rights, thereby tying all such rights to the Crown. In other words, he didn't just add a new law on top of existing ones: he cleaned house first. In the case of the United States, the Constitution was developed after the Articles of Confederation hadn't worked: and it wasn't an add-on, it was a replacement. And, of course, with the French Revolution, the constitution emerged from the ashes of the Old Regime.

In the Pluto in Aquarius period which mainly featured Neptune in Aries, the principal events were the expansion and consolidation of Protestantism, and the continued exploration and exploitation of the New World. At least Paul III issued an edict declaring that the Native American had souls, and hence, that there were limits to their exploitation.

The religious wars started under Pluto in Pisces. And the warfare piece seems to apply to both tracks of Pluto in Pisces: whether Neptune in Taurus is the dominant placement, or Neptune in Scorpio. I can see a real similarity between religious warfare and Napolean's conquest of Europe – on behalf of a new political system.

Pluto in Pisces has shown a pattern of the re-assertion of hierarchies, sometimes violently. And this should not seem surprising, because Jupiter itself is mythologically king of the gods. In the 16th century, the Catholic Church reacted to Protestantism, and then in the early 19th century, the world-conquering ambitions of the Emperor Bonaparte emerged from the French Revolution. Under Mars-ruled Pisces (through Triplicity) and then Aries (through sign), the Old Order (Empire) strikes back – or at least tries to.

The Third Pass
(1995-2066)

In this pass, we are back to virtually the same Neptune-Pluto "structure" as the pass that opens this chapter. This means that we are back to Neptune proposing, and Pluto disposing, when first Neptune runs a sign, and then Pluto runs the same sign a couple of decades later.

So, thinking about these past passes, I propose the following addition to our understanding of Pluto's transit through a sign: *Pride goeth before a fall.*[245] For example, while the Pluto in Virgo engineers succeeded spectacularly in getting us to the Moon – we didn't stay there! We *didn't* develop a colony, we *didn't* follow up with an observatory. The moon landing became a dead end instead of becoming the gateway to the exploration of our solar system, and the stars. President Kennedy perfectly embodied the Pluto in Leo call to put a man on the moon – but he said it while Pluto was in Virgo. The vision that got us there couldn't encompass the concept of knowledge and engineering for its own sake – once the deed was accomplished, the funding was cut. We went for the wrong reason, and having gotten there, couldn't sustain it. Pluto in Leo was gone, Pluto in Virgo spent, and the needs of Pluto in Libra would direct our attention elsewhere. In the words of President Lyndon Johnson: *"It's unfortunate, but the way Americans are, now that they have developed all of this capability, instead of taking advantage of it, they'll probably just piss it all away."*[246]

It's very interesting that Neptune went into Libra at the beginning of 1970 – just before the Apollo 13 mission rated a "partial failure" because the explosion in an oxygen tank (air!) and the failure of an engine aborted the landing mission, and tested the theory that the Lunar Module could be used as a lifeboat. One would think that the ingress of Neptune into an air sign would have made space that much more appealing, since it's "up there." It was – but in science fiction, not "real" science. *Star Trek* (The Original Series, to its fans) had premiered in 1966, under Pluto in Virgo/Neptune in Scorpio – the configuration of the Space Race itself. During its original run, it was not wildly popular. It achieved cult status once Neptune went into Sagittarius, with the first three *Star Trek* movies coming under Neptune there. The first *Star Wars* trilogy also launched at this time. Even the all-star cast version of *Dune* came out in 1984, the last year of Neptune in Sagittarius. Bookstores followed this trend, with large science fiction sections.

Our usual concept of Pluto in a sign is that it totally disrupts and reforms matters relating to the affairs of that sign. As we have seen, it is just as likely that the affairs of that sign have a free hand for most of the transit – and then the fruits of that transit are "tested" at the very end of the sign. So it was pretty obvious with Pluto going into Sagittarius that the most likely candidate for this treatment was organized religion. And we can make a great case for the period of Pluto in Sagittarius as being the triumph of the Religious Right – and then its rejection. Pluto went into Sagittarius in 1995 – during Clinton's presidency. Now one might at first wonder what Clinton had to do with this Pluto in Sagittarius trend. There was a visceral reaction of a religious Right minority who loathed Clinton – and we saw this manifest with his second term in the form of the Impeachment, where the issues had absolutely nothing to do with his Presidency, and *everything* to do with his morality. This outrage, fanned by paid hate-mongers like Rush Limbaugh, resulted in the "election" of George W. Bush, who, along with his followers, saw no Christian conflict with lying about weapons of mass destruction, and torturing individuals savagely and repeatedly, but who, as far as we know, was absolutely faithful to his wife.

Table 8-6 shows us the sign distribution of the planets from Saturn out, for the period of Pluto in each of the four signs of interest. The Neptune line is identical to the first pass. Uranus has shifted backward by two signs, and Saturn is one sign forward. Pluto in Capricorn corresponds to a remarkable amount of dignity for its dispositor Saturn, comprising Virgo (same nature but peregrine), Libra (Exaltation and Triplicity), Scorpio (peregrine), Sagittarius (Triplicity), Capricorn (Rulership), Aquarius (Rulership and Triplicity), and Pisces (peregrine). This is as dignified a run of Saturn as it's possible to get, and it further avoids either Saturn in Leo or Aries, its Detriment and Fall.

In 2008, just after the Religious Right celebrated the nomination of Sarah Palin, and when Pluto had retrograded back into Sagittarius for its final pass, the economy fell apart, the Republicans lost the election, and the Religious Right was left looking even more tarnished. So one can legitimately ask: what about financial matters? Is the Pluto sign ingress a contributing factor to the economic collapse?

About ten years ago, I had a master class of private students in Atlanta intensely interested in financial matters: Penny Shelton, Fran Rackow, Ralph Cannizzaro, and Agnes Moscrip. They did a lot of study of financial cycles, and one thing that did emerge was that the transit of outer planets through the signs was *not* a useful indicator of financial success or failure. In other words, the 2008 financial debacle should not be attributed solely or primarily to Pluto's ingress into Capricorn. There are other factors to consider. Penny did find some correlation between market bottoms and the 21st degree of the cardinals – but we're not there yet – a possibly depressing thought.

One possible contributing factor that comes to mind immediately has been the Saturn-Uranus. There is some evidence that this is a combination which produces volatility. Interestingly, the peak of the dot-com crisis came in February 2000, just as the Triple Conjunction of Mars, Jupiter and Saturn was forming, along with Uranus square to the whole group.

Perhaps a better recent pattern for consideration in interpreting the immediate future is 1989. This was the year when Saturn, Neptune, and Uranus were all circling around each other in late Sagittarius, and then early Capricorn. So events during that time should be a good signature for those anticipated over the next few years.

1989 was the fall of Communism and the break-up of the Soviet Union. It was the Savings and Loan Crisis. It was Tiananmen Square. And then of course there was the *Exxon Valdez*. Clearly, that year highlighted crises in all the areas we can expect to continue to be hotspots: political instability, religious instability, financial instability, and environmental instability.

Pluto	Sagittarius	Capricorn	Aquarius	Pisces
Neptune	Capricorn – Aquarius	Aquarius – Pisces	Pisces – Taurus	Taurus-Cancer
Uranus	Capricorn – Pisces	Pisces – Taurus	Taurus – Leo	Leo – Scorpio
Saturn	Taurus – Virgo	Virgo – Pisces	Pisces – Scorpio	Scorpio – Leo

Table 8-6. Outer Planet signs: Third pass, 1995-2066

But what is the difference between a crisis and a meltdown? Because this is the essence of understanding the *context* of these celestial events. And it's worth asking whether this is a question that can be always or even usually answered astrologically at all, or whether it is also a function of the stability of the political, religious, or other structures in question. For example, the previous pass of Pluto into Capricorn before the 16th century did not result in the breakdown of the Catholic Church. It was the time of Thomas Aquinas and Roger Bacon. The Catholic Church didn't self-destruct in this era: if anything, it produced some of its greatest theologians. However, in Asia, this was the time of the Mongols, and their expansion had considerable impact on the expansion of Buddhism. Strong institutions don't automatically fall apart, even if they are ruled by the sign Pluto transits. Pluto's passage is more like a stress test! And it's worth always remembering that astrological events are not the only events happening in a particular time period. *The existence of celestial influence does not preclude other kinds of influences!*

Recent Events

Much of the pass of Sagittarius and Pluto in the 1500s concerned the Church. Our age is a more secular one, but the attribution of Jupiter to church hierarchy is a deep one, although other readings of Jupiter that are more secular are possible. As I am writing this in 2010, the child molestation scandal within the Catholic Church has been eclipsed by the explosion of the British Petroleum deep water drilling platform in the Gulf of Mexico. Both events, however, are ruled by the same Aries Ingress. If we were following the history of religion as our major theme, that chart calculated for Vatican City would indeed be a colorful discussion. But our theme is the environment. While we will shortly examine the chart for the explosion and sinking of the *Deepwater Horizon*, the crisis has impacted primarily the United States, so it seems appropriate to begin by studying the Aries Ingress for Washington, DC, Chart 68.

You will recall how in Chapter 4, we explored the historical connection of petroleum to Mars – and its possible co-rulership by Pluto. Here we have the Sun-Saturn opposition very close to the MC/IC axis, thereby indicating that this is one of the hot spots where the Aries Ingress will have a great effect. This angularity alone suggests that the U.S.A. will be highlighted as an exemplar for the meaning of this Ingress. That Sun is not only applying to Saturn, but to square Pluto, as it is in a partile trine to Mars. The Moon exalted rules the 1st, which does include accidents according to Lilly.[247] Being in Taurus, we would expect this to be wonderful – but this Moon in Taurus is conjunct Algol.

The last hit of Saturn to the IC in an Aries Ingress in the U.S.A. was 2005, the year Hurricane Katrina hit the Gulf states. This is the disaster that keeps being referred to as the comparison with the sinking of the *Deepwater Horizon*, presumably because both were Gulf events that required federal intervention. Conjunctions of Saturn with the IC are not extremely rare – and most of the time, the effect does not seem to be primarily environmental. But then, since the founding of the U.S., there was never one that was opposite the Sun at the same time.

The involvement with both Mars and Pluto may not be predictive of petroleum problems, but it is a consistent reading. Saturn conjunct the IC is not something one would expect for good things for the land, and this argument is fortified by the 4th house sign ruler, Venus, in Detriment and closely square the Nodes. That 10th house Venus is going to bring issues with the land to light.

It's hard to decide upon a ruler for BP, in part because of the confusion about the responsibility for the *Deepwater Horizon*

NATAL CHART
Sun enters Ari 3-20-2010
March 20, 2010
1:32:12 PM
Washington, D.C.
38N53'42" 77W02'12"
Daylight Saving Time
Time Zone: 5 hours West
Tropical Regiomontanus

Chart 68. Sun enters Aries 2010, Washington, DC

Day of ♄	Hour of ☽
Last Hr ☿	- 16 mins
Next Hr ♄	+44 mins

FIXED STARS	
As☌Castor	0°50's
☉☌Scheat	0°28's
☽☌ Algol	0°06'a
☊☌Rukbat	0°41'a
♃☌ Achernar	0°51'a

Hs	Alm. (Dor)
1	☽
2	☉
3	☿
4	♄
5	♂
6	♃
7	♂
8	♄
9	♀
10	☉
11	♀
12	☿♄

ESSENTIAL DIGNITIES (Dorothean)

Pl	Ruler	Exalt	Tripl	Term	Face	Detri	Fall	Score
☉	♂ m	☉ +	☉ +	♃	♂	♀	♄	+12
☽	♀	☽ +	♀	♂	♄ m	♂	--	+4
☿	♂	☉	☉	♀ m	♂	♀	♄	- 5 P
♀	♂	☉	☉	☿ m	☉	♀ -	♄	- 10 P
♂	☉ m	--	☉	♄	♄	♄	--	+0 P
♃	♃ +	♀	♀	☿	♃ +	☿	☿	+6
♄	♀	♄ +	♄ +	♄ +	☽ m	♂	☉	+9
☊	♄	♂	♀	♃	♂	☽	♃	--
⊗	☿	☿	♀	♃	♀	♃	♀	--
As	☽	♃	♀	♀	☽	♄	♂	--
Mc	♂	☉	☉	♃	♂	♀	♄	--
☋	☽	♃	♀	☿	☿	♄	♂	--

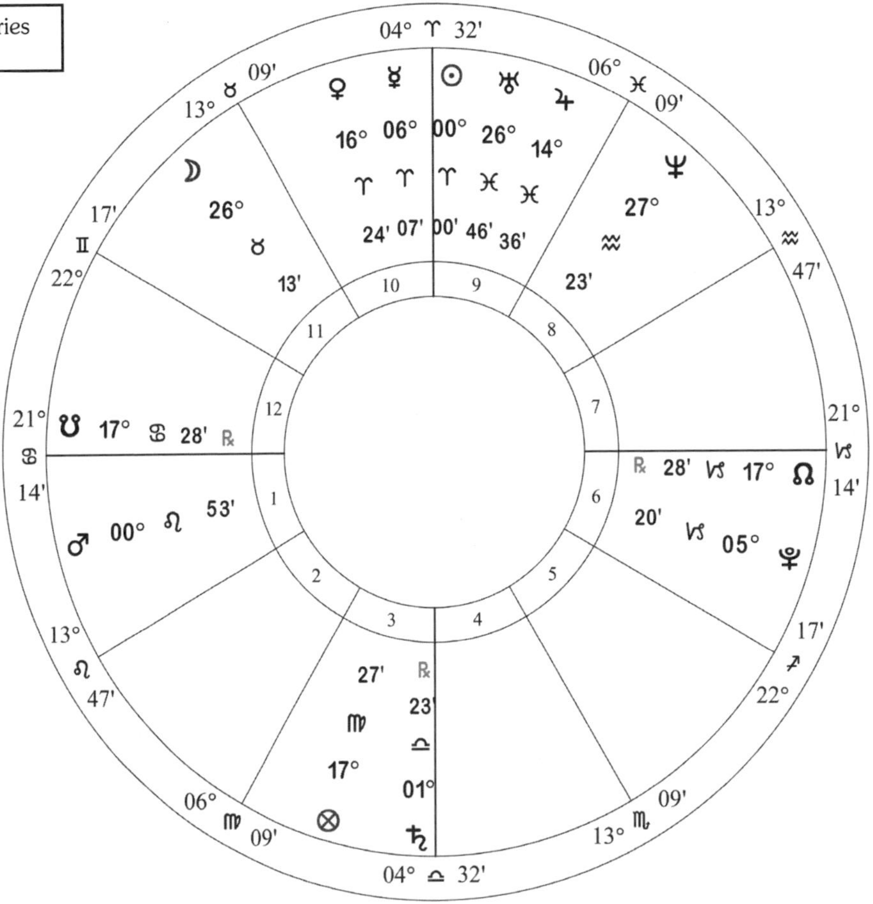

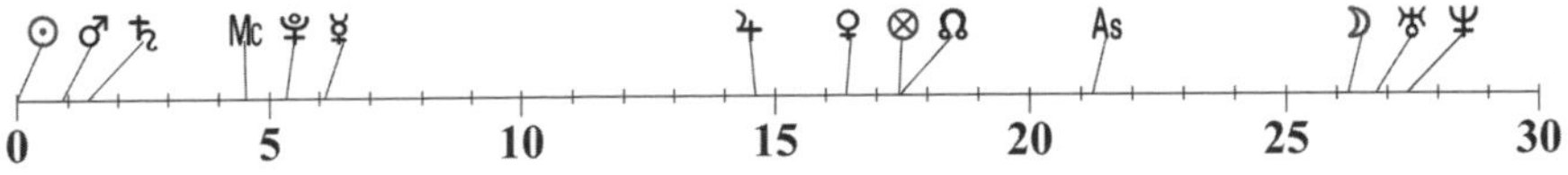

and drilling equipment at the time of the explosion and pipeline collapse. I would nominate Jupiter, as ruler of the 9th and in the 9th, because such a big deal has been made about BP being *British Petroleum*. The attitude of the CEO in the wake of the problem – the seeming cluelessness about how his yachting exploits would be perceived – makes Jupiter a good candidate. Jupiter is well dignified: and this makes sense, because BP is a *very* wealthy company – and all that's being proposed in terms of damages truly is trivial compared to their balance sheet. Jupiter opposite the Part of Fortune does seem to fit.

We have already examined charts for shipwrecks, and this event, Chart 69, can be considered a combination of shipwreck and explosion – something not unlike the sinking of the *Maine*. Returning to Lilly's model on this, we see that this time, the angular malefics are Saturn and Uranus, themselves in a doubly approaching opposition. The Ruler of the Ascendant is also the ruler of the 4th, and in the 4th, approaching Uranus, although Uranus reached Aries before Jupiter came to conjunction, making this a refranation. Jupiter did come to oppose Saturn, however.

According to Lilly's list, Cancer rules the bottom of the ship.[248] Lilly states that when Mars, Saturn, or the South Node is in Cancer, there is the danger of drowning or leaking. Here, the Moon and South Node are in the 8th in Cancer, and this part is sadly the signature for the people who died on the rig. He refers to the signs occupied by those three as the unfortunated signs. In that case, those signs are Cancer, Leo, and Virgo: one of those signs on the MC and unfortunated by Mars makes fire. Unlike the other shipwrecks we have examined, Mars is not so prominent here. The usual meaning Lilly gives for Saturn so prominent is theft of the cargo. Here, there wasn't a cargo – yet! Of this configuration, Lilly says:

If Saturn instead of Mars do denunciate Dammage, and be placed in the Mid-heaven, the Ship shall received prejudice by contrary Winds, and by leaks in the Ship, by rending or using of bad Sailes; and this misfortune shall be greater or lesser, according to the potency of the significator of that misfortune, and remoteness of the Fortunes.[249]

As I write this, the preliminary cause given for the accident was that drilling mud, which acts as a drag against leaks, was removed during the final stages of the drilling operation. This was evidently done as both a cost-savings and time-savings procedure, but high pressure had built up in the drilled shaft, pressure that overwhelmed what remained of the safety protocols, exacerbated by the fact that the alarms were turned off. The prominence of the sign earth in this chart is consistent with that explanation, now that we have established that this chart is actually fairly dangerous by Lilly's rules.

Stepping out of Lilly's immediate considerations for a minute, with that angular Saturn ruling the 2nd, and Pluto and the North Node there, one can immediately see how expensive this mistake will be.

Asia

So far, this book has been mainly centered on Western Europe and North America. If we are serious about One Earth, then we cannot presume that this zone speaks for the globe. It doesn't. This is even more true as the post-World War II era saw the emergence of two economic giants in Asia: China and Japan. Furthermore, India emerged as one of the most populous countries, and Korea developed an extremely impressive economy.

In fact, go to Asia now, and you will see an exuberance that followed the collapse of Communism in 1989 – or characterized

NATAL CHART
Deepwater horizon spill
April 20, 2010
9:45 PM
near New Orleans
28 N 44 88 W 23
Daylight Saving Time
Time Zone: 6 hours West
Tropical Regiomontanus

Day of ♂	Hour of ♂
Last Hr ♃	- 35 mins
Next Hr ☉	+20 mins

FIXED STARS	
☊☌Rukbat	0°59's
♀☌ Capulus	0°40's
☉☌Mirach	0°21's
☊☌Vega	0°20'a
⊗☌Zosma	0°53'a
☽☌ Pollux	0°54'a

Chart 69. Deepwater Horizon Spill

Hs	Alm. (Dor)
1	♃
2	♄
3	♄
4	♃
5	☉♂
6	☽♀
7	☿
8	☽
9	☉
10	☿
11	♀♄
12	♂

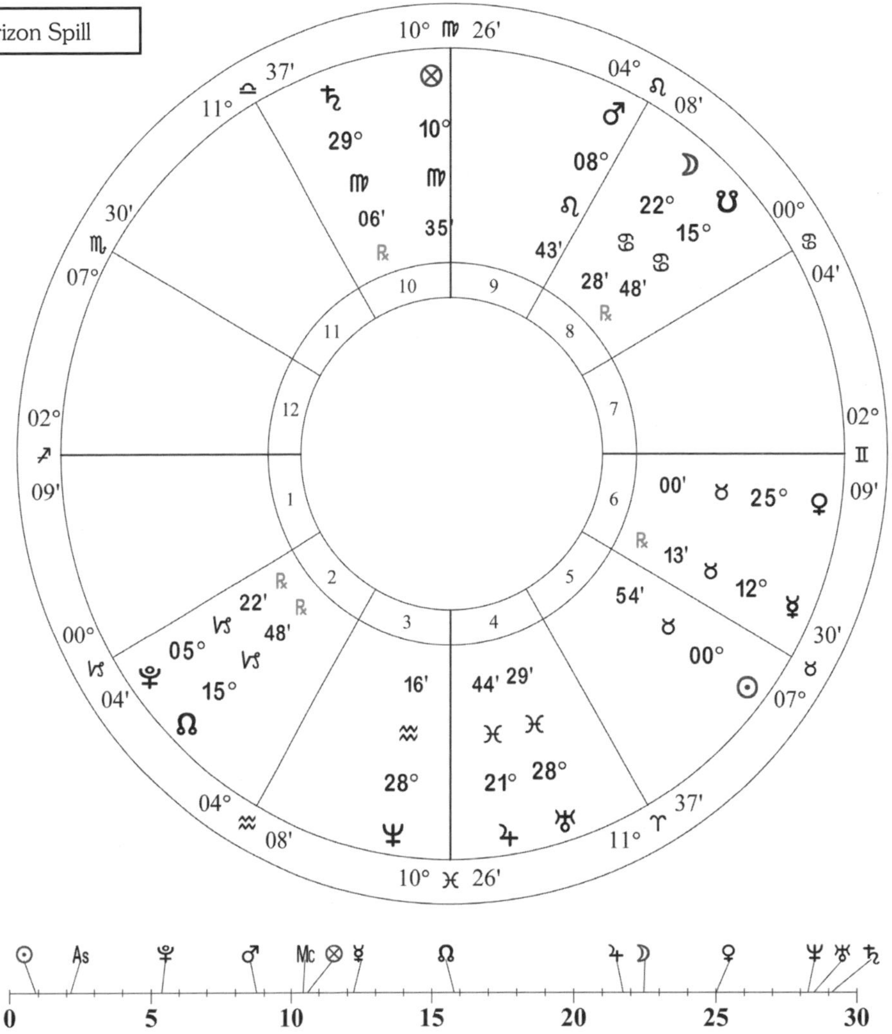

ESSENTIAL DIGNITIES (Dorothean)

Pl	Ruler	Exalt	Tripl	Term	Face	Detri	Fall	Score
☉	♀	☽	☽	♀	☿	♂	--	- 5 P
☽	☽ +	♃	♂	♀	☽ +	♄	♂	+6
☿	♀	☽	☽	☿ +	☽	♂	--	+2
♀	♀ +	☽	☽	♄	♄	♂	--	+5
♂	☉	--	♃ m	☿	♄	♄	--	- 5 P
♃	♃ +	♀	♂ m	☿	♂	☿	☿	+5
♄	☿	☿	☽	♂	☿	♃	♀	- 5 P
☊	♄	♂	☽	♃	♂	☽	♃	--
⊗	☿	☿	☽	♀	♀	♃	♀	--
As	♃	☋	♃	♃	☿	☿	--	--
Mc	☿	☿	☽	♀	♀	♃	♀	--
☋	☽	♃	♂	☿	☿	♄	♂	--

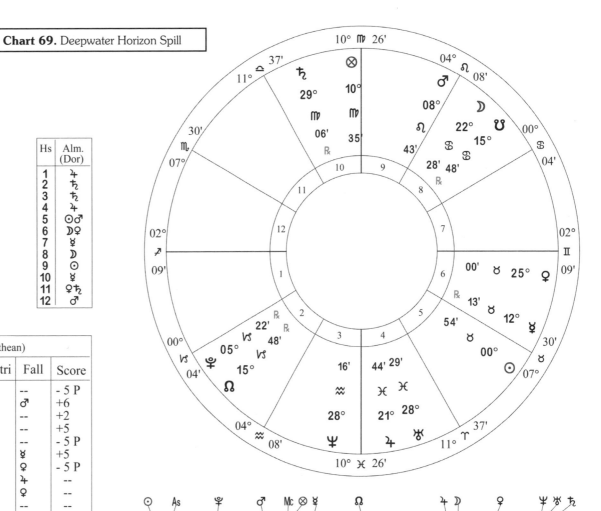

England or the United States in the 1920s. This enthusiasm is for the same reason. Here are the emerging economies of the 21st century, where manufacturing is still king. Emerging economies become dominant economies if they continue to successfully produce and compete. By contrast, much of the West slipped into extolling the benefits of the service economy in the latter half of the 20th century

After the death of Mao Tse Tung and his inner circle, the Chinese wanted to develop. They wanted, within slightly outdated parlance, to go from being a Third World Country to a First World one. But they had a problem: too many people. So they created a social contract with their people: if the people would adopt the One Child Policy, in turn, the government would create the infrastructure for economic development. Both sides have kept their end of the bargain. The One Child Policy has been estimated to have reduced the Chinese population by 250 million – that's the equivalent of the entire U.S. population twenty years ago! China has gone from being the world's most populous state to the second most populous – India is now the largest. More Chinese have access to education and consumer goods than ever before.

But there's still a problem – because, even with this massive shift, China still cannot find the resources on the planet to develop fully. It's been estimated that it would take the equivalent of 2 to 3 entire earth-sized planets to provide the resources for the entire world to develop to the level of the First World – and that's at today's level of population, which is still increasing. The Chinese were supposed to end the One Child Policy in about a decade. I don't need astrology to tell me that that won't happen.

As one indicator of this challenge: China's petroleum usage is increasing at 12% a year, in a global economy in which the mining of oil has been mostly stagnant since 1980.[250] Given that, despite increased price incentives, world oil mining has *not* increased. The conclusion is obvious: China can only increase her oil consumption at the expense of somebody else. And *everywhere* on the globe, increased population growth means *decreased* oil consumption per person. In a global economy such as ours, there is no rational way this will not result in both price increase, and eventually, a noticeable decrease in standard of living *unless* either huge increases in non-petroleum-based consumption occur, or a technological miracle occurs.

And yet – in the midst of this negative news, China is rushing ahead with more green projects than any other country. In the midst of massive pollution, they are converting their food supply toward, first low-level organic, and increasingly higher levels. They are developing wind energy. They are developing cleaner automobiles. They are caught in dual priorities: rapid development, and sustainable development. The two don't mix well.[251]

The Chinese have almost completed the deforestation of Southeast Asia. The reliance of Chinese development on township and village enterprises has vastly increased development, but this local control is also outside national control as far as contamination and pollution standards are concerned – much to the dismay of the world when first confronted with pet food contamination, and then dried milk contamination.

China, like a number of other countries, is running out of land for farming. Why? Like other developed or developing countries, they are losing farmland to urbanization or other land uses. And as population grows, both industrial and domestic water use cuts the availability of farm irrigation water. So China has joined Saudi Arabia, South Korea, Kuwait, Libya, India. Egypt, Jordan, the United Arab Emirates, and Qatar in either buying or leasing land in a series of poor countries, most of whom have hunger issues themselves.[252]

And as we move slowly toward Pluto in Aquarius (the Water Bearer), ecologists are already focusing on the observation that freshwater ecosystems are seeing much higher rates of biodiversity decline than other systems.[253] This consensus has been forming with Neptune in the Water Bearer! It's easy to say that Neptune has a delusion component, but I think we can make the case for it also having something to do with the fashions in ideas. Suddenly everybody believes the same thing – and nobody knows why. It's rather like trying to understand who made the hemlines go up or down. Right now, everybody in the business is starting to talk about water. We can anticipate that these issues will become yet more apparent as Neptune moves into Pisces, where it will be for most of the time before Pluto moves into the Water Bearer. In fact, with the progression of Neptune signs in this Pluto pass where Neptune anticipates Pluto, people are feeling the issues before they really become manifest.

The Triad of Passes

Now that we have completed our survey of three passes through the same Pluto signs, what can we conclude? Obviously, a huge difference between the 16th century pass and the one today is that ours is a more secular society. Yet it is fascinating to see how the same themes can resonate across nearly five hundred years.

Can the themes of the 16th century shed any light on the problems of sustainability that we must cope with today? That depends upon how you frame the issue. By the 16th century, there had certainly been enough instances of deforestation for people to be aware of the effects. The only policies that had been implemented in Europe were to restrict forest use (meaning gathering firewood or cutting trees) by the *poor*. Part of the effect of colonization was to relieve population pressure. Jared Diamond made the same argument for the Norse centuries earlier – that when the good estates are occupied, there has to be a place for second (and third and fourth) sons to go. It is doubtful that contemporaries viewed it so much as overpopulation, as an inheritance issue, and an economic opportunity. There is no evidence that there was the slightest perception that any of these matters was anything other than an inconvenience, certainly not a threat to civilization.

One is hard pressed to see any sense of limitation at all in any of the cultural activities of Europeans of this time period. One could make an excellent case for the reverse having been true: that this was a period where the *Zeitgeist* was precisely that there *were* no limits. Is the modern experience of limitation the opposite side of the coin? It would seem to be axiomatic that one has to explore one's territory before one discovers limits.

Since the 19th century historians adopted the polemics of the Renaissance in describing the Middle Ages, there tends to be an excessive devaluation of the earlier era's accomplishments. Gradually through the Middle Ages, windmill and water wheel technology, and a host of other technologies gradually improved. All of these technological innovations led to greater exploitation of the land – whether because superior plows opened up new areas to cultivation, or as deforestation proceeded. Deforestation was an inevitable process, as long as wood was the major fuel for fires and heating. By 1560-1600, the industrial revolution itself was driving the market to coal by its rapid deforestation. With Pluto being in Pisces until 1577, we see that the industrial revolution began with Pluto in Pisces, then continuing (and accelerating) with Pluto in Aries – rather like our picture of the first half of the 19th century *So even almost five hundred years ago, the same clash of priorities was playing out that we see today.*

Earth, Air, Fire, Water – soil erosion, air pollution, fossil fuel consumption, and water pollution. In our current era, the Four Horsemen of the Apocalypse wear different clothing. Five hundred years ago, Europeans were just coming to grips with the concept that animals were not there merely to serve man. Can we now truly understand the same for the Earth?

In introductory astronomy books, the authors often like to illustrate the universe showing orders of magnitude: the very small and the very large. This serves the debunking polemic of denying astrology, since our solar system is such a paltry average thing at the periphery of an average galaxy. The thing is – our very consciousness always puts us at the center, no matter how much we try to understand the very big and the very small. Can we come to understand that we are wired to see the world from a human perspective, and that this need not imply that *we* are all that matters? Can we learn that true civilization means that we must think in a multi-generational mode, and not use up that which will allow our children, grandchildren, and generation to come, a decent standard of living? Time will tell.

Endnotes: Chapter 8

212. See Harvey in Baigent, Campion and Harvey, pp 182-183 for a description of this cycle. Harvey specifically singles out André Barbault for first equating Communism to the Saturn-Neptune cycle.

213. Harvey, Charles. *Anima Mundi : The Astrology of the Individual and the Collective.* CPA Seminar Series. London: Centre for Psychological Astrology Press, 2002, p 134.

214. If the idea of genocide sounds new to you, I suggest you consult Loewen, James W. *Lies My Teacher Told Me : Everything Your American History Textbook Got Wrong.* New York; London: New Press ; Turnaround [distributor], 2008. This work systematically critiques the complete misrepresentation of American history in high school textbooks.

215. Menocal, Maria Rosa. *The Ornament of the World : How Muslims, Jews, and Christians Created a Culture of Tolerance in Medieval Spain.* 1st Back Bay paperback ed. Boston: Little, Brown, 2002.

216. Thomas, Keith. *Man and the Natural World : Changing Attitudes in England 1500- 1800.* 1983. London: Penguin Books, 1984.

217. Thomas, 1984, pp 30-31.

218. Thomas, 1984, p 29.

219. Thomas, 1984, p 26.

220. Thomas, 1984, p 49.

221. Thomas, 1984, pp 51-70.

222. Lehman, J. Lee. *Essential Dignities.* Atglen, PA: Schiffer Press, 1989, pp 67-93.

223. Thomas, 1984, p 65.

224. Thomas, pp 105-110.

225. Thomas, p 121.

226. Thomas, pp 193-197.

227. Lilly, p 115.

228. American readers may be somewhat shocked with my language, having become accustomed through their history books to regard people like Columbus as heroes. This is a sad reflection of the level of propaganda perpetrated on children to protect a country's self-image. While the slavery of Black Americans is now treated more fairly, there is a tendency to skip over the atrocities of the colonial period. For more information on this, please see: Loewen, 2008.

229. For a history of slavery, see Meltzer, Milton. *Slavery : A World History.* 1st Da Capo Press ed. New York: Da Capo, 1993.

230. Luther, Martin. *Three Treatises*. Philadelphia: Fortress Press, 1970, p iv.

231. Thomas, pp 223-224.

232. For a discussion of the tulip craze from a later period, but a good source to explain how plants have been viewed in various times, see Pollan, 2003.

233. Thomas, 1984, p. 39.

234. Thomas, 1984, p 45.

235. Thomas, 1984, p 170.

236. Thomas, 1984, p 168.

237. Gould, Stephen Jay. *Rocks of Ages : Science and Religion in the Fullness of Life*. The Library of Contemporary Thought. 1st ed. New York: Ballantine Pub. Group, 1999.

238. Thomas, p 243.

239. Thomas, p 260.

240. Arendt, Hannah. *On Revolution*. New York: Viking Press, 1963.

241. Rousseau, Jean-Jacques. *The Social Contract*. Washington, D.C.: Regnery Pub., 2009.

242. See Wilson, A. N. *God's Funeral*. 1st American ed. New York: W.W. Norton, 1999.

243. For a good discussion of this history see Porter, Theodore M. *The Rise of Statistical Thinking, 1820-1900*. Princeton, N.J.: Princeton University Press, 1986, pp 23-33..

244. Thomas, 1984, p 297.

245. Proverbs 16:18.

246. *www.historicspacecraft.com/quotes.html*

247. Lilly, CA, p 130.

248. Lilly, p 158.

249. Lilly, page 160.

250. Austravicius, Petra and John Boozman. China's Development Challenge. NATO Parliamentary Assembly Committee Reports. *www.nato-pa.int/default. asp?SHORTCUT=1001*, 2006. Also see *www.hubbertpeak.com* and the Energy Watch Group, *www.energywatchgroup.org*.

251. An excellent appraisal of how these priorities are working in practice can be found in: Ho and Vermeer, 2006.

252. Brown, 2009, p 10.

253. Vaughn, Caryn C. "Biodiversity Losses and Ecosystem Function in Freshwaters: Emerging Conclusions and Research Directions." *Bioscience* 60.1 (2010): 25-35.

9

Summary, Suggestions and Conclusions

That's a pretty thin hope.
I've never known Hope when it wasn't on a diet.
—Babylon 5, *The Lost Tales*

Now that we have gotten this far, I want to return to the time period of Chapter 8, and examine another way to view these three periods together by using the cyclic analysis discussed by Harvey in *Mundane Astrology*.[254] Modern astrologers have reasserted the importance of cyclic analysis, again stressing the importance of the conjunctions. It's just that in the modern context, there are so many more of them!

In Chapter 1, I briefly presented the Mars-Jupiter and Mars-Saturn cycles, but then we mostly dropped that material out of our discussion, because the periods of these two planets are so short compared to the Pluto sign ingresses we have been discussing throughout this book. At this stage, I would suggest that we drop three of the four Jupiter conjunction cycles out too for exactly the same reason. Harvey gives all ten outer planet cycle lengths on p. 177 of *Mundane Astrology*. These three Jupiter cycles are:

Jupiter-Uranus:	14 years
Jupiter-Neptune:	13 years
Jupiter-Pluto:	12 years

The reason these periods are so short is that a synodic cycle measures the time it takes two bodies to come back to conjunction. When there is a huge discrepancy between the two orbits, the cycle length will begin to approximate the synodic period of the faster body. Thus, when Jupiter and Saturn combine to get twenty years for their synodic cycle, this really does look like the "midpoint" between Jupiter's cycle of 12 years and Saturn's of 29. But Uranus has 84 years, and this is already so much longer than Jupiter's cycle, that the combined cycle time is scarcely one year longer than Jupiter's cycle by itself! Then when you combine Jupiter with Neptune and Pluto, with their centuries long cycles, the result gets increasingly short. These Pluto sign ingresses run 13-16 years for Sagittarius, and increasingly more for the other three signs. Accordingly, we can drop out the three shortened Jupiter cycles using the logic that there will *always* be a conjunction of each of these three combinations under a given Pluto sign. This, by the way, is why I have so seldom mentioned Jupiter, except where it specifically relates to an Ingress interpretation. In any given Pluto sign, Jupiter will appear in all twelve of its signs. It is the fact that Uranus and Neptune *don't* go through all the signs under one Pluto sign that makes each Pluto ingress different. The fact that Neptune shares certain sign combinations with Pluto repeatedly is what makes these combinations so interesting.

The outer planet conjunctions within each Pluto sign for Sagittarius through Pisces are shown in Table 9-1. This table allows us to evaluate these three periods in yet another way. The theory of examining the superior planet conjunctions is that they represent beginnings, going right back to all the discussion on the Jupiter-Saturn cycle in Chapter 1. The other three hard aspects (opening square, opposition and closing square) represent crisis points in the cycle – where an existing cycle may change course. The presumption is: a new cycle is – *new*! A hard aspect within an existing cycle means that the reaction is to something existing. This is not to say that crisis points are not difficult: there's no question that some may be. But people are not really looking for new solutions, even if they are presented with novel situations. Let's take the information in this table and recontextualize it with the information we have already covered in Chapter 8.

	PL in SG	PL in CP	PL in AQ	PL in PI
1st Pass	1500-1516	1516-1532	1532-1550	1550-1572
	Ju cj Sa (1504)	Sa cj Pl (1518)	Sa cj Ur (1533	Sa cj Pl (1552)
		Sa cj Ne (1523)	Ju cj Sa (1544)	Ju cj Sa (1563)
		Ju cj Sa (1524)		
2nd Pass	1748-1762	1762-1777	1777-1797	1797-1822
	Sa cj Pl (1750)	Ju cj Sa (1762)	Ju cj Sa (1782)	Sa cj Ur (1805)
	Sa cj Ur (1761)	Sa cj Ne (1773)	Sa cj Pl (1786)	Sa cj Ne (1809)
				Sa cj Pl (1819)
				Ur cj Ne (1820)
				Ju cj Sa (1821)
Current Pass	1995-2008	2008-2023	2023-2043	2043-2066
	Ju cj Sa (2000)	Sa cj Pl (2020)	Sa cj Ne (2026)	Sa cj Pl (2053)
		Ju cj Sa (2020)	Ju cj Sa (2040)	Ju cj Sa (2060)
				Sa cj Ne (2061)

Table 9-1. Major conjunctions from Saturn out and Jupiter-Saturn conjunctions within the period of Pluto in Sagittarius – Pisces, three passes given in Chapter 8. Years given are for the first pass of the conjunction, if there was more than one, unless a conjunction overlaps two Pluto signs. In each Pluto sign, the other three conjunctions between Jupiter and the other outer planets will always occur.

Pass One by Major Conjunctions 1500-1572

Despite the expectation we might have that the discovery of the New World was a profound new experience, Table 9-1 suggests that it wasn't. Only the Jupiter-Saturn conjunction occurred during the Pluto in Sagittarius period when Spain and Portugal were at the height of their New World exploration/exploitation. Since the Greeks, all educated people in Europe already knew that the world was round, so the ability to reach the East by sailing West was no profound discovery. Spain wasn't learning anything new in the New World. We commented earlier (and not based on this analysis) on how Spain's encounter with the New World didn't seem to raise an intellectual hair, as far as new ways of thinking were concerned. It raised no theological or philosophical insights. Francis Bacon would call for new ways of compiling research on the New World – but this was initially based on the need to process more information, not ways to understand it differently.

Pluto in Capricorn does present a new front, with both Saturn-Pluto and Saturn-Neptune cycles restarting while the debates that led to the Protestant split were occurring. Harvey notes that the Saturn-Neptune has overtones relating both to democracy and to spirituality.[255] He did not cover this pass in his discussion, but this would seem true here. Luther's appeal to the German princes was to achieve control over their own domains, thereby increasing democracy among princes, if not among subjects. Harvey called Saturn-Pluto a time for "...*emerging nations and very deep cultural transformations, purgations and 'resurrections.'*"[256] The whole theme of the emergence of the German princes seems palpably evident. We saw in Chapter 8 exactly how explosive the Aries Ingresses were during this period of time. Now we can add the change in cycles of these two outer planet pairs to further demarcate why Luther succeeded in reforming the Church when those before him had not. Change was in the winds from multiple directions.

When we examine Pluto in Aquarius, we see the conjunction of Saturn-Uranus. Harvey pointed to the work of André Barbault, who had studied the period from 1625 forward (*i.e., after* this period), and from which Barbault concluded that this cycle is right-wing, conservative, and imperialistic. In our examination of this period in the last chapter, we found it to be a period of consolidation. One might add here that, since Protestantism had already begun before this cycle started, it was "fixed" during this phase. It is interesting that Henry VIII, who only created the Church of England during the time of Pluto in Aquarius, did not repeat the more radical approach of Luther and Calvin.

Just as Pluto moved into Pisces, there was a Saturn-Pluto conjunction – the very next cycle after the one that had marked Luther's objections. It is at this phase that the religious wars began. We have already mentioned the violent tendencies of this synodic cycle in relation to World Trade Center bombings in the U.S.A. And this is interesting that it should occur in the *next* cycle, not the same cycle. Saturn in the 1518 conjunction was dignified: Saturn in the 1552 one was not. Without dignity, the worst of the prejudicial tendencies of this planet occurred.

Pass Two by Major Conjunctions, 1748-1822

Pluto in Sagittarius in the next pass was more active than in our first pass, featuring the Saturn-Uranus conjunction (1761-1762).

We have seen that this was essentially a conservative cycle. This conjunction occurred during the War of the Austrian Succession, a rather pointless war that ended primarily in a stalemate. Nothing was seriously challenged at this time.

Pluto in Capricorn had the Saturn-Neptune (1773). Here, the theme is democracy in the Colonies. This was the build-up to the American Revolution.

During Pluto in Aquarius, there is the same conjunction of Saturn and Pluto which marked Luther's rebellion as well as the later religious warfare. Already, we can see why the French Revolution was scarier to the Europeans than the American one.

During this pass, it was Pluto in Pisces that had the largest number of conjunctions, not Pluto in Capricorn, as with the earlier pass. Pluto in Pisces had Saturn-Uranus (1805), Saturn-Neptune (1809), Saturn-Pluto (1819), and Uranus-Neptune (1820). We have seen that Saturn-Uranus is conservative: in 1804, Napoleon had declared himself Emperor, after first rising as a general of the French Revolution, then declaring himself Consul. Shall we classify this shift to a monarchy as reactionary on his part? The time of the Saturn-Neptune was a depression in the U.S.A., economic downturn being another common effect of this conjunction, although not one mentioned by Harvey. Saturn-Pluto was our Luther aspect, and here we have the New World Order of Metternich, which lasted for most of the century. Then we have the Uranus-Neptune, which Harvey discussed as possibly relating to changes in either religious, socio-economic, or belief systems.[257] So we see that, whereas it was the Pluto in Capricorn part of the first pass that had the most significant outer planet conjunction activity, in the second pass, it was the Pluto in Pisces stage. In each pass, the Pluto sign with the largest number of outer planet conjunctions does seem to represent the focus of that period.

Pass Three by Major Conjunctions 1995-2066

In our third pass, we can see qualities of both of the last two, from which we can derive the theory that we will experience some qualities of each. Where this pass resembles the 15th century pass is that both Pluto in Capricorn and Pluto in Pisces experience the Saturn-Pluto conjunction – in 2020, and in 2053-2054. But like the U.S./French Revolutionary pass, the major period of outer planet conjunctions occurs in the Pluto in Pisces stage.

But back to that Saturn-Pluto: the radical idea occurs toward the end of the Pluto in Capricorn stage, not the beginning as with Luther. What does this mean? There is no question that there was a big bump that occurred when Pluto went into Capricorn in 2008. However, watching various governments attempt to deal with the economic crisis shows that the world governments are seeing the problems as incremental. In other words, they are acting as if nothing extraordinary happened when Pluto went into Capricorn that cannot be fixed by the usual means. They are waiting for business to get back to *normal*, back to Pluto in Sagittarius, but without the derivatives bubble and the mortgage bubble. They are Pope Leo X, still thinking he can go to the well one more time.

This actually tracks with what a number of astrologers are saying – but not exactly. There has been a tendency to get caught in all the hard aspects of the outer planets in 2010-2012 without fully noticing that there are no conjunctions except for the relatively frequent Jupiter-Pluto. This is not a time when people can really break out of the box: they are still reacting to what has already occurred, rather than striking out in a new direction. They are waiting for a normality which the Pluto in Capricorn should tell us cannot return. It will take until 2020 when the new series of *conjunctions* allows them to finally grasp that a new era has dawned.

This does not mean universal and constant misery until 2020, though. But it does mean that nothing is fundamentally repaired – and that one cannot act as if things will return to what they were.

Look at the rhetoric of politics. When people talk about a *return* to some mystical period of the past when things were better, they may be at a crisis point, but they are not embracing a conjunction. Hard aspects can bring awareness of something not working, but are people really willing to let go of what they have in order to grasp something new? The problem is that people mostly want to hold on to what they have and get more.

It's like what happens when people inherit a medium amount: not enough to make you feel rich, but enough to spend in more than one place. What do you do with it? Pay off the house, take a vacation, and buy a car. Now you have the same lifestyle, but somewhat better economically. Chances are, within a couple of years, nothing will seem any different.

Some fewer people may do some of the above, but will invest at least part of the money in something different that they wanted to do. Now, a few years later, there really are changes, because that something new has had a chance to sprout. This the conjunctional approach: setting forth in a new direction without knowing whether that direction will be successful or not.

Either way, life is experienced in part as having a drag from the road already taken. Whether at the personal or the governmental level, we are constantly cleaning up from decisions made in the past. The government gets into a war, and then finds it much easier to stay than to leave, as the war turns into a cesspool of conflicting interests, rather than a series of surgical strikes. A family still is recovering from buying a house just at the peak of real estate prices before a crash. Even when confronted with a new possibility like a sign change of an outer planet, how does one make time for it when there is so much stuff already going on?

Conjunctions, like sign ingresses, require a leap into the unknown, which includes unburdening some of the freight from one's existence as usual. Often, it's hard to figure out which is harder: the leap, or the unburdening.

The period of Pluto in Aquarius also only has one major outer planet conjunction: Saturn-Neptune in 2026. Again, an economic downturn is one possible reading of this aspect, but so is a change in democracy, or the symbolism of communism, which could relate to the balance between individuals and government in a particular society. This occurs just after Neptune has shifted into Aries, its typical pairing with Pluto in Aquarius. One specific thought relating to this in the U.S.A.: as of 2010, births of non-Caucasians now exceed births of Caucasians. By 2026, this trend may have become so obvious that there will be no choice but to have a new synthesis in the social fabric because of it. Pluto went into Capricorn in 2008 – but the outer planet conjunctions don't occur for another twelve years. 2026 is only two years after Pluto first enters Aquarius. There is much more time for the effect of the Saturn-Neptune to be felt before Pluto and Neptune change signs.

Finally we arrive at Pluto in Pisces in 2043 – the powerhouse of outer planet activity in this pass. This period is not so active as during the Revolutionary pass: it's a recapitulation of two prior outer planet conjunctions from the earlier phase of this four sign grouping: Saturn-Pluto (2053-2054), and Saturn-Neptune (2061). This means that both the challenges and syntheses of Pluto in Capricorn and Pluto in Aquarius are on the table once again.

The Current Pass and the Environment

Of late, the speculative environmental rhetoric has switched to talking about a so-called tipping point: that if we allow certain critical processes such as the release of greenhouse gases to exceed some magic number, the process of global warming will become irreversible. While there may be some truth in this statement, the problem is that it has the ring of Chicken Little to it: it sounds like a moral admonition as much or more than a scientific one.

In Europe, the connection between population and sustainability has been acknowledged, even as most European countries have dropped into negative population growth. The European Union has begun to incorporate green thinking and acting into its governmental activities much more consistently than the U.S.A. has.

It is the U.S.A. and many developing countries that have dragged their heels about population. In developing countries, one of the driving factors of population growth is a long-held view that children are the backbone to a farm economy. In the U.S.A., the reasons are more complex, but include religious objections, the sense that everyone has a "right" to have as many children as they can afford, and a outmoded belief by many economists that population growth is the basis for economic growth.

It may well be because of despair over these strongly held beliefs that many American environmentalists have issued the most extreme apocalyptic predictions about population growth and environmental decay and devastation. It is simply hard to envision an American turn-around on this issue. But I would respond that it was impossible to envision the birth drop in European countries in the 1960s and 1970s. People change their behavior when they feel motivated to do so.

As Ho and Vermeer point out, the tendency of the environmental movement to issue dire projections of societal collapse that then don't happen has severely damaged the prestige and credibility of the movement to those who might otherwise be inclined to take it more seriously.[258] I think their criticism is a completely valid one, because the simple fact is, no matter how much we may believe that a global collapse is imminent, we really have no certainty at all about an exact date. The environmental movement has sometimes needlessly looked like a doomsday cult, predicting the end of the world for next Tuesday, and then giving some feeble excuse when it doesn't happen.

Overpopulation

We are still faced with some basic facts. Unless a miracle occurs, the Earth is a ball of mineral and rock that has finite land area, limited water, limited atmosphere, limited minerals, and limited fossil fuels, no matter how vast the size of those resources may seem.

By this logic, there truly is a limit to human population and resource consumption. Once we can accept this premise, then we can see that the arguments are about how close we are to the realization that we need to worry about these facts.

There have been many societies that have faced either overpopulation or resource limitation in the past. But really, it's the same thing: too many people competing for too little of something – arable land, food, wood for fuel, pasture land. If the scarcity comes on quickly, and travel to a new viable location isn't feasible, people starve, and the entire population can die off. If the limitation comes on gradually, people may emigrate, and the population may decline until it is viable again within the changed environmental circumstances, or continued emigration can bring the population to zero. Or of course, the problem could have been temporary, as with a bad harvest, and then things go on as before.

It's hard to tally these past events, but it appears to me that emigration has generally been the solution of choice when a society has been threatened over a long enough period that a few good harvests can't solve the problem. Starvation isn't any victim's idea of a good solution.

But here's the problem. Where can you go? The world has been parceled out into discrete units: of countries, counties, cities, and private property. These different levels are defended. That means you have to buy your way to emigration, and that means you have to have resources left to sell in order to do it, unless you want to be a refugee in a camp, or a statistic in a squatter city, which is also nobody's ideal plan. Human density on this planet is now such that there aren't too many spots left that are unoccupied. Human migration in the past always depended on being able to find empty space *somewhere*. That's simply gone.

Which Issue goes with Which Pluto Sign?

I would frame the challenges of this time period with Pluto in Capricorn as follows. In addition to the usual suspects (religious, economic, and political conflict), we have issues that have resulted in the global lifestyle we created in the process of industrialization. These are problems that people either did not have to solve, or did not have to grapple with at this level of intensity before, including:

- The population of the globe has exceeded its carrying capacity without substantial energy inputs in the form of fossil fuel or nuclear energy. This is because we would be incapable of producing enough food even for our current population without mechanization. This sounds like Pluto in Capricorn from the agricultural side, and Pluto in Aries for the energy side.

- Fossil fuel is finite, although even the most pessimistic estimates on coal suggest centuries of supply. Fuel is metaphorically fire, so this is a Pluto in Aries topic too.

- Nuclear energy produces toxic waste products that, despite over a century of working with radioactivity, we still don't know how to dispose of safely and permanently. The waste side of this is Pluto in Capricorn, since we've tried to solve the problem by burying the radioactive waste.

- One of the most invisible environmental issues has been the massive increase in the usage of groundwater pumped from underground reservoirs. It was estimated in 2009 that nearly all global groundwater reservoirs were being overpumped.[259] Many of these reservoirs may dry up in the next few decades. Without pumpable groundwater, agriculture immediately reverts to only what is sustainable by rainfall alone, which would represent a substantial and virtually instantaneous catastrophic decline in productivity. I am betting on this being a major problem by Pluto in Pisces, if not Pluto in Aquarius. After all, the "Water Bearer" sounds awfully metaphoric for pipelines, doesn't it?

- Agricultural productivity increases have been declining. Genetic modification, quite apart from environmental concerns, was supposed to be the next great increase in productivity – and it hasn't been. This one sounds like a Pluto in Capricorn issue, doesn't it?

- Pollution, which continues to increase, impacts both agricultural productivity and human health. The air pollution has the potential to be a problem with Pluto in Aquarius. Water pollution can wait for Pluto in Pisces. Land pollution, though, is Capricorn.

- Production of biofuels has so far served mainly to increase the price of food, because biofuel and food have been in direct competition on a market level. This is probably another agenda item for Capricorn, because of the unfortunate choice that is being presented between food and fuel.

- The Third World wants to develop, which means achieving the lifestyle of the developed world. As I mentioned with regard to China in Chapter 8, there aren't the resources on the Earth for this to happen, so something will have to give. I expect it to give during Pluto in Capricorn, because this is first and foremost a material issue.

Until 2043, we will be experiencing Pluto in a Saturn-ruled sign. It is the easiest prediction in the world to say that it is under Saturn's rulership that we as an Earth will have to come to grips with the fact that we have no more places to hide or run. We will as a total species have to do something we have never done before: consciously decide where and how to limit ourselves. Frankly, this is going to be a very bitter discovery, and human nature dictates that people and politicians will stay in denial as long as they can, so the means will become more draconian than they would need to be otherwise.

All of the signs are with us now, and astrologers are one of the groups of people trained at reading signs. In 2010, China became the largest oil *consumer*, surpassing the U.S.A. There isn't even a ghost of a chance this trend is likely to change anytime soon.

U.S. economic policy, at least in its aspects that are paraded out for the general public, has always assumed that our economy stops at our national boundaries, rather like a lot of weather maps. In fact, this hasn't been true for years. But T-shirts saying "What is Our Oil doing Under Your Sand?" are both silly and dangerous.

Peak Oil

Besides, it is entirely possible that what has been styled the Great Recession may have been caused by oil prices, not home mortgages – in which case, we are back to the resource issues that we have been discussing throughout this book. Jeff Rubin, who has not only followed the oil industry, but made correct predictions relating to the issue of peak oil, has presented evidence that it was the increase in oil prices past $100 per barrel that sparked the recession – not the housing market and derivatives.[260] If he is correct, then this recession will be longer than the other ones he believes were caused by oil: in 1973-1974, and 1979-1982.

Is this plausible? As astrologers, we can use what we have studied so far to try to find out. I have shown the Aries Ingress charts for 1973, 1979 and 2008, Chart 70. While the charts are done for Washington, that fact may be at least partially arbitrary, since the U.S.A. was hardly the only country impacted by these petroleum prices and recessions.

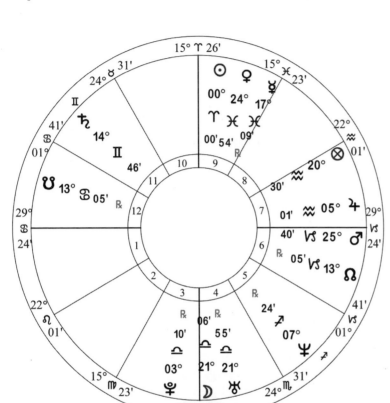

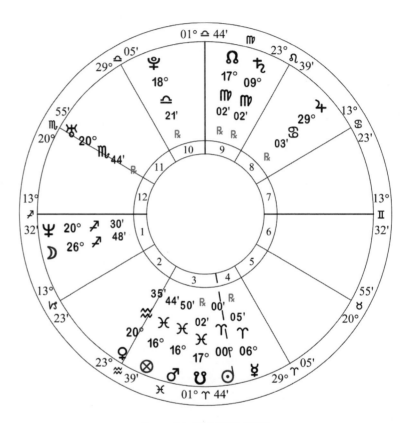

Sun enters Ari 3-20-1973
March 20, 1973
1:12:28 PM
Washington, D.C.
38N53'42" 77W02'12"
Standard Time
Time Zone: 5 hours West
Tropical Regiomontanus
NATAL CHART

Sun enters Ari 3-21-1979
March 21, 1979
12:21:57 AM
Washington, D.C.
38N53'42" 77W02'12"
Standard Time
Time Zone: 5 hours West
Tropical Regiomontanus
NATAL CHART

Chart 70. Aries Ingress 1973, 1979, and 2008, Washington, DC

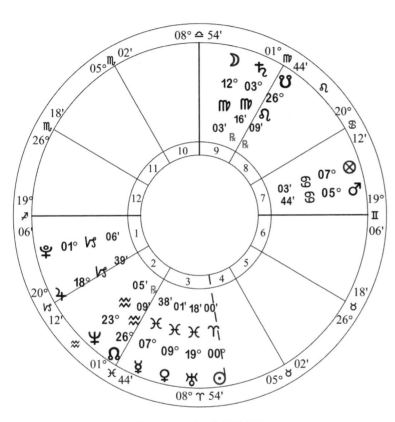

Sun enters Ari 3-20-2008
March 20, 2008
1:48:18 AM
Washington, D.C.
38N53'42" 77W02'12"
Daylight Saving Time
Time Zone: 5 hours West
Tropical Regiomontanus
NATAL CHART

In each case, we have yet more reminders of the Mars-Pluto co-rulership of petroleum that we have already discussed. In 1973, we observe the partile conjunction of Moon and Uranus, with the Moon coming to square Mars – a telling signature for a "new" phenomenon, namely oil-based global recession.

In 1979, Mars happened to be conjunct the Part of Fortune in Washington, but it was also conjunct the South Node, and approaching the square to Neptune. In 2008, Mars had just departed from opposing Pluto, with the Sun going to square both of them.

And yet, there is almost no mention of petroleum prices as a causative factor of the recession – let alone as *the* causative factor. We will know soon if Rubin's theory is correct. His theory makes the following assumptions and predictions:

• Oil "production" (remember: mining of a finite resource?) has leveled off, despite periods of considerable demand. Using conventional economic theory, increased demand should result in increased supply. Since this hasn't happened, Rubin concludes that there is no more "easy" oil.

• Rubin presents data to show that most of the Middle East producers have vastly increased their own internal petroleum consumption for such matters as desalinization of water, which is hugely energy-intensive. Desalinization is so energy-intensive that it is unlikely to ever be a serious contender for reversing water shortages. However, this internal use of petroleum reduces the amount of oil the OPEC countries are willing to sell.

- While at first, one would assume that the price of oil would permanently rise because of shortages – this isn't true. When supply becomes too scarce or too expensive, people find ways to conserve, which then drops demand, and then price drops. When this triggers a recession, the drop is especially acute. What Rubin is predicting is permanent volatility of oil price, not the stable prices that allowed for the development of the global economy over the last fifty years.

- By his model, we are looking at a decade of such economic volatility, at least – and most likely, when the current recession begins to ease, it will trigger another price spiral of oil, which will then send the world back into recession. Notice that Rubin's decade of volatility would take us to the 2020 conjunctions.

However, by the end of that decade, it should be pretty clear that there is less available oil. In other words, oil production is past peak, but Pluto in Capricorn will illustrate it.

Is Pluto in Saturn's Signs our New Social Contract?

In the modern era, psychological astrologers have discussed the significance of the first Saturn return as a point when the individual finally settles into her or his body. Astrologically, it's a rite of passage that marks the Native's acceptance of the "contract" with this life. Parenthetically, it explains what appears to be a peak of mortality that coincides with the combination of progressed lunar return and the Saturn Return. Our existence in the material world may be something that people interested in spirituality may see as a bit base – but material existence sure seems to be part of that contract. Could it be that this long period of Pluto in Saturn's signs marks the renewal of the "corporate" contract: our species being stripped back to the essence of material existence before we can again embark on the journeys that so characterize what it means to be human?

It is only since the Enlightenment – that intellectual child of the last period of Pluto in Saturn's signs – that the West has attempted to "solve" its existential problems in a secular fashion. For it was in the still previous passage of Pluto through Saturn's signs that the Western myth of universal Christianity shattered, challenging Western peoples to seek solutions in another way.

What has remained through these two great transitions was that archaic admonition: be fruitful and multiply. Is this a command for all time – or was this simply a good idea *at* the time? And if modern biblical scholars like Ellen Davis can experiment with phrases like "artful mastery" to replace "dominion," then it truly is time to posit that this re-think may well be part of the paradigm for our age.[261]

As astrologers, perhaps we need to re-vision the cycle. Linear thinking assumes that growth can be infinite. Cyclic thinking knows that what comes up, later comes down. Linear thinking is at the core of the Enlightenment – the kind of "rationality" that destroys wetlands because waterfowl habitat has no economic value. Linear thinking believes that economies can grow indefinitely – except, perhaps for occasional hiccups. Cyclic thinking allows us to envision waxing and waning – breathing in, breathing out – and right now, as a species, we need to wane quite a bit!

The typical human tendency is for the waning portion of a cycle to be experienced as a catastrophe, whether through disease or war.

The Chinese have managed to pull off one of the first voluntary population reductions in history. However, their determination to full development results in economic policies which are producing devastation for their own population, as well as the entire globe.

But we can hardly be smug. U.S. economists and others are still acting as if the U.S. population can continue to grow indefinitely. Can the so-called Developed World join the Chinese in their demographic policy, but add still greater environmental awareness? That's not as far-fetched as it sounds. Most of Europe is inching toward an average of 1 child per family voluntarily. It's the United States that's the big question at this point. While our average number of children per family has decreased, it hasn't decreased enough. Our laws remain pro-natalist.

This will be a very difficult struggle, because it runs up against religious beliefs that many people hold sincerely. I believe there is still the possibility that time has not run out for us. The clock is ticking. Now, the world population is 6.8 billion. Still, that 6.8 billion is about half of what the 1970 projected estimates of world population would be in 2010. That is an extremely hopeful sign, although still not enough in the long run.

The pattern is that the period of Pluto in Pisces has tended toward large-scale warfare. If we have not made substantial progress on our environmental challenges by then, the outcome could be grim.

The Meaning of the Outer Planets in Our Lives

Our esoteric colleagues have spoken often about the increase in consciousness implied by the discovery of the outer planets. Let us hope that they are not only right about this, but that this greater consciousness will allow a great enough cohort of world citizens to keep the focus on these issues. Therein lies our greatest hope.

To this point, I haven't said much about what I think of the consciousness-enhancing theory of the outer planets: or even about the scheme into which the outer planets should fit. Here's my personal take. Until the early modern era (*i.e.*, the Renaissance, or roughly 1500), the primary unit of humanity was the tribe: different from our closest primate ancestors in form somewhat, and certainly in technology. These enhancements allowed tribes to ally themselves into feudal units, based on many of the same kinds of glue as tribes. The inability to have rapid and complete mixing over vast distances prevented the formation of a strong state, leaving smaller units still the primary social unit. This is the boundary of Saturn. Mythologically, we see this in the *Lord of the Rings*, when Sam remarks that he has never traveled beyond a certain point in the Shire, and that, crossing that boundary, he is proceeding into the unknown. This is the challenge of Uranus: breaking out of one's normal patterns of reality. Tolkien also portrayed this in *The Hobbit*, when Bilbo was called to his great adventure by Gandalf.

The Aries Ingress, or any other chart, interpreted rigorously classically, meaning without the outer planets, works perfectly fine for our levels of reality that exist within the Saturn boundary. What has happened since the Early Modern Period is that our technological improvements in travel and communication broke down the boundaries that kept people who lived further apart from being able to mingle, almost at will. Travel over vast distances did occur – but the average person probably didn't go much beyond the neighboring village. Sam's trepidation at crossing into the unknown illustrates perfectly the traditional suspicion that "out there" is dangerous.

And yet these voyages of discovery did occur. Trading routes over thousands of miles developed. Ideas percolated from region to region, as we are well aware with astrology, with the mixing of Hellenistic and Vedic ideas, for example. There were people like al-Biruni who clearly enjoyed traveling over great distances, and talking to strangers from distant lands. Curiosity is not a new human trait.

Improvements in ship building and design in the Early Modern Period sent Europeans on vast voyages of discovery – and the world grew smaller. A number of scholars have noted that Chinese ships – vastly superior technologically to the Medieval European fleet – could have engaged in exploration: *they simply didn't want to*. The European Renaissance ignited the desire to see what was out there – the same call that kept millions of *Star Trek* fans engaged in that fictional voyage of discovery.

This stepping out into the unknown – the focal issue for Uranus – is only so monumental as the choices made by people who step out. We have seen these times of stress: in the 1840s and 1960s with the Uranus-Pluto conjunction, when the world seemed to crack and be on the verge of a new era: and yet, once the stress was released, life went mostly back to the same old ways. Uranus doesn't guarantee change, it only presents the possibility.

Beyond Uranus is Neptune. Here, the issue is even more subversive, because Neptune dissolves dichotomies, as well as other boundaries. The world of Saturn requires that we think in dichotomies, because they have survival value. Neptune takes these easy choices away.

I think the modern astrological understanding of Pluto isn't quite correct, because it developed viewing Pluto as a single body, not a representative – and I would argue, emissary, of the Plutinos. Lacking the understanding of the context, ideas on the meaning of Pluto in isolation don't quite work.

As we have started to become acquainted with other members of the Plutino group, the meanings that have been proposed so far fit into the very old category of deities known as chthonic. These energies and archetypes are timeless more than old, beyond the bounds of individuality and reason, imperatives that we can barely attempt to understand, much less control. I believe it is precisely the fact that Pluto's orbit takes it inside the orbit of Neptune that gives us some small chance to understand at least a piece of its message, and that inner orbit, along with its close harmonic relationship with Neptune, allows it a louder voice than other Plutinos.

The image for the stepping down of their energy to our level of existence is a conduit. When Reiki masters speak of being a conduit to healing energy, they may not be speaking to the Plutinos, but the image holds. As a conduit to Plutino energy, we are principally acting beyond our own egos, whether we recognize this or not.

In a number of different story arcs by different sci fi authors, a common theme emerges: until sentient life on a planet can evolve to a certain level of societal and technical proficiency, they are uninteresting to the rest of the sentient life of the galaxy. This is where we find ourselves with Uranus, Neptune, Pluto, and beyond – until we can form stable units past the tribe, these energies have no meaning for us. They *will* operate, but beyond the realm of human knowledge and understanding, much less control.

The Challenge of Pluto in Capricorn – and Beyond

Since the 18th century, we have been given a dangerous gift: the gift of knowledge and the glimmer of potential understanding. Uranus was discovered in 1781, when Pluto was in Aquarius and

Neptune was in Libra. We have also been given a task: to learn how to make decisions as a much larger collective than ever before. As we go toward the first Pluto return of that gift, we are being challenged to voluntarily limit ourselves for the greater good, not to mention, the ultimate survival of our species at a cultural level beyond the Medieval.

I am hopeful, even if Hope is slim and always on a diet. When I was growing up, the kids of farmers were ridiculed as hicks by the townies. As the U.S. population had shifted from rural to urban, this sort of devaluation of traditional lifestyles becomes commonplace. Now, fifty years later, I find myself going to farmers' markets, supporting community agriculture, growing some of my own food again, and enjoying knowing the farmers who grow my food. Times change. Values change.

If we as astrologers can break our mundane astrology away from merely the prediction of the next war or assassination, to examining our priorities on Spaceship Earth, we will have accomplished a great deal. In order to do this, we will have to exercise ourselves as global citizens, not merely astrologers.

One of the biggest causes of environmental devastation remains war. Whether the horrors of genocide in Africa, or the burning of the oilfields in the Middle East, massive amounts of our economies are devoted to killing people. In 17th century France, a war could be ruinous to the treasury, as well as cause starvation among the peasants, whose harvest was disrupted. Now, in our times, we can destroy cropland for decades with herbicides. When we talk about wasting resources, I cannot imagine anything more wasteful than wanton destruction. And sadly, the U.S.A. is one of the leading world exporters of weapons.

Sustainability will involve more than changing lightbulbs and buying electric cars. There will be some major decisions that people will have to make in their lifestyle choices. But as astrologers, I challenge you to examine these charts for the coming years and to ask: will life go back to the way it was in 2007? I think you will find that the answer is *no*. We have moved on to another part of the cycle.

History can be a useful indicator of the possible. But all of these issues of overpopulation and resource utilization are new – at least on a global scale. It is here that we need to return to the symbolism of Earth, Air, Fire, and Water to bring us ideas and symbols with which to construct our new world.

In this book we have examined how to delineate charts for the Aries Ingress. We have examined the Neptune-Pluto cycles from the standpoint of sustainability. We have concluded that Pluto's transit through Capricorn and Aquarius will almost undoubtedly produce further issues related to resource limitations.

It is extremely likely that, with Pluto in either Aquarius or Pisces , there will be global water shortages. It is also likely that political entities will find it easier to deal with these problems through denial and war than through conscious adaptation to changed circumstances. At this point we have reached the limitation of what astrology can tell us. If you have followed my logic so far than you will realize that the consequences of everything you've seen in this book is that our society will be forced to adopt radically different strategies. Appendix C gives resources that you can consult to help you to use your astrology to stay ahead of this inevitable curve.

The challenge for 21st Century astrology is to see whether we are up to the task of engaging the heavenly writing as the Babylonians did. The writing is already there, whether we choose to read it or not; and most importantly, whether we choose to have a dialog about this, or, through denial, force these issues upon us in a completely ruthless way. Do we have the honesty and courage to create a world of what *can* be before we are condemned to a world of what *must* be?

Humans have shown themselves to be mentally lazy. *All of us* like to laze around in our minds, thinking the same old thoughts, living today like yesterday. We react poorly to change, hence the curse about living in interesting times.

From what I can see, all of us living now will spend most of the rest of our lives in interesting times. Can we bring the *consciousness* that we have talked about so much over the past few decades to the issues of the here and now? If we can, then maybe Hope can eat a square meal!

Endnotes: Chapter 9

254. Harvey in Baigent, Campion and Harvey, pp 176-188.
255. Harvey in Baigent, Campion and Harvey, pp 182-183.
256. Harvey in Baigent, Campion and Harvey, pp 183-184.
257. Harvey in Baigent, Campion and Harvey, pp 178-181. I should point out that this work was published in 1984: the 1993 conjunction of these bodies does not seem to represent a watershed year – but then, neither, really does 1820 – Harvey relates how Barbault associated it with the growth of capitalism, but I see no evidence that 1820 represents any particular turning point related to capitalism. There are some tantalizing new beginnings: the voyage of Darwin's ship *The Beagle*, and the Missouri Compromise in the U.S. which precipitated the Civil War in the 1860s. Both set up major events of years later.
258. Ho & Vermeer, p 5.
259. Brown, 2009, p 14.
260. Rubin, Jeff. *Why Your World Is About to Get a Whole Lot Smaller : Oil and the End of Globalization*. New York: Random House, 2009.
261. c.f., Davis, Ellen F. *Scripture, Culture, and Agriculture : An Agrarian Reading of the Bible*. New York: Cambridge University Press, 2009.

Glossary

Accidental Dignity: a mix of conditions, all of which relate to the strength of a planet being increased (or decreased, with accidental debility) because of the planet's placement, apart from its tropical zodiacal position. The kinds of factors which are included in the tables of accidental dignity include: house placement, whether oriental or occidental, in conjunction to fixed stars, aspects to benefics or malefics, closeness to the Sun, and speed.

Almuten/Almutem: There are five Essential Dignities for any degree of the zodiac: the rulership (+5), exaltation (+4), triplicity (+3), term (+2), and face (+1). If you take a particular house cusp, find the planet which rules each of the five essential dignities of the position, and assign the points to the planet. The planet with the highest point value is the Almuten. For example: for 8 Aries 15: Mars is the ruler (+5), the Sun rules the exaltation (+4), the triplicity (+3) and the face (+1) = +8, and Venus the terms (+2): the Sun is Almuten. Arabic sources give the word as "Almutem," but by the 17th Century, the word was consistently being translated and used as "Almuten."

Angles: the angular houses, 1, 4, 7 and 10.

Antiscion/Antiscial: "*Some of the learned in this Art do hold that the Antiscions of the Planets be equivalent unto a Sextile or a Trine-aspect, especially if they were beneficial Planets; and their Contrantiscions to be of the nature of Quadrate or Opposition. How to know the Antiscions is no more than this; first, know the Antiscions of the signs, which is no more but a sign being equally distant with another from Cancer and Capricorn the two Tropicks; as Gemini hath its Antiscion in Cancer, Taurus in Leo, Aries in Virgo, Pisces in Libra, Aquarius in Scorpio, and Capricorn in Sagittary; for when the Sun is in 1° of Gemini, he is as far from the Tropick point of Cancer as when he is in 29° of Cancer; and in the 5° of Taurus, as when the 25° of Leo, &c.... The Contrantiscion is known thus; look in what sign, degree and minute your Antiscion falls, and your contrantiscion will be in the same degree and minute as your opposite sign to your Antiscion.* [RA]

Application: "*is when two Planets approach each other, either by Body or Aspect; and this may be three several ways: First, when both Planets are direct, for Example, Jupiter in 11 deg. of Aries, and Mars in 9 degrees of Aries, both of them direct; here Mars apples to a conjunction of Jupiter.*

"*The second is when two Stars are Retrograde, and apply to each other by a Retrograde motion; thus Jupiter in 9 degrees of Aries. Retrograde, and Mars in 11 degrees of the same Sign Retrograde also, here Mars applies to the body of Jupiter by Retrograde motion.*

"*Thirdly, when one Planet is Retrograde in more degrees of a Sign, and another direct in fewer; as suppose Mars in 12 degrees of Aries Retrograde, and Venus in 10 degrees of Aries, here Mars applies to Venus and Venus applies to Mars, and this kind of application is of great force and efficacy in all manner of Astrological Resolutions; but this must be remembered also, that a Superior Planet cannot apply to an Inferior one, unless he be Retrograde.*"[PA]

Aries Ingress chart: a chart drawn for the moment of the onset of Spring, defined as zero Aries in the present definition of tropical astrology. This has sometimes been called the Chart of the Year, because the quadruplicity of the Ascendant generally defines how many ingress charts are necessary to interpret the year.

Astrometeorology: forecasting the weather using astrological tools such as the phases of the Sun and Moon or the solar months.

Autotrophs: the plants and certain bacteria that "fix" carbon and store energy from radiant or chemical processes.

Axial Age: a term coined by Karl Jaspers for the time period from roughly 800 - 200 BCE. The reason for naming the period was that Jaspers noted what he considered parallel developments in religion and philosophy in China, India and Greece.

The Bendings: the points square the Nodal axis. If a planet square the Nodes is zodiacally between the North Node and the South Node (i.e., start counting at the North Node), then it is at the Northern Bending; if between the South Node and the North Node, it is at the Southern Bending. The problem at the Northern Bending tends to be that of being ahead of one's time. The crisis at the Southern Bending is being blamed for what has already occurred. See *Classical Astrology for Modern Living*, Chapter 10.

Benefics: traditional placement that would produce good unless afflicted: Venus, the Lesser Benefic, Jupiter, the Greater Benefic, and the North Node.

Besieging: "*this I think need no Explanation, for every Souldier understands it; as suppose Saturn in 10 deg. Jupiter in 1 deg. and Mars in 13 deg. of Leo; here Jupiter is besieged by Saturn and Mars.*" [PA]

Biomes: major climatic regions such as grasslands, tropical rainforests, desert, and tundra, that share similar temperature and rainfall, and have similar species worldwide.

Bioregenerative: self-sustaining, in that the biological and non-biological components of the biosphere recycle into each other.

Biosphere: the region of the Earth where life is possible.

Bode's Law: a proposal, now rejected by astronomers, that expressed the mean distances of the planets from the Sun as a ratio.

Carnivores: eat other animals, whether herbivore or carnivore

Carrying capacity: the population level of a particular species where a stable population results. This may vary from ecosystem to ecosystem, and over time.

Cazimi: "*is when a Planet is in the heart of the Sun; that is, not distant from him above 17 min. as Mars in 10 deg. 30 min. of Aries, the Sun in 10 deg. 15 min. of Aries; here Mars is in Cazimi.*" [PA]

Clear-cutting: a lumbering strategy in which all the trees of an area are cut, regardless of age or species. The theory is that wholesale removal of this nature will result in lumber equipment causing less permanent damage to the land. The argument against is that it can accelerate erosion.

Climata: a system of assigning geographical rulerships, based on zones radiating out from the Mediterranean. The system broke down with the discovery of the New World, and the need to more precisely consider Asian nations.

Combustion: *"A Planet is Combust when he is not distant from the Sun 8 deg. 30 min. either before or after him; for Example, Jupiter in 10 deg. of Aries, the Sun in 14 deg. and Mars in 18, here both Jupiter and Mars are Combust; and observe that a Planet going to Combustion is more afflicted than when departing from it."* [PA].

Conjunctional chart: the name for a chart that allegedly is calculated for the moment of a conjunction of two bodies. Historically, there have been huge methodical problems with accomplishing this, and the error factors have been large enough to seriously compromise house placements.

Consumers (or heterotrophs): these organisms eat other organisms or dead organisms in order to gather their carbon and energy

Cosmos: it's easy now to define Cosmos as the Greek word for universe: except that the modern concept of universe doesn't pre-date the 20th century. *Cosmos* is What Is; that which was created by the Prime Mover, which we could describe as matter, energy, and the laws that govern them.

Diurnal motion: using the typical chart wheel, this would refer to the actual way that the Sun or other bodies "moves" around the chart throughout the day. Diurnal motion is clockwise within the chart wheel. The Sun at dawn is at the Ascendant, and then moves through the 12th, 11th, 10th, 9th, 8th, 7th, 6th, 5th, 4th, 3rd, 2nd, and finally through the 1st house until the next dawn.

Diurnal planets: Sun, Jupiter, Saturn, and Mercury as the morning star in Hellenistic; Mercury may not be so defined in Medieval.

Diurnal signs: the masculine signs: the fire and air elements.

Eclipse: defined astrologically, eclipses occur when a Full Moon (solar) or New Moon (solar) occur near enough to the [Moon's] nodal axis, which means that either the Sun or the Moon is fully or partially invisible. There are two major variations in calculation: the astronomical and the astrological methods. The astrological method computes the time when the Sun and the Moon are precisely conjunct or opposite each other in ecliptic longitude. Astronomers calculate when the angle between the two bodies is shortest, which isn't necessarily the same in three dimensional space as when it is projected to the ecliptic. A chart for an eclipse is a standard mundane method in use since the Hellenistic period.

Ecology: from the Greek for the study of one's house, ecology is the branch of biology devoted to the study of organisms and populations of organisms within their environment, both living and nonliving.

Ecosystem: a community of organisms that live together. This is usually understood through studying the different species that comprise the ecosystem, and the "roles" they perform within the ecosystem. The specific species may change over time, but the "roles" tend to remain the same.

Elevation: proximity to the Midheaven.

Essential Dignity: essential dignity was a system for assessing the strength of a planet by its placement in the zodiac alone. There were five essential dignities: by sign, exaltation, triplicity, term, and face. A planet with dignity can act or do as it wants, whereas a planet without dignity has difficulty getting from Point A to Point B except by a very circuitous route.

Evolution:: a biological theory proposed by Charles Darwin and Alfred Wallace that proposes that new species are formed by the following means: (1) there is variability within a species; (2) more offspring to any existing are born than could possibly survive, setting up (3) a struggle for survival, which results in (4) the establishment of successful traits. Eventually, there may be enough change to result in new species. While this concept was taken over into spirituality by Blavatsky, the "struggle for existence" part was seldom discussed from a spiritual perspective.

Face: one of the minor dignities, also called Chaldean decanates. The faces are 10° slices of the signs, marked by planetary rulers falling in the sequence known as the Chaldean order. The Face is given +1 point.

Five degree (5°) rule: consider the movement of the planets diurnally. For example, the Sun "rises" by going from the 1st House to the 12th House. A planet on the 12th House side of the Ascendant may be said to be angular if it is within 5° of the Ascendant: this is the so-called 5° rule. Depending on the source, this may actually entail anywhere from 2° to 7-8°, depending on the source, and whether the House moved into is Angular, Succedent, or Cadent (largest for Angular; smallest for Cadent). Generally, Medieval sources give 7° for angular cusps, 5° for succedent cusps, and 3° for cadent cusps.

Fossil Groundwater: All groundwater exists below the water table in a saturated zone; i.e., it fills all available spaces. Fossil groundwater was accumulated a very long time ago from ancient sediments. It is not replenished by rain. Many reservoirs of fossil groundwater have been pumped for agricultural purposes since the 1930s.

Gaia Hypothesis: the theory of James Lovelock that says that, since the biosphere is self-sustaining, in that the biological and non-biological components of the biosphere recycle into each other, that the living components regulate the nonliving substrate, thereby changing it. It is *as if* the entire biosphere were one large organism.

Global warming: the observation that the average temperature of the Earth is increasing.. The controversy is concerning how much of the observed temperature increase is a result of human activity, and whether this will continue to the point of creating a runaway greenhouse effect.

Great conjunctions: are those between any superior bodies from Mars on out. A conjunction between an inferior and a superior or between two inferiors is called a lesser or minor conjunction. As of this writing, the term major conjunction has not been agreed upon by astrologers as referring to either the centaurs such as Chiron, or the Plutinos apart from Pluto. The original classical definition only applied to the combinations of Mars, Jupiter, and Saturn, but with the discovery of the outer planets, these additional bodies were immediately included in the definition. Traditionally, the meaning of outer planet conjunctions was delineated two ways: first, through either an ingress or lunation which occurred close to the precise conjunction, and secondly, by using the degree of the conjunction as a sensitive point. The first attempt to interpret a chart drawn for the actual moment of the Jupiter-Saturn conjunction occurred in 1603, but astrologers for the rest of that century cautioned about the accuracy of such a computation. Since the late 19th century, astrologers have switched to attempting to do a chart for the conjunction, often completely unaware that their tools (including computer programs!) were not up to the task, resulting in charts that could easily be wrong by hours.

Great mutation: applied primarily to the Jupiter-Saturn conjunctional cycle, astrologers had computed that there was a cycle relating to the location of subsequent Jupiter-Saturn conjunctions by element, theoretically lasting 960 years, with twelve conjunctions within each element, before the next element takes over. In fact, the actual period between successive cycles is closer to 794 years, because there simply isn't such a neat allocation of three conjunctions per sign. Also, it is very common that, once there is a mutation between elements, that the next conjunction, or even two conjunctions later, may be in the prior element. These "retrograde element" conjunctions are interpreted as anomalies.

Greenhouse effect: the condition, such as on the surface of Venus, where the presence of sufficient greenhouse gases has altered the climate, resulting in a much higher atmospheric temperature.

Greenhouse gases: those gases which absorb and radiate energy within the thermal range, thus potentially allowing the temperature of the atmosphere to increase; these gases include ozone, water and carbon dioxide, as well as nitrous oxide and methane.

Hayz: a system of assessing strength based on the diurnal and nocturnal placements and natural conditions of the planets. A planet is in Hayz when it is a diurnal planet in a diurnal chart in a diurnal sign placed diurnally, or a nocturnal planet in a nocturnal chart in a nocturnal sign placed nocturnally. See diurnal or nocturnal planets and signs. The placement piece is related to visibility: a diurnal planet above the horizon (houses 12 to 7, counting in diurnal motion) is diurnally placed: it is "visible," except that the Sun prevents its viewing. A nocturnal planet in a nocturnal chart nocturnally placed is also above the horizon, because it too can be seen.

Herbivores eat producer organisms (generally plants).

Heterotrophs: these organisms eat other organisms or dead organisms in order to gather their carbon and energy

Hydrosphere: the water more or less at the surface of the earth. This also includes ground water.

Imbecilic: a planet was judged imbecilic when it was either combust or retrograde.

Inferior Planets: Mercury and Venus, whose orbits are inside the Earth's heliocentrically, or inside the Sun's, geocentrically. Inferior planets appear to oscillate around the Sun, because they can never be very far from it.

Infortune: a synonym for malefic.

Judicial astrology: literally, the astrology of judgment; these are the forms of astrology like most natal and horary that was considered sinful under Medieval Christianity because their tenets were believed to interfere with the free will necessary for salvation.

Law of Unintended Consequences: doing something which on the surface seems right, moral, or just a good idea, often produces effects that are the reverse, because of the interdependence of elements of the system that don't act in anticipated ways.

Lithosphere: the soil and surface rocks that provide the substrate for life, and many chemicals necessary for life to exist.

Lord of the Year: an attempt, principally in the Arabic and Latin periods, to compute one planet as the primary significator of the year. Whether Abu Ma'shar or Bonatti, the aphorisms were rather complex, and the extent to which this system was rigorously applied is unknown.

Lots: the Hellenistic name for what is also called the Arabic parts. These are points calculated on the formula A + B – C, where the three components my be planets, house cusps, or either house or planetary rulers.

Major conjunction: defined originally as when all three of the original superior planets, Mars, Jupiter and Saturn, occurred within the same Face (i.e., 10 degrees of a sign) at the time of a Jupiter-Saturn conjunction. The last one occurred in 2000 and the next one will occur in 2040.

Malefics: bodies or points which will denote evil or problems unless dignified: Mars, the Lesser Malefic, Saturn, the Greater Malefic, and the South Node. Most neoclassical astrologers classify Uranus, Neptune and Pluto as malefic as well.

Monoculture: the exclusive or near-exclusive cultivation of a single plant species in a given area.

Mutation: in the Jupiter-Saturn conjunctional cycle, anytime the conjunction series changes elements. 1980 was the last mutation. See "Great mutation" for a description of the entire cycle.

Natural ruler: an object can be said to be ruled by a house, as is common especially in horary astrology (as in: marriage is ruled by the 7th house), or by a natural ruler, as in: Mercury is the natural ruler of keys. These two systems can produce different rulers, as keys in the house system would be the 2nd house, which might not be ruled by Mercury.

Nocturnal planets: Moon, Venus, Mars, and Mercury as the evening star in Hellenistic; Mercury may not be so defined in Medieval.

Nocturnal signs: the feminine signs: the water and earth elements.

Occidental: "is when a Planet or Star sets after the Sun is down." [PA]

Old field succession: an ecological concept that describes how, when many ecosystems are disturbed by fire or other means, the recovery of the ecosystem will proceed through a series of predictable phases involving different plant and animals species.

Omnivores: sometime eat plants, and sometimes eat animals

Oriental: "is when a Planet riseth before the Sun." [PA]

Overgrazing: a term in ecology which refers to damage caused by herbivorous animals on the grass or other plant cover of an area. Usually, this is caused by humans allowing too many animals to graze upon the available plant population, without regard to the ability of the plants to sustain themselves and reproduce.

Parapegmata: a calendar of predictions, usually of weather predictions, most frequently organized by Moon phase.or the rising of stars.

Partile: within the same degree number. Notice that this is not an orb size. The Moon at 6 Leo 01 is partile conjunct Mars at 6 Leo 59. If the Moon were in the same place, with Mars at 5 Leo 59, they are within a degree, but are not partile. Aspects which are not partile, are called platic.

Peak oil: a concept developed by M. King Hubbert, this posits that oil production in a region or globally occurs exponentially, until reaching a peak, and then declines exponentially. He correctly predicted when U.S. oil production would peak and then decline. His estimate for global peak production was 2000-2010, although he mentioned various factors that could delay it by perhaps a decade. The United States Geological Service predicts peak oil in the 2021-2112 range, depending on various assumptions.

Peregrine: "a Planet is Peregrine when he is in a Sign and degree where he hath no Essential dignity, as Mars in 26 degrees of Gemini is Peregrine, because he hath no dignity there, &c." [PA]

Photosynthesis: the series of chemical reactions carried on within a plant which capture energy from light into organic compounds and stored energy

Portals of Death: this is a Greek term for the 7th house cusp. The reference is to the idea that the As-cendant is the origin of life (hence, Portals of Life), thereby making its opposite point a place of death. We see the same idea in the use of metaphors of birth for the dawn, and death for sunset.

Producers (also called autotrophs): the plants and certain bacteria that "fix" carbon and store energy from radiant or chemical processes.

Quality: the Greek system of components that underlaid their elemental and physical systems: the qualities are hot & cold (active), and wet & dry (Passive). Please refer to the table shown under "temperaments" to see how these qualities corresponded to the system of elements.

Reception *"is when two Planets are in each other's dignities, as the Sun in Aries, and Mars in Leo, here is a Reception by House, it may be also by Exaltation, Triplicity, Term and Face."* [PA]

Rendered/Rendering: this occurs when an imbecilic planet (either combust or retrograde) is aspected by one of its dispositors – and that dispositor in turn is dignified. The effect is that the disposing planet saves the imbecilic planet from its own stupidity.

Replacement fertility: a term in population studies that refers to the number of children two parents must have in order for the population to remain exactly stable: neither growing, nor shrinking. Because of deaths of children, that number is a bit more than 2, typically in the range of 2.2.

Retrogression of the Conjunction: In the Jupiter-Saturn conjunction series, any appearance of a conjunction in the Triplicity prior to the current elemental series; as for example, once the 1980 conjunction shifted into Air, the 2000 conjunction in Earth is a retrogression, and the 2020 conjunction resumes the series in Air. A retrogression is treated as unnatural in effect.

Revolution: a return chart. This can either be an Ingress chart in mundane, or a solar return in natal.

Runaway Greenhouse effect: a planetary climate disaster in which the greenhouse gases like carbon dioxide, nitrous oxide and carbon monoxide do not block sunlight coming in, but prevent heat from escaping the planet, resulting in a catastrophic increase in temperature of the planet and atmosphere. This is what is believed to have happened to create such hot temperatures on Venus.

Saprovores consume dead organisms, or dead organic matter

Scapulimancy: literally, divination by shoulder blades. In China, this was the shoulder blade of a tortoise, virtually driving the species to extinction, since so many questions were asked.

Scientific method: the process which scientists use to do their experiments. The exact methods differ by discipline, and have changed over time, but most typically, the experimenter enunciates a hypothesis that is stated negatively (the "null hypothesis"), such as, "There is no relationship between the length of the index finger and one's Sun sign." Then, one or more experiments are designed to test this hypothesis. Once the scientists is satisfied that the results are comprehensible (whichever way the experiment goes), then these results are typically written up and presented to the scientific community for further comment and replication. While even this method may be morphing, one commonality is that the data must be collected objectively.

Sect: whether diurnal or nocturnal. The primary sect of a chart is whether the chart itself is by day or night. A night chart has the Sun posited in the 1st through 6th Houses; a day chart has the Sun in the 12th through 7th Houses: right on the Ascendant-Descendant is anyone's guess! In addition, planets were considered to have intrinsic sect (Sun, Jupiter and Saturn: diurnal; Moon, Venus and Mars: nocturnal; Mercury: mixed); signs had intrinsic sect (Masculine = diurnal, Feminine = nocturnal), and planets had sect placement, according to whether they were diurnally or nocturnally placed in the chart in question.

Sect Light: the Sun, for a day chart; the Moon for a night chart.

Self-sustaining community or ecosystem: one in which the building blocks that the aggregate of organisms need is either generated internally, or where what comes in and goes out is roughly the same.

Sensitive point: this is a modern name for the concept of using a zodiacal degree from a prior astrological event as producing an impact if another body transits that point. Common examples are the degree of an eclipse, or, in a classical use, the degree of the prior Jupiter-Saturn conjunction, especially if it was for a change in element.

Separation: "*is when two Planets have been in Conjunction or Aspect and are going from it as Jupiter in 6 degrees of Aries and Mars in 7 degrees; here Mars separates himself from Jupiter; but yet he is not quite separated from him till they are distant from each other 8 degrees 30 minutes, which is the moiety of both their Orbs; what their Orbs and Aspects are.*" [PA]

Sesquialter: a harmonic relationship in music known as the fifth, but a general expression for a relationship between two notes that are in a 3:2 relationship to each other, which is the same relationship as the angle sesquiquadrate, or 135 degrees.

Sesquiquadrate: the aspect of 135°

Significator of the King: an Arabic and Latin system for calculating which body should have rulership over the King in an Ingress; later, this was simplified to being the 10th house ruler or Almuten. The reason for the more complex system was that it was held that the king could not be represented by a planet that might not be that royal or dignified – but the counter-argument would be that sometimes the king really isn't as strong as the attempt to always create the most regal option would imply.

Stellium: this is a modern astrological concept that refers to three or four or more bodies being in either the same sign or house.

Superior Planets: those whose orbits are outside that of the Earth, or the Sun, if defined geocentrically. This would be Mars out.

Systems theory: pioneered in ecology (not its only academic home) by Howard and Eugene Odum, systems theory is an inter-disciplinary approach which attempts to develop general procedures to understand and characterize how a "system" works. The Odums attempted to define the chemical and energy inputs and outputs of an ecosystem, a community of organisms that live together.

Term: one of the five essential dignities. The Term ruler was said to be "of the body" of that planet, so if the Ascendant is in the Terms of Saturn, it would represent a person serious, older, in a saturnine profession, etc. – primarily physical or outward appearance. The Term was given +2 points, and is considered a minor dignity.

Tipping point: in an environment, a tipping point occurs when the build-up of some substance or condition results in a catastrophic failure of a control system, resulting in a systems collapse.

Triplicity: one of the five essential dignities. Triplicities run by element, so there is one set of rulers for the fire signs, another for earth, etc. Triplicity is worth +3 points on the scale of essential dignities. The trick is that there are three different systems. Two of them utilize a day, night, and mixed ruler; the third, which was in common use by English astrologers in the 17th Century, used only day and night. Among the most obvious differences between the two that will be seen in this work is Jupiter being the mixed Triplicity ruler of Air: thus, for a year with Jupiter In Aquarius, Jupiter will often be the most dignified planet, and will virtually always be a contender for use because of the dignity.

Under the Sun's Beams: "*a Planet is said to be under the Sun's beams, till he is full 17 degrees distant from him.*" [PA]

Void of Course: "*is when a Planet is separated from one, and doth not apply to any other while he is in that Sign, and it is most observable in the Moon.*" [PA]

Water table: the depth at which all the spaces in the soil are filled with water. It may be associated with an aquifer, which is an underground water deposit within the rock. Water below the water table is called ground water.

B

Table of Essential Dignities

	Ruler	Exalt.	Triplicity			Terms					Faces		
			Day	Night	Mix						0-10	10-20	20-30
♈	♂D	☉19	☉	♃	♄	0 ♃ 6	6 ♀ 14	14 ☿ 21	21 ♂ 26	26 ♄ 30	♂	☉	♀
♉	♀N	☽3	♀	☽	♂	0 ♀ 8	8 ☿ 15	15 ♃ 22	22 ♄ 26	26 ♂ 30	☿	☽	♄
♊	☿D	☊3	♄	☿	♃	0 ☿ 7	7 ♃ 14	14 ♀ 21	21 ♄ 25	25 ♂ 30	♃	♂	☉
♋	☽DN	♃15	♀**	♂	☽	0 ♂ 6	6 ♃ 13	13 ☿ 20	20 ♀ 27	27 ♄ 30	♀	☿	☽
♌	☉DN		☉	♃	♄	0 ♄ 6	6 ☿ 13	13 ♀ 19	19 ♃ 25	25 ♂ 30	♄	♃	♂
♍	☿N	☿15	♀	☽	♂	0 ☿ 7	7 ♀ 13	13 ♃ 18	18 ♄ 24	24 ♂ 30	☉	♀	☿
♎	♀D	♄21	♄	☿	♃	0 ♄ 6	6 ♀ 11	11 ♃ 19	19 ☿ 24	24 ♂ 30	☽	♄	♃
♏	♂N		♀**	♂	☽	0 ♂ 6	6 ♃ 14	14 ♀ 21	21 ☿ 27	27 ♄ 30	♂	☉	♀
♐	♃D	☋3	☉	♃	♄	0 ♃ 8	8 ♀ 14	14 ☿ 19	19 ♄ 25	25 ♂ 30	☿	☽	♄
♑	♄N	♂28	♀	☽	♂	0 ♀ 6	6 ☿ 12	12 ♃ 19	19 ♂ 25	25 ♄ 30	♃	♂	☉
♒	♄D		♄	☿	♃	0 ♄ 6	6 ☿ 12	12 ♀ 20	20 ♃ 25	25 ♂ 30	♀	☿	☽
♓	♃N	♀27	♀**	♂	☽	0 ♀ 8	8 ♃ 14	14 ☿ 20	20 ♂ 26	26 ♄ 30	♄	♃	♂

* Dorothean Triplicities and so-called Ptolemaic or Chaldean Terms.
** Lilly gives both day and night in the water signs to Mars.
Font used is ET AStro, compliments of Esoteric Tehnologies Pty, lttd

C

Further Readings in Environmental Issues

UNFORTUNATELY, THIS BOOK IS ALREADY BIG ENOUGH WITHOUT ALSO TAKING UP THE PRACTICAL SIDE OF WHAT YOU CAN DO TO ADDRESS SUSTAINABILITY ISSUES IN YOUR OWN LIFE. I would like to address this issue myself in a book in the future. For now, I would like to point you to additional books and web sites beyond the references I used in the text to help you to both understand many of the issues I have addressed, but more so, constructive things you can do yourself.

But before we get very far, I want to specifically address the issue of green-washing. Green-washing is a term that refers to fake green. While the 1970s may have marked a time when a lot of legislation was passed relating to the environment, what never has passed in the U.S.A. is a legal definition of what something has to achieve in order to be "green." As a result, all sorts of claims can be made about a product or process being green where no substantiation is necessary. This is a definite "let the buyer beware" market.

Furthermore, even when there are legitimate measures which indicate that something is green, then the next question is: which green?

Is it green because it is more energy efficient?

Is it green because it's more chemically benign?

Is it green because it's biodegradable?

Is it green because it's made of all "natural" components?

Is it green because it's produced locally?

Is it green because the weight and amount of packaging has been minimized?

Is it green because it's designed to last longer?

All of the above are arguably green. We have seen already that one of the challenges is that ecology and other forms of systems theory point out that it really is impossible to consistently maximize two variables. A house designed for high energy efficiency may use plastic materials in its construction which can outgas, thereby not being chemically benign.

In the 1970s, the concept of the Environmental Impact Statement was built into law for various major projects. Attempting to do this on a personal level is hideously difficult, in great part because it is impossible to acquire accurate, useful information about all the possible components that need to be considered in making a decision.

Take cars. Maybe if you have an old car that's leaking everything and getting three miles per gallon, it seems obvious that the greener solution is to get a new hybrid. But is it really? Your old car goes into the landfill before it has really fallen apart. What impact is that? Your new hybrid has batteries: do you know how long they are expected to last? What happens to those dead batteries? Are they recharged? Do they go into the landfill? They have toxic substances in them: how is that dealt with from an environmental standpoint? Suddenly that decision about the hybrid vehicle isn't quite as clear.

There is one simple idea that I can suggest: but a lot of people won't like it. If you simply take the attitude that everything you buy, you agree to use longer, you are making a significant impact in a positive way. Part of what got us into this mess is our insatiable appetite for stuff. Stuff ends up in landfills, it often has toxic components, and there's the energy cost of producing it, marketing it, and transporting it in the first place. If we are going to find our way out, we have to break that habit. This also reminds us that, when it comes to sustainability, we cannot solve our problems by simply buying something new. That is a habit we have to break.

So enough of the soapbox. The rest of this Appendix lists places to go, whether for information or political action, within several different categories. These are works apart from those in the general bibliography of sources used in this book. After the list of references, I also include places to find organizations that address the issues we have discussed in this book.

Books

Green Building

Chiras, Daniel D. *The New Ecological Home : The Complete Guide to Green Building Options*. Chelsea Green Guides for Homeowners. White River Junction, Vt.: Chelsea Green Pub. Co., 2004.

Clark, William H. *Energy Conservation in Existing Buildings*. Troy, Mich.: Business News Pub. Co., 1996.

Crume, Richard V., and Yoko Crume. The Simply Solar House : Green Building on a Budget. Duvall, Wash.: Counterbalance Books, 2007.

Ehrlich, Chuck. *Intelligent Building Dictionary Terminology for Smart, Integrated, Green Building Design, Construction, and Management*. San Francisco: Hands-on-Guide, 2007.

Ester, P. *Consumer Behavior and Energy Conservation: A Policy-Oriented Experimental Field Study on the Effectiveness of Behavioral Interventions Promoting Residential Energy Conservation*. Dordrecht [Netherlands] ; Boston; Hingham, MA., U.S.A.: M. Nijhoff Publishers ; Distributors for the U.S. and Canada Kluwer Academic Publishers, 1985.

Freed, Eric C. *Green Building & Remodeling for Dummies*. 1st ed. Indianapolis, IN: Wiley Pub., Inc., 2007.

Frej, Anne B., William D. Browning, and Urban Land Institute. *Green Office Buildings : A Practical Guide to Development*. Washington, D.C.: ULI-Urban Land Institute, 2005.

Gause, Jo Allen, Richard Franko, and Urban Land Institute. *Developing Sustainable Planned Communities*. Washington, D.C.: Urban Land Institute, 2007.

Gevorkian, Peter. *Sustainable Energy Systems in Architectural Design : A Blueprint for Green Building*. New York: McGraw-Hill, 2006.

Glavinich, Thomas E. *The AGC Contractor's Guide to Green Building Construction : Management, Project Delivery, Documentation, and Risk Reduction*. Hoboken, N.J.: John Wiley, 2008.

Kibert, Charles J. *Sustainable Construction : Green Building Design and Delivery*. 2nd ed. Hoboken, N.J.: Wiley, 2007.

Susanka, Sarah. *Creating the Not So Big House : Insights and Ideas for the New American Home*. Newtown, CT; [Emeryville, CA]: Taunton Press ; Distributed by Publishers Group West, 2000.

Susanka, Sarah, and Kira Obolensky. *The Not So Big House : A Blueprint for the Way We Really Live.* Newtown, CT; [Emeryville, CA]: Taunton Press ; Distributed by Publishers Group West, 1998.

Susanka, Sarah, and Marc Vassallo. *Not So Big Remodeling : Tailoring Your Home for the Way You Really Live.* Newtown, CT: Taunton Press, 2009.

Biodiversity

Barrow, Mark V. *Nature's Ghosts : Confronting Extinction from the Age of Jefferson to the Age of Ecology.* Chicago: University of Chicago Press, 2009.

Chivian, Eric, et al. *Sustaining Life : How Human Health Depends on Biodiversity.* Oxford; New York: Oxford University Press, 2008.

Xu, Haigen, et al. "China's Progress toward the Significant Reduction of the Rate of Biodiversity Loss." *Bioscience* 59.10 (2009): 843-52.

Zeigler, David. *Understanding Biodiversity.* Westport, Conn.: Praeger, 2007.

Water Issues

Lang, Damon, and Darlene Claire Preussner. *The Sustainable Landscape : Recycling Materials, Water Conservation.* Atglen, PA: Schiffer Pub., 2010.

Postel, Sandra L. "Water for Food Production: Will There Be Enough in 2025?" *Bioscience* 48.8 (1998): 629-37.

Postel, Sandra L. "Entering an Era of Water Scarcity: The Challenges Ahead." *Ecological Applications* 10.4 (2000): 941-48.

Timm, Ulrich. *Creating Ponds, Brooks, and Pools : Water in the Garden.* A Schiffer Design Book. Atglen, PA.: Schiffer Pub., 1999.

Wallace, Terry. *The Rain Garden Planner : Seven Steps to Conserving and Managing Water in the Garden.* Atglen, PA: Schiffer Pub., 2009.

Climate Change

Crist, Eileen, and H. Bruce Rinker. *Gaia in Turmoil : Climate Change, Biodepletion, and Earth Ethics in an Age of Crisis.* Cambridge, Mass.: MIT Press, 2010.

Lin, Brenda B., Ivette Perfecto, and John Vandermeer. "Synergies between Agricultural Intensification and Climate Change Could Create Surprising Vulnerabilities for Crops." *Bioscience* 58.9 (2008): 847-54.

Lovejoy, Thomas E., and Lee Jay Hannah. *Climate Change and Biodiversity.* New Haven: Yale University Press, 2005.

Population Issues

Biller, Peter. *The Measure of Multitude : Population in Medieval Thought*. Oxford; New York: Oxford University Press, 2000.

Easterlin, Richard A. *The Reluctant Economist : Perspectives on Economics, Economic History and Demography*. Cambridge, UK; New York: Cambridge University Press, 2004.

Ehrlich, Paul R., and Anne H. Ehrlich. *The Population Explosion*. New York: Simon and Schuster, 1990.

Ehrlich, Paul R., and Anne H. Ehrlich. *One with Nineveh : Politics, Consumption, and the Human Future*. Washington: Island Press : Shearwater Books, 2004.

Graham, Otis, Jr. "Immigration and America's Unchosen Future." *Negative Population Growth Forum Series* 117.October (2009): 8 pages.

Hardin, Garrett. "The Tragedy of the Commons." *Science* 13 Dec 1968: 1242-48.

Milwertz, Cecilia Nathansen. *Accepting Population Control : Urban Chinese Women and the One-Child Family Policy*. Nordic Institute of Asian Studies Monograph Series, No. 74. Richmond, Surrey: Curzon, 1997.

Neurath, Paul. *From Malthus to the Club of Rome and Back : Problems of Limits to Growth, Population Control, and Migrations*. Columbia University Seminar Series. Armonk, N.Y.: M.E. Sharpe, 1994.

Taylor, Dorceta E. *Environment and the People in American Cities, 1600s-1900s : Disorder, Inequality, and Social*. [S.l.]: Duke Univ Press, 2009.

Business Matters

Freedman, David H. *Wrong : Why Experts* Keep Failing Us--and How to Know When Not to Trust Them : *Scientists, Finance Wizards, Doctors, Relationship Gurus, Celebrity Ceos, High-Powered Consultants, Health Officials, and More*. New York: Little, Brown and Co, 2010.

Larsson, Mats. *The Limits of Business Development and Economic Growth : Why Business Will Need to Invest Less in the Future*. Houndmills, Basingstoke, Hampshire; New York: Palgrave Macmillan, 2004.

Townsend, A. K. *Business Ecology : Why Most Green Business Practices Don't Work-- and What to Do About It*. Atglen, PA: Schiffer Pub. Ltd., 2009.

Green Energy

Cohn, Jeffrey P. "How Ecofriendly Are Wind Farms." *Bioscience* 58.7 (2008): 576-78.

Gillis, Christopher. *Wind Power*. Atglen, Pa.: Schiffer Pub. Ltd., 2008.

Patrick, Dale R. *Energy Conservation Guidebook*. 2nd ed. Lilburn, GA: Fairmont Press, 2006.

Pimentel, David, and Marcia Pimentel. *Food, Energy, and Society*. 3rd ed. Boca Raton, FL: CRC Press, 2008.

Simpson, Tom. "Biofuels: The Past, Present, and a New Vision for the Future." *Bioscience* 59.11 (2009): 926-27.

Townsend, A. K. *Exploring Sustainable Biodiesel*. Atglen, Pa.: Schiffer, 2008.

Societal Collapse

Allen, T. F. H., Joseph A. Tainter, and T. W. Hoekstra. *Supply-Side Sustainability*. New York: Columbia University Press, 2003.

McAnany, Patricia Ann, and Norman Yoffee. *Questioning Collapse : Human Resilience, Ecological Vulnerability, and the Aftermath of Empire*. Cambridge; New York: Cambridge University Press, 2010.

Tainter, Joseph A. *The Collapse of Complex Societies*. New Studies in Archaeology. Cambridge, Cambridgeshire; New York: Cambridge University Press, 1988.

Vale, Lawrence J., and Thomas J. Campanella. *The Resilient City : How Modern Cities Recover from Disaster*. New York: Oxford University Press, 2005.

Pollution and Toxicity

Baker, Nena. *The Body Toxic : How the Hazardous Chemistry of Everyday Things Threatens Our Health and Well-Being*. New York: North Point Press, 2009.

Davis, Devra Lee. *The Secret History of the War on Cancer*. New York: BasicBooks, 2007.

Watts, Jonathan. *When a Billion Chinese Jump How China Will Become the World's First Green Superpower or Its Last Environmental Assassin*. Scribner, 2010.

Resources

Heinberg, Richard. *Peak Everything : Waking up to the Century of Declines*. Gabriola, BC: New Society Publishers, 2007.

Meadows, Donella H., Jørgen Randers, and Dennis L. Meadows. *The Limits to Growth : The 30-Year Update*. White River Junction, Vt: Chelsea Green Publishing Company, 2004.

Pirages, Dennis, and Ken Cousins. *From Resource Scarcity to Ecological Security : Exploring New Limits to Growth*. Cambridge, Mass.: MIT Press, 2005.

Organizations

**Environmental Defense Fund
(www.edf.org):**
a group dedicated to solving problems

**Negative Population Growth
(www.npg.org):**
not just zero, but negative. This
organization addresses the
overpopulation issue.

**Population Reference Bureau
(www.prb.org):**
This organization has been providing
outstanding statistics related to
demographics for decades.

**Sierra Club
(www.sierraclub.org):**
the oldest grassroots environmental
organization in the U.S.A.

**Worldwatch Institute
(http://www.worldwatch.org)**
This has been one of the premier
organizations for providing
information relating to sustainability.
You have seen Lester Brown's name
in this work: this is his organization.

THERE ARE MANY ORGANIZATIONS THAT OPERATE ON A GRASSROOTS LEVEL. This is so appropriate,
given that local action is so necessary to solve local needs. You can easily find many
organizations in your local area that will have programs to suit your interests.

Index